T&T Clark Studies in Systematic Theology

Edited by

John Webster
Ian A. McFarland
Ivor Davidson

Volume 19

JONATHAN EDWARDS'S THEOLOGY

A Reinterpretation

by
Kyle C. Strobel

B L O O M S B U R Y
LONDON • NEW DELHI • NEW YORK • SYDNEY

Bloomsbury T&T Clark
An imprint of Bloomsbury Publishing Plc

50 Bedford Square   1385 Broadway
London   New York
WC1B 3DP   NY 10018
UK   USA

www.bloomsbury.com

Bloomsbury is a registered trade mark of Bloomsbury Publishing Plc

First published 2013
Paperback edition first published 2014

British Library Cataloguing-in-Publication Data
A catalogue record for this book is available from the British Library.

ISBN: HB: 978-0-567-17110-8
PB: 978-0-567-65575-2

Library of Congress Cataloging-in-Publication Data
A catalog record for this book is available from the Library of Congress.

Typeset by Fakenham Prepress Solutions, Fakenham, Norfolk NR21 8NN

For my loving parents, Lee and Leslie Strobel, whose encouragement, support and excitement have been unwavering throughout this long journey of my education. As cliché as this is, it is true, I truly could not have done it without you!

And to my wife Kelli, who loved, encouraged and blessed me throughout the many stages of this project. Without your support I never could have completed this. Ours truly is an uncommon union.

Contents

Acknowledgements   xi

Abbreviations   xiii

Introduction   1
  Edwards's Theological Vision   3
  Edwards's Theological Project   5
  Argument Overview   12
      Section 1. Edwards's Doctrine of the Trinity   14
      Section 2. Emanation to Consummation   15
      Section 3. Redemption as Remanation   15

Section 1 Jonathan Edwards's God   **21**

1. Personal Beatific-Delight: An Account of the Trinity   23
    I   Overview: A Model of the Beatific   26
    II Background of Edwards's Doctrine   31
    III Overview of Edwards's Argumentation – The *'Discourse on the Trinity'*   35
      1. The Divine Essence and the Divine Persons   40
         Conclusion   65
    IV Categorizing Edwards's Doctrine of the Trinity 65

Section 2 Emanation to Consummation   **73**

2. The End For Which God Created the World   75
    I   God Creates for His Own Glory   78
    II God's Disposition to Create   83
      1. God Creates because of Who He Is   87

    III   God's Intention to Create   94
    IV   Revelation of Glory   99
    V   The Dogmatic Task of God's End in Creating   102

3. Heaven Is a World of Love   105
    I   The Changing Realm of the Unchangeable God   107
          1.   First Era: From Creation to Christ's Ascension   109
          2.   Second Era: From Ascension to Consummation   113
          3.   Third Era: Consummation of All Things   120
    II   Edwards and the Beatific   125
          1.   John Owen: Reforming Aquinas   126
          2.   Francis Turretin and the Beatific   130
          3.   A Happifying Sight: Jonathan Edwards and the
               Beatific   132
          Conclusion   144

Interlude: The Heuristic Key   145

Section 3 Redemption as Remanation   **147**

4. Spiritual Knowledge   149
    I   Seeing God: The Beatified Pilgrim   152
    II   Reformed Backdrop: Archetypal and Ectypal   155
    III   Edwards's Use of the Archetypal/Ectypal Distinction   157
          1.   Sanctified Sight   161
          2.   A Christologically Mediated Vision   166
          3.   Modes of Knowing   171
          4.   A Heavenward Journey   174

5. Regeneration   177
    I   The Spirit's Work: Illumination   180
          1.   The Effect of Illumination on the Soul   186
    II   The Spirit's Work: Infusion   196
          1.   The Spirit Functioning as Principle of Grace   198
          2.   Grace as God's Nature Infused in the Soul   202
          Conclusion   205

6.   Religious Affection as Remanation unto Glory   209
     I   Religious Affection   211
     II   Religious Affection within Edwards's Theology   217
          Conclusion   225
          Recapitulation   225
          Evaluation   228

Appendix: Divine Attributes and Essence   234
          Conclusion   242

Bibliography   243

Index   251

Acknowledgements

I start these acknowledgements by focusing on the community of Edwards scholars I now find myself a part of. The Edwards community is warm, generous and encouraging, even while there are hard-fought debates for the true interpretation of Edwards. I appreciate dearly that you have welcomed me into this world. That said, in this volume I 'go after' almost everyone! This should not be taken as a criticism of the level of work achieved in this field nor a comment on my indebtedness to their work. In fact, Sang Hyun Lee, who is critiqued throughout this entire volume, has been one of the most important figures for me in coming to my conclusions. Lee's work is of the highest order and his contribution to Edwards scholarship goes far beyond the school of thought he has developed. Without his work I never could have come to some of my most fundamental conclusions. This goes for those figures like Gerald McDermott and Michael McClymond who are in Lee's school of thought. Their individual and co-written works were key to help me wrap my mind around the mess of Edwards's corpus. There were, furthermore, Edwards scholars who befriended me and, in one way or another, helped guide me in this process. Maybe most importantly was my time at the Jonathan Edwards Center at Yale Divinity School where Ken Minkema and Adriaan Neele were always gracious enough to interact with me on all things Edwards. Doug Sweeney provided helpful feedback on very early and extremely rough material, and his insights and critiques helped me form my chapter (and conclusions) on Edwards's elusive doctrine of the Trinity. Oliver Crisp has always been generous with his time and companionship, and continues to embody the generosity, grace and light-heartedness to which all scholars should strive.

This volume started out as a dissertation, a long and arduous journey into the unknown. As in all great pilgrim journeys in life there are many who travelled alongside of me who deserve, if nothing else, to be named here. I would like to thank my supervisor Philip Ziegler, whose guidance and wit helped this project (and my own sanity) immensely. It was always helpful to have someone else find Edwards's language as odd as I did! Similarly, John Webster and Stephen Holmes, my examiners, offered helpful and insightful feedback on my dissertation and provided much fodder for my thinking on Edwards's theology. Along with these figures, I had several friends and scholars who were willing to read portions of his work. All of these figures, in various ways, provided differing views on my argument, which only helped to strengthen it in the long run. James Merrick, Chris Green, and Rhys Bezzant all read at least a chapter of the work (no small task!), and all provided insights which, in the end, helped form how I thought about this project. My time with Rhys at Yale was a particularly blessed time. At Aberdeen I was the lone 'Edwards guy', while at Yale Rhys and I were able to banter about all things 'JE'. I should add that my wife Kelli took on the thankless task of reading for formatting issues, even perusing the smooth prose of my bibliography(!), and Jeff Reimer for his invaluable help on formatting and editing.

One of God's great graces to me in my life generally and this season of life specifically, has been great friends to help push my thinking and help my writing. My friend Jamin Goggin has proven, time and again, to be an incredible encouragement in all I do. Likewise, Kent Eilers, James Merrick and Mark McDowell all provided much-needed friendship, plus generous critique of my work and their insight and passion for the theological task was always encouraging and convicting. Furthermore, Chris Green, Benj Foreman, the original KCS5 and Gerrard Street Baptist Church provided friendships, laughs, and in the case of Chris, another theological mind in which to engage in fruitful conversation. Lastly, my parents along with Alison, Dan, Abby and Penny, as well as my in-laws, have given up much for Kelli and I to be in Scotland, and their support and encouragement cannot be underestimated. And, of course, Kelli, whose companionship, love and grace helped this season to be a truly blessed time.

Abbreviations

Y1   Edwards, Jonathan. *Freedom of the Will.* Vol. 1, ed. Paul Ramsey.

Y2   —*The Religious Affections.* Vol. 2, ed. Perry Miller.

Y3   —*Original Sin.* Vol. 3, ed. Clyde A. Holbrook.

Y4   —*The Great Awakening.* Vol. 4, ed. C. C. Goen.

Y5   —*Apocalyptic Writings.* Vol. 5, ed. Stephen J. Stein.

Y6   —*Scientific and Philosophical Writings.* Vol. 6, ed. Wallace E. Anderson.

Y8   —*Ethical Writings.* Vol. 8, ed. Paul Ramsey.

Y9   —*A History of the Work of Redemption.* Vol. 9, ed. John F. Wilson.

Y10   —*Sermons and Discourses, 1720–1723.* Vol. 10, ed. Wilson H. Kimnach.

Y11   —*Typological Writings.* Vol. 11, ed. Wallace E. Anderson and David H. Watters.

Y13   —*The 'Miscellanies': A-500.* Vol. 13, ed. Thomas A. Schafer.

Y14   —*Sermons and Discourses, 1723–1729.* Vol. 14, ed. Kenneth P. Minkema.

Y15   —*Notes on Scripture.* Vol. 15, ed. Stephen J. Stein.

Y16   —*Letters and Personal Writings.* Vol. 16, ed. George S. Claghorn.

Y17   —*Sermons and Discourses, 1730–1733.* Vol. 17, ed. Mark R. Valeri.

Y18   —*The 'Miscellanies': Entry Nos. 501–832.* Vol. 18, ed. Ava Chamberlain.

Y19   —*Sermons and Discourses, 1734–1738.* Vol. 19, ed. M. X. Lesser.

Y20   —*The 'Miscellanies': Entry Nos. 833–1152.* Vol. 20, ed. Amy Plantinga Pauw.

Y21   —*Writings on the Trinity, Grace, and Faith.* Vol. 21, ed. Sang Hyun Lee.

Y22   —*Sermons and Discourses, 1739–1742.* Vol. 22, ed. Harry S. Stout and Nathan O. Hatch.

Y23   —*The 'Miscellanies': Entry Nos. 1153–1320.* Vol. 23, ed. Douglas A. Sweeney.

Y24 — *The 'Blank Bible'.* Vol. 24, ed. Stephen J. Stein.
Y25 — *Sermons and Discourses, 1743–1758.* Vol. 25, ed. Wilson H. Kimnach.
Y26 — *Catalogues of Books.* Vol. 26, ed. Peter J. Thuesen.
JEC   Jonathan Edwards Center Transcriptions.

Introduction

'True weanedness from the world don't consist in being beat off from the world by the affliction of it, but a being drawn off by the sight of something better.'[1]

Few thinkers have ascended to the highest echelon of theological thought as *slowly* as Jonathan Edwards. His voice, drowned out by cultural shifts and thinkers who have demurred at his apparently outmoded theocentrism, was, admittedly, never fully silenced. Edwards has always retained devoted followers (mainly his relatives and disciples!), maintaining his vast corpus of unpublished writings and raising a defence if anyone bothered to level a complaint. In one of the great turns of irony in God's providential plan, it was an atheist who resurrected Edwards from obscurity, disregarding the church's neglect and raising him as an example of a thinker of the highest order. Perry Miller was that atheist, and since his work on Edwards in the mid-twentieth century there continues to be an ever-increasing interest in Edwards.

Unfortunately, Miller bequeathed more to Edwards studies than the revival of one of the great thinkers of the church. Miller, rather, presented a thinker who transcended even himself – an isolated genius whose work we are only now catching up with – a thinker whose theological depth was secondary, rather than primary, to his brilliance. This imprint on Edwards studies has coloured modern interpretation to the degree that the flood of monographs and articles has not resulted in an equally overwhelming deluge of knowledge of the true Edwards.

---

[1] Jonathan Edwards, '*Miscellanies* 724: Preparatory Work', in *The 'Miscellanies': Entry Nos. 501–832* (ed. Ava Chamberlain; The Works of Jonathan Edwards, vol. 18; New Haven: Yale University Press, 2000), 352 (after the initial reference for each volume, references for the Yale edition will be abbreviated with a Y followed by the volume number, work cited, and page number: e.g. Y18, '*Miscellanies* 724: Preparatory Work', 352). For a full listing of abbreviations, see the abbreviations page.

This volume seeks to cut through the fog of Edwards interpretation by offering an interpretative scheme to understand Edwards's thought. This interpretative key, like all others, is not neutral, but is discovered through prolonged meditation on Edwards and the God he served. In other words, rather than positing philosophical, scientific or artistic motivation as the primary engine that propelled Edwards's impressive literary output, I suggest that Edwards was a true theologian. In this sense, a true theologian is one who is compelled by the mystery of the gospel and its God, overcome by the deepest dimensions of God's self-revelation in Christ. As a true theologian of the highest order, then, Edwards wandered into the desert of theological discourse, searching for the only fountain that would offer him eternal sustenance. The fountain Edwards found, the spring that nourishes his thought, is the triune God of glory. What propelled Edwards was a desire to speak meaningfully about the God who confronted him as the beautiful one who took on flesh for the sake of his beloved.

Grasping Edwards's true vocation as a theologian enables us to see that Edwards's thought is, ultimately, *theologically* oriented. Along these lines, I suggest that the Jonathan Edwards of history is the Jonathan Edwards found in his corpus – a *Reformed* theologian, pastor, apologist and missionary who interpreted all reality through the lens of the gospel and, ultimately, God's own life, what Edwards depicted as 'the supreme harmony of all'.[2] This harmony, *in nuce*, provides both the teleology for Edwards's theological task and the imperative for any interpretative scheme. Rather than seeing this theological task as secondary to the breadth of his thought, I take it to be the centrepiece, the fountain from which all else flows.

This book is a description of that fountain. It shows how Edwards's theocentric vision of reality was the forming influence of his theology. Rather than establishing an interpretative key that claims to unlock Edwards's thought and then finishing the volume and moving on, I show how this key unveils the inner logic to his theological vision. This book is, in other words, a demonstration of Edwards's larger body of *Reformed* theology through its coherence and inner-relation to a specific doctrine of God. As such, this volume stands in contrast to many that have come before, most often touting Edwards as a philosopher first and theologian second. This is, in the mind of this interpreter, a disastrous error. Rather,

---

[2] Jonathan Edwards, '*Miscellanies* 182: Heaven', in *The 'Miscellanies': A–500* (ed. Thomas A. Schafer, The Works of Jonathan Edwards, vol. 13; New Haven: Yale University Press, 1994), 329.

what we find epitomized in Edwards's thought is a deeply spiritual theology driven by the identity of a God who transcends creaturely time and order as the true alpha and omega of all created things. We find in Edwards's thought a pastor at work, wielding the highest of thoughts for the greatest purpose – addressing the reconciling work of God to a people who are lost.

Turning our attention more narrowly to the confines of this introduction, what follows is a brief overview of Edwards's theological vision and then an equally brief overview of Edwards's theological project. These sections highlight the main features of his thought, which in turn serve as the foundation for this project. After the completion of this overview, I offer an overview of the volume itself, mapping the argument through terse summaries of my conclusions.

Edwards's Theological Vision

In his missive to the trustees of the College of New Jersey (what would eventually become Princeton), Edwards wrote what is arguably his most tantalizing statement for later interpreters, claiming his systematic theology would be:

> thrown into the form of an history, considering the affair of Christian theology, as the whole of it, in each part, stands in reference to the great work of redemption by Jesus Christ which I suppose is to be the grand design, of all God's designs, and the summum and ultimum of all the divine operations and decrees; particularly considering all parts of the grand scheme in their historical order. The order of their existence ... beginning from eternity and descending from thence to the great work and successive dispensations of the infinitely wise God in time, considering the chief events coming to pass in the church of God, and revolutions in the world of mankind, affecting the state of the church and the affair of redemption, which we have an account of in history or prophecy; till at last we come to the general resurrection, last judgement, and consummation of all things.[3]

Edwards's untimely death prevented him from seeing this theological vision to completion. Even so, several key elements come to the foreground,

---

[3] Jonathan Edwards, 'To the Trustees of the College of New Jersey', in *Letters and Personal Writings* (ed. George S. Claghorn, The Works of Jonathan Edwards, vol. 16; New Haven: Yale University Press, 1998), 728–9.

both in this statement and elsewhere in his corpus, that illuminate how he understood his task and the interconnection of his thought. Taking these in their 'order of existence', as Edwards suggests, I offer four key points, which I expound more fully below. First, Edwards's theology begins with God, in his eternal life as Trinity, as the ontological principle which grounds his systematic task. Second, Edwards begins 'from eternity' and then 'descends' to address God's work in time, or, in other words, God's economic movement to create and sustain. Third, this work in time is the work of redemption, directing the 'revolutions in the world' and guiding it toward resurrection, judgement and consummation. Fourth and finally, Edwards's theology is a theology of redemptive history, grounded in and formed by the God who is redeeming, or more specifically, the God who redeems *in, through* and *as* Christ.

First, Jonathan Edwards's theology is fundamentally trinitarian. Edwards's account of the Trinity is the anchor, or in his words, the *fountain* of all that is. Edwards's theology traces the contours of the Trinity so that the ordering, emphasis and teleology of his thought finds its home in his trinitarian analysis. Several key concepts come into focus as a result of this ordering. First, Edwards emphasizes personhood. This emphasis grounds his depiction of the Trinity and organizes his discussions concerning God's attributes and his work of redemption. The formal demarcations of the processions are not addressed through origin (e.g. begottenness) but through personhood (i.e. understanding and will). Second, Edwards develops his formal analysis of the processions in terms of the beatific vision. The Father gazes upon the Son and the Son upon the Father, not in a detached fashion, but with delight (the Spirit's spiration). In other words, the 'happiness' of the Father and Son *is* the Spirit, and the vision of God, shared by Father and Son, is, in Edwards's phrase, 'happifying'. Last, as an account of mutual beholding in the Godhead leading to affection, Edwards's depiction of the Trinity serves as the archetype for creaturely knowledge of God. Knowing God, in other words, requires apprehension that 'happifies'.

Second, God 'descends' to create the world and sustain it. Edwards refers to this as God's emanation. God is diffusive; he is communicative in both his immanent and economic existence. God is a God who reveals himself in the world for the purpose of affectionate knowledge, which is an image of his own inner-trinitarian self-knowing. This grounds the third point, that God sustains creation for the purpose of perfecting this affectionate knowledge as well as perfecting the union believers have with Christ. God is guiding creation to resurrection, judgement and consummation, which, for the elect, entails the full beatific vision of God, or true participation in God's self-knowing and self-loving. The parallel of God's emanation is thus, in Edwards's terminology, 'remanation', the glory of God received and communicated back to its divine source.

The Trinity, as the fountain, gives shape to all theology so that the beatific thread formed in his doctrine of the Trinity is woven throughout the whole until it finds its perfection in consummation. Edwards's theology, in this sense, is cyclical. Everything moves from God, and everything returns to him in judgement. The elect continue on this trajectory (past judgement) to God, while the reprobate do not. Along with being cyclical, Edwards's thought is teleological. The elect do not disappear into God, but commune with God eternally, because this eternal union is asymptotic – always growing closer without collapsing into a singular identity. Fourth, Christ, as the image of God, is the locus of revelation to the creature and as God-man is the point of mediation between God and man. Affectionate knowledge of God, as noted above, entails beholding God. Christ reveals God in his excellencies, calling the elect to behold and see his goodness and beauty. Redemption, through Christ's work, is the central thread that shapes Edwards's entire theological project.[4] Redemption is what the world was created for, and redemption entails God's revealing himself in Christ with affectionate creaturely response.

Edwards's Theological Project

Based upon this overview, it is necessary to explain why I address Edwards this way and not another. Edwards's depiction of his 'great work', and subsequent notes, suggests three important tendencies, which I highlight here. First, as noted above, Edwards's theology is a theology of redemption. Yet it would prove short-sighted to conclude that this theology of redemption encompasses the novelty of his method. There has been confusion over this fact because Edwards's sermon series 'A History of the Work of Redemption' bears the same title as his great work and would have provided something of an overall structure for this magnum opus. Importantly, Edwards's sermon series itself was not an innovation. In fact, Edwards's sermon series

---

[4] 'His works at the same time are wonderful, and cannot be found out to perfection; especially the work of redemption, which is that work of God about which the science of divinity is chiefly conversant, is full of unsearchable wonders.' Jonathan Edwards, 'The Importance and Advantage of a Thorough Knowledge of Divine Truth', in *Sermons and Discourses, 1739–1742* (ed. Harry Stout and Nathan Hatch; The Works of Jonathan Edwards, vol. 22; New Haven, Conn.: Yale University Press, 2003), 95.

follows van Mastricht move for move.[5] Second, in the case of his great work, Edwards could have utilized the same overall framework as the sermon series, which I believe was his intention, portraying God's redemptive activity through time as the structure of his work. The problem, again, is that this was not wholly new (as Edwards claimed his method was). John Owen's work *Biblical Theology* does just this, following contours broadly similar to Edwards's sermons series 'A History of the Work of Redemption'.[6]

Edwards's sermon series advances along an outline of redemption through three main periods: Fall to incarnation, incarnation to resurrection and resurrection to the end of the world. The sermons move toward glory with each step, through greater and greater knowledge of God's work of redemption and ever-expanding revelation (Flood to Abraham, Abraham to Moses, Moses to David, etc.). Owen likewise demarcates several of his chapters ('Books') along similar lines as Edwards's sermons: Book II: Theology from Adam to Noah; Book III: Theology from Noah to Abraham; Book IV: Theology from Abraham to Moses; Book V: Theology from Moses to Christ.[7] Therefore, as a covenant theologian with commitments to Christ's work of redemption as God's greatest work, Edwards found, like Owen and van Mastricht before him, that a historical mode proves advantageous to developing doctrine in a way which forms theology along the specific contours of God's work of redemption.[8]

Unlike Owen, however, it is clear that Edwards's trinitarian thought is the engine of his theology, and his division into similar epochs of time (Fall to Flood, Flood to Abraham, Abraham to Moses, etc.) would have served as the structure by which he would delineate, *doctrinally*, God's

---

[5] Jan van Vliet states, 'Indeed, Edwards's entire program, from conceptual framework to content, "from the fall of man to the end of the world" reveals, with some modification, a construct almost identical to that of Voetius' successor at Utrecht [van Mastricht].' Jan van Vliet, 'William Ames: Marrow of the Theology and Piety of the Reformed Tradition' (unpublished doctoral dissertation, Westminster Theological Seminary, 2002), 411.

[6] This is not to say that Edwards's projects would have been identical to Owen's, but only that the overall scheme was similar.

[7] See John Owen, *Biblical Theology, or, the Nature, Origin, Development, and Study of Theological Truth, in Six Books: In Which Are Examined the Origins and Progress of Both True and False Religious Worship, and the Most Notable Declensions and Revivals of the Church, from the Very Beginning of the World* (Morgan: Soli Deo Gloria Publications, 1994), 169–590.

[8] Robert Brown states, 'Rather than intending it [his great work] to serve as merely another treatment of religious revival or Protestant soteriology, he conceived the "Work of Redemption" as a comprehensive, systematic exposition of doctrine.' Robert E. Brown, 'Edwards, Locke, and the Bible', *The Journal of Religion* 79 (1999) 361–84; Brown, *Jonathan Edwards and the Bible* (Bloomington: Indiana University Press, 2002), 166. Brown argues that Edwards's task was born out of a response to problems with the critical-historical approaches to the Bible. In contrast, I believe Edwards was following his standard line, viz. creatively reworking the insights of his forebears. I would, however, broadly speaking, agree with Brown's analysis of Edwards's future work on redemption.

work of redemption. Their differences notwithstanding, the following quote from Carl Trueman concerning Owen could very well be said of Edwards: 'Underlying this choice of organization is Owen's fundamental belief that theology is relational; that is, it depends upon the nature of the relationship that exists between God the revealer and the one revealed, and humans, the recipients of that revelation.'[9] Edwards, in unpacking his relational theology, puts his trinitarian thought to work for his development of creation, redemption and ultimately consummation. History, in other words, is saturated by God's action – revealed in the movements of redemption from creation to consummation – and is the teleological plotline for creation as the theatre of glory. The result, as John F. Wilson notes, is that 'eternity actually is brought within time ... and time is endowed with significance by being taken up into eternity'.[10]

The second notable piece of Edwards's project, expounding upon the 'God-saturated' aspect of redemption history, is his use of Ezekiel's wheels.[11] Edwards pictured the whole of created reality like a huge clock, and just as the sun, stars and planets rotate in their orbits, so ages of history, and even individual lives, are part of a cyclical movement careening toward God's end – the 'striking of the hammer at the appointed time', as Edwards would prophetically utter.[12] Like a symphony, each wheel moves according to its role within the largest wheel – a cacophony of glorifying revolutions – accomplishing one ultimate turn of time and inaugurating God's eternal

---

[9] Carl Trueman, *Claims of Truth: John Owen's Trinitarian Theology* (Carlisle: Paternoster, 1998), 49.

[10] John F. Wilson, 'Editor's Introduction', in *A History of the Work of Redemption*, ed. John F. Wilson, The Works of Jonathan Edwards, vol. 9 (New Haven: Yale University Press, 1989), 56.

[11] In his 'Work of Redemption' notebooks, Edwards places Ezekiel's wheels in parallel with other images that describe how, in his words, 'all things in the foregoing periods are preparations for the next'. John Owen notes the origins of this move (using Ezekiel's chariot) in his *Biblical Theology*. He claims that Maimonides, in his mind the 'most learned of their [Jewish] theologians', divided theology into two parts: 'the work of creation, and the work of the chariot. The first is natural, and the second mystical theology, the latter title being taken from Ezekiel chapter one.' Owen, *Biblical Theology*, 3. Edwards showed interest in Maimonides. According to the editors of the typology notebooks, 'His notebooks give evidence of his interest in this and related traditions as well as his own application of the mystical approach. For example, an early entry in the "Catalogue", under the heading "Books to be inquired for", reads, "the best that treats of the cabalistic learning of the Jews" (4, no. 56). Entries elsewhere in his reading list include such standards as the Hebrew Bible, "the Chaldee Paraphrast", and the works of Moses Maimonides.' Wallace E. Anderson and David Watters, 'Editor's Introduction to "Image of Divine Things" and "Types"', in *Typological Writings* (ed. Wallace E. Anderson and David Watters; The Works of Jonathan Edwards, vol. 11; New Haven, Conn.: Yale University Press, 1993), 26.

[12] Jonathan Edwards, 'An Humble Attempt to Promote Explicit Agreement and Visible Union of God's People in Extraordinary Prayer', in *Apocalyptic Writings* (ed. Stephen J. Stein; The Works of Jonathan Edwards, vol. 5; New Haven, Conn.: Yale University Press, 1977), 346.

consummation. In his 'Notes on Scripture', Edwards explains, 'Things in their series and course in providence, they do as it were go round like a wheel in its motion on earth. That which goes round like a wheel goes from a certain point or direction, till it gradually returned to it again. So is the course of things in providence.'[13] He uses the zodiac, the changes in season and the yearly calendar to note the cyclical nature of time, never neglecting to highlight its fundamental teleology. Most importantly, all these 'wheels' are interconnected:

> So the monthly changes are by the revolution of another lesser wheel within that greater annual wheel, which, being a lesser wheel, must go round oftener to make the same progress. Ezekiel's vision was of wheels within wheels, of lesser wheels within greater, each touching the circumference of its respective wheel, and all making the same progress, keeping pace one with another.[14]

Edwards sees this movement in everything from the calendar to the circulation of blood in human bodies. As one epoch falls toward the earth, so another begins to rise, just as a wheel simultaneously hits the ground and rises from it.[15] Likewise, all of the lesser wheels are gears within one giant wheel representing all of time. This wheel makes only one great revolution, from God and back to God (see Figure 1 page 13).[16] The organization and

---

[13] Jonathan Edwards, '389. Ezekiel 1', in *Notes on Scripture* (ed. Stephen J. Stein; The Works of Jonathan Edwards, vol. 15; New Haven, Conn.: Yale University Press, 1998), 373. Importantly, Edwards's musings on Ezekiel's wheels are not solely relegated to his notes but are permeated throughout his work. See Jonathan Edwards, *Freedom of the Will*, ed. Paul Ramsey; The Works of Jonathan Edwards, vol. 1; New Haven, Conn.: Yale University Press, 1957), 250–1; Edwards, *Dissertation I: Concerning the End for which God Created the World*, in *Ethical Writings* (ed. Paul Ramsey; The Works of Jonathan Edwards, vol. 8; New Haven, Conn.: Yale University Press, 1989), 508; Y9, *The History of the Work of Redemption*, 118, 128, 282, 492, 519, 525; Y22, 'God's Care for His Servants in Time of Public Commotions', 349; Edwards, 'Approaching the End of God's Grand Design', in *Sermons and Discourses, 1743–1758* (ed. Wilson H. Kimnach; The Works of Jonathan Edwards, vol. 25; New Haven: Yale University Press, 2006), 121–2, 124.

[14] Y15, '389. Ezekiel 1', 373. See also: Y8, *Dissertation I: Concerning the End for which God Created the World*, 508; and Edwards, 'Miscellanies 867: Christian Religion. Immortality of the Soul. Future State. That This World Will Come to an End', in *The 'Miscellanies': Entry Nos. 833–1152* (ed. Amy Plantinga Pauw; The Works of Jonathan Edwards, vol. 20; New Haven: Yale University Press, 2002), 108.

[15] See Y15, '389. Ezekiel 1', 374. Edwards highlights that this can often be confusing for the church: 'The course of things seems to be backward, away from the proposed and promised end; but 'tis a mistake. God is still constantly making progress towards the church's promised glory.' Jonathan Edwards, 'Deuteronomy 33:26', in *The Blank Bible* (ed. Stephen Stein; The Works of Jonathan Edwards, vol. 24; New Haven: Yale University Press, 2006), 316; and Y24, 'Ecclesiastes 3:11', 586.

[16] The movement of this one wheel is the second section of this work, focusing on God's end

driving force behind every other wheel is this one; everything coming from God, and everything ultimately going back to him in judgement. Notably, Edwards maps the structure of *History of Redemption* onto his development of Ezekiel's wheels. Each section of the redemption sermon series is represented by a wheel within the great wheel: 'The course of things from the beginning of the world to the flood may be looked upon as the revolution of a wheel .... The course of things from the flood to Abraham was as it were the revolution of another wheel, or another revolution of the same wheel.'[17] This epochal motion in creation, ushering created reality toward eternity, narrates the broad movement of Edwards's theological vision. The eternal motion of the divine processions in the Godhead is the engine for his development, driving the economic activity of the Son and the Spirit, out of which flows the scheme of redemption. In other words, these wheels of time diligently perform their specific part according to the conductor's movement, the movement of the inner-triune life of God, who wills his economic existence for the redemption of his creation. As such, this organizing framework for Edwards's theology revolves around redemption and ultimately Christ, its centrepiece. Just as each demarcation of *History of Redemption* corresponds to a wheel (or revolution of that wheel), so this image would serve the theocentricity of Edwards's systematic portrayal of doctrine. His project would be 'thrown into the form of an history', but as a systematic theology, it was held together through a careful and expansive notion of the immanent and economic life of God.

This leads us to the final point about Edwards's work of divinity. Edwards's work was to have a tri-level structure. In his own words:

> This history will be carried on with regard to all three worlds, heaven, earth, and hell: considering the connected, successive events and alterations, in each so far as the Scriptures give any light; introducing all parts of divinity in that order which is most scriptural and most natural: which is a method which appears to me the most beautiful and entertaining, wherein every divine doctrine, will appear to greatest advantage in the

---

in creating the world and the consummation of all things – the first turning of the wheel and its final resting point in eternity. Michael McClymond is helpful at this point: 'In understanding God's work in history, the whole has epistemological priority over the part; that is, one cannot interpret the part without having at least a bare outline or sketch of the whole in one's mind .... Human beings understand the course and direction of history insofar as they participate in God's panoramic vision of the whole.' Michael J. McClymond, *Encounters with God: An Approach to the Theology of Jonathan Edwards* (Oxford: Oxford University Press, 1998), 75.

[17] Y15, '389. Ezekiel 1', 376.

brightest light, in the most striking manner, showing the admirable contexture and harmony of the whole.[18]

This was Edwards's great contribution to theology – his 'entirely new method' – whose scope seems to borrow, mutatis mutandis, from Dante's tri-level vision. His hope was to navigate God's redemptive activity in relation to three interconnected realms, each of which depends upon redemption history. Importantly, Edwards's interest was not history as such, but history *as redemptive history*, as God's movement in Christ to redeem and judge.[19] Edwards's new method is 'thrown into the form of a history' because heaven, earth and hell were three realms whose history develops Christologically and redemptively (as I show specifically in relation to heaven). Heaven, earth and hell are not isolated realms on this view. Heaven and hell, to be truly understood, are understood in relation to redemption. Edwards again invokes the chariot and wheels from Ezekiel 1 to narrate this reality:

> The church in heaven, in the progress it makes in its state of glory and blessedness, keeps pace with the church on earth, that the glory of both is advancing together …. For heaven and earth are both framed together. 'Tis the same chariot; one part has relation to another, and is connected with another, and is all moved together. The motion of one part depends on the motion of the other. The upper part moves on the wheels of the lower part, for heaven is the room and seat of the chariot that is above the firmament, that moves on the wheels that are under the firmament, and that go upon the earth.[20]

This will be fleshed out in our development of the ages of heaven. Importantly, one can see Edwards's tri-level vision, here a twofold vision of heaven and earth, come to the fore. Hell, the third level of Edwards's tri-level vision, is not addressed directly in this volume, but it too corresponds with redemption, in contrast rather than in parallel. The saints

---

[18] Y16, 'To the Trustees of the College of New Jersey', 729.

[19] This is in contrast to the many interpreters who seek to make Edwards's argument somehow subsumed *under* history as such. Harry Stout makes this mistake when he states, 'Whatever distance the reformers may have traveled from Rome, they had retained a Thomistic sense of systematic theology as the queen of the sciences. Edwards would substitute history.' Harry Stout, 'Jonathan Edwards's Tri-World Vision', in *The Legacy of Jonathan Edwards: American Religion and the Evangelical Tradition* (ed. D. G. Hart, Sean Michael Lucas and Stephen J. Nichols; Grand Rapids: Baker Academic, 2003), 28. In contrast, John F. Wilson correctly states, 'Beyond doubt, the Redemption project remained primarily a theological program in his mind.' Y9, *A History of the Work of Redemption*, 70.

[20] Y15, '391. Ezekiel 1', 385.

and angels in heaven, far from being removed from hell, visually or cognitively, are said to increase in happiness as they see the damned souls in punishment, thereby witnessing God's wrath and justice and growing in their knowledge of God.[21] Just like heaven, hell is a pilgrimage of eternal increase, but unlike heaven, it is increase unto misery rather than happiness.[22] The souls in hell will, like the saints in heaven, have heightened faculties and eternal 'affectionate knowledge' of their circumstance, saints unto glory and sinners unto depravity.[23] In this sense, the saints' eternal life is built on faith, what Edwards defines as 'closing with Christ', such that heaven will entail an eternal closing with God in Christ by the Spirit. Hell, by contrast, is the solidification of pride in the hearts of sinners, so that hell entails pride unto greater and greater rebellion, hardening and darkness.[24]

In short, Edwards's tri-level vision hinges on the work of Christ and its outpouring wake careening through time to God's creatures, either unto glory or damnation. The work of redemption is the driving force of Edwards's theological interests because it is the work of God in the world through Christ. This great work of Christ reveals who God is and, in turn, what God's ends are. The history of redemption is the shape that God's trinitarian movement of self-glorification takes – it is the motion that drives the wheels of time toward eternity. In Edwards's words, the work of redemption is the end and sum of all God's works, 'it was the end of the creation of the whole universe, and of all God's works of providence'.[25] Furthermore, Edwards focuses on God's nature as overflowing and diffusive, using the sun as an analogy. God's 'illumination' in the world is either illumination unto glory or hardening unto damnation. God's economic activity is never without creaturely effect; God is the sun that either illuminates or burns.[26]

---

[21] See *Miscellanies* 279, 407; and sermons: Mt. 10:28, Mk. 9:44, Mt. 25:46, Jn. 3:16 and Isa. 66:23–24.

[22] See *Miscellanies* 478 and 491.

[23] See *Miscellanies* 493, 505, 545, 921, 926, 927, 929 and 1004, and sermons: Lk. 16:24; 16:25.

[24] See *Miscellanies* 258. For similar, see sermons: Isa. 38:18, and Mt. 13:30; 18:8–9.

[25] Y20, *Miscellanies* 952: 'Consummation of All Things. New Heavens and New Earth. Progress of the Work of Redemption. Heaven Shall Be Changed, and Exalted to Higher Glory at the End of the World', 220. In *Miscellanies* 930 Edwards states, 'But God's end is to be obtained chiefly in the final disposal of mankind, who are that creature for whom the whole creation was made: it is to glorify himself in their eternal state. He will, therefore, without doubt glorify his perfections – his power, his majesty, his holiness, his wrath and love – in a very high degree indeed, in that happiness and misery.' Y20, *Miscellanies* 930: 'Misery of the Damned and Happiness of Heaven', 175.

[26] This is Edwards's main point in his sermon on Mal. 4:1–2 (see Y22, 'Christ the Spiritual Sun', 50–63). In *Miscellanies* 931 Edwards states that the sun is an image of God's relation to the world in two things: 'viz. as a fountain of light and life and refreshment, and also in being a consuming fire, an immense fountain as it were of infinitely fierce and burning heat'. Y20, '*Miscellanies* 931: Hell Torments. Conflagration', 180.

Utilizing this tri-level structure, Edwards claims, would have the 'greatest advantage in the brightest light', and would expose the 'harmony of the whole'.

While the focus of this volume is not to exposit Edwards's theological *project* as such, these three features help outline and detail Edwards's theological outlook. My task here is to trace the 'metanarrative' of Edwards's theology and address the broad strokes of redemption. Because of space considerations (and my nocturnal dream states), we ignore the doctrine of hell, the third level of Edwards's tri-level scheme, as well as certain key doctrines such as atonement, justification and sanctification. Furthermore, Edwards's metanarrative would have encapsulated the arts and sciences, showing how divinity is truly the queen discipline, but that will not be addressed here either.[27] Here, rather, I offer an exposition of Edwards's theology that is centred upon God's beatific self-glorification (sections 1 and 2), and then I demonstrate the heuristic power of this reading by reconsidering three important aspects of Edwards's theology of redemption (section 3). Edwards's theological vision, as worked out in anticipation of his unfinished theological project, provides a metanarrative to which all his theologizing conforms. Failure to take this metanarrative seriously is to reject Edwards's own theological moorings and self-confession.

Argument Overview

Based on the foregoing development, three key realities order discussion of Edwards's theology: first, his understanding of God's existence *in se*; second, his understanding of God's work to create and consummate that creation; and third, his vision of the trinitarian work of redemption (see fig. 1). It is my contention that any reconstruction of Edwards's theology must be directed by the relationship of the immanent Trinity to *this* work of

---

[27] Edwards made a note to himself to put in his preface to this great work, 'to shew how all arts and sciences, the more they are perfected, the more they issue in divinity, and coincide with it, and appear to be as parts of it. And to shew how absurd for Christians to write treatises of ethics distinctly from divinity as revealed in the Gospel.' Jonathan Edwards, 'Outline of "A Rational Account"', in *Scientific and Philosophical Writings* (ed. Wallace E. Anderson; The Works of Jonathan Edwards, vol. 6; New Haven: Yale University Press, 1980), 397. Likewise, 'But there is one science, or one certain kind of knowledge and doctrine, which is above all the rest, as it is concerning God and the great business of religion: this is divinity; which is not learned, as other sciences, merely by the improvement of man's natural reason, but is taught by God himself in a certain book that he hath given for that end, full of instruction.' Y22, 'The Importance and Advantage of a Thorough Knowledge of Divine Truth', 87.

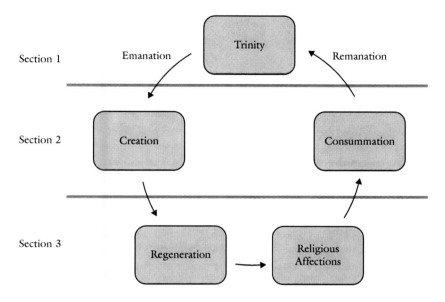

Figure 1: The structure of the book.

redemption, as Edwards himself states in his letter to the Princeton trustees and as we show below.

The structure I propose for an adequate reading of Edwards entails a top-down movement, depicted by the three sections in Figure 1, which correspond to the three sections of this volume. Each section governs the next, highlighting the teleological (or 'historical') and cyclical nature of Edwards's theology. As Figure 1 highlights, God emanates his glory to creation and, in the work of Christ and the Spirit, regenerates the elect to remanate that glory back to God, ultimately finding its perfection in consummation. This structure *anchors* redemption in God's trinitarian life and his end in creating and *orients* redemption proleptically in consummation.

The three sections of this volume expound the three levels of Figure 1 as summarized below. In advancing Edwards's theology as fundamentally *trinitarian*, we start with God *in se*, as the 'fountain' from which history and reality flows. Second, we place God's economic movement in creation in parallel with the saints' participation in the beatific life of the Godhead in eternity.[28] God's act and purpose in creation parallels his act and purpose in

---

[28] Edwards, in delineating the contours of his 'Work of Redemption' states: 'Concluding my work, with the consideration of that perfect state of things, which shall be finally settled, to last for eternity.' Y16, 'To the Trustees of the College of New Jersey', 729.

consummation, thereby bracketing and governing the work of redemption. Last, we broadly answer the question: 'How does God redeem the elect?' by addressing spiritual knowledge, regeneration and religious affection.

Section 1. Edwards's Doctrine of the Trinity

The first section of this work is constituted by a single chapter addressing Edwards's doctrine of the Trinity in light of its polemical context. Doing so raises three themes. First, Edwards's argument *moves from* a specific concept of divine personhood (through a psychological analogy) and *advances to* a conception of divine personhood through perichoresis. More poignantly, Edwards presupposes that a person is a being with understanding and will. Building upon this idea, Edwards develops his account of the Father as a person (with understanding and will) and then attributes the Son and Spirit to those 'subsistences'. Edwards commandeers perichoresis to explain how attributes (understanding and will) can be persons, claiming that the Father, Son and Spirit have personhood only insofar as they exist in perichoretic union. A subsistence of the divine essence, in other words, is a necessary but not sufficient condition for divine personhood.

Second, as noted above, the conceptual vehicle Edwards utilizes to talk about the processions is the beatific vision (the Father and Son gazing upon one another with a 'happifying' result). God, as eternal, infinite and pure act, eternally knows (or beholds) himself and loves himself. As perfect being and pure beauty, God beholds himself as perfect and beautiful, the greatest possible being, and therefore inclines to himself. To put this in terms more central to the Edwardsian corpus, one could say that God's eternal life is infinite religious affection in pure act.

Third, because Edwards's main category for talking about the Trinity is personhood, he translates the attributes according to his conception of a personal God. Therefore, just as God the Father is a person by having understanding and will, the Son and the Spirit respectively, so God's attributes must be conceived as attributes proper to persons. To do so, Edwards provides a twofold demarcation of God's attributes, first 'real', and second, 'relational'. Real attributes are God's understanding and will (or anything that can fall under those categories) and relational attributes are extrinsic attributes which do not obtain essentially in God. Edwards claims that relational attributes are 'modes' of God's being, such as eternality (this is developed most fully in the appendix).

Therefore, I argue that a sufficient development of Edwards's understanding of the immanent Trinity must be an account of persons, delighting in their own infinite beauty and perfection. All ontological, aesthetic and ethical discussion must take place in the light of triune persons delighting in infinite beauty and love. This is the source of history and, as will be shown below, the goal of history, which is oriented toward eternity.

Section 2. Emanation to Consummation

God's purpose in creation is the second ground of theological reflection and is exposited in parallel with God's uniting believers to himself for eternal union and communion in glorification. Redemptive history, therefore, is understood as God enacting his ends in creation toward consummation. As Edwards was apt to say, God is the alpha and omega in the affairs of history. History, as Edwards conceives it, is both teleological and cyclical; it is always aiming toward a given end, God's end, and flows back to God through cyclical movements of time. Creation and consummation, therefore, serve to locate and govern Edwards's doctrine of redemption. In short, God creates for his own glory, which he brings to pass through creaturely participation in his own beatific-delight.

God, as the God of personal beatific-delight, presses redemption into the mould it takes in consummation – the church, the bride of Christ, participating within the Father's love to the Son and the Son's love to the Father.[29] This union is consummated in heaven, where the church participates in the very beatific vision that defines the eternal life of the Godhead. The emanation of God's communicative overflow stems from a desire for his own self-glorification, which results in remanation. Therefore the beginning and the end are ordered by God's own inner-trinitarian vision and his redemptive purpose to share that vision with creatures.

Section 3. Redemption as Remanation

Edwards's account of redemption is a trinitarian scheme of union and communion. All of redemption is a single turn of history's wheel, starting with God, perfect in union and delight, and ends with God, uniting the church to himself as the spouse of the Son, partaking and participating through the Son in God's personal beatific-delight. Redemption, as seen

---

[29] In Edwards's words, 'The world is the chariot of Jesus Christ, the Son of God, in which he makes his progress to that glory, that glorious marriage with his spouse, that eternal feast, that everlasting kingdom of rest, and love, and joy, which the Father hath designed him.' Y15, '389. Ezekiel 1', 378.

above, is ordered by the concepts of emanation and remanation, grounded in God's act of creation and oriented toward God's act of glorification.

For the purposes of this volume, I suggest that this beatific self-glorification of God serves as a heuristic key to God's redemptive activity. We apply this interpretative scheme in the final section, expositing spiritual knowledge, regeneration and religious affection. First, spiritual knowledge is governed by the kind of knowledge God has of himself, which is constituted by sight and affection. Therefore, true knowledge of God entails an ectypal knowledge based on the trinitarian archetype. Creaturely knowledge of God is lived by faith in the mode of pilgrim knowledge, itself oriented by a vision of God in Christ by his Spirit through the dark glass of the gospel. This darkened sight is unquestionably sight nonetheless as it grasps with increasing clarity God's beauty for eternity.

Second, regeneration is the means by which one experiences this vision of Christ. On the one hand, regeneration entails illumination and infusion. Infusion is the work of the Spirit to unite God's love to the elect, thereby making them holy. Illumination, on the other hand, is the action of the Spirit to enlighten the person to truly see God. This movement of illumination and infusion corresponds to the missions of the Son and Spirit. The triune God of beatific-delight is the self-revealing God of the gospel, revealing himself in his Son, his own understanding, sent so that the elect can truly know God by *seeing him.* Furthermore, since archetypal knowledge is affectionate knowledge – i.e. perfect sight and infinite *delight* – ectypal knowledge also functions in the register of affection, as God sends his Spirit so that the elect can *truly* know, not only understand, but incline their wills to the God of history. Furthermore, the Spirit unites creatures to Christ, so that they become one with him and within that union see him through the Spirit's illuminating work and incline to him habitually through an infusion of *Holy* Spirit.

Third, I close out this section by addressing religious affection. God's redemption of humanity is governed by the beatific life of God. Redemption, therefore, demands that both human understanding and human will be thoroughly renovated. Spiritual knowledge entails creaturely correspondence to God's life *ad intra,* the archetype of creaturely knowledge, and that correspondence is religious affection. Spiritual knowledge is oriented by the teleological nature of Edwards's thought, which is a movement toward the unadulterated beatific knowledge of God in consummation. Pilgrim theology, for Edwards, because it is knowledge *of God,* entails, according to the points made above, that it is *beatific*-pilgrim theology. Edwards's doctrine of the 'sense of the heart' is grounded within an understanding of knowledge that is 'sensible' and governed by its divine object. The divine sense is the echo of eternity, grounded by the beatific nature of the trinitarian life, forcing all knowledge of God into a beatific form (i.e. affectionate knowledge). Religious affections, therefore, call out the image of God in the regenerate as those who have a new divine sense and participate in God's own understanding and love. As God's life is eternal, infinite and the pure action of understanding and loving, the regenerate, in a finite and limited sense, mirror God's life by receiving his communication and in turn 'flowing out' in their inclination, truly knowing and loving God with their whole beings.

In addressing Edwards's trinitarian theology of redemption in this manner, I provide a dogmatic sketch of redemption, what I refer to as Edwards's trinitarian metanarrative of redemption (i.e. God's beatific self-glorification). This volume, in other words, is a systematic reconstruction of Edwards's metanarrative, a reconstruction that entails thorough exposition of materials across Edwards's corpus, focusing primarily on the inner coherence of Edwards's trinitarian theology. To do so necessitates, at times, detailed exposition of texts that are ordered according to their 'weight'.[30] The 'weightiest' material in Edwards's corpus are published works, followed by sermons and then, last, his notebook entries. At times, such as with the doctrinal material on heaven, Edwards's notebooks and sermons concur and are therefore used in parallel to fill out an account beyond anything he provided in one specific text. More often, however, Edwards's notebooks are used to supplement the explication or else used to highlight shifts in his thought.[31] As a systematic reconstruction, this volume's emphasis is neither on polemical engagement with the secondary literature nor on contrasting the view proposed here with other readings. That said, throughout my argumentation I highlight errors commentators have made by failing to take the weight of Edwards's various materials seriously, as well as enter into critical engagement with other views for the purpose of clarity.[32] In an attempt to minimize polemical engagement, I have pushed the bulk of this material, as well as the areas where my position inevitably contrasts other

---

[30] Michael McClenahan, 'Jonathan Edwards's Doctrine of Justification in the Period up to the First Great Awakening' (unpublished doctoral dissertation, University of Oxford, 2006), 36–7, raises this issue as well.

[31] Many accounts of Edwards's theology fail to follow these shifts of thought. Examples will be provided in their context below.

[32] As is shown below, a failure to take seriously the weight of a document leads to a misunderstanding or misuse of the document itself. With the increase in accessibility to Edwards's note material, unpublished sermons and fragmentary work, there is an even greater need to consider how Edwards's thought progresses and how the individual documents relate.

overarching interpretative proposals, to footnotes and an appendix to keep the focus on the exposition and reconstruction of Edwards's theology. However, I highlight the main competing interpretation here.

Without question, the most influential interpretative proposal of Edwards's thought is Sang Hyun Lee's discussion of the philosophical theology of Jonathan Edwards.[33] Lee has not only devised an interpretative model for Edwards's theology and philosophy, but he has also built the only real 'school' of thought in Edwards studies.[34] Because of the influence Lee has wielded through his project it is important to highlight several key moments where my project runs contrary to his own.[35] First, and most importantly, I believe that Lee's interpretative scheme is ultimately misguided because his approach fails to be robustly *theological.* Lee develops an account of Edwards's philosophy and then applies that philosophy wholesale to his doctrine of God. As I have noted in the foregoing material, however, God stands alone as the foundation of Edwards's thought. To advance a distinctively *theological* philosophical theology, I believe it necessary to start with Edwards's doctrine of God and only then move to address his philosophical convictions.[36] In other words, Edwards's theocentricity has real methodological import. This point is the most substantive in my criticism of Lee and the interpretative power of his project. If I am correct, Lee fails to interpret Edwards as Edwards – failing

[33] Sang Hyun Lee, *The Philosophical Theology of Jonathan Edwards* (Princeton: Princeton University Press, 2000).

[34] The major figures working within what could be called the 'Lee school' are, of course, Sang Hyun Lee himself, Gerald R. McDermott and Anri Morimoto, the latter's work, *Jonathan Edwards and the Catholic Vision of Salvation*, sought to take Lee's program and apply it to Edwards's account of salvation. In contrast to Lee's school, both Stephen Holmes and Oliver Crisp have sought to provide alternative readings, focusing on the systematic, confessional and philosophical difficulties (they would no doubt say 'errors') of Lee's analysis. See: Anri Morimoto, *Jonathan Edwards and the Catholic Vision of Salvation* (University Park: Pennsylvania State University Press, 1995); Gerald R. McDermott, *One Holy and Happy Society: The Public Theology of Jonathan Edwards* (University Park: Pennsylvania State University Press, 1992); Gerald R. McDermott, *Jonathan Edwards Confronts the Gods: Christian Theology, Enlightenment Religion, and Non-Christian Faiths* (Oxford: Oxford University Press, 2000); Oliver Crisp, 'Jonathan Edwards's Ontology: A Critique of Sang Hyun Lee's Dispositional Account of Edwardsian Metaphysics', *Religious Studies* 46, no. 1 (2010), 1–20; Stephen Holmes, *God of Grace and God of Glory: An Account of the Theology of Jonathan Edwards* (Grand Rapids: Eerdmans, 2001); Stephen Holmes, 'Does Jonathan Edwards Use a Dispositional Ontology? A Response to Sang Hyun Lee', in *Jonathan Edwards: Philosophical Theologian* (ed. Oliver Crisp and Paul Helm; Aldershot: Ashgate, 2004), 99–114.

[35] In the most recent scholarship on Edwards's philosophy, there seems to be a move away from Lee's interpretative schema. See Crisp, 'Jonathan Edwards's Ontology', 1–20; and John J. Bombaro, *Jonathan Edwards's Vision of Reality: The Relationship of God to the World, Redemption History, and the Reprobate* (Princeton Theological Monograph Series; Eugene: Wiph & Stock, 2012).

[36] One such project would be: Oliver Crisp, *Jonathan Edwards on God and Creation* (Oxford: Oxford University Press, forthcoming).

to weigh issues and texts appropriately according to Edwards's own estima-
tions – and therefore maligns his thought. These issues become clear
when both Lee and those in his school utilize his interpretative scheme
to address specifically *theological* loci. In short, I suggest Lee champions
Edwards as a philosopher, whereas my account claims that Edwards is, first
and foremost, a theologian.

Second, Lee's use of Edwards's corpus is unhelpful at best and misleading
at worst. By failing to demarcate between various genres of texts and
their weight (i.e. published works, sermons, *Miscellanies*), and by failing
to address Edwards's theological development, Lee inevitably finds texts
to substantiate his position and reads Edwards's theological language
through a peculiar philosophical filter. Because of the nature of Edwards's
corpus, addressed throughout this work, interpreters must give priority to
published works over notebooks, and they must focus their attention on the
development of Edwards's thought. Third, building on the previous two
points, I do not find Lee's account of God in Edwards's work to be either
plausible or accurate, and I provide a competing interpretation in Chapter
1 below. I do not find it *plausible*, as Stephen Holmes points out, because
Edwards would have been wrong about his own theological commitments
(Reformed), and because it would have made Edwards, in both his mind
and the tradition, a heretic (specifically in terms of God's aseity).[37] Likewise,
I do not find Lee's analysis of Edwards's *The End for Which God Created the
World* to be an *accurate* portrayal of Edwards's concerns or analysis (see my
second chapter). Rather than seeking to rebut Lee's claims one by one
in this volume, which would be both cumbersome and tiring, we offer
the following analysis, *in toto*, as a more adequate account of Edwards's
theology and method. It should be said that this volume does not attack or
address Lee's philosophical insights but rather focuses on how he wields
those insights to solve theological problems – most specifically, God's own
eternal life and God's relation to the world.[38] Some of Lee's philosophical
insights may very well be accurate. My contention is that they function as
a result of his trinitarian theology and should not be allowed to govern it.

In short, I propose that Edwards's trinitarian theology forms the overall
contours of redemption by focusing on the redemption of *persons* by God's
self-revelation of his inner life. God's glory, as the reality of his own beatific-
delight, is the grounding of creation, redemption and consummation,

[37] Holmes, 'Does Jonathan Edwards Use a Dispositional Ontology?', 99–114.
[38] It should also be noted that this does not take away in the slightest from Lee's stature as
an Edwards scholar and his impact on the field. Since Perry Miller, no one has influenced
Edwards scholarship as much as Lee.

determining the *kind of redemption* that must take place. Ultimately, God redeems by revealing his beatific-glory in Christ, through the regenerating activity of the Spirit, so that the elect experience God's own personal delight and thereby truly know God.

Section 1

Jonathan Edwards's God

'Those doctrines which relate to the essence, attributes, and subsistencies of God, concern all; as it is of infinite importance to common people, as well as to ministers, to know what kind of being God is.'[1]

'And therefore seeing he is an infinite Being, it follows that he is an infinite fountain of love. Seeing he is an all-sufficient Being, it follows that he is a full and overflowing and an inexhaustible fountain of love. Seeing he is an unchangeable and eternal Being, he is an unchangeable and eternal source of love.'[2]

---

[1] Y22, 'The Importance and Advantage of a Thorough Knowledge of Divine Truth', 92.
[2] Y8, 'Charity and Its Fruits', 369.

Chapter 1

Personal Beatific-Delight: An Account of the Trinity

To advance the position I developed in the introduction, the necessary starting point in Edwards's theology is theology proper. This chapter therefore examines Edwards's understanding of the Trinity, answering the statement quoted above: what kind of being is God? This, I propose, lays the groundwork for how Edwards develops his understanding of God's economic activity (establishing the contours of redemption) and provides a robust trinitarian grammar with which to parse Edwards's theology. Detailed discussion of Edwards's trinitarian thought, in other words, sets the stage for understanding the *ad extra* movement of God, from creating to consummating, the origin and *telos* of redemption, and thereby appropriately orders our analysis. This approach follows Edwards himself, who, in his outline of 'A Rational Account', wrote of his intent to 'explain the doctrine of the Trinity before I begin to treat of the work of redemption'.[1]

In starting with the Trinity as the fountain of Edwards's thought, I am placing myself in line with the overwhelming consensus of contemporary Edwards commentary. Interpreters find in Edwards a robust trinitarian foundation orienting the whole of his theological programme. This is in part because of Edwards's understanding of the interconnectivity of God's internal life and his work within creation. Sang Hyun Lee writes:

What is striking about Jonathan Edwards' writings on the Trinity is that there is none of this bifurcation between the doctrine of the Trinity and the Christian life of faith and practice. Everything Edwards wrote about the Trinity expresses the intertwining connectedness of the Trinity and

[1] Y6, 'Outline of "A Rational Account"', 396.

the Christian's experience of God as the Creator, Savior, and Sanctifier, and thus between the immanent and the economic Trinity.[2]

The emphasis on the Trinity as an interpretative key for Edwards's thought summarizes the majority opinion of Edwards scholars. William J. Danaher, in his book *The Trinitarian Ethics of Jonathan Edwards*, starts with a lengthy discussion of Edwards's work on the Trinity in order to ground and explain his theological ethics. In discussing this task, Danaher states, 'what is distinctive in Edwards's writings on the Trinity is that he integrates the moral life with the life of the Trinity such that understanding the nature and character of God is inseparable from understanding the nature of morality'.[3] Likewise, Amy Plantinga Pauw, in her book *'The Supreme Harmony of All': The Trinitarian Theology of Jonathan Edwards*, writes, 'Edwards's trinitarianism provides an unusually wide view of his deepest philosophical, theological, and pastoral inclinations. The Trinity was for Edwards "the supreme harmony of all", and in his trinitarian thought the various facets of his life and genius ... moved toward harmonious resolution.'[4]

What Lee, Danaher and Pauw suggest is what contemporary commentators on Edwards commonly affirm: Jonathan Edwards's theology is truly trinitarian.[5] In following this line, I also take seriously Edwards's practical orientation, yet remain attuned to the theological nature of his pastoral task. In Edwards's words:

I used to think sometimes with myself, if such doctrines as those of the Trinity and decrees are true, yet what need was there of revealing of them in the gospel? what good do they do towards the advancing [of] holiness? But now I don't wonder at all at their being revealed, for such doctrines as these are glorious inlets into the knowledge and view of the

[2] Sang Hyun Lee, 'Editor's Introduction', in Jonathan Edwards, *Writings on the Trinity, Grace, and Faith* (ed. Sang Hyun Lee; The Works of Jonathan Edwards, vol. 21; New Haven: Yale University Press, 2003), 3.

[3] William J. Danaher, *The Trinitarian Ethics of Jonathan Edwards* (Columbia Series in Reformed Theology; Louisville: Westminster John Knox, 2004), 11.

[4] Amy Plantinga Pauw, *The Supreme Harmony of All: The Trinitarian Theology of Jonathan Edwards* (Grand Rapids: Eerdmanns, 2002), 3.

[5] There are several other published works of note that could have been used alongside Lee, Danaher and Pauw, such as Robert W. Caldwell, *Communion in the Spirit: The Holy Spirit as the Bond of Union in the Theology of Jonathan Edwards* (ed. David Bebbington *et al.*; Studies in Evangelical History and Thought; Waynesboro: Paternoster, 2006); Robert W. Jenson, *America's Theologian: A Recommendation of Jonathan Edwards* (Oxford: Oxford University Press, 1988); Stephen Holmes, *God of Grace and God of Glory: An Account of the Theology of Jonathan Edwards* (Grand Rapids: Eerdmans, 2001); and Steven Studebaker, 'Jonathan Edwards' Social Augustinian Trinitarianism: An Alternative to a Recent Trend', *Scottish Journal of Theology* 56, no. 3 (2003), 268–85.

spiritual world, and the contemplation of supreme things; the knowledge of which I have experienced how much it contributes to the betterment of the heart.[6]

Edwards's thought in this area is heavily debated, so I engage the contemporary discussion of specific issues for the purpose of clarity, the bulk of which will be relegated to footnotes and an appendix. As the fountain of his thought, the Trinity is the most important piece for grasping the inner logic of Edwards's theology. In other words, a failure to grasp Edwards's doctrine of the Trinity – a reality that I argue continues to plague contemporary scholarship – is a failure to truly understand his theology.[7]

There are several necessary components to address in adequately detailing Edwards's doctrine of the Trinity: his view itself, his view as developed in argumentation, the polemical issues behind his view, and the centrepiece of his analysis; there is also the contemporary discussions and debates concerning his view, its categorization, and some more intricate aspects of his development. In order to navigate this complex terrain, I start by sketching a brief overview of my categorization and understanding of Edwards's work in this area. Following this précis, I look specifically at the background issues leading up to and defining Edwards's context, highlighting key issues and ideas that would have influenced his view. In doing so, I hope to give the reader a strong understanding of Edwards's thought itself and the impetus for its development. I build on this analysis by working through Edwards's *Discourse on the Trinity* (hereafter *Discourse*) to highlight my view and reveal how Edwards goes about arguing for his doctrine. This examination raises to the surface key debates concerning the divine essence and persons, which have particular import for the processions and relations within the Godhead. It is only after I work through these issues that I contrast my account with other contemporary categorizations. In so arguing, I suggest a different way of talking about the issues in Edwards's thought, a way which grounds our latter development of redemption, as well as offer clarifying distinctions in Edwards's understanding of the Trinity broadly and for his *trinitarian* theology specifically.

---

[6] Y13, '*Miscellanies* 181. Trinity and Decrees', 328.

[7] Note Michael McClymond's comments: 'A fair appraisal of his [Edwards's] theology must therefore answer the question: *What sort of God* did he propound? A mistaken answer to this question could have repercussions in construing the various theological loci, such as anthropology, Christology, soteriology, ecclesiology, and eschatology.' Michael J. McClymond, 'Hearing the Symphony: A Critique of Some Critics of Sang Lee's and Amy Pauw's Accounts of Jonathan Edwards' View of God', in *Jonathan Edwards as Contemporary: Essays in Honor of Sang Hyun Lee* (ed. Don Schweitzer; New York: Peter Lang, 2010), 67.

In the appendix at the end of this volume I offer a more in-depth treatment of Edwards's idiosyncratic account of the divine attributes in the *Discourse* and set my position in discussion with the debate between Stephen Holmes and Oliver Crisp.

Admittedly, starting with the broad picture and then descending into what can appear to be minutiae runs the risk of feeling like a backward attempt at argumentation. For the sake of clarity, I believe this is a necessary risk. My overall hope for this structure is that the broad picture will provide the clarity necessary for the individual aspects to be recognized not as gratuitous minutiae but as necessary thumbnails in a complex mosaic.

I Overview: A Model of the Beatific

It is my contention that the best way to talk about Edwards's understanding of the Trinity is in terms of 'personal beatific-delight'. There are two ways we must proceed to explicate this view. First, it is important to exposit the view itself in isolation from Edwards's development of it in his *Discourse*. The polemical thrust of the *Discourse*, as well as its undeveloped nature, often complicates the task of clarification if it is treated as his view simply stated. In brief, Edwards posits *personhood* as the delineation of the divine essence. The divine essence exists with personal properties – understanding and will – which define and establish the character of the deity. Furthermore, rather than developing the triune personhood of God in terms of subsistence alone, Edwards posits personhood through perichoresis. The central defining conceptual feature of Edwards's analysis of the Trinity is personhood, which both initiates his argument (i.e. God has understanding and will) and completes it by establishing tri-personhood through perichoresis.[8]

The term 'personal beatific-delight' pulls together three images into one composite image or model. First, 'personal' highlights his use of a psychological analogy, highlighting his claim that a person is a being with understanding and will. Second, 'beatific' is the mechanism he

---

[8] The bulk of my interaction with Lee comes in the following chapter, but here it is important to note that I focus on persons rather than dispositions. Lee makes the case for Edwards's dispositional ontology but then moves from there directly into his doctrine of God. In doing so, Lee ushers in dispositions as a category with its own 'life', so to speak. Instead, I focus on Edwards's explicit discussions of God and argue that person(s) is a more fundamental category in his doctrine of God than dispositions. (Lee would no doubt agree with this, but my point here is more methodologically important than simply the content of the claim.) In the following chapter, I focus on how dispositions function in Edwards's thought, but it is not meaningless to claim that Lee's analysis and mine part ways on this point.

uses to explicate the processions. This is done in terms of an archetypal beatific envisaging within the inner life of God, where the Father gazes upon himself, or his perfect idea (Son), and the Son gazes back, spirating perfect happiness (Holy Spirit). Last, the category of 'delight' finds its home in Edwards's aesthetics as well as in his discussion of the beatific life of God, calling out the Spirit's emanation as the happiness and love of the Godhead. Each of these three images can be accommodated to one specific person of the triune three, although each necessarily entails the others. For instance, *personhood* calls out the Father specifically as the *fons et origo* of the Son and the Spirit, the understanding and the will respectively. Likewise, the Son is the image on which the Father gazes *beatifically*, being both subject and object of the vision shared with the Father. Last, *delight* is the specific role of the Spirit as the spirated love of God in the beatific vision. Personal beatific-delight, therefore, does justice to his use of classic imagery (psychological analogy, beatific, God's eternal delight) within a broader 'narrative' of the pure actuality of God.

Second, the bulk of our exposition attends to the development of Edwards's view in the *Discourse* itself. Again, in brief, Edwards starts with the concept of a personal God as his guiding assumption and builds his argument upon that foundation, thus highlighting the unity of the Godhead. His initial analysis begins with a singular person, who, as God, is infinite, simple, and understands and loves in pure act.[9] Edwards, having grounded the discussion in unity and singularity, pushes his argument forward to talk about a personal God who has two *real* attributes true of his nature – understanding and will. Edwards, furthermore, develops threeness from the top down. (It is not until later in the *Discourse* that he introduces his understanding of the tri-personed nature of God and how this one God is actually three.) He invokes the notion of perichoresis, arguing that the subsistences all partake in each other personally; therefore, the Son (understanding) and the Spirit (will) are both persons insofar as they partake in one another. In this sense, personhood drives Edwards's exposition from two angles: God's singular personhood establishes the contours of the divine essence, doing what the psychological analogy does best, namely, looking at personhood in terms of a mind that understands and loves, the two 'faculties' or 'principles' of the soul.

---

[9] Oliver Crisp's recent work has emphasized the *actus purus* line in Edwards's thought, arguing that Edwards's view can best be described as '*pure act panentheism*'. Oliver Crisp, 'Jonathan Edwards on the Divine Nature', *Journal of Reformed Theology* 3, no. 2 (2009), 175–201 (175). Oliver continues this line of thought in his forthcoming book, *Jonathan Edwards on God and Creation* (Oxford: Oxford University Press, forthcoming).

Likewise, from the opposite angle, Edwards runs personhood through the machinery of perichoresis, establishing the reality that the personhood of the Father, assumed at the outset, is personhood *only insofar as God is triune.* Notably, these are not two definitions of personhood, but are one analysis, argued from a singular person to triune persons (emphasizing a logical rather than temporal development).[10]

In other words, according to Edwards's argumentation, one starts with a single person and 'arrives' at a trinitarian account of persons. Therefore, instead of Father, Son and Spirit as persons in their own right, Edwards offers a trinitarian interpretation of personhood through perichoresis. This is the 'twist in the plot', as it were, in his trinitarian narrative that begins with the singular personhood of God. The great 'twist' is that the triune persons are not persons *individually.* Therefore, in his development, he seeks a certain amount of rhetorical slack, focusing on the Father as a single person, generating a perfect idea and will eternally. Just as the Father is not a person without understanding and will, Edwards's argument will establish, so also the Father is not a person without the Son or the Spirit. As will be discussed later, Edwards's statements can be difficult to categorize precisely because these images of personhood, beatific and delight are interwoven into and flow out of his thought in such a way that his theology consistently intermingles them.

What this analysis does make clear, however, is that Edwards's concern, possibly his main concern, is to establish the *trinitarian* personhood of God. Wanting to use personhood for polemical reasons, as shown below, Edwards affirms that God is personal and that the Son and the Spirit are also both persons and divine in their own right. Note his explicitness concerning the Spirit's personhood: 'He [the Spirit] is often spoken of as a person, revealed under personal characters and in personal acts, and it speaks of his being acted on as a person; and the Scripture plainly ascribes everything to him that properly denotes a distinct person.'[11] Edwards emphasizes the personhood of the Spirit in response to the degradation, common in his day, of the Son and Spirit's distinct personhood and divinity. In fact, most importantly for his work on the Trinity, Edwards was working within an age where anti-trinitarian sentiments in general were growing in popularity.[12] By viewing the Trinity as the Father, his

---

[10] Studebaker, as is highlighted below, mistakenly posits two definitions of personhood. Rather, what is found in the *Discourse* is a singular definition of personhood that ultimately drives Edwards to utilize perichoresis.

[11] Y21, *Treatise on Grace*, 181.

[12] Establishing Edwards's opponents is not the particular burden of this chapter. Nevertheless,

understanding and his love united together to form three persons (as persons in their perichoretic union), Edwards corrects the very idea the anti-trinitarians were seeking to attack. He argues that if God is a person, *their very point of agreement*, then, assuming what Christian divines have always assumed – that the trinitarian persons only have one understanding and one will – God can still very well be triune. Even by starting with God's singularity, Edwards seeks to remedy talk about God the Father in distinction from the other two triune members.[13] Christian *God* talk, for Edwards, is *trinitarian* God talk.[14]

In choosing to talk about Edwards's trinitarianism as personal beatific-delight, I am rejecting all other contemporary categorizations of Edwards's trinitarian thought.[15] This move will, I propose, prove less controversial

I believe that Edwards's polemical eye was aimed at the several versions of anti-trinitarianism in vogue in his day (viz. Socinians, Deists, Arians, etc.), but he understood them all as secondary targets behind Samuel Clarke's subordinationism. See Samuel Clarke, *The Scripture-Doctrine of the Trinity: In Three Parts* (London: Printed for James Knapton, 1712). Admittedly, when writing the *Discourse*, Edwards would not have had a copy of Clarke's work. Nevertheless, it is beyond question that Edwards would have known of the work and been privy to its argumentation (even if not in strict detail). Thomas Schafer notes that in the *Miscellanies* Table, Edwards quotes Clarke's Boyle lectures more than any other work, and Edwards would no doubt have been interested in his newly published 'heretical' writings. Y13, 'Notes on the Table', 120n1. Clarke's work, published in 1712 (about 18 years prior to Edwards's *Discourse*), created a major stir that would not have escaped Edwards's attention. Furthermore, after the publication of Clarke's work, there was a flurry of books written on both sides of the debate, including a convocation of the Church of England in 1714 to investigate Clarke's views. See Thomas C. Pfizenmaier, *The Trinitarian Theology of Dr. Samuel Clarke (1675–1729): Context, Sources, and Controversy* (New York: Brill, 1997), 185. Edwards, who saw himself as an international figure and defender of orthodoxy, would no doubt have wanted to have his name appear in the debate that was waged for years after the initial publication of Clarke's book. Several times throughout this chapter, I will highlight places where Edwards is responding to a specific position of Clarke's. I should also mention that through the convocation, the Upper House resolved not to proceed further against Clarke. This decision was made on July 5, 1714, the same day that Clarke clarified his position to the Bishop of London. Pfizenmaier, *Trinitarian Theology of Dr. Samuel Clarke*, 186–7. One wonders if it is a coincidence that 264 years later I was born on that same day. The implications, no doubt profound, will be left to the reader to decipher.

[13] 'The Son, whatever his metaphysical essence or substance be, and whatever divine greatness and dignity is ascribed to him in Scripture; yet in this he is evidently subordinate to the Father, that he derives his being and attributes from the Father, and the Father nothing from him.' Clarke, *Scripture-Doctrine of the Trinity*, 304 – my edits (any quotation of Clarke's work has had the italics and capitalizations edited for readability).

[14] Edwards states that "tis as natural to God to subsist in three persons as 'tis to be wise and to be holy as to be omnipresent and unchangeable'. Jonathan Edwards, 'Jesus Christ Is the Shining Forth of the Father's Glory', in *The Glory and Honor of God: Volume 2 of the Previously Unpublished Sermons of Jonathan Edwards* (ed. Michael D. McMullen; Nashville: Broadman & Holman, 2004), 228–9.

[15] It is noteworthy that Edwards's view helps him avoid 'sliding' toward the opposite errors of tritheism and modalism, the two errors Clarke is so worried about. The greater emphasis on persons necessitates stronger union and coinherence without diminishing their personhood.

than it seems at face value and will in fact allow for greater clarity of his purpose and explication of the doctrine. Commentators, generally speaking, tend to grasp one or two facets of Edwards's composite imagery and attempt to read his entire conception through that lens. In the end, these analyses either constrain Edwards's view, offering a truncated image, or undermine the conceptual structure and unity of Edwards's composite imagery.

I believe that there are three major factors why Edwards's view has proved elusive to commentators: First, and most importantly, Edwards changes his view of the Trinity as he writes the *Discourse* itself. The failure to recognize this shift is ubiquitous in the secondary literature. Second, commentators have proved too determined to categorize Edwards in terms of the tradition rather than first allowing him to, as it were, 'speak for himself'. This has tended to either 'flatten' Edwards's view or else bifurcate his position unnecessarily into two models held in tension. And third, for the reasons noted above, the secondary literature fails to find a unified account of the Trinity in Edwards's development.

My categorization of Edwards's doctrine of the Trinity as personal beatific-delight is therefore admittedly idiosyncratic, but the conceptual foundation of personal beatific-delight finds widespread support throughout the secondary literature. Amy Plantinga Pauw states concerning Edwards's *Miscellanies* entries, 'There he made the daring assertion that "if God loves himself and delights in himself, there is really a triplicity." '[16] Likewise, William J. Danaher, in talking about God's unity in plurality, states that 'Edwards's idealism emphasizes the objective "happiness", "complacency", "delight", and "love" that exists between the mind and its idea.'[17] Likewise, Robert W. Jenson states, 'He [God] is absolute in that in him the elements of the consciousness make a communal Harmony in themselves; thus he can ... delight in his own beauty within himself.'[18] As these commentators bear witness, Edwards's God is the God of personal-delight, and I argue he exists eternally as the subject, object and experience of the beatific vision itself.

[16] Pauw, *Supreme Harmony of All,* 4–5.
[17] Danaher, *Trinitarian Ethics of Jonathan Edwards,* 30.
[18] Jenson, *America's Theologian,* 98.

II Background of Edwards's Doctrine

Polemically, Edwards's work on the Trinity addresses the theological 'misfits' of his day.[19] By moving from the singular personhood of God, Edwards starts where his polemics almost always do, on common ground with his opponents.[20] Edwards moves from a singular person to trinitarianism through his invocation of simplicity, *actus purus*, and eternality.[21] This makes sense of the structure of his *Discourse* and fits with Edwards's posture as a polemicist. As Ken Minkema notes, Edwards was certainly attuned to the fact that 'anti-trinitarianism, in the forms of Arianism and Socinianism, was … spreading throughout Europe'.[22] Samuel Clarke, one of the church leaders on whom Edwards kept close watch, 'renounced the Athanasian Creed's formulation of three co-equal and co-eternal persons as unscriptural and treated the trinitarian question as non-essential to

---

[19] Much later in his life, in 1757, Edwards wrote a letter to Dr. Edward Wigglesworth at Harvard concerning Dr. Jonathan Meyhew's book which 'ridicules the doctrine of the Trinity'. Y16, 'To Dr. Edward Wigglesworth', 698. Likewise, his five lectures delivered at the Thursday lecture between February 15 and March 22, 1750, called 'Lectures on the Qualifications for Full Communion in the Church of Christ', mentioned both Arianism and Socinianism, clearly choosing examples of heresy known by the people. Y25, 'Lectures on the Qualifications for Full Communion in the Church of Christ', 349, 432. Peter J. Thuesen states: 'At least 10 percent of the titles in both the "Catalogue" and the "Account Book" stem from the many post-Restoration debates in England over atheism, natural religion, deism, and the Trinity.' Y26, 'Editor's Introduction', 55.

[20] Clarke's work starts with a strong understanding of the personhood of the Father, Son and Spirit, using that to force every other position against the rocks of tritheism or modalism. Note his usage concerning the wording of the Athanasian Creed: 'Because it is so worded, as that many of the common people cannot but be too apt to understand it in the sense favouring either Sabellianism or Tritheism; viz. either that the three persons are merely different denominations of the same individual, or that they are three absolutely co-ordinate beings; neither of which, is consistent with the doctrine of Scripture, seeing the one takes away the very being of the Son and Holy Spirit, and the other introduces manifestly a plurality of Gods.' Clarke, *Scripture-Doctrine of the Trinity*, 447. Edwards seems to take this argument as something of a challenge, showing exactly how a strong understanding of personhood actually leads to orthodox trinitarian grammar.

[21] One of the reasons Stephen Studebaker mistakes the overall structure of Edwards's *Discourse* is that he fails to recognize the polemical nature of the document. Instead, Studebaker highlights Edwards's other polemical projects, such as his material against Deists in the *Miscellanies* and Edwards's use of the *prisca theologia*. By missing his specific polemical mode, Studebaker also misses how Edwards develops his argument. Studebaker, *Jonathan Edwards's Social Augustinian Trinitarianism*, 212–27, and also Steve Studebaker, 'Jonathan Edwards' Trinitarian Theology in the Context of the Early-Enlightenment Deist Controversy', in *The Contribution of Jonathan Edwards to American Culture and Society: Essays on America's Spiritual Founding Father (The Northampton Tercentenary Celebration, 1703–2003)* (ed. Richard A. S. Hall; Lewiston: The Edwin Mellen Press, 2008), 281–301.

[22] Kenneth Minkema, 'Preface to the Period', in *Sermons and Discourses, 1723–1729* (ed. Kenneth P. Minkema; The Works of Jonathan Edwards, vol. 14; New Haven: Yale University Press, 1997), 43.

the faith'.[23] Likewise, in 1692, Cotton Mather argued against 'ancient Sabellianism' and 'Quakerism' as denying God's triune nature.[24] Edwards, in his sermon series 'A History of the Work of Redemption' (hereafter *Work of Redemption*), describes Arianism thus: 'They denied the doctrine of the Trinity, and denied the divinity of Christ and the Holy Ghost, and maintained that they were but mere creatures.'[25] Later in the treatise he goes on to bemoan: 'Of late years this heresy has been revived in England, and greatly prevails there both in the Church of England and among Dissenters.'[26]

This anti-trinitarianism stemmed from an anti-philosophical stance as well as an emphasis upon God's economic work over and against any true knowledge of God in his immanent life.[27] Edwards's engagement with this stance comes through in *Miscellanies* 94 which commences by saying, 'There has been much cry of late against saying one word, particularly about the Trinity, but what the Scripture has said.'[28] Edwards's work on the Trinity, far from being conceived in academic isolation, was born into an arena of polemical engagement. Carl R. Trueman, in a work on John Owen, suggests that Biddle, Owen's chief Socinian counterpart, concentrated his attack on trinitarian issues of personhood and essence. Substance language, Biddle argued, necessitates an impersonal God, while utilizing 'essence' language necessitates *one* person rather than three.[29] It is important to note

[23] Minkema, 'Preface to the Period', 43n3. See Clarke, *Scripture-Doctrine of the Trinity*, 144–57, 180–5, 219, 245–9, 270–80, 287–8, 441–7. It is important, for my purposes here, to bracket Clarke's actual view and focus more on what it was perceived to be. Clarke's position is a tightly argued 'Eusebian' account, whose detailed analysis has been consistently undermined because of the nature of the polemical situation in which he found himself. For a detailed analysis of the 'Eusebian' character of Clarke's trinitarian thought, see Pfizenmaier, *Trinitarian Theology of Dr. Samuel Clarke*. Clarke has been seen as Arian, which is not technically correct, but he would no doubt have been a concern of Edwards. Clarke was a much better theologian than the bulk of the anti-trinitarians, so if Edwards could go toe to toe with Clarke's account he could indirectly attack the Arian position that had been gaining steam.
[24] Cotton Mather, *Blessed Unions* (Boston: B. Green and J. Allen, 1692), 46.
[25] Y9, *A History of the Work of Redemption*, 405–6.
[26] Y9, *A History of the Work of Redemption*, 432.
[27] See Fred Sanders, *The Image of the Immanent Trinity: Rahner's Rule and the Theological Interpretation of Scripture* (Issues in Systematic Theology; New York: Peter Lang, 2005), 40–1. See also Richard A. Muller, *The Triunity of God* (Post-Reformation Reformed Dogmatics, vol. 4; Grand Rapids: Baker Academic, 2nd edn, 2003), 59–142. Muller persuasively shows that the radical interpreters of *sola scriptura* understood the doctrine of the Trinity as an area where the Reformers neglected reforming. By turning to Scripture alone, the question for trinitarian theology became: How does the creedal language interact with the biblical language, and how is it justified to use nonbiblical philosophic terminology?
[28] Y13, '*Miscellanies* 94. Trinity', 256. Clarke's argument depends on his attack of 'metaphysical speculation'. See Clarke, *Scripture-Doctrine of the Trinity*, xxvi–xxvii, 185, 243, 272, 373, 459, 465.
[29] Carl Trueman, *John Owen: Reformed Catholic, Renaissance Man* (Great Theologians Series;

that Biddle was far from being a lone radical; he was embedded in an era of Biblicists who sought to wield *sola scriptura* against orthodox (mainly metaphysical) doctrines such as the Trinity.[30] Deists, Socinians and Arians, in varying degrees, brought into question the Son and Spirit's divinity, the biblical foundation for the Trinity, as well as the usefulness of the councils' statements and classic trinitarian grammar. Moreover, these groups tended to adopt a subordination in the Trinity, denying the full deity of Christ and often the full deity (if not also personhood) of the Spirit.[31] God the Father was the only God (fully), and he was the only figure who had the divine attributes.[32] Furthermore, as an attack on Christ's deity, these Biblicists argued that singleness of essence *necessarily* entails singleness of

Aldershot: Ashgate, 2007), 49. This issue was certainly not isolated to Biddle. Pfizenmaier, in his substantial study of Clarke's trinitarian thought, notes that in the polemical tirades that followed the publication of Clarke's books, the issue of three persons and one substance became *the* central issue. This point was highlighted by Edward Potter, Stephen Nye, Richard Mayo, Thomas Bennet and Daniel Waterland. Pfizenmaier, *Trinitarian Theology of Dr. Samuel Clarke*, 184–206.

[30] Muller states, 'Virtually all of the sixteenth century antitrinitarians were biblicists. They lacked not a reverence for the text as the norm of doctrine but rather a traditionary norm for the regulation of their exegesis. They believed quite strongly that they had simply taken the next logical step beyond that of the Reformers: they accepted the Reformers' attack in the name of *sola scriptura* on the doctrinal accretions characteristic of medieval theology and turned the new, non-allegorical, textual, and literal exegesis on a wider array of traditional dogmas, most notably, the doctrine of Christ and the doctrine of the Trinity.' Muller, *Triunity of God*, 79. Clarke quotes Chillingworth approvingly, 'The Bible, I say, the BIBLE only, is the religion of Protestants. Whatsoever else they believe besides it, and the plain, irrefragable, indubitable consequences of it; well may they hold it as a matter of opinion: but as a matter of faith and religion, neither can they, with coherence to their own grounds, believe it themselves; nor require the belief of it of others, without most high and most schismatical presumption.' Clarke, *Scripture-Doctrine of the Trinity*, x–xi.

[31] Preaching on Heb. 1:3 in April 1734, Edwards writes, 'Though we can't comprehend the eternal generation of the Son of God, yet there are two things that we may know of it, wherein it differs from creation: 1. That it is not an arbitrary production but a necessary emanation …. 2. Another difference wherein the generation of the Son of God differs from creation is that which is created has a beginning, but the generation of the Son is eternal.' Jonathan Edwards, Unpublished sermon, Heb. 1:3, Transcription 321, April, 1734. Jonathan Edwards Center, Yale University, New Haven, CT [L. 4r–L. 4v.] – my edits (All remaining unpublished sermons will have my edits, unless otherwise specified, and are referenced by 'JEC, Unpublished sermon', transcription number and leaf). I quote the transcription of the Heb. 1.3 sermon here rather than the version found in *The Glory and Honor of God* because their edits confuse the meaning of the text. Importantly, this too is a direct attack on Clarke's position, which attempts to give an account of the *willed* procession of the Son. See Clarke, *Scripture-Doctrine of the Trinity*, 276.

[32] Clarke argues, 'The words, one and only, are used, by way of eminence, to signifie [*sic*] Him who is absolutely supreme, self-existent, and independent; which attributes are personal, and evidently impossible to be communicated from one person to another.' Clarke, *Scripture-Doctrine of the Trinity*, 245. Furthermore, 'The Son (or second person) is not self-existent, but derives his being or essence, and all his attributes, from the Father, as from the supreme cause.' Ibid., 270. See also 261–5, 296–9, 428.

person.[33] This last point could very well have been the rhetorical impetus for Edwards's polemics.

Edwards developed his trinitarian reflection in an ethos saturated with denials of classic trinitarian language, including the deity and personhood of the Son and Spirit, the idea of persons subsisting in a unified essence and processions without subordination. The concepts of personhood, unity and the dangers of tri-theism (which these heresies saw themselves as protecting against) were central to these divisions.[34] It is not surprising, therefore, to find Edwards, known for his thorough and pervasive defence of Reformed orthodoxy, developing a doctrine of the Trinity that is emphatic on all of these points.[35] Edwards rethinks the relationship between persons and essence, and is adamant that the divinity of the Son and the Spirit are *necessary* aspects of the Father's own personhood and life. In contrast to seeing the Father as the only person in whom the divine attributes obtain, Edwards posits that the divine attributes *actually are* the Son and the Spirit! In emphasizing the divinity and personhood of the Son and Spirit, Edwards grounds them in the personhood of the Father and utilizes biblical and rational support for his view. In doing so, Edwards develops a model of the Trinity that emphasizes oneness *only in so far* as it emphasizes threeness, undermining the heretical views through the very affirmation they make of the Father's personhood and singularity.[36]

---

[33] See Muller, *Triunity of God*, 59–142, esp. 60–2, 79, 95, 98, 130–3. Likewise, Studebaker notes that William Sherlock 'defined *person* as an intelligent being. A person is a mind. Distinct persons are distinct minds and to multiply persons is to multiply minds.' Studebaker, 230. Likewise, he claims that Samuel Clarke only allowed for the term 'God' to refer to one divine person. Studebaker, *Jonathan Edwards' Social Augustinian Trinitarianism*, 249. These kinds of arguments, in the air in Edwards's day, are exactly what he sought to undermine. Notably, Clarke does not question the Son or the Spirit's personhood, but subordinates them from the Father, who eternally wills their creation from himself (as opposed to *ex nihilo*). Clarke, *Scripture-Doctrine of the Trinity*, 276.

[34] Clarke was specifically concerned with tritheism and Sabellianism. See Clarke, *Scripture-Doctrine of the Trinity*, xxviii, 85, 157, 447.

[35] In supplemental material believed to be additions to the *Discourse*, Edwards writes himself a note to 'consider that question, whether Christ is to be worshipped as mediator'. Y21, *Discourse*, 143. One of Clarke's main polemical points concerned the worship of Christ, and he focuses specifically on worshipping Christ as a mediator. It seems likely that Edwards continued to take notes in response to Clarke. Pfizenmaier, *Trinitarian Theology of Dr. Samuel Clarke*, 127. This is all the more interesting because Edwards's comment to himself is in the midst of a note about prayer being primarily to the Father. Clarke's point about worship to Christ as mediator arises within a discussion concerning prayer as ultimately to the Father. Furthermore, it seems likely that Edwards's fragmentary work, 'On the Equality of the Persons of the Trinity', was meant as a notebook to build up a defence against Clarke's work. There, for instance, Edwards states, 'To show and prove out of Scripture how that it cannot be that Christ is called the wisdom of God only in a figurative sense ... but that he is the real proper wisdom of God.' Y21, 'On the Equality of the Persons of the Trinity', 148.

[36] Clarke provides three options of the affirmation that the Word was God: (1) it is the same person as the Father (Sabellianism); (2) the Word is another self-existent, 'underived' and

III Overview of Edwards's Argumentation – The *'Discourse on the Trinity'*

Before moving into exposition, it will prove instructive to walk through the major steps of Edwards's argument in the *Discourse*, pausing for preliminary reflections on the question of persons and essence. In arguing that Edwards's view of the Trinity was governed by personal beatific-delight, I give preference to Edwards's *Discourse* over notes preceding this work. Following this overview, I will track closely with the argumentative flow of the *Discourse*, which at times, will necessitate thorough exposition of the material. In the end, this will clarify a document and doctrine plagued by nearly as many viewpoints as commentators. Edwards's *Miscellanies* entries concerning the Trinity run parallel to the *Discourse*. These notes are mainly utilized because they offer insight into Edwards's doctrinal development. Stephen Holmes rightly states that the *Miscellanies* 'cannot be considered as Edwards's final word on any subject, but must rather be seen as his "rough workings". These books are the place where he jotted down interesting ideas that he felt the need to think more about; where he sketched new statements of arguments to see if they worked.'[37]

It is noteworthy that the *Discourse* itself was never readied for publication and therefore, it could be argued, maintains the status of a working note. While it was indeed never readied for publication, any reading of the *Miscellanies* entries prior to his writing of the *Discourse* will show that Edwards compiled, organized and synthesized his notes in such a way as to compose a 'final' thought on the subject. Therefore, it seems reasonable to suppose that the doctrine he proposes therein, while fragmentary and unpolished, represents his mature understanding of the Trinity, though not necessarily his mature development of argumentation.[38] While this

---

independent person (polytheism); and (3) the Word is a person deriving from the Father – his being, attributes and authority. Clarke, *Scripture-Doctrine of the Trinity*, 86. The third position is Clarke's, and was often seen as a type of Arianism. See Y9, *A History of the Work of Redemption*, 432, for Edwards's concerns about the 'Arian heresy' in the Church of England. Clarke believed that the Father was the only true God, with the Son and the Spirit deriving 'divinity' in some sense from him. They were created, but were created eternally by the *will* of the Father. Clarke's position depends upon understanding the Father to have all the divine attributes, glory and existence applied to him absolutely, and to the Son and Spirit relatively. His position depends upon his understanding of personhood, and how three persons in one divine essence is tritheism. Edwards's *Discourse* picks up these themes to show the opposite to be the case.

[37] Holmes, *God of Grace and God of Glory*, 36.

[38] Robert Caldwell argues that the *Miscellanies* entries dealing with Christ's two natures bring both theological and exegetical clarity to his stated view in the *Miscellanies* entries themselves, and therefore represents his mature position. Caldwell, *Communion in the Spirit*, 85. Something similar could be said here. The solidification of his notes into one major

assumption has become standard for Edwards commentators, below I argue even further that while the *Discourse* is the main source for Edwards's doctrine, his view decisively shifted *as he wrote it*, demanding that the document be understood in light of his new-found conclusions.[39]

The development of Edwards's argument in the *Discourse* follows a basic outline:[40] first, Edwards states his thesis and main idea; second, he articulates the divine self-understanding (the Son's generation), advancing rational and biblical support; third, he addresses the divine love (the Spirit's spiration) and offers biblical support for the concept; and fourth, he engages possible issues and objections, affirming that his analysis is complete, biblical, and orthodox.[41]

Edwards begins his essay with an overview:

> When we speak of God's happiness, the account that we are wont to give of it is that God is infinitely happy in the enjoyment of himself, in perfectly beholding and infinitely loving, and rejoicing in, his own essence and perfections. And accordingly it must be supposed that God perpetually and eternally has a most perfect idea of himself, as it were an exact image and representation of himself ever before him and in actual view. And from hence arises a most pure and perfect energy in the Godhead, which is the divine love, complacence and joy.[42]

Here Edwards lays out in carefully chosen language his understanding of

---

document on the Trinity, as well as the remaining notes bringing exegetical and authoritative evidence to his aid, show that this is Edwards's mature position.

[39] I will develop this below. It seems likely that the reason Edwards wrote the *Discourse* in the first place was to readdress his view based on his new conclusions. This explains why the *Discourse* tends to link together previous *Miscellanies* notes on the topic, offering some expanded thoughts and direction.

[40] The outline I suggest is based upon my own analysis rather than Edwards's personal outlining that is often found in his material, a point which could argue against seeing this document as anywhere near a final manuscript.

[41] The remaining material digresses rapidly into note material highlighting more biblical resources. This is noteworthy since Edwards would have had to bulk up this material to adequately combat Clarke's analysis. Furthermore, Edwards continued to address the Trinity in his *Miscellanies* entries after the *Discourse*, again building up his scriptural evidence. Edwards talks about Christ as the face of God (no. 446), the Holy Spirit as oil (no. 680), and the Holy Spirit as ointment poured forth onto Christ. He focuses in no. 1008 on the fact that in Scripture Christ is called the 'Word of God', showing that words are thoughts, which for Edwards means that they are ideas and therefore support his thesis that Jesus is the perfect idea of God. In no. 1047 Edwards states that God's holiness 'consists in' the Holy Spirit, saying that the original biblical passages should be rendered, 'the Spirit of his holiness', focusing on the perichoretic nature of personhood in the Godhead and the equality of the persons of the Trinity.

[42] Y21, *Discourse on the Trinity*, 113.

God's existence: God is eternally *happy*, in that he perfectly and infinitely *beholds himself*, his perfect idea, and love arises in the *mutual beholding* of his idea, emanating in complacence and joy. Edwards will be more specific with his language, but the breadth of his thesis is found here, however bare and simple.

Edwards starts by grounding his understanding and explication of the Trinity in God's eternal happiness, what I refer to as God's delight, and he takes it to be axiomatic that God is 'infinitely happy in the enjoyment of himself', which entails that he perfectly *beholds*, *loves* and *rejoices* in 'his own essence and perfections'.[43] This is the palate with which Edwards paints his view of the Trinity, offering important middle ground between himself and his anti-trinitarian opponents. It does not take much detailed reflection to notice the key words for the beatific vision in Edwards's initial overview. 'The sight of God that makes one happy' simply is the beatific vision. For the Reformed in this period, the beatific vision was not relegated to creaturely life in glory but was the nature of God's life *in se* – the *beatitudo Dei*. Richard Muller makes an important note concerning the use of 'blessedness' as a way to describe the *beatitudo Dei* in Post-Reformation dogmatics:

> In the era of orthodoxy, however, the topic of divine beatitude and felicity returns to the theological systems .... The concept of divine blessedness is, moreover, conveyed, not through a single term, but through several predicates that are used almost interchangeably by the Reformed orthodox: blessedness or beatitude (*beatitudo*), joy or happiness (*felicitas*), delight (*delectatio*), and contentment or self-fulfillment (*complacentia*).[44]

None of Edwards's opponents will deny that God is a person, and as a person, however composed, he lives in eternal self-delight. Importantly, Edwards's initial statement is not, at first glance, *trinitarian*. God is infinitely happy in the enjoyment of *himself*, rather than of the Son, and this happiness stems from viewing his perfect *idea*. The Father's object and delight, therefore, in his starting point here, is his inner life. Edwards's point of attack, then, starts with God's singular personhood, and the shared agreement that God

---

[43] The language of beholding is particularly relevant for my understanding of the *beatific-delight* of God.

[44] Richard A. Muller, *The Divine Essence and Attributes* (Post-Reformation Reformed Dogmatics, vol. 3; Grand Rapids: Baker Academic, 2003), 381. Muller then refers to van Mastricht, stating that 'these definitions follow as a consequence of the goodness and sufficiency of God, who alone of all beings finds contentment in himself and whose blessedness is, therefore, the final goal of all creaturely existence: God is both blessed *in se* and the source (*fons*) of all blessedness.' Ibid. This is exactly what we find in Edwards's development.

exists in delight eternally, perfectly and infinitely.[45] The 'great twist', noted above, is that the Father's own personhood is derivative, constituted by the Son and the Spirit as his understanding and will respectively, but Edwards refuses to reveal his hand just yet.

Edwards's polemical strategy requires that he first show that God's perfect idea of himself *actually is* the divine essence generated and repeated.[46] This move necessitates robust development and argumentation, which then does the conceptual heavy lifting in arguing for the 'pure and perfect energy' to arise in love. But this initial move – that God has an idea of himself (however that is understood) and in so having that idea he has eternally generated a divine subsistence – is the first and major hurdle Edwards has to cross.[47]

By defining the divine understanding as idea, Edwards draws a relation between the divine and human: 'Though the divine nature be vastly different from that of created spirits, yet our souls are made in the image of God: we have understanding and will, idea and love, as God hath, and the difference is only in the perfection of degree and manner.'[48] The

---

[45] Edwards advances his argument along similar contours as Clarke, who starts with God the Father as the supreme and absolute God and then goes on to explain the Son and the Spirit. Edwards, by contrast, starts with God the Father but then moves on to analyse the personhood of the Father who is eternal, infinite, etc. Edwards turns to biblical argumentation only after securing the eternal idea and will of God. Edwards thus shows Clarke's argumentation to be superficial. See Clarke, *Scripture-Doctrine of the Trinity*, 352, 359, 373, 415–16, 428, 441–2, 447, 465. Pfizenmaier, in narrating the debates after Clarke's initial publication, compares Clarke and Waterland on this very issue: 'Clarke was concerned to work from the language of scripture itself in which he found that the term "God" was always used of a person, (never referring to substance, essence, or being) and that both the Father and Son were so named. For him the problem was not "how three persons can be one God" (Waterland), but rather how the infallible teaching of scripture that there is only one God can be maintained in the face of scripture's ascription of the term "God" to the Son.' Pfizenmaier, *Trinitarian Theology of Dr. Samuel Clarke*, 203.

[46] Clarke states, 'And why two persons, of (or, as the schoolmen speak, in) one nature, (if they are co-ordinate and equally supreme,) should not be as properly two Gods, (that is, two supreme governours,) as two persons in two distinct natures would be; no intelligible reason can be given.' Clarke, *Scripture-Doctrine of the Trinity*, 349, see also 428, 441–2, 447, 459–70.

[47] Clarke notes that some have tried to argue for the Son being an attribute of the Father, but disregards the idea that an attribute of 'reason' could somehow take on flesh and dwell among creatures. Clarke, *Scripture-Doctrine of the Trinity*, 85. Furthermore, Clarke attributes this to an ancient position: 'Of the writers before the time of the council of Nice [Nicaea], Theophilus, Tatian and Athenagoras, seem to have been of that opinion, that … the word, was … the internal reason or wisdom of the Father; and yet, at the same time, they speak as if they supposed that word to be produced or generated into a real person. Which is hardly intelligible: And seems to be the mixture of two opinions: The one, of the generality of Christians; who believed the word to be a real person: The other, of the Jews and Jewish Christians; who personated the internal wisdom of God, or spake of it figuratively (according to the genius of their language) as a person.' Ibid., 287–8. Clarke's position assumes that an attribute and a person are mutually exclusive categories – Edwards's *Discourse* seeks to argue the opposite.

[48] Y21, *Discourse on the Trinity*, 113. This could be Edwards's attempt to circumnavigate Clarke's

focus here is not on the second *person* of the Trinity but simply on God's perfect idea of himself. Therefore, as a singular personal God, Edwards argues, God has ideas like we do. Edwards will follow these same basic contours in developing the spiration of the Spirit. Being singular persons as we are, we can understand how God would have an idea of himself in which he delights. Importantly, this move, if accepted, entails the recognition that the divine essence has a real 'property'. (This usage will be explored in the appendix.) Edwards's attack on the anti-trinitarians thus starts with attributes of the essence, which exist in the infinity, immutability and simplicity of God, rather than starting with the personhood of the subsistences.

But how is this development an account of the Trinity rather than simply a personal God? Edwards's solution, explained below, entails, first, simplicity: whatever is in God is God;[49] second, infinity: God is infinite and perfect, and therefore his attributes – again, understanding and will – are infinite and perfect; third, *actus purus*: God is wholly act, and therefore the generation of God's idea and the emanation of his will/love are eternal and without potential; and fourth, perichoresis: God's understanding is the Son, his will is the Spirit, and personhood obtains because they commune *in* one another; the Father is a person because he has understanding (the Son) and will (the Spirit). Therefore, the denouement of Edwards's trinitarian narrative is his use of perichoresis, and it is only at that point that the document as a whole can be understood. After grasping these four points, Edwards's first paragraph is not unitarian, however much it may appear so at first glance, but is in fact robustly trinitarian. Edwards takes on the claim that one essence equals one person by arguing that one essence, if infinite,

---

criticism of 'metaphysical speculation'. Edwards turns to persons and analogy rather than metaphysics as such.

[49] There has been some question as to Edwards's commitment concerning simplicity. Amy Plantinga Pauw, for instance, suggests that Edwards was ambivalent to the simplicity tradition. I agree with Helm that her critique does not stand and that Edwards utilizes simplicity as a central aspect of his argument within the *Discourse*. Pauw argues that Edwards's discussion of the generation of the Son breaks with the tradition of simplicity. As Helm argues in the aforementioned paper, if Edwards fails here, he does so with the entire tradition. See: Pauw, *Supreme Harmony of All*, 59–80; Pauw, '"One Alone Cannot Be Excellent": Edwards on Divine Simplicity', in *Jonathan Edwards Philosophical Theologian* (ed. Oliver Crisp and Paul Helm; Aldershot: Ashgate, 2003), 115–26; Holmes, 'Does Jonathan Edwards Use a Dispositional Ontology?', 99–114; Crisp, 'Jonathan Edwards on Divine Simplicity', 175–201; Steven M. Studebaker, 'Supreme Harmony or Supreme Disharmony? An Analysis of Amy Plantinga Pauw's "The Supreme Harmony of All": The Trinitarian Theology of Jonathan Edwards', *Scottish Journal of Theology* 4, no. 57 (2004), 479–85; Paul Helm, 'Edwards on the Trinity' (paper delivered at the Edwards Tercentenary Conference, Princeton Theological Seminary, 2003), and Sang Hyun Lee, in Y21, 'Editor's Introduction', 22–6.

simple and existing as person in pure act, can just as easily be conceived as three persons (and with Scripture's support, should be).

1. The Divine Essence and the Divine Persons

Before moving on to discuss the processions of the divine idea and will in detail, I address the key issue that drove Edwards to compile and analyse his previous insights on the Trinity, namely, the relationship of the divine essence to the divine persons.[50] Admittedly, doing so here breaks up our analysis of the *Discourse* in a way that might not be obviously helpful. This is a necessary evil, in that the remaining argumentation is clarified only once we address this particular issue, which was likely the impetus for Edwards's compiling and reworking his earlier material into one main document. The argument of the whole must therefore be read in light of these conclusions. Furthermore, Edwards's understanding of the relationship between the divine essence and the divine persons changed as he was taking notes for and even putting together the *Discourse* itself. This change is subtle but decisive and changes the tenor and *telos* of Edwards's account of the Trinity. In brief, Edwards moves away from understanding the divine persons as receiving personhood (understanding and will) from the divine essence and instead argues that the divine essence iterates and 'breathes out' as understanding and will respectively, grounding personhood in their perichoretic union. Furthermore, talk of the divine essence is relegated to discussions of 'spiritual substance' and therefore becomes subdued in Edwards's analysis.[51]

The issue of the divine essence comes to the fore in the *Discourse* when

---

[50] We should not be surprised to find Edwards focusing on this very issue. The divine essence was central to major debates in the generation before Edwards as well as his own. For instance, John Owen states concerning the anti-trinitarians of his day, 'At the first entrance upon their undertaking, some of them made no small advantage, in dealing with weak and unwary men, by crying out that the terms of *trinity, persons, essence, hypostatical union, communion of propetia*, and the like, were not found in the Scriptures, and therefore were to be abandoned.' John Owen, *The Gospel Defended* (ed. William H. Goold; The Works of John Owen, vol. 12; Edinburgh: Banner of Truth, 1966), 46. As noted above, this was the major point of contention for the orthodox theologians against Clarke. Clarke refused to allow for three persons to subsist in an individual essence. It is not an overstatement to say that this issue was *the* issue that plagued trinitarian thought in the eighteenth century.

[51] Crisp's analysis of Edwards's ontology, contra Lee, is insightful: 'Edwards's ontology is a rather strange thing – there is no denying that. He believed in a version of idealism coupled with something like what I have called a Berkeleyan bundle theory that yields a phenomenalism with regard to perceptible objects. Yet he did believe that there were substances, God being the only "true" substance, strictly speaking, with created substances (minds or souls) being ultimately merely the occasions of divine action.' Oliver Crisp, 'Jonathan Edwards's Ontology: A Critique of Sang Hyun Lee's Dispositional Account of Edwardsian Metaphysics', *Religious Studies* 46, no.1 (2010), 14–15.

Edwards addresses the *personhood* of the Spirit. The parallel *Miscellanies* entries address the divine essence as well, but proceed in a contrary direction. In the *Discourse,* Edwards argues that personhood entails understanding and will and that the divine essence is predicated of the subsistences, reiterating that we are dealing with *one* God, and then goes on to argue that the Father has understanding and will, namely, the Son and the Spirit. It is clear in his development of the perichoretic union that the purpose of perichoresis is to achieve a *trinitarian* account of persons. The personhood that exists in the Trinity, on his view, exists as each member interpenetrates the other and is truly *of* the other. Edwards's God is the personal God known through revelation, a God whose *understanding* took on flesh and whose *will* is cast abroad into the hearts of believers. Edwards, then, is not trying to rationally deduce a doctrine of God but is developing a way to talk about a God who, while one, still exists triunally as persons in beatific-delight.

What we initially find in Edwards's *Miscellanies* entries, however, does not track this understanding of divine essence as found in the 'final' version of the *Discourse.* In *Miscellanies* 308, Edwards states:

> In the first place, we don't suppose that the Father, the Son, and the Holy Ghost are three distinct beings that have three distinct under-standings. It is the divine essence [that] understands, and it is the divine essence [that] is understood; 'tis the divine being that loves, and it is the divine being that is loved. The Father understands, the Son under-stands, and the Holy Ghost understands, because every one is the same understanding divine essence; and not that each of them have a distinct understanding of their own.[52]

Just as in the *Discourse,* Edwards affirms that there are not three under-standings but one. His solution is not the Son who *is* the understanding, but the 'divine essence' itself understands.[53] The 'persons', as Edwards

---

[52] Y13, '*Miscellanies* 308. Trinity', 392. Studebaker invokes Edwards's texts without discernment and therefore fails to recognize progression in Edwards's thought. That mistake is most detrimental to his project on this point specifically. At several key places he uses *Miscellanies* 308 as evidence for his position, rather than using the *Discourse,* which suggests a different view. See Studebaker, *Jonathan Edwards' Social Augustinian Trinitarianism,* 237 and 252 for representative usages.

[53] Richard Muller notes, 'In an argument that had broad significance for the later Reformed orthodox exposition of the divine essence and attributes, Zanchi pointed out that, since God is most simple essence, not being composite or having accidents and separable qualities, the so-called attributes of God are intended to indicate this most simple essence without essential or real distinction between them: the essence itself is good, powerful, just, merciful, and so forth.' Richard A. Muller, *Divine Essence and Attributes,* 217.

posits here, *are persons* as they partake in an underlying 'personal' (having understanding and will) reality that can be predicated of God, namely, his being or essence. Therefore the problem, as I understand it, is the very problem Edwards addresses in the *Discourse*. How then are these subsistences persons?[54]

Edwards wrote entry 308 sometime in 1729–30, immediately prior to writing the *Discourse*.[55] If this were his final position, Edwards would hold to a standard view of appropriation, with the Son and the Spirit simply appropriating understanding and will respectively. Sometime in 1729–30, Edwards shifted away from this position and wrote the *Discourse*, altering his account of the persons and attributes so that understanding and will were actually the subsistences themselves. This alteration generates the problem that Edwards could use the same language before or after this development and mean very different things – appropriation on the one side, and full being on the other.[56] Even in entry 308 Edwards discusses the Son as the divine understanding, although he makes it clear that it is the divine essence that actually understands rather than understanding existing as a subsistence of the essence. While *Miscellanies* 308 works through a different issue than the one in the *Discourse* (the *Discourse* is dealing with the person of the Spirit, while entry 308 is dealing with how there are only three persons in the Trinity rather than an infinite number), the two are clearly related. This interrelation becomes evident in the *Discourse* when he states: 'But I don't pretend fully to explain how these things are, and I am sensible a hundred other objections may be made,'[57] and in entry 308, 'But I would not be understood to pretend to give a full explication of the Trinity, for I think it still remains an incomprehensible mystery.'[58] So in answering a similar question, and in using similar material, Edwards, on the two occasions, addresses the problem of essential unity and personal plurality with a different solution.

The key to this change regards the use of 'person' that he has brought into his account. In the *Discourse* he categorically states, 'A person is that which hath understanding and will. If the three in the Godhead are persons, they

---

[54] Edwards's specific question concerns the Spirit, but, on my account, the issue of personhood was a central concern for Edwards in general.

[55] Edwards offers a similar explanation in a sermon series titled 'The Threefold Work of the Holy Ghost', given in 1729, that supports the view found in *Miscellanies* 308. See Y14, 'The Threefold Work of the Holy Ghost', 379, 434.

[56] It could be that Edwards believed he was making a category fallacy in attempting to talk about understanding and willing, necessarily personal actions, by talking about the divine essence. In the end, essences do not understand or will, only persons do.

[57] Y21, *Discourse on the Trinity*, 134.

[58] Y13, '*Miscellanies* 308. Trinity', 393.

doubtless each of 'em have understanding.'[59] Starting with God the Father, Edwards has to assume that as a person, he has understanding and will. The architecture of 'person' does not change based on the capacity, quality or attributes of the person, human or divine; a person is simply a being with understanding and will, full stop, while the greatness and goodness of a person are dynamic categories. The 'essence' of God in this sense is the Father, the fountain of deity, who is discussed not as being *qua* being, but as being *qua* person (thereby maintaining common ground with the anti-trinitarians). In entry 308, however, the persons of the Trinity partake in the one divine essence that *has* understanding and *has* will, which is to say that being a person necessitates partaking in the divine essence which has the personal properties of understanding and will. And yet, the Son appropriates the divine understanding, there described as an understanding of the divine essence, rather than being the divine essence *as* understanding.

The emphasis in *Miscellanies* 308 is not personhood, but a singular divine essence which grounds personhood. So in entry 308 God's understanding and will are only truly predicable of the divine essence, while in the *Discourse* they are the divine essence *as* individuated subsistences, intertwined in perichoresis (as persons). In entry 308 Edwards's God is not composite because he *is* the divine essence, which has all his attributes predicated of it; the divine persons are God because they partake of the divine essence. The problem in *Miscellanies* 308, one could argue, is that Edwards posits a monadic God who has everything a person needs to be a person (understanding, will, essence, etc.) and yet, for some reason, is three persons. (He argues that it cannot be more, based on his psychological delineation, again seeking to use personhood to help determine God's architecture.) In the *Discourse*, Edwards has developed an allergy to talking about the divine essence as 'having' understanding and will, now describing the Father generating and spirating subsistences of understanding and willing. Again, in response to the quote at the beginning of the chapter, Edwards parses the 'kind of being God is' through trinitarian personhood rather than 'essence'.[60]

---

[59] Y21, *Discourse on the Trinity*, 133.
[60] Karl Barth proves instructive here: 'It is also hard to see how what is distinctive for this God can be made clear if, as has constantly happened in Roman Catholic and Protestant dogmatics both old and new, that question who God is, which it is the business of the doctrine of the Trinity to answer, is held in reserve, and the first question to be treated is that of the That and the What of God, as though these could be defined otherwise than on the presupposition of the Who.' Karl Barth, *Church Dogmatics: The Doctrine of The Word of God* (ed. G. W. Bromiley and T. F. Torrance; vol. I/1; New York: T&T Clark International, 2004), 300–1.

If this shift is true, in the year or so preceding his writing of the *Discourse*, Edwards questioned his understanding of the relationship between the divine essence and the persons. Therefore, Edwards's early *Miscellanies* have to be qualified; now the Son *actually is* the divine idea – he is truly God's understanding – and not merely appropriated as understanding. The understanding that the Father and the Spirit have *is the Son*, and likewise, the love shared by the members *is the Spirit*.[61] The triune persons are not persons by partaking in the divine essence, but through perichoretic union.

This view finds support in several *Miscellanies* entries written after 308, as well as in the composition of the *Discourse* itself. In *Miscellanies* 309, Edwards takes the first step toward a position more akin to the one found in the *Discourse*. In contemplating the language used of Jesus – namely, that he is called the Logos of God – Edwards states, 'If we translate it the "word" of God, he is either the outward word of God or his inward. None will say he is his outward. Now the outward word is speech, but the inward word, which is the original of it, is thought.'[62] Here Edwards formulates, for what appears to be the first time in his notes, the idea that the Son is the 'thought' of God, the 'inward word'. Previously, understanding was predicated of the essence, and so the understanding was the essence's understanding – it was only 'appropriated' to the Son. But in entry 309, Edwards uses personal language which pushes beyond the idea/understanding appropriation he had been using. Likewise, in the very next entry, Edwards claims the Holy Spirit 'is God's love and the love of God'.[63] Here Edwards adds both the subjective and objective element to the Spirit *qua* love. The Spirit is God's love – namely, the love that the Father has, as well as love of God – because the Spirit is God's self-love and delight.

The next relevant *Miscellanies* entry is 330, where Edwards states, 'It appears that the Holy Spirit is the holiness, or excellency and delight of God.'[64] This statement differs little from previous material, but Edwards qualifies his point, stating, 'Communion with God is nothing else but a partaking with him of his excellency, his holiness and happiness.'[65]

---

[61] This is possibly true of the *Discourse* as well. In other words, even though he made statements about the divine essence prior to landing on his 'final' view, the earlier uses of divine essence need to be understood in light of the later development. Therefore, earlier references which would have fallen under the category of appropriation are now forced to take on an ontological status not true of them before.

[62] Y13, '*Miscellanies* 309. Trinity', 393.

[63] Y13, '*Miscellanies* 309. Trinity', 393.

[64] Y13, '*Miscellanies* 330. Holy Ghost', 409.

[65] Y13, '*Miscellanies* 330. Holy Ghost', 409.

Communing with God can be accomplished *through* a partaking of the Spirit. The fact that Edwards reconsiders these issues and their implications justifies the idea that his thought is shifting. In the next *Miscellanies* entry, Edwards states, 'God is said to be light and love. Light is his understanding or idea, which is his Son; love is the Holy Spirit.'[66] Once again, these statements are not new in Edwards's corpus, but he is reading them through new trinitarian lenses – God's essence exists in pure act as understanding and loving, his own personal beatific-delight – rather than conceiving of understanding and will as predicated of God's essence, and then abstracting 'persons' from that essence.[67]

In one of the last relevant notes in the proto–*Discourse Miscellanies*, Edwards muses upon how the word 'spirit' is predicated of God. In entry 396 he states,

> So the word 'spirit,' when it [is] used concerning God: when it is not used to signify the divine essence (as sometimes it is, as when we read that God is a Spirit) it signifies the holy temper, or disposition or affection of God, as when we speak of the Spirit of God … so when we read of the good Spirit or holy Spirit of God, we should likewise understand it of the divine temper and affection …. Now the temper and disposition or affection of God is no other than infinite love …. As God's understanding is all comprehended in that, that he perfectly understands [himself], so his temper or disposition is perfectly expressed by that, that he infinitely loves himself.[68]

In this passage, Edwards once again moves toward the belief that the Spirit is in fact God's character and disposition rather than just a partaker of the divine essence's character. These *Miscellanies* focus on scriptural texts specifically, dealing with the biblical and theological implications of his new position. Edwards continues, 'The word "spirit" … in Scripture is

---

[66] Y13, '*Miscellanies* 331. Trinity', 409.
[67] In *Miscellanies* 341, Edwards addresses the issue of why the apostle Paul fails to mention the Spirit when he says, 'Grace and peace to you in the name of God the Father and the Lord Jesus Christ.' Y13, '*Miscellanies* 341. Trinity', 415. Because the Holy Spirit is the grace, peace and love of God, Edwards reasons, he is left out and replaced by grace and peace. Edwards finds this significant concerning the nature of the Spirit, noting that Paul often sends grace and love from the Father and the Son but offers communion in the Spirit. While the blessings come from the Father and the Son, the blessing actually is the Holy Spirit. Edwards goes on in *Miscellanies* 376 to make a similar point, that our fellowship with God and Jesus consists in communion with the Holy Ghost, and ties this in with human fellowship as well. Y13, '*Miscellanies* 376. Trinity', 448.
[68] Y13, '*Miscellanies* 396. Trinity', 462.

used in these two senses, either for a spiritual substance or mind, or for the temper of the individual.'[69] The Holy Spirit therefore, according to Edwards, is God's *holy* disposition, focusing on the *Holy* Spirit rather than the Holy *Spirit*. Classically, a 'disposition' would seem to be less ontologically weighty than one's 'material' status (e.g. being spiritual substance), but for Edwards, who is determined to talk about God as persons, disposition is actually weightier. In other words, it is more immediately relevant to talk of God as 'whom' rather than 'what'.

Edwards's composition of the *Discourse* is an important last point in this discussion of the *Miscellanies* material. It is impossible to know the exact dates of all the *Miscellanies* entries, as well as the exact dating of the *Discourse*, and therefore it is impossible to know if Edwards was struggling through these issues even as he was writing. But one piece of evidence leads toward the idea that Edwards was still wrestling with issues related to essence and persons *as he was writing*. In the original manuscript of the *Discourse*, at the point where Edwards begins to answer the question concerning the personhood of the Holy Spirit, Edwards crossed out two paragraphs, which he later replaced. These ideas, originally meant to be in the *Discourse*, were certainly close to the last, if not the last ideas on the subject prior to finishing the work, and therefore prove relevant to our examination.

In this 'deleted' section, Edwards engages possible objections concerning the personality of the Holy Spirit, stating:

> One of the principal objections that I can think of, is that this scheme don't seem well to agree with the personality of the Holy Ghost. A person is that that hath an understanding, and hath a will, and love: and how can the understanding and love themselves be said to be persons? The three that are in the Godhead, if they are persons, they doubtless all understand and all love.[70]

Here Edwards asks the questions that eventually incline him to take the position he takes in the *Discourse*. He reasons that if a person has understanding and will, and these are predicated of the Son and the Spirit, how is it that the understanding and will are *actually* persons? Then, on the flipside of the coin, what could it mean to say that they all somehow have these 'attributes'? In other words, if each member of the Trinity is a person

---

[69] Y13, '*Miscellanies* 396. Trinity', 461.
[70] Y21, *Discourse on the Trinity*, 132–3. Edwards's polemical concerns come through here, addressing the Spirit's equal status as a person.

(therefore having understanding and will), how is it that *understanding* can be identified as the Son and *will* the Spirit, and yet all share in that understanding and will? Edwards proceeds by addressing the tradition: '*The divines* have not been wont to suppose that those three are three distinct minds, but they are all the same mind in three distinct ways of subsisting.' He continues, still channelling the divines, by answering that God does not have three distinct understandings or wills, 'because they have all the same essence, and the attributes are not distinct from the essence'.[71] Continuing in the deleted section, Edwards undermines his older position, suggesting his account of perichoresis, and rebutting the divines: 'To this I answer, that there is such an union of the persons in the Trinity, [and] that after an ineffable and inconceivable manner, one in another, so that one hath another and one is as it were predicable of another ... and that because they are all the same divine essence.'[72]

The divines, as Edwards understands them, argue against tritheism by invoking the divine essence. There are not three understandings or three wills because there is only one divine essence, and, according to his older position, it is the divine essence that understands and wills. In contrasting his position to that of the divines here, however, Edwards shows that his view has changed. His newer position utilizes both perichoresis and the divine essence to talk about plurality and unity, unity grounded by one essence and personhood existing through perichoresis. At this point, Edwards can now show how there is one divine essence and three persons without somehow becoming tritheistic or falling victim to criticisms that one essence must equal one person. Here, his use of the divine essence seems much closer to what he ends up using in the *Discourse* when he states,

> In order to clear up this matter, let it be considered, that the whole divine essence is supposed truly and properly to subsist in each of these three – viz. God, and his understanding, and love – and that there is such a wonderful union between them that they are after an ineffable and inconceivable manner one in another; so that one hath another, and they have communion in one another, and are as it were predicable one of another .... And the Father understands because the Son, who is the divine understanding, is in him. The Father loves because the Holy Ghost is in him .... So the Holy Ghost, or the divine essence subsisting in divine love, understands because the Son, the divine idea, is in him.

---

[71] Y21, *Discourse on the Trinity*, 133 – my emphasis.
[72] Y21, *Discourse on the Trinity*, 133.

Edwards's original position, stated in *Miscellanies* 308, argues for a bifurcation in theology proper: the divine essence and the divine persons.[73] As
noted above, one of the major critiques from the anti-trinitarians was that
one essence necessarily equalled one person. Edwards realized his original
view was susceptible to this critique. It seemed, one could argue, somewhat
arbitrary to assign to a 'divine essence' everything the Godhead needed
to be *one* God, but then maintain three persons subsisting regardless
(rather than four or five). Edwards's final position addresses this neglect.
In responding to the divines, Edwards treats the divine essence as the
'spiritual substance' of God, and the divine persons as instances *of* that
spiritual substance, existing as persons in perichoresis – subsisting, it
should be noted, as the personal predicates of understanding and will. His
answer to the question of personhood is not that each member subsists
in the divine essence (that is how they are united as deity); his answer is
that 'there is such a wonderful union between them that they are after an
ineffable and inconceivable manner one in another'. In this same time
period, conceivably upon completion of the *Discourse*, Edwards offers
a definition of communion in *Miscellanies* 404 as 'a common partaking
of benefits, or of good, in union or society'.[74] Likewise, in talking about
persons, Edwards invokes 'communion in' rather than 'partaking of', as in
his earlier analysis.

Interestingly, in both the penultimate deleted sections, as well as
in the *Discourse* itself, Edwards is responding to 'the divines'. In the
deleted section, he states, 'To this I answer', after considering what the
tradition has handed him, while in the *Discourse* he states, in the same
context, 'In order to clear up this matter'. As noted in the background
section above, the issue of the divine essence and persons was central
to the anti-trinitarian debates leading up to Edwards's time, with Samuel
Clarke as the most noteworthy offender. Richard Muller summarizes
Clarke's view:

> Clarke hypothesized that the Son was begotten by an act of will and not
> by necessity. As for the Spirit, it is nowhere given the divine name and
> is subadviate not only to the Father but also the Son – as both Scripture
> and the fathers indicate. Clarke insisted that the idea of coequal and
> coeternal persons was necessarily tritheistic. He also denied the idea of

---

[73] Crisp attempts to maintain this bifurcation in his discussion of the divine attributes (see
appendix). I believe, as evident here, that this neglects to follow the shift in Edwards's
thought.
[74] Y13, '*Miscellanies* 404. Communion', 468.

one indivisible divine substance or essence: the essence was divisible and the three persons all partook of it, the Son and the Spirit being derived from the Father and therefore subordinate to him.[75]

The question of God's essence and person(s) was thus central to Edwards's theological milieu. At the heart of the attack on orthodoxy was the idea that God could be one essence and three persons, with various groups decrying every attempt at trinitarian thought. Edwards, I am suggesting, recognized this attack and attempted to develop a trinitarian structure based on God's inherent personhood that would navigate past this kind of critique from Clarke, the Socinians and the Deists. It is noteworthy that in the *Discourse* itself, Edwards mentions people who misunderstand the idea of the Father being called God by insisting that only the Father is 'truly and properly God'.[76] Furthermore, his revised position emphasizes that the triune members are eternal and equal in honour. Their honour is based, not simply upon their having the divine essence, but equally upon their coinherence in infinite delight: 'The honour of the Father and the Son is, they are infinitely happy and are the original and fountain of happiness; but the honour of the Holy Ghost is equal, for he is infinite happiness and joy itself.'[77]

While it is impossible to reconstruct exactly what Edwards was thinking as he worked through his view, there is an interesting *Miscellanies* entry that might lean the direction I am pointing. It is possible that Edwards wrote this note prior to completing the *Discourse*, but whatever the circumstance, it was written within the same time period as the *Discourse* itself. This entry, number 405, was written soon after what I consider (most obviously) Edwards's last entry prior to the *Discourse*. In it, he states, 'It may be thus expressed: the Son is the Deity generated by God's understanding, or having an idea of himself; the Holy Ghost is the divine essence flowing out, or breathed forth, infinite love and delight. Or, which is the same, the

---

[75] Muller, *Triunity of God*, 131. See also Pfizenmaier, *Trinitarian Theology of Dr. Samuel Clarke*, 89–176.

[76] This is a clear reference to Clarke's view. See Clarke, *Scripture-Doctrine of the Trinity*, 182, 245–9, 261–5, 280–2, 298–9, 304, 332–3, 349–52, 359, 428, 441–2, 447, 455, 465.

[77] Y21, *Discourse on the Trinity*, 135. This is a direct attack on Clarke's position. It is interesting that Edwards turns to his account of the beatific – the internal happiness of God – in an attempt to undermine Clarke's claims. Clarke turns to the issue of honour as a way to separate the Son and Spirit from the Father, focusing on honour in the economy rather than in God's immanent life (which is only had absolutely by the Father). Edwards shows just the opposite, that God's honour is wrapped up in God's eternal life as necessarily triune. See Clarke, *Scripture-Doctrine of the Trinity*, 352–80, 441.

Son is God's idea of himself, and the Spirit is God's love to and delight in himself.'[78]

In entry 405, we find a revised summary statement of Edwards's main image concerning his understanding of the Trinity. It is fruitful to inquire why Edwards would focus further note entries on his main image of the Trinity immediately after compiling his previous notes into the *Discourse*. The language of understanding and loving the divine essence is now dropped for the divine essence flowing out *as* love and generated *as* understanding of God *himself*. Edwards has shifted his view away from the impersonal abstraction of 'divine essence' to God's personal relationship of communion in delight of himself. Likewise, the Son is God's idea and the Spirit is God's love in a way that was not the case when he first started making notes on the Trinity. The divine essence is a way to talk about *what God is*; it is what is true of each person that makes the word 'God' predicable of them. But it is their being predicable of one another, their truly perichoretic nature, that makes them three persons rather than merely attributes of a singular person.

By failing to acknowledge this shift in Edwards's thought, commentators read Edwards's early material against his later and therefore misunderstand the *Discourse* itself.[79] The major interpreters of Edwards's doctrine of the Trinity, Amy Plantinga Pauw, William Danaher and Steven Studebaker, all in one way or another bifurcate Edwards's view as a result of their failure to recognize this shift. Pauw and Danaher, on the one hand, posit two models of the Trinity, one a psychological, the other a social.[80] Studebaker, on the other hand, repeatedly asserts that Edwards *uses only* a mutual-love model, then backpedals to assert, mistakenly, that Edwards employs two theories of a person, a psychological and an ontological.[81] Such accounts fail to follow the polemical flow of Edwards's *Discourse* and thus also fail to recognize the shift in Edwards's trinitarian thought, and all three commentators continue to pit Edwards's early note material against his more mature position, thereby unnecessarily bifurcating his view.

Any adequate explication of Edwards's view of the Trinity must take this shift into account. Therefore, it is necessary to understand that the fundamental image Edwards uses to engage in the anti-trinitarian debates is personal beatific-delight. Edwards starts firmly on the soil of

---

[78] Y13, '*Miscellanies* 405. Trinity', 468.
[79] This mistake is ubiquitous in the secondary literature.
[80] See Pauw, *Supreme Harmony of All*, 30–55; and Danaher, *Trinitarian Ethics of Jonathan Edwards*, 16–116.
[81] See Studebaker, *Jonathan Edwards' Social Augustinian Trinitarianism*, 237–8.

the anti-trinitarians, who affirm God *as necessarily one person*, using their foundation to argue that their use of necessity fails. Edwards's fundamental image is not, as many have claimed, simply the image of the soul or mind, though his account does make use of a psychological analogy. Arguing along these lines is not only overly reductionistic, but Edwards, in the *Discourse* itself, talks about *other* possible images and includes the image of the soul as one of them, clearly indicating that this was not the fundamental image he was using.[82] In Edwards's analysis, the idea of 'soul' parallels his understanding of the divine essence, which, in light of the shift I have described, is not his main concern.[83] Edwards did not look primarily for a *vestigia trinitatis* for the sake of explaining the Trinity, but argued that a perfect personal God is actually the perfect tri-personed God of the Bible, who exists in beatific-delight, thereby eroding the very foundation his opponents assumed.

1.3.1.1 The Divine Idea

The foregoing material allows us to return to the flow of Edwards's argument in the *Discourse*. As we do, it is necessary to keep three things in mind: (1) the big picture I described at the outset of this chapter; (2) the polemical issues Edwards was addressing; and (3) the analysis above of the primary issue that led Edwards to revise his thoughts concerning the Trinity (i.e. how the divine persons and essence relate). Factoring these three elements into the flow of the *Discourse* clarifies the somewhat convoluted development of Edwards's argument. Therefore, without offering mere exposition, we backtrack to the beginning of the *Discourse* by focusing here on Edwards's argument pertaining to the Son's eternal generation. It is not within the scope of this section to offer a critique of Edwards's position or to engage in contemporary

---

[82] Many commentators seem to miss this. For example, William J. Danaher, in *Trinitarian Ethics of Jonathan Edwards*, 17, states: 'Edwards considers the "soul" as the "image of God", and he believes "one of the most eminent and remarkable images of the Trinity" is "the mind, and its understanding or idea, and the will or affection or love" (H:126; Y13:435).' Danaher, in making a point about Edwards's Augustinianism (specifically his use of the psychological analogy), quotes Edwards for support, but Edwards is actually distinguishing his view from the one Danaher is proposing. (Danaher is quoting from the *Discourse* specifically here rather than the *Miscellanies* entry he claims to quote, which contains a similar but not exact remark.) I believe the difference to be subtle but important. If Edwards does not believe he is doing this in the *Discourse*, it seems important to believe him.

[83] Edwards uses 'soul' in the *Discourse* almost exclusively to talk about what 'flows forth' in man, paralleling his discussion of the divine essence, or he uses it in reference to the biblical material, explicating the biblical usage of the term.

debates concerning the validity of Edwards's metaphysical manoeuvring. Instead, it is most relevant to note the movement of the argument itself with reference to his overall project (as canvassed above). It is also important at the outset of this section to clarify what Edwards is and is not trying to accomplish.[84]

Based on my previous exposition, it should be clear that Edwards's goal in engaging the concept of God's perfect idea of himself is not to argue for the generation *of a person*, but to argue for the generation of a perfect idea for the purpose of expositing a real act (or reiteration) of the divine essence. This is why, contra Helm and Crisp, I would deny that Edwards is offering an a priori proof for the second *person*.[85] Edwards's goal at this stage is much more minimal. All Edwards is doing in this section is addressing God's perfect idea of himself, which he will later build upon with his argument for personhood through perichoresis. In other words, Helm and Crisp fail to see the importance of perichoresis as the 'twist' in Edwards's narrative of the Trinity. Once Edwards reads the triune persons' personhood through perichoresis, the whole document changes; it is the gestalt which reveals his true intentions. Edwards begins with the Father as a person who begets an idea of himself, but does not mention that God's personhood *depends on that idea* to be a person. Therefore, for trinitarian personhood to obtain, in an Edwardsian conception, all he has to argue for here is that God can and does have perfect self-understanding. By failing to recognize the polemical nature of the *Discourse*, and how those polemics form Edwards's argumentation, commentators force his argument to do more than he needs it to.

Edwards begins by explaining his thesis that God exists in personal self-delight, by drawing similarity and dissimilarity through analogy. His analogy serves to show that while the language we use of God has actual reference – we can talk about God having an idea and understand what

---

[84] I believe that Helm is mistaken on this point when he states, 'Edwards does not blink at the idea that God the Father begets another God.' Helm, 'Edwards on the Trinity'. Edwards is addressing the divine essence in subsistence qua idea/understanding. This subsistence is God, not because a person is begotten (a new God) but because this subsistence is 'within' the undivided divine essence. Helm is mistaken because he assumes Edwards needs to argue for the second person (the Son), when, on my view, all Edwards needs to argue for is the divine understanding. This confusion comes through when Helm suggests Edwards confuses (and combines) the replication of the divine essence with the generation of the Son. Edwards is clear that there is not a new divine essence, and since personhood exists through perichoresis, it is hard to understand how one undivided essence could possibly entail another God.

[85] Helm addressed this proof in a revised paper presented at the Edwards Tercentenary Conference at Princeton Theological Seminary in April 2003 titled, 'Edwards on the Trinity', and Crisp makes this same move. See Crisp, 'Jonathan Edwards's God', 83–103.

that means – God is nevertheless infinite and wholly other.[86] Edwards seeks to maintain our personhood and God's without diminishing the infinite gap between the two. Edwards invokes the doctrine of simplicity, infinity and *actus purus* to protect the creature-Creator distinction. Edwards states:

> The perfection of the manner will indeed infer this, that there is no distinction to be made in God between power and habit and act; and with respect to God's understanding, that there are no such distinctions to be admitted as in ours between perception or idea, and reasoning and judgement ... but that the whole of the divine understanding or wisdom consists in the mere perception or unvaried presence of his infinitely perfect idea. And with respect to the other faculty, as it is in God, there are no distinctions to be admitted of faculty, habit and act, between will, inclination and love: but that it is all one simple act.[87]

Edwards, we see here, avoids expressing what he will later state explicitly concerning God's attributes:

> It is a maxim amongst the divines that everything that is in God is God, which must be understood of real attributes and not mere modalities.... But if it be meant that real attributes of God, viz. his understanding and love, are God, then what we have said may in some measure explain how it is so: for Deity subsists in them distinctly, so they are distinct divine persons.[88]

At the very beginning of his treatise, Edwards admits that while his own ideas of himself are imperfect, God's are perfect. Edwards draws the reader

---

[86] Helm states, 'For Edwards the godhead is not like a Lockean mind, it is a case of a Lockean mind, tweaked by the application of the principle of perfection, and modified by the recognition of the pure spirituality of God.' Helm, 'Edwards on the Trinity'. Helm suggests that Edwards's use of a modified Lockean understanding is why he avoids the classical expressions of the Trinity (substance, nature and person). I disagree with Helm's conclusions on several fronts: First, Edwards's analogy in this context is simply a psychological analogy that is functioning to serve a beatific end. Edwards consistently defines a person as 'that which hath understanding and will', and establishes God's beatific-delight as central to his trinitarian discourse. Helm's suggestion that Edwards does not use the term 'person' seems to come from his misunderstanding of the text itself, as well as the overall argument Edwards is making. Edwards downplays this language at the beginning, where he focuses on the subsistences qua divine essence, and then later employs his understanding of perichoretic personhood, which, I argue, is based on the polemical nature of the document. Second, while Helm's suggestion is possible, I think it is more probable that Edwards avoided classical language because of the nature of the anti-trinitarian polemic.
[87] Y21, *Discourse on the Trinity*, 113.
[88] Y21, *Discourse on the Trinity*, 132.

into an analogy about ideas: 'The reflection, as we reflect on our own minds, carries something of imperfection in it. However, if God beholds himself so as thence to have *delight and joy* in himself, he must become his own object: there must be a duplicity.'[89] Edwards believes that the analogy holds – we can understand this duplicity – and even argues that someone could experience this duplicity as well, assuming the possibility of an absolutely perfect idea of oneself.[90] Edwards continues, 'There is God and the idea of God, if it be proper to call a conception of that that is purely spiritual an idea.'[91] Edwards, bringing his reader into a discussion about spiritual things, draws them in with likenesses to their own spiritual selves, but draws careful demarcations between creature and Creator, fleshing out the implications that follow.[92] In doing so, Edwards is building upon earlier *Miscellanies* entries dealing with spiritual ideas and the Trinity. In entry 238, Edwards states, 'So certainly it is, in all our spiritual ideas. They are the very same things repeated, perhaps very faintly and obscurely .... if the idea be perfect, it is only the same thing absolutely over again.'[93] This conception is now put to work when Edwards asserts, 'This idea of God is a *substantial* idea and has the very essence of God, is truly God, to all intents and purposes, and that by this means the Godhead is really generated and repeated.'[94] The 'Godhead' or 'deity' is nothing more than the divine essence, and therefore as a perfect idea the divine essence 'repeats'. God's self-understanding is perfect, infinite and, most importantly, 'substantial'. Edwards states,

> Therefore as God with perfect clearness, fullness and strength understands himself, *views* his own essence (in which there is no distinction of

---

[89] Y21, *Discourse on the Trinity*, 114 – emphasis added.

[90] Y21, *Discourse on the Trinity*, 116. Again, at this point, the emphasis is on a perfect idea and not another person.

[91] Y21, *Discourse on the Trinity*, 114.

[92] Paul Helm rightly notes that Edwards is invoking a Lockean concept of 'ideas of reflection'. He states, 'Ideas of sensation are derived from "external sensible objects", ideas of reflection are "about the internal operations of our minds, perceived and reflected on by ourselves". Among the ideas of reflection are "thinking, doubting, believing, reasoning, knowing, willing, and all the different acts of our own minds" obtained by the mind "reflecting on its own operations within itself". Because God is pure spirit, Edwards confines his application of Locke's views to the Trinity to ideas of reflection.' Helm, 'Edwards on the Trinity'. It should be emphasized, though, that this language was not without precedent in the tradition. Keckermann states that 'thus God's knowledge returns and bends back from eternity upon itself, i.e. upon God. Just as the soul thinks of itself ... and this thought or intellection is called reflex.' Quoted in Heinrich Heppe, *Reformed Dogmatics* (ed. Ernst Bizer; Eugene: Wipf & Stock, 2008), 106.

[93] Y13, '*Miscellanies* 238. Trinity', 354.

[94] Y21, *Discourse on the Trinity*, 114 – emphasis mine.

substance and act, but it is wholly substance and wholly act), that idea which God hath of himself is absolutely himself. This representation of the divine nature and essence is the divine nature and essence again. So that by God's thinking of the Deity, [the Deity] must certainly be generated.[95]

There are two important points to highlight here. First, to partake in a beatific view of himself, the Father must generate his perfect *idea*. Second, Edwards immediately goes on to affirm that this essence and 'deity' generated is the second *person* of the Trinity, but refrains from addressing how it is that God's perfect 'idea' is a person. This 'generation' is the generation of the divine essence as subsistence, and the personhood of that subsistence is not explained until Edwards unveils his account of perichoresis. Notably, there is a true distinction to be drawn in the divine essence because of God's idea, but it is a distinction within one essence (not divided) as an infinite spiritual substance. Along these lines, Turretin proves instructive: 'About the nature of this distinction theologians are not agreed. Some maintain that it is real; others formal; others virtual and eminent ...; others personal; others, finally, modal.'[96]

Edwards later clarifies that there are real distinctions between the subsistences based on his psychological analogy.[97] Likewise, Edwards does use the term 'modal', but he uses it in a circumstantial sense, in other words, as extrinsic to God.[98] Their *proprietas*, in other words, is based on personhood rather than based on being *paternitas*, *filiatio* and *spiratio*.[99] The properties

---

[95] Y21, *Discourse on the Trinity*, 116 – emphasis mine.

[96] Francis Turretin, *Institutes of Elenctic Theology* (ed. James T. Dennison; trans. George Musgrave Giger, vol. 1; Phillipsburg: P&R, 1992), 278.

[97] 'There are but these three distinct real things in God; whatsoever else can be mentioned in God are nothing but mere modes or relations of existence.' Y21, *Discourse on the Trinity*, 131.

[98] See Y21, *Discourse on the Trinity*, 114, 132.

[99] See the discussion in Francis Turretin, *Institutes of Elenctic Theology* (ed. James T. Dennison; trans. George Musgrave Giger, vol. 3; Phillipsburg: P&R, 1992), 17, as well as Muller, *Triunity of God*, 187. I disagree with Pauw when she argues that Edwards 'showed striking lack of interest in the traditional terminology of processions within God, or of the "real relations" within God (fatherhood, sonship, spiration) that these implied. In fact, he characteristically rejected the use of the terms *relation* and *mode* to signify the real distinctions within the Godhead.' Pauw, *Supreme Harmony of All*, 73. Pauw neglects that Edwards addresses the processions, but addresses them under personhood, focusing instead on understanding and love as true processions within the Godhead. Edwards's rejection of the terms *relation* and *mode* for 'real' is not without precedent in the tradition as well. Zanchi, for instance, uses the term 'real' to talk about the distinctions within the Godhead. Muller, *Triunity of God*, 192.

that call out the second member of the Trinity, therefore, are personal properties.[100]

In closing his discussion of the divine idea, Edwards engages the biblical material, offering justification for his position based on scriptural language concerning the Son. The focus of this material is on God seeing his perfect idea, face and image – in other words, his Son – and delighting infinitely in him. Edwards summarizes, 'And joining this with what was observed before, I think we may be bold to say that that which is the form, face, and express and perfect image of God, in beholding which God has eternal delight, and is also the wisdom, knowledge, logos and truth of God, is God's idea of himself.'[101]

His Biblicist opponents always in view, Edwards emphasizes common ground and points to the Scriptures as evidence of his model of personal beatific-delight. He can reasonably assume that his opponents affirm that God is a person, that he exists in self-delight and that he has a perfect idea of himself. Edwards argues in his biblical exposition that the Bible talks about Jesus as if he were truly God's perfect idea, seeking to undermine his opponents' claim to the biblical higher ground. Assuming he has shown that God has a perfect idea that is somehow 'real', and that this perfect idea corresponds to Jesus, all Edwards needs to show is that an idea can somehow be a person. He leaves off this latter task to perichoresis, turning his attention first to the Spirit.

1.3.1.2 The Divine Love

Now that the Father has a perfect image to behold, there is 'motion' in the deity. Edwards states,

> This is the eternal and most perfect and essential act of the divine nature, wherein the Godhead acts to an infinite degree and in the most perfect manner possible. The Deity becomes all act; the divine essence itself flows out and is as it were breathed forth in love and joy. So that the Godhead therein stands forth in yet another manner of subsistence, and

---

[100] In a sermon on Heb. 1:3 given in April 1734, in the middle of developing concepts on the Trinity, Edwards states, '"Tis not only as 'tis by Christ that the brightest manifestations of the glory of the Father has been to men, that he is called the shining forth of his glory. But he is so in himself by nature of his personal properties .... This is not merely an honor conferred upon him by the good pleasure of God, but 'tis what he is himself necessarily.' Edwards, 'Jesus Christ Is the Shining Forth of the Father's Glory', 226.

[101] Y21, *Discourse on the Trinity*, 120.

there proceeds the third person in the Trinity, the Holy Spirit, viz. the Deity in act: for there is no other act but the act of the will.[102]

Edwards returns to his initial suggestion that God exists in eternal self-delight, and again, invoking psychological imagery, notes that God qua person wills. To put it in terms I will flesh out later in this volume, God has affectionate self-knowledge through a vision of his own self. It is beatific, or 'happifying', in that happiness itself spirates. Edwards has argued that God must have a perfect idea of himself, and in light of that idea, because God is perfect, beautiful and true, he must also love that perfect idea; and that idea, as God's self-understanding, loves the Father. Here again the argumentative flow of the *Discourse* seems forced beyond Edwards's deductions, necessarily invoking personhood without explanation. His focus for the initial generation was upon the Father contemplating himself, but to maintain the *filioque* clause, the Son must gaze back at the Father; so Edwards, just as with the divine idea, moves into the realm of persons without explanation.[103] Edwards now uses personhood language in a more robust manner than before but still has yet to argue for how the divine essence generates actual persons. While this is all true, having to move back and forth between divine unity, properties and persons is a necessary evil plaguing any account of eternal realities, and therefore we should not push too hard for clarity just yet.

Edwards, perhaps attempting to skirt potential criticisms of his overzealous logic, moves rapidly to biblical exposition as further evidence for his view. Here his initially strong person language gives way to a discussion of the Spirit as God's love, disposition and holiness (which are merely three ways of affirming the same reality). The way the Bible uses 'spirit' (when concerning minds), Edwards argues, is not for substance, but for disposition, inclination or temper of the mind. Edwards's argumentation here parallels his discussion of the generation of the Son. He argues that since there is no distinction between habit and act or disposition and exercise, the Holy Spirit, as God's loving disposition, is truly the Godhead in eternal 'motion'. It is because of this, Edwards reasons, that the Spirit is the beautifier, the sanctifier and the means of the elect's partaking of the divine nature. Preceding the beatific vision of the saints, which Edwards deems a 'happifying sight', is the Spirit as the emanation of that happiness; or, in the words of Francis Turretin, 'Vision begets love.'[104]

---

[102] Y21, *Discourse on the Trinity*, 121.
[103] The *a*temporal nature of the *ad intra* discussion seems to necessitate this.
[104] Turretin, *Institutes of Elenctic Theology*, vol. 3, 609.

The Spirit, therefore, acts economically as he acts immanently, as a disposition of love and union.

> God's Spirit, or his love, doth but as it were come and dwell in our hearts and act there as a vital principle, and we become the living temples of the Holy Ghost; and when men are regenerated and sanctified, God pours forth of his Spirit upon them, and they have fellowship or, which is the same thing, are made partakers with the Father and Son of their good, i.e. of their love, joy and beauty.[105]

In a passage designed to argue the deity of the Spirit, that fellowship in the Spirit is necessarily fellowship with God, Edwards offers the reader a glimpse into his trinitarian vision of redemption. Regeneration is having God's own love dwelling within one's heart, allowing one to partake of God's communal love, joy and beauty, and to truly *be godly*.[106] Edwards finds abundant scriptural support for his conclusion, arguing that the Spirit of God *is actually* God's own love. Edwards once again levels his attack on the anti-trinitarians, who wish to affirm the reality of the Son and the Spirit but to deny their divinity.[107] Furthermore, Edwards establishes a twofold distinction in a unified Godhead and links the attributes of each, understanding and will, to the biblical accounts of Jesus and the Spirit respectively, seeking to undermine any solid scriptural footing the anti-trinitarians assume they have.[108]

---

[105] Y21, *Discourse on the Trinity*, 124.

[106] Edwards states, 'But the Holy Ghost, being the love and joy of God, is his beauty and happiness; and it is in our partaking of the same Holy Spirit that our communion with God consists …. In partaking with the Father and the Son of the Holy Ghost, we possess and enjoy the love and grace of the Father and the Son: for the Holy Ghost is that love and grace.' Y21, *Discourse on the Trinity*, 130.

[107] Take Biddle for instance. Richard Muller offers this helpful summary: 'In his "XII Arguments drawn out of the Scripture", Biddle set himself to the task of offering syllogistic arguments against the divinity of the Spirit: "He that is distinguished from God is not God: The Holy Spirit is distinguished from God: Ergo …. He that hath a will distinct in number from that of God is not God: The Holy Spirit hath a will distinct in number from that of God, Ergo.' Biddle denied the divinity of Christ and of the Spirit but affirmed, on the grounds of their distinct wills, their personal identity or subsistence – arguing Christ to be an inspired human being and the Spirit to be an angel.' Muller, *Triunity of God*, 95. It is interesting that Biddle's line of argumentation is that the Spirit has a different will from God the Father, when Edwards argues that the Spirit *is in fact* the Father's own will.

[108] This, again, is a frontal attack on Clarke, who assumes that the Son and the Spirit, by necessity, have to be *willed* into creation by the Father. Clarke assumes that any other position will either be tritheism, Sabellianism, or else make the absurd claim that an attribute of God can be a person. This, I argue, is what Edwards sets out to do. See Clarke, *Scripture-Doctrine of the Trinity*, 183, 219, 276, 280–2, 351–2.

1.3.1.3 The Divine Persons

Immediately following the explication of the Spirit's procession, Edwards makes a decisive shift. His argument has been minimalist, seeking to argue that God, in his perfection and simplicity, has two distinct realities predicated of his being, namely, that he has a perfect idea of himself and that he loves that idea, admittedly bringing in persons, however mysteriously, to explain that reality.[109] By starting with a God that is truly personal, and by invoking infinity, simplicity and *actus purus*, Edwards lays the foundation to talk about God, not only as *a* person, but also as *persons*. Given the polemical nature of his task, as well as his utilization of the doctrine of simplicity, Edwards first addresses the nature of the divine attributes. In a summary and transition paragraph, Edwards states:

> And this I suppose to be that blessed Trinity that we read of in the holy Scriptures. The Father is the Deity subsisting in the prime, unoriginated and most absolute manner, or the Deity in its direct existence. The Son is the Deity generated by God's understanding, or having an idea of himself, and subsisting in that idea. The Holy Ghost is the Deity subsisting in act, or the divine essence flowing out and breathed forth, in God's infinite love to and delight in himself. And I believe the whole divine essence does truly and distinctly subsist both in the divine idea and divine love, and that *therefore* each of them are properly distinct persons.[110]

It is this 'therefore' in the last clause to which Edwards directs his attention in the next phase of argumentation.[111] He has shown that there are 'real' distinctions in God, or more appropriately, subsistences. Therefore, in addressing questions about God, the appropriate answers do not concern immateriality or 'spiritual-substance' (essence), but the inner life of the Godhead as *persons*. By taking this line, Edwards focuses on attributes properly predicated of personhood rather than essence: 'There are but these three distinct real things in God; whatsoever else can be mentioned in God are nothing but mere modes or relations of existence. There are

---

[109] Or, more exactly, that love emanates between God and his idea.

[110] Y21, *Discourse on the Trinity*, 131 – my emphasis.

[111] It is possible that this idea is a leftover piece of Edwards's earlier material. If, as I have suggested, Edwards changed his view while writing the *Discourse*, it is not surprising to find this kind of material. Here, he seems to suggest that the divine essence brings personhood with it rather than through perichoresis. It is not until later in the *Discourse* that Edwards addresses the central problem and shifts his view as exposited above. Furthermore, it is possible that the force of this claim is on *properly distinct* persons rather than properly distinct *persons*.

his attributes of infinity, eternity and immutability: they are mere modes of existence.'[112]

Edwards does not deny that God is infinite, eternal or immutable but rather denies that these can somehow be predicated of God *intrinsically*. 'Reason' confirms to Edwards that these three, God (absolutely considered), God's perfect idea of himself and his love and delight, are necessary and real attributes in God.[113] The scriptural testimony, Edwards believes, reinforces this assumption. Therefore, for a perfect, spiritual, simple and eternal God, the only *real* attributes and distinctions which obtain of his being are the attributes and distinctions necessarily predicable of his self-existence qua persons. Any *real* attribute in God is subsumed under the categories of understanding and will; in other words, the Father's attributes are true of him only insofar as *they actually are* the Son and the Spirit.[114] This account of the divine perfections aims to reorient theology proper around the Trinity, focusing on personal being rather than spiritual substance.[115] Furthermore, Edwards's divine psychology functions through his use of simplicity. He explains,

> It is a maxim amongst divines that everything that is in God is God, which must be understood of real attributes and not of mere modalities.

---

[112] Y21, *Discourse on the Trinity*, 131. Elsewhere, Edwards expands his discussion of the attributes, again affirming that only God's understanding and willing are 'real' attributes. He continues to explain 'relational' attributes, claiming, 'God's infinity is not so properly a distinct kind of good in God, but only expresses the *degree* of the good there is in him. So God's eternity is not a distinct good; but is the duration of good. His immutability is still the same good, with a negation of change.' Y8, *End of Creation*, 528. 'Relational' attributes, therefore, are extrinsic attributes. See the appendix for a more complete development of these issues.

[113] By shifting the discussion away from relational attributes of begottenness and spiration, Edwards can accuse Clarke of 'metaphysical speculation' when Clarke argues, 'For a person who is not self-existent, cannot, without a manifest contradiction, be said, strictly and properly, and in the metaphysical sense of the phrase, to be of the same essence with a person who is self-existent, and of whose essence that self-existence must of necessity be a principal character.' Clarke, *Scripture-Doctrine of the Trinity*, 465.

[114] Clarke argued that the Father, as the one who had the divine attributes, was the only one fully and absolutely divine. Muller, *Triunity of God*, 130. Edwards's argument goes a long way to show that it is impossible merely to assert scriptural attributes of the Father, when, on his view, those attributes are only truly predicated of the Father because of the Son and the Spirit.

[115] Stephen Holmes offers some helpful thoughts on this subject: 'There is, then, in Edwards, a move to subsume the doctrine of the divine perfections under the doctrine of the Trinity. In this move we see that he takes with full seriousness the warnings in the tradition (that Barth claims the tradition itself was unable to heed) that the perfections of God are truly the being of God – the position Barth is arguing for – and offers a way of understanding it built on the doctrine of the Trinity, gathering all the perfections of God up into the Son and the Spirit. Let me immediately say that this is radical within the tradition.' Holmes, *God of Grace and God of Glory*, 70.

If a man should tell me that the immutability of God is God, or that the omnipresence of God and authority of God [is God], I should not be able to think of any rational meaning of what he said .... But if it be meant that the real attributes of God, viz. his understanding and love, are God, then what we have said may in some measure explain how it is so: for Deity subsists in them distinctly, so they are distinct divine persons.[116]

The predication of attributes follows the contours of God's essential *quiddity*. By grounding his discussion in the *personhood* of God, and affirming a specific definition of persons (understanding and will), Edwards recasts the divine attributes accordingly.[117] Notably, Edwards here seems to push against his view of perichoresis by claiming that 'Deity subsists in them distinctly, so they are distinctly divine persons.'[118] 'Deity', which Edwards

[116] Y21, *Discourse on the Trinity*, 132. Amy Plantinga Pauw oddly suggests that this passage reveals Edwards has 'self-consciously departed from the scholastic and Puritan consensus regarding the identity of all of God's attributes with God'. Pauw, *Supreme Harmony of All*, 72. Pauw mistakes the emphasis of Edwards's point. Edwards is not radicalizing the simplicity tradition; rather, he is conceiving attributes through God's personhood. His point is that God-talk must be talk of the trinitarian God rather than abstracting away the divine essence as something of a god in its own right. Oliver Crisp tries to critique Edwards's view of simplicity as well, but does so irrespective of the Reformed tradition (this is also Helm's critique of Pauw). Therefore, if his critique of Edwards holds, it holds for the tradition as well (a line of argument Edwards loved to use against his opponents). See Oliver Crisp, 'Jonathan Edwards on Divine Simplicity', *Religious Studies* 39, no. 1 (2003), 23–41. Holmes provides a helpful definition forged within the tradition: 'To describe God as "simple" means that God is ontologically basic. Any attribution of ontological complexity, any postulation of distinction or division into ontological parts, is excluded by this doctrine. If we accept the linked scholastic account of God's nature as dynamic, as pure act, then this doctrine means that God does one thing, and that is to be God – perfectly, eternally, and incomprehensibly.' Stephen R. Holmes, '"Something Much Too Plain to Say": Towards a Defence of the Doctrine of Divine Simplicity', *Neue Zeitschrift für Systematische Theologie und Religionsphilosophie* 43, no. 1 (2001), 137–54 (139). Thus, the one thing God eternally does is beatifically know himself. McClymond, in defending Pauw, makes the same mistakes. Furthermore, McClymond's defence of Pauw shows itself to be on shaky ground when he counts the times that Edwards uses the term 'simplicity' as a way to defend his position! This is, as should be obvious, not the way to make an argument. McClymond, 'Hearing the Symphony,' 89–48. For a more recent addition to Helm's argument for simplicity in Edwards, see Paul Helm, 'The Human Self and the Divine Trinity', in *Jonathan Edwards as Contemporary: Essays in Honor of Sang Hyun Lee* (ed. Don Schweitzer; New York: Peter Lang, 2010), 93–106.

[117] Muller states, 'Thus, in answer to the question of "What" or "Who" God is, the orthodox set themselves first to describe the "nature" or "essence" of God and to encompass in the discussion the topics of the divine essence, the divine attributes, and the Trinity. There is a single topic, namely, the doctrine of God, which is divided for purposes of discussion.' Muller, *Divine Essence and Attributes*, 232. For Edwards, God's 'nature' is personal beatific-delight, and therefore the attributes, nature and Trinity discussion is actually one discussion about *these persons'* inner life of unity, simplicity and pure act.

[118] Again, as noted above, Edwards has yet to reach the point in the *Discourse* where he changes his position, and the emphasis here seems to be the real distinctions drawn rather than the personhood of those distinctions.

previously used to call out the divine essence, is now read through simplicity to highlight that whatever is in God is God. What is *in* God, because of his psychology, is personal properties. What God essentially is, as we have stated, is a person. Therefore it is fitting that a personal property, itself infinite, simple and eternal, exists in personal-perichoresis within the divine life. Edwards develops his conception of perichoresis to explain this.

Richard Muller, in addressing the problem of predication and the attributes of God, states,

> Once we have been led by Scripture and reason to affirm and deny certain things of God, we are led to the further question of the meaning of the attribution: does it indicate an intrinsic or an extrinsic characteristic of the object under consideration and how does the attribute or predicate belong to the thing as one of its actual properties.[119]

This is the very issue Edwards sets out to answer. The question of predication is not lost in the mire of finite capacities of knowledge, communicable and incommunicable attributes, or the attributes of the essence versus the life of God.[120] On the contrary, Edwards's discussion of God finds its moorings in personhood.[121] The real properties/attributes are intrinsic to the nature of persons, while the extrinsic properties are instantiated precisely as Edwards describes – as modes or relations.[122] Edwards's analysis builds on the fact that we know what persons are and we can therefore talk about God accordingly.

Edwards reveals his final understanding of the relation of the divine essence to the divine persons as exposited above – God's essence cannot be abstracted from his tri-personed being. As I have been indicating, it is

---

[119] Muller, *Divine Essence and Attributes*, 197. Dividing the attributes 'personally', by intellect and will, is not without precedent in the tradition. Richard Muller states, 'Despite his primary division of the subject into divine names, incommunicable attributes, and communicable attributes, Cocceius also has recourse to the faculty of psychology in his classification of attributes …. The attributes of the divine life Cocceius further divides into attributes of intellect and attributes of will.' Muller, *Divine Essence and Attributes*, 219–20.

[120] Richard Muller has an excellent discussion of these. Muller, *Divine Essence and Attributes*, 216–26.

[121] Thus Edwards could agree with Calvin: 'What is God? Men who pose this question are merely toying with idle speculations. It is more important for us to know of what sort he is and what is consistent with his nature.' John Calvin, *Institutes of the Christian Religion* (ed. John T. McNeill; trans. Ford Lewis Battles; vol. 1; Louisville: Westminster John Knox, 1960), 1.2.2 (41). The 'sort' that God is is persons, and his nature is persons in beatific-delight.

[122] This seems to follow the distinction Muller posits when he states, 'To say that God has "attributes", in the strictest sense, is simply to state that various characteristics have been attributed to or predicated of God – to identify the attributes as "properties", which is the typical orthodox approach, is to indicate that they are genuinely in God in some sense.' Muller, *Divine Essence and Attributes*, 215.

here where Edwards finally deploys his understanding of perichoresis. The difficulty, Edwards recognizes, is showing how the subsistences are persons after demarcating them as understanding and love. In his own words, 'One of the principal objections that I can think of against what has been supposed is concerning the personality of the Holy Ghost, that this scheme of things don't seem well to consist with that, [that] a person is that which hath understanding and will.'[123] Edwards has argued that the divine essence truly subsists in each of these by necessity. A personal God must necessarily have understanding and will, and those must be substantial because of God's infinite perfection and simplicity. Edwards finally unveils what he has until this point kept hidden:

> The Father understands because the Son, who is the divine under-standing, is in him. The Father loves because the Holy Ghost is in him. So the Son loves because the Holy Spirit is in him and proceeds from him. So the Holy Ghost, or the divine essence subsisting in divine love, understands because the Son, the divine idea, is in him. Understanding may be predicated of this love, because it is the love of the understanding both objectively and subjectively.[124]

Each *real* distinction in the Godhead is a person because they each have understanding and will.[125] Edwards's position undercuts the anti-trinitarian view by arguing that a singular personal God, in his perfections, *is actually three.* He avoids the anti-trinitarian claim that singularity of essence equals singularity of person and that three persons necessitates tritheism. Edwards, recognizing the difficulty his audience may have conceiving understanding and will as persons, not to mention their mutual predication, immediately states,

> Nor is it to be looked upon as a strange and unreasonable figment that the person should be said to have an understanding or love by another

---

[123] Y21, *Discourse on the Trinity*, 132–3.

[124] Y21, *Discourse on the Trinity*, 133.

[125] This move is distinct from how the tradition tended to posit persons. Richard A. Muller, in analysing the post-Reformation dogmatics, states, 'Thus, as implied by the definition of person as one not sustained by another, the divine persons have their essence and existence from themselves, at least in the sense that the divine essence is neither multiplied nor divided, but rather possessed entire and without division by each of the persons.' Edwards could affirm Muller's statement concerning the subsistences, but because he develops personhood through perichoresis he could not affirm that persons have their existence from themselves. Persons, according to Edwards, are able to be predicated of one another if a being is infinite, simple and perfect. Muller, *Triunity of God*, 189–90.

person's being in 'em: for we have Scripture ground to conclude so concerning the Father's having wisdom and understanding or reason, that it is by the Son's being in him; because we are there informed that he is the wisdom and reason and truth of God. And hereby God is wise by his own wisdom being in him.[126]

The persuasive viability of Edwards's view is for a different discussion, but his answer is clear: this is what it looks like in the Bible. The triune members are not three *individuals* of the same abstracted deity; there is not the Father existing as a person in his own right only to sustain the existence of the other two members. Instead there is one indivisible essence, which exists as subsistences, whose interconnection entails three true persons. There is one understanding and one will that each share together, and yet, each is truly a person in their own right. If pushed further on this, I believe Edwards would point to the tradition and ask, 'What else could it mean to say that God is three persons who have one understanding and one will?' God eternally lives in threefold communion and therefore lives in pericho-retic personal delight.[127] If pushed even further, Edwards was not hesitant to point to mystery in the realm of spiritual unions. In *Miscellanies* 184, on spiritual unions, Edwards states,

What insight I have of the nature of minds, I am convinced that there is no guessing what kind of union and mixtion, by consciousness or otherwise, there may be between them. So that all difficulty is removed in believing what the Scripture declares about spiritual unions – of the persons of the Trinity, of the two natures of Christ, of Christ and the minds of saints.[128]

---

[126] Y21, *Discourse on the Trinity*, 134.

[127] Oliver Crisp argues: 'But although he invokes perichoresis, he does not explain how this is compatible with his distinction between "real" and "relational" attributes. Nor does he attempt to explicate the relations that exist in the immanent Trinity, which make such a doctrine viable in light of his analysis of "real" Trinitarian relations. For, presumably if a concrete particular P has an intrinsic essential attribute x and another concrete particular Q has another intrinsic essential attribute y, then it is difficult to see how P and Q can remain distinct individuals whilst sharing a perichoretic relation such that what can be predicated of P (namely x) can also be predicated of Q and vice versa.' Crisp, 'Jonathan Edwards on Divine Simplicity', 41. While this may be true, for Edwards, it seems, the protocol for talking about God's being *ad intra* is to start with a theological reality, namely, God's beatific-delight as well as the *sui generis* eternality of God. As shown in the appendix, Crisp misunderstands Edwards's position and builds his critique based upon this misrepresentation.

[128] Y13, '*Miscellanies* 184. Union, Spiritual', 330.

Conclusion

Before moving on to a brief categorization of Edwards's view, we conclude this discussion of the divine persons. It is important to keep in mind the subtle interplay between the psychological image of a person (understanding and will) and Edwards's use of perichoresis. Furthermore, commentators have struggled with the relationship of the persons to the divine essence. As we have already noted, the psychological analogy serves to parse the nature of the divine essence, showing anti-trinitarians that if God is a person, he has two attributes that correspond to the biblical account of the missions of Christ and the Spirit. Furthermore, the divine essence itself, like the soul of a person, is the substantial foundation for personhood. God's perfect idea, as noted, is substantial – it is truly the divine essence repeated – but only because it is a *personal* property. Therefore, as shown below, *real* attributes in God are read through the lens of personhood.

IV Categorizing Edwards's Doctrine of the Trinity

Because of the nature of this project, the issue of categorization plays a very minor role. That said, based on my idiosyncratic categorization of Edwards's view as personal beatific-delight, it seems appropriate to set my view against the major commentators. This section will not be expansive, but instead focuses simply on why I consider other categorizations to be less helpful. On the continuum of major interpretations concerning Edwards's doctrine of the Trinity, the two major poles are, on one side, that Edwards was Augustinian (in utilizing a psychological analogy and/or the mutual-love model) and, on the other, that alongside Augustinianism Edwards also utilizes a social analogy.[129] The latter position is best represented by Amy Plantinga Pauw and William J. Danaher, who affirm that while Edwards's main explication of the Trinity utilizes a psychological analogy, he went beyond Augustine by invoking a social analogy as a parallel model. Studebaker, who represents the former position, argues that Edwards's view is solely Augustinian, specifically in reference to Augustine's mutual-love model.[130]

---

[129] Caldwell describes Edwards's trinitarianism as having an 'Augustinian flavor'. This, like the other categorizations, is true but otherwise unhelpful. Caldwell, *Communion in the Spirit*, 33.

[130] I agree with much of Studebaker's assessment but find his categorization unhelpful. He is desperate to keep Edwards categorized as Augustinian and therefore fails to do justice to Edwards's idiosyncratic approach to the issue, the polemical emphasis or how Edwards understood his own view. Studebaker offers five points that act as necessary and sufficient conditions for being Augustinian: (1) theologians within the Augustinian tradition employ

I believe that calling Edwards 'Augustinian' is unhelpful for meaningful categorization for the following reasons: first, as I have just shown, Edwards does employ, with Augustine, a psychological analogy but does so within a much broader model and in the context of his polemic against the anti-trinitarians. Likewise, I would hold, with the majority of commentators, that Edwards's thought *just isn't that Augustinian*.[131] Second, in light of Studebaker's assertion, it is difficult, if not impossible, to lay out the necessary and sufficient conditions for what it would mean to hold the 'mutual-love model', or, as well, to make a view truly 'Augustinian'. Studebaker does attempt to offer conditions for what being Augustinian would be, but doing so necessitates a certain level of arbitrariness. For instance, Pauw affirms that the mutual-love model is the main model that Edwards uses, even going so far as to call it Edwards's 'default trinitarian model', but denies this can encapsulate Edwards's thought.[132] Importantly, in response to Studebaker, she shows that Edwards's affirmations concerning persons directly contradicts Augustine's view of what constitutes a divine person, *which Augustine lays out within the mutual-love model itself*. In book 15, chapter 5 of *De Trinitate*, Augustine states:

> But now I have already argued earlier on in this book that the trinity which is God cannot just be read off from those three things which we have pointed out in the trinity of our minds, in such a way that the Father is taken as the memory of all three, and the Son as the understanding of all three, and the Holy Spirit as the charity of all three; *as though the Father did not do his own understanding or loving, but the Son did his understanding*

the mental aspects of the mind (e.g. memory, understanding and will) to illustrate the immanent Trinity. This is done because they represent the *imago Dei*; (2) The Father is understood as the source of divinity. He is the *fons et origo* of the Son and the Spirit; (3) The Father's generation of the Son is understood in terms of an act of intellection, corresponding to an idea or word in the mind by an act of understanding; (4) The procession of the Holy Spirit corresponds to the highest exertion of the will, which is love; (5) The activities of the divine persons in the economy of redemption correspond to the immanent processions of the divine persons. Steven M. Studebaker, 'Jonathan Edwards' Social Augustinian Trinitarianism: A Criticism of and an Alternative to Recent Interpretations' (unpublished doctoral dissertation, Marquette University, 2003), 123. It is unclear to me that these can be understood to be necessary *and* sufficient for calling a position Augustinian in any meaningful sense.

[131] See Sang Hyun Lee, Amy Plantinga Pauw and William J. Danaher as a representative sample. Caldwell talks in terms of 'broadly Augustinian categories' and Edwards's trinitarianism having an Augustinian 'flavor'. Caldwell, *Communion in the Spirit*, 33–40.

[132] Amy Plantinga Pauw, 'A Response from Amy Plantinga Pauw', *Scottish Journal of Theology* 57, no. 4 (2004), 487. Helm denies that this is an adequate use of Augustine's claim here, but his assertion seems to be unfounded. See Helm, 'The Human Self and the Divine Trinity', 103.

for him and the Holy Spirit his loving .... It is rather that all and each of them has all three things each in his own nature.[133]

Yet this view, which Augustine goes on to call absurd, is Edwards's position almost verbatim. Again, as Edwards states: 'The Father loves because the Holy Ghost is in him. So the Son loves because the Holy Spirit is in him and proceeds from him. So the Holy Ghost, or the divine essence subsisting in divine love, understands because the Son, the divine idea, is in him.'[134] Edwards's understanding of personhood through perichoresis seems to break the boundaries of what could be called a specifically 'Augustinian' mutual-love model, but according to Studebaker's conditions, this is not problematic.[135] Importantly, Edwards's earlier view fits much closer, if not

---

[133] Augustine, *The Trinity* (ed. John E. Rotelle, O.S.A.; trans. Edmund Hill, O.P.; The Works of Saint Augustine: A Translation for the 21st Century; New York: New City Press, 1991), 419 – emphasis mine.

[134] Y21, *Discourse on the Trinity*, 133.

[135] Studebaker seems to succumb to his own critique. His major thrust against Pauw is that she arbitrarily forces Edwards to choose between two streams of thought ('Western' and 'Social' or, as Studebaker terms it, the 'threeness-oneness paradigm') that he argues are anachronistically applied by contemporary theologians (a point, I should note, that is correct). But in placing the Augustinian mantle so firmly on Edwards's shoulders, Studebaker ends up diminishing the very areas in Edwards's thought that are idiosyncratic, namely, personhood and his account of perichoresis. Adding to his confusion, Studebaker claims that Edwards holds two theories of personhood: a psychological and an ontological. He also claims that these two notions of personhood introduce tension into Edwards's trinitarian theology. Studebaker, *Jonathan Edwards's Social Augustinian Trinitarianism in Historical and Contemporary Perspectives* (Gorgias Studies in Philosophy and Theology; Piscataway: Gorgias Press, 2008), 237. By failing to recognize the overarching model of personal beatific-delight, as well as his failure to recognize Edwards's ideological shift, Studebaker ultimately fails to portray Edwards's view. The tension Studebaker discerns is his own – his attempt to hold on to 'early Edwards' to keep his view within a psychological analogy in the line of Augustine – and he therefore misses the thrust of Edwards's argument. In light of this misconception, it is unclear how Studebaker's analysis avoids succumbing to a similar fate as his opponents. Edwards, in both his notes and the *Discourse*, emphasizes the personhood of the Holy Spirit, and yet Studebaker tries to turn Edwards's comments into an admission of conflict between an ontological and psychological understanding of personhood (237–8). Studebaker, comparing the ontological and psychological, states, 'A psychological theory portrays a person as a self-conscious agent and an ontological one as a subsistence of nature or an unique mode of being. Although Edwards' thought reflects both, his primary concept of the divine persons is the ontological one. This is the case because the status of the divine persons in the mutual love model shapes their identities.' Studebaker, *Jonathan Edwards's Social Augustinian Trinitarianism*, 238. The force of Studebaker's critique becomes clear when he states, 'In my opinion, the traditional metaphysical notion of person is preferable to the psychological notion of subjectivity. The metaphysical theory allows the ascription of *person* to the Father, the Son, and the Holy Spirit because they are distinct subsistences or individuations of the divine essence without at the same time severally assigning to each of them attributes of a subject. Moreover, I prefer the metaphysical theory to the psychological because if the divine persons are defined as discrete subjects, tritheism seems unavoidable.' Studebaker, 'Jonathan Edwards' Social Augustinian Trinitarianism', 233. It is unclear how Studebaker's personal opinion on trinitarian thought comes into an adequate description of Edwards's position, but as I have tried to show here, if nothing else,

identical, to Augustine, and Studebaker continues to invoke the earlier material over against Edwards's redescription.

While it would not be technically wrong to place Edwards's view, in some sense, within a broad sphere of positions utilizing psychological analogies, to do so exclusively is overly simplistic, disregards shifts in Edwards's position and ultimately fails to be either helpful or meaningful for the sake of categorization. Based on the fact that Augustine refers to (what would become) Edwards's position on the subsistences as 'absurd', his development of the *beatitio Dei*, and the idiosyncratic nature and task of Edwards's polemic, I find it unhelpful at best and misleading at worst to categorize Edwards's view of the Trinity as Augustinian. This kind of categorization, generally speaking, and Studebaker's analysis specifically, ends up being either too 'clean' of a distinction, cutting off the rough edges of Edwards's account, or else fails to read Edwards in his own right prior to reading him alongside others.

On the other side of the continuum, Danaher and Pauw argue that Edwards offers a model alongside the psychological analogy to balance out the 'limited' nature of the psychological model. On their understanding, Edwards felt too restricted in Augustinianism and so adopted a tradition stemming from Richard of St. Victor to help draw out a more holistic understanding of the Godhead.[136] I think that this view suffers from several weaknesses as well. First, Edwards offers no hint or allusion that he was offering two distinct models of the Trinity. At the end of the *Discourse*, Edwards offers two other 'images' of the Trinity, neither of which is a social analogy. If Edwards wanted to introduce a new image of the Trinity, this point certainly seems like his best opportunity.

Second, Studebaker rightly critiques Pauw (and indirectly Danaher) for assuming from the outset that a psychological (or Western) depiction is socially anaemic (what Studebaker calls the 'threeness-oneness paradigm') and that any social language must point beyond the psychological analogy to another model.[137] Neither of these assumptions is clear. Many of the texts Pauw utilizes to argue that Edwards was a social trinitarian seem to

---

it seems to have skewed Studebaker's understanding of Edwards. Studebaker's preference is early Edwards, which evidently blinds him to Edwards's ideological shift.

[136] See Pauw, *Supreme Harmony of All*, 11–17, and Danaher, *Trinitarian Ethics of Jonathan Edwards*, 6, 68. Studebaker rightly shows that this kind of categorization is anachronistic and contrived.

[137] See Studebaker, 'Supreme Harmony or Supreme Disharmony? An Analysis of Amy Plantinga Pauw's "the Supreme Harmony of All": The Trinitarian Theology of Jonathan Edwards', 479–85; and Steven M. Studebaker, 'Jonathan Edwards' Social Augustinian Trinitarianism: An Alternative to a Recent Trend', *Scottish Journal of Theology*, no. 56 (2003), 268–85.

be texts where Edwards was simply utilizing social language he believed was adequately developed by a psychological analogy. For instance, in *Miscellanies* 117 Edwards states that 'if God is excellent, there must be a plurality in God; otherwise, there can be no consent in him'. If Pauw is willing to admit that an image utilizing a psychological analogy can accommodate person language, which she does, it seems odd to argue that this text cannot be used to substantiate his view in the *Discourse*, but she continually uses it as one of the major texts in support of Edwards's use of the social analogy.

Furthermore, apart from the assumption that the psychological analogy cannot adequately handle social language, Pauw provides no actual argumentation that Edwards uses a social analogy in his thought. Instead, she gives examples of texts where Edwards uses social language with reference to the Trinity. This kind of argument fails because the account in Edwards's *Discourse* was, in his mind, 'exceedingly analogous to the gospel scheme' and provided adequate theological space to talk about social inter-action.[138] His development of personhood through perichoresis provides the resources to talk about both the Son and the Spirit as *actual persons*, and therefore we can assume that social language can be used to describe them. Arguing from Edwards's works (beyond the *Discourse*) that mention the society of God, and using these instances as examples of a social analogy in parallel to his analysis in the *Discourse*, is equally unhelpful for the reasons just stated. In addressing the covenant of redemption in *Miscellanies* 1062, for instance, where Edwards is expositing how the trinitarian 'society' functions (a key text used for the supposed 'social analogy'), he still regards the Holy Spirit as the 'bond of union' between the Father and the Son, a problematic inclination for social trinitarians.[139] In light of these critiques, I see no reason to think that Edwards somehow thought the view he had developed in the *Discourse* was lacking.

Against these accounts, I have proposed that Edwards described the procession of the Son and Spirit with the image/narrative of personal beatific-delight, which more adequately accounts for Edwards's argumentation and anti-trinitarian polemics. Importantly, my view is built upon Edwards's *own progression of thought* and does not pit Edwards's early position against his mature thought, a move now standard in the secondary literature but that only muddies the waters in the task of categorization, whose purpose is clarification. Failure to track the progression of Edwards's

---

[138] The 'mutual free agreement' among the persons of the Trinity is an example of this. See Y20, '*Miscellanies* 1062. Economy of the Trinity and Covenant of Redemption', 430–43.
[139] Y20, '*Miscellanies* 1062. Economy of the Trinity and Covenant of Redemption', 443.

argument in its own right, prior to categorization, results in either an oversimplification of his task or an overfragmentation of his purpose. That said, 'personal beatific-delight' is not necessarily the clearest categorization for a doctrine of the Trinity. For my purposes here I use this terminology to keep the three key images (i.e. the *persons* of Father and Son gazing *beatifically* in the *delight* of the Spirit) always before our sight. Admittedly, a more adequate categorization for Edwards's view, drawn from the depths of his own emphases and terminology, is that the Trinity is religious affection in pure act. Personal beatific-delight is simply a way to highlight the key features of religious affection as the very life of God.

As shown here, Edwards's *Discourse* provides the major contours of his thought on the Trinity and, importantly, reveals a key shift in Edwards's thinking at the moment of compiling and synthesizing his note material. As suggested earlier, the *Discourse* should take the status of a working note and not that of a final work. That said, it is clear that Edwards's position on the Trinity shifted from his earlier view as he wrote the *Discourse*, to the view found in the *Discourse*, which established the position he would hold for the remainder of his life. What follows in this volume, therefore, will help to substantiate the claims of this chapter by showing how Edwards's understanding of the Trinity forms his theological task and, more specifically, orients the contours of God's redemption of his elect. In Edwards's theology, it is *this* God who creates, redeems and communes with humanity eternally, which means that Edwards's theology of redemption will take on the trinitarian contours outlined here. This tri-personed God redeems persons qua persons and reconciles them to his life of personal beatific-delight; or, God reveals himself to creatures such that they experience the religious affection that characterizes his own life.

Edwards has, as noted above, a threefold emphasis on *personhood*, the *beatific* reality of God's self-knowing and the *delight* God experiences as love emanating between the Father and the Son.[140] This description of God's inner life serves as the grammar for Edwards's theological analysis of redemption. God's character of knowing and delighting in his own beatific envisaging serves as the ground and explication of glory, the end for which God created the world and the end for which God created creatures. To fulfil this end, God brings the elect to himself to partake in his own knowledge, love and delight, a knowledge which necessitates *vision* to behold. Furthermore, the elect, made in the image of God, must

---

[140] In something of an oversimplification, whereas Lee ushers in the idea of disposition as the fundamental framework in which to read Edwards's view of God, I suggest the personal beatific-delight of God.

mirror the *delightful* knowing that God experiences to truly know God, being 'affected' in their knowledge of him. As an account flowing out from *this* God only to return back to him, we must take seriously how these categories cohere in Edwards's trinitarian theology of redemption.

Section 2

Emanation to Consummation

'Here is both an emanation and remanation. The refulgence shines upon and into the creature, and is reflected back to the luminary. The beams of glory come from God, and are something of God, and are refunded back again to their original. So that the whole is of God, and in God, and to God; and God is the beginning, middle and end in this affair.'[1]

''Tis rational to suppose that this blessing should be immediately from God; for there is no gift or benefit that is in itself so nearly related to the divine nature, there is nothing the creature receives that is so much of God, of his nature, so much a participation of the Deity: 'tis a kind of emanation of God's beauty, and is related to God as the light is to the sun.'[2]

---

[1] Y8, *End of Creation*, 531.

[2] Jonathan Edwards, 'A Divine and Supernatural Light', in *Sermons and Discourses, 1730–1733* (ed. Mark Valeri; The Works of Jonathan Edwards, vol. 17; New Haven: Yale University Press, 1999), 422.

Chapter 2

The End For Which God Created the World

Advancing beyond the convoluted development Edwards offered in his unfinished work on the Trinity, we now move to its polar opposite, a lapidary analysis on God's end in creating the world.[1] At various points throughout this volume we do 'low-flying' textual work, analysing specific texts and arguments in parallel with other material in Edwards's corpus, similar to our exposition of the *Discourse* and our detailing the appropriate *Miscellanies* material. This chapter, focusing on God's purpose in creating, advances a more economical treatment. While other commentary on Edwards's doctrine of creation builds its case on an interpretation of key texts and terms, my approach here is to look closely at the argument and terminology within the context of his own work. The bulk of this exposition details Edwards's argument for the sake of clarity, and I contrast my exposition with other commentary. This material will culminate in a short but focused section on the dogmatic traction Edwards gains through his account, setting up the following elucidation of heaven, which displays the inherent *teleology* of Edwards's theological vision. There we trace the effects and culmination of God's emanation for eternity (emanation rebounding in remanation). Proceeding from this analysis, I frame spiritual knowledge, regeneration and religious affection with God's self-glorification and consummation, whose grammar and constitutive principles find their origin in God's personal beatific-delight.

While Edwards's doctrine of the Trinity stands at the forefront of his thought, guiding his understanding of God's economic movement through to redemption and consummation, his audience would not have been privy to his trinitarian reflection expounded in the previous chapter.[2] Edwards,

---

[1] This being said, this work was posthumously published. Hopkins, who edited and published the work, believed Edwards would have revised it at points (presumably for greater clarity). See Y8, 'Hopkins' Preface', 401.

[2] This is in contrast to Marsden's comment that Edwards's *End of Creation* 'might be seen as the logical starting point for all of this thinking'. George Marsden, 'Challenging the

in other words, had to weave his trinitarian logic into his published work
in a way that was conceptually potent but subtle enough that a previous
discussion of the Trinity would not be necessary.[3] What follows builds upon
my development of the ground and grammar of Edwards's theology – the
personal beatific-delight of God – and exposits why *this* God created the
world as ground for analysing glorification. In short, the fullness of God's
life as personal beatific-delight *grounds* God's external emanation of that
life and *guides* it back to God's own self for eternity.

Edwards's *Concerning the End for which God Created the World* (hereafter
End of Creation) has been one of his most neglected works historically.[4]
Upon realizing this error, contemporary commentators have focused on
the centrality of this work for Edwards's theology and have done much to
turn the tide against former neglect. For our purposes I turn our attention
more fully to the main thrust of Edwards's proposal: that God created the
world for his own glory and in doing so created creatures as reciprocal
personal agents to receive his glory and remanate it back to him.[5]

Presumptions of the Age', in *The Legacy of Jonathan Edwards: American Religion and the Evangelical Tradition* (ed. D. G. Hart, Sean Michael Lucas and Stephen J. Nichols (Grand Rapids: Baker Academic, 2003), 101. I will not engage this directly, but the ordering of my thesis and the necessary backdrop of aseity should show this to be misguided.

[3] Robert Caldwell notes, 'Among the many purposes of *End of Creation*, Edwards intended it as a work of apologetics to an enlightened community that was growing increasingly hostile to the Trinity as a rational doctrine. By accepting the argument in chapter one of the work … one basically becomes committed to a trinitarian view of reality without making an explicit reference to the Trinity.' Robert W. Caldwell, *Communion in the Spirit: The Holy Spirit as the Bond of Union in the Theology of Jonathan Edwards* (Studies in Evangelical History and Thought; Waynesboro: Paternoster, 2006), 60n2. This work is therefore building upon the same polemical realities as the *Discourse* itself.

[4] Holmes notes this neglect, pointing to McClymond and Jenson as short but insightful engagements, and offers his own account as a corrective to this neglect. Michael J. McClymond, *Encounters with God: An Approach to the Theology of Jonathan Edwards* (Oxford: Oxford University Press, 1998), 50–64, Robert W. Jenson, *America's Theologian: A Recommendation of Jonathan Edwards* (Oxford: Oxford University Press, 1988), 38–43, Stephen Holmes, *God of Grace and God of Glory: An Account of the Theology of Jonathan Edwards* (Grand Rapids: Eerdmans, 2001), 45n45. John Piper has sought to popularize this work in his book *God's Passion for His Glory*. Holmes's work inaugurated a reversal of this neglect: Danaher, for example, offers a detailed and expansive discussion in his *The Trinitarian Ethics of Jonathan Edwards* (Columbia Series in Reformed Theology; Louisville: Westminster John Knox, 2004), 201–49, arguing that the *Two Dissertations* are polemical works engaging moral sense philosophy, Danaher, *Trinitarian Ethics of Jonathan Edwards*, 201–2. Likewise, Lee offers an account of this in his chapter 'God's Relation to the World', in *The Princeton Companion to Jonathan Edwards* (ed. Sang Hyun Lee; Princeton: Princeton University Press, 2005), 59–71. Patricia Wilson-Kastner contrasts Edwards's work with Gregory of Nyssa. See Patricia Wilson-Kastner, 'God's Infinity and His Relationship to Creation in the Theologies of Gregory of Nyssa and Jonathan Edwards', *Foundations* 21, no. 4 (1978), 305–21.

[5] It is important not to separate *True Virtue* from *End of Creation*, but this is more important for reading *True Virtue*. See Holmes, *God of Grace and God of Glory*, 44–5; Y8, 'Editor's Introduction', 5–6.

In short, Edwards argues that God is the *weightiest* and most excellent of beings, existing without potential and having the greatest regard for himself. God's perfections, his excellency and fullness, are able to be communicated, and it is amiable and valuable that they are, therefore God *wills* his economic existence. God's economic diffusion is the communication of his understanding and his will, the image of his triune processions.[6] It is furthermore both *fit* and *desirable* for God's glory to be known, i.e. God's understanding and will to be communicated to the creature, so that the creature will be conformed to his image. In other words, God's external life is emanation seeking remanation; the elect receive knowledge of who God is and incline to God as the fundamental beauty. Therefore God's original end in creating the world, based upon his own fullness, is the outpouring of that fullness. Only upon willing these ends does God decide to create creatures in his image who can have his glory communicated to them. God's chief end in creating the world, therefore, is his own glory, known in his inner life, diffused in the economy, and reflected back to him in remanation. This perspective is, as I argue below, a typical (albeit robust) Reformed answer to the question of why God created: God, in his eternal fullness, *willed* to create for his own glory.

Central to Edwards's discussion is his delineation of chief ends, ultimate ends and subordinate ends.[7] One's actions stem from a chain of ends, subordinate, ultimate (what may be called terminal ends) and chief (the end in which all other ends find their purpose). A subordinate end is an end chosen for another purpose; it is not sought for its own sake, in contrast to an ultimate end, *which is* sought for its own sake. A chief end, furthermore, is what Edwards deems a 'highest end' and is the primary ultimate end. Importantly, God's end in creating the world was an *original* ultimate end, independent of creatures or circumstance, and therefore is the grounding factor of all circumstantial or consequential ultimate ends (ends dependent on God's prior original end). The key example of these ends in the history of redemption is God's providential action. Providential

---

[6] In Holmes's words, 'For Edwards, the economic Trinity is not so much identical with the immanent Trinity as coherent, or harmonious: it is a relationship of order and beauty, rather than identity (always remembering that beauty is a key category of ontology).' Holmes, *God of Grace and God of Glory*, 134.

[7] 'A chief end is opposite to an inferior end; an ultimate end is opposite to a subordinate end. A subordinate end is something that an agent seeks and aims at in what he does; but yet don't seek it, or regard it at all upon its own account, but wholly on the account of a further end, or in order to some other thing which it is considered as a means of …. An ultimate end is that which the agent seeks in what he does for its own sake; that he has respect to, as what he loves, values and takes pleasure in on its own account, and not merely as a means of a further end.' Y8, *End of Creation*, 405.

action *is a kind* of ultimate end, a consequential end based on his decision to create and redeem, derived from, and subordinated to, the *original* ultimate end to which his providential action points.[8] This distinction, as we will see, is essential for understanding the thrust of Edwards's position.[9]

I God Creates for His Own Glory

Edwards grounds his argument in *End of Creation* in the belief that God exists in his own fullness, without need or potential, and nonetheless eternally wills to create. Initially, I will trace the key steps of Edwards's argument before turning to address issues of clarification and theological import. Edwards begins by focusing on *God's* end in creating the world, making six qualifications:[10] First, no notion of God's last end could imply any insufficiency or mutability in God, and Edwards therefore entirely rules out an end which necessitates potentiality or need intrinsic to God.[11] Second, God's end must be good and valuable in itself, and it must be a proper candidate for God's act of creation. In other words, it must serve as a grounding for subordinate ends. Third, the ultimate end for God's creating must be that which was most valuable *originally* (note the original ultimate end above) and prior to willing creation. Fourth, if God himself is capable of being his own end in creation, then it is most reasonable to suppose that, as the infinitely greatest and most worthy of beings, he is in fact his chief

---

[8] Y8, *End of Creation*, 414.

[9] Edwards suggests that a man may go on a journey with more than one ultimate end, but always one chief end. His example, I suggest, is not irrelevant to the discussion. The man, Edwards claims, could go on a journey for two ultimate ends, for the purpose of obtaining a bride, as well as to gratify his curiosity by looking at a new telescope. The chief end, of course, is to obtain his bride. This is, as Edwards often remarks, Jesus's end, to obtain for himself a spouse, the church. But this end cannot be God's chief end, unless it is understood that this is an ultimate *consequential* end. In other words, it is truly an ultimate end, but is only insofar as it rests upon the *original* ultimate end of why God created in the first place. The scenario offered, of obtaining a spouse, presupposes that there is a spouse to obtain. Y8, *End of Creation*, 407.

[10] Edwards takes these six points as obvious to 'reason' itself. Y8, *End of Creation*, 419–20.

[11] Holmes, in his critique of Lee, outlines Edwards's broad commitments in his doctrine of God: 'God does not change (immutability), is sufficient to his own existence (aseity) and totally unaffected by anything done by any created being (impassibility), is not subject to change over time (immutability, eternity), and is sufficient to all effects that he should intend (omnipotence). Finally, God on this account is not doing many things, but is one act: being Father, Son and Spirit, eternally, perfectly and unchangeably. This is the doctrine of divine simplicity.' Stephen Holmes, 'Does Jonathan Edwards Use a Dispositional Ontology? A Response to Sang Hyun Lee', in *Jonathan Edwards: Philosophical Theologian* (ed. Paul Helm and Oliver Crisp; Aldershot: Ashgate, 2003), 108.

ultimate end.[12] God's economic working, for Edwards, offers a picture of 'what kind of being he is', and iterates his 'moral excellence' which consists in the 'disposition of his heart'.[13] God is infinitely excellent, morally perfect and the greatest of all beings. His disposition is love, and his love is oriented to the greatest moral goodness – himself. Here, importantly, Edwards refers back to his notion of the wheels within the wheels of God's providential ruling over time (from Ezekiel 1). Comparing the wheels to the various ends, he states,

> The whole universe, including all creatures animate and inanimate, in all its actings, proceedings, revolutions, and entire series of events, should proceed from a regard and with a view to *God*, as the supreme and last end of all: that every wheel, both great and small, in all its rotations, should move with a constant invariable regard to him as the ultimate end of all; as perfectly and uniformly as if the whole system were animated and directed by one common soul.[14]

Fifth, after a long explication of the fourth point, Edwards claims it is necessary that God must aim at himself in his creation of the world. In other words, it is necessary that God value himself as the only true *original* ultimate end because he is the only object/subject that is inherently (not to mention infinitely) perfect and worthy. Sixth, and last, whatever is good and valuable in and of itself and 'is actually the effect or consequence of the creation of the world', is an ultimate end of God's creating the world.[15]

Edwards's next move addresses why, if God exists in infinite beatific-delight, he ought to create at all? Edwards suggests that God has certain attributes that remain stagnant, having no reason to be exercised in his eternal perfection, such as infinite power, wisdom, righteousness and

---

[12] Y8, *End of Creation*, 420–1. 'Therefore a proper regard to this Being is what the fitness of regard does infinitely most consist in. Hence it will follow that the moral rectitude and fitness of the disposition, inclination or affection of God's heart does chiefly consist in a respect or regard to himself infinitely above his regard to all other beings: or in other words his holiness consists in this.' Y8, *End of Creation*, 422.

[13] Y8, *End of Creation*, 422.

[14] Y8, *End of Creation*, 425.

[15] Y8, *End of Creation*, 426. This sixth point is fleshed out more fully later in his analysis. Edwards states, 'Here God's acting for himself, or making himself his last end, and his acting for their sake, are not to be set in opposition; or to be considered as the opposite parts of a disjunction: they are rather to be considered as coinciding one with the other, and implied one in the other. But yet God is to be considered as first and original in his regard; and the creature is the object of God's regard consequentially and by implication as being as it were comprehended in God; as shall be more particularly observed presently.' Y8, *End of Creation*, 440–1. This point addresses how God can act for himself and for man at the same time, and yet ordering these ends appropriately (i.e. God is always the highest end).

goodness.[16] These are attributes extrinsic to God, or, as Edwards's delineates them, they are *relative*. Nonetheless, God's excellency, in part, refers to
these attributes.[17] Therefore, Edwards explains, 'As God therefore esteems
these attributes themselves valuable, and delights in them, so 'tis natural
to suppose that he delights in their proper exercise and expression.'[18]

---

[16] In *Miscellanies* ww, Edwards states that 'wisdom, power, goodness, and justice' are 'the
four attributes of God that have [to do] with the world, and these only; the rest concerns
himself'. Y13, '*Miscellanies* ww. Four Beasts', 191–5. Paul Ramsey notes that 'these are the
four living creatures, and the four faces, that manage the wheels of providence (Ezek.
1:5–20); but only goodness moved God to create the world'. Y8, *End of Creation*, 428. See
also *Miscellanies* 3, 87. Later in the dissertation, Edwards states, 'The whole universe is a
machine which God hath made for his own use, to be his chariot for him to ride in; as is
represented in Ezekiel's vision. In this chariot God's seat or throne is heaven, where he sits,
who uses and governs and rides in this chariot, Ezek. 1:22, 26–28. The inferior part of the
creation, this visible universe, subject to such continual changes and revolutions, are the
wheels of the chariot, under the place of the seat of him who rides in this chariot. God's
providence in the constant revolutions and alterations and successive events, is represented
by the motion of the wheels of the chariot, by the spirit of him who sits in his throne on
the heavens, or above the firmament. Moses tells us for whose sake it is that God moves
the wheels of this chariot, or rides in it sitting in his heavenly seat; and to what end he is
making his progress, or goes his appointed journey in it, viz. the salvation of his people.'
Y8, *End of Creation*, 508.

[17] Y8, *End of Creation*, 428. See *Miscellanies* 445, 553; Y8, *End of Creation*, 503. See also Holmes,
God of Grace and God of Glory, 41–2, for helpful discussion. Crisp highlights this as a failure of
Edwards's account, claiming that 'if God is a pure act he cannot have unrealized attributes'.
Oliver Crisp, 'Jonathan Edwards on the Divine Nature', *Journal of Reformed Theology* 3, no. 2
(2009), 175–201 (190). This is where Crisp's account of the attributes and divine essence (as
noted in the appendix) fail in accordance with Edwards's statements here. God's unrealized
attributes, on Edwards's account, are merely 'relational' attributes, and therefore are not
constitutive of God's pure act, simplicity or immutability. God's pure act is simply the
procession of understanding and will as self-knowledge/beholding and love. As Holmes
highlights, in Edwards's note material, Edwards is consistently trying to protect God's aseity.
He makes a distinctive move to do this in *Miscellanies* 332, where he develops the concept
of communication. Holmes, *God of Grace and God of Glory*, 40. In this entry, Edwards states,
'The great and universal end of God's creating the world was to communicate himself. God
is a communicative being .... God created the world for the shining forth of his excellency
and for the flowing forth of his happiness. It don't make God the happier to be praised,
but it is a becoming and condecent and worthy thing for infinite and supreme excellency
to shine forth: 'tis not his happiness but his excellency so to do.' Y13, '*Miscellanies* 332. End
of the Creation', 410. James Beilby's critique of Edwards fails at this point as well, assuming
that God, from eternity, had an 'unfulfilled need' only met in the divine creative act. This
is a misunderstanding of Edwards's position, which becomes clear when he suggests the
solution that 'if God's glory is understood in terms of the expression of attributes already
given full expression within the Trinity, there is no problem in saying that God creates with
the purpose of displaying his glory.' Ironically, this is Edwards's exact position. James Beilby,
'Divine Aseity, Divine Freedom: A Conceptual Problem for Edwardsian-Calvinism', *Journal
of the Evangelical Theological Society* 47, no. 4 (2004), 647–58 (657, see also 654). Studebaker
falters at the same point, following both Lee and Beilby. Studebaker, *Jonathan Edwards'
Social Augustinian Trinitarianism in Historical and Contemporary Perspectives* (Gorgias Studies
in Philosophy and Theology; Piscataway: Gorgias Press, 2008), 201–3.

[18] Y8, *End of Creation*, 430. Furthermore, 'This is the necessary consequence of his delighting
in the glory of his nature, that he delights in the emanation and effulgence of it.' Y8, *End
of Creation*, 447.

Later in the work, Edwards picks back up on these unexercised attributes, claiming that God's glory partially consists in these being expressed *ad extra*, as wisdom is enacted in wise workings, power in great effects, justice in acts of righteousness and goodness in communicating his happiness. He continues, 'His having delight herein does not argue that his pleasure or happiness is not in himself, and his own glory; but the contrary.'[19] These are attributes with corresponding effects, and therefore, as God delights fully in having these attributes, it is fitting that he delight in their exercise.[20]

Advancing his case that it is good for God to exercise dormant attributes, Edwards asserts that it is 'fit' and 'desirable' that God's unrealized perfections should be known by those outside of himself.[21] Therefore, God's *original* ultimate end is in view of himself diffused, or his fullness existing economically, and based on that, the *consequential* ultimate end is that creatures can receive that communication in knowledge and love. In other words, God has perfect understanding, and the exercise of his perfections does not add to God's understanding. God's perfections qua perfections are worthy to be valued and desired in and of themselves. God, furthermore, truly delights in creatures, but this delight is not separate from the infinite delight and happiness God has in his unchangeable, independent and self-sufficient existence.[22]

This consequential ultimate end is instructive in respect to the second half of this chapter. For interpretative clarity, I suggest God's *ad extra* movement be read in parallel with God's eternal life with the creatures in heaven (creation in parallel with glorification), where creatures participate in God's own life. In light of this parallel, it is far from irrelevant that Edwards states,

'Tis a thing infinitely good in itself that God's glory should be known by a glorious society of created beings. And that there should be in them an increasing knowledge of God to all eternity is an existence, a reality

---

[19] Y8, *End of Creation*, 447.
[20] Y8, *End of Creation*, 429.
[21] Y8, *End of Creation*, 430–1.
[22] Y8, *End of Creation*, 445–6. This is the main answer to the objection Edwards poses to himself. He states, 'Though it be true that God's glory and happiness are in and of himself, are infinite and can't be added to, unchangeable for the whole and every part of which he is perfectly independent of the creature; ... God may have a real and proper pleasure or happiness in seeing the happy state of the creature: yet this may not be different from his delight in himself; being a delight in his own infinite goodness; or the exercise of that glorious propensity of his nature to diffuse and communicate himself, and so gratifying this inclination of his own heart.' Y8, *End of Creation*, 445–6.

infinitely worthy to be, and worthy to be valued and regarded by him ... which, of all things possible, is fittest and best.[23]

God's glory is worth being communicated in its own right, as a good in itself, but is also worthy to be known in an increasing degree by others. This knowledge is what the created universe *is for*.[24] It is the greatest good because it is knowledge of the infinite, perfect being. This is why, as we will see, God created *persons*. God's processions of understanding and will, which are exercised by God *ad extra*, correspond to personal beings. The elect receive knowledge through God's self-revelation and incline toward God in delight and happiness.[25] Therefore, when Edwards later states, 'Understanding and will are the highest kind of created existence .... If they be valuable, it must be in their exercise', he is pointing to the way in which the elect are redeemed, through God's image of understanding and will *overflowing* in spiritual knowledge and love.[26]

Following his discussion of the knowledge of God, Edwards states, 'As it is a thing valuable and desirable in itself that God's glory should be seen and known, so when known, it seems equally reasonable and fit, it should be valued and esteemed, loved and delighted in, answerably to its dignity.'[27] Once again, Edwards iterates the inner life of the Trinity as a picture of reality. In the triune processions, God not only has perfect self-knowledge but also perfect love/will. Mirroring this reality, the purpose of creation is not only knowledge of God but also love of God (affectionate knowledge). Redemption entails a participation in God's economic life, in order that one day the elect may participate in God's inner life.[28] Therefore, in

---

[23] Y8, *End of Creation*, 431–2.

[24] *Miscellanies* 1063 offers a representative example: "Tis an evidence that the work of redemption is the great thing, the grand event of things that God had ultimately in view in his creation, of all the things that he has made in heaven and earth, and consequently the last aim and end in all his works.' Y20, '*Miscellanies* 1063. The Work of Redemption the End of All God's Works', 443–4.

[25] Edwards, near the end of this work, states, 'It hence appears that here is no other variety or distinction, but what necessarily arises from the distinct faculties of the creature, to which the communication is made, as created in the image of God; even as having these two faculties of understanding and will. God communicates himself to the understanding of the creature, in giving him the knowledge of his glory; and to the will of the creature, in giving him holiness, consisting primarily in the love of God: and in giving the creature happiness, chiefly consisting in joy in God. These are the sum of that emanation of divine fullness called in Scripture, "the glory of God"'. Y8, *End of Creation*, 529.

[26] Y8, *End of Creation*, 454. This will be discussed in the final section of this thesis. God's inner life pours forth in infinite perfection of understanding and will, delighting in his beatific glory, while the truly religious person receives and flows out in imperfect and finite knowledge and love.

[27] Y8, *End of Creation*, 432.

[28] To make explicit what is simply implicit here, Edwards develops his soteriology according to

Edwards's words, 'God in seeking their glory and happiness, seeks himself: and in seeking himself, i.e. himself diffused and expressed (which he delights in, as he delights in his own beauty and fullness), he seeks their glory and happiness.'[29] Likewise, 'The whole of God's internal good or glory, is in these three things, viz. his infinite knowledge; his infinite virtue or holiness, and his infinite joy and happiness.'[30]

It is not irrelevant that Edwards wrote *two* 'dissertations' to be read together, the first of which engages God's reason for creating, establishing the ground, as we see here, for humankind to have true knowledge and true love, and the second of which develops a theology of virtue. Edwards claims, 'In God, the love of what is fit or decent, or the love of virtue, can't be a distinct thing from the love of himself – because the love of God is that wherein all virtue and holiness does primarily and chiefly consist.'[31] Therefore, God created persons who could correspond to his own personal life, receiving his understanding and his love, mirroring God's own love of virtue in both religion and society. All virtue, as we will see, is built upon God's holiness, which is love to himself. Man's holiness is therefore necessarily built upon his love of God, itself a participation in God's self-love.[32]

II God's Disposition to Create

At this point in our exposition, we focus on three issues needing clarification: first, we address God's nature as a fountain of fullness; second, we provide clarity concerning Edwards's use of the terms 'disposition' and 'property' in reference to God's eternal nature; and third, we exposit Edwards's use of the term 'nature'. Turning our attention to God's fullness, Edwards states,

> As there is an infinite fullness of all possible good in God, a fullness of every perfection, of all excellency and beauty, and of infinite happiness. And as this fullness is capable of communication or emanation *ad extra*; so it seems a thing amiable and valuable in itself that it should be

a doctrine of *theosis*. For more on this, see Michael McClymond, 'Salvation as Divinization: Jonathan Edwards, Gregory Palamas and the Theological Uses of Neoplatonism', in *Jonathan Edwards: Philosophical Theologian* (ed. Paul Helm and Oliver Crisp; Aldershot: Ashgate, 2003), 139–60, and Kyle Strobel, 'Jonathan Edwards and the Polemics of *Theosis*', *Harvard Theological Review* 105:3 (July 2012): 259–79.

[29] Y8, *End of Creation*, 459.
[30] Y8, *End of Creation*, 528.
[31] Y8, *End of Creation*, 455.
[32] See discussion on Y8, *End of Creation*, 456.

communicated or flow forth, that this infinite fountain of good should
send forth abundant streams, that this infinite fountain of light should,
diffusing its excellent fullness, pour forth light all around. And this is in
itself excellent, so a disposition to this in the Divine Being must be looked
upon as a perfection or an excellent disposition; such an emanation of
good is, in some sense, a multiplication of it; so far as the communication
or external stream may be looked upon as anything besides the fountain,
so far it may be looked on as an increase of good.[33]

Because this statement has proven provocative, I pause momentarily for
some preliminary reflections. To do so, I put *Miscellanies* 1218 in parallel
with *End of Creation* because it covers similar ground, and was marked either
to be used, or because it was used, in Edwards's writing of *End of Creation*.[34]
Importantly, this *Miscellanies* entry helps to flesh out two of our already-
emphasized points: First, God's fullness, which is his own eternally perfect
life, is the foundation for his willing (finding it 'amiable' and 'valuable' to
communicate or 'flow forth'). God's aseity takes precedence, as seen both
in his first qualification of the six noted above and in his doctrine of the
Trinity.[35] Glory exists, and is known, within God's life of personal beatific-
delight. Second, God's *original* ultimate end is the diffusion of that fullness
ad extra. This end is an *original* end because it is had without reference to
creaturely reality or anything extrinsic to his nature. In his words, "Tis true
that we must suppose that, *prior to the creatures' existence*, God seeks occasion
to exercise his goodness, and opportunity to communicate happiness, and
that this is one end why he gives being to creatures.'[36] Therefore creation
of the world, and creaturely reality in general, is a consequential ultimate
end with the aim of glorifying God (participating in God's original ultimate
end) through the receiving, knowing and loving of God's economic
communication of himself.[37]

---

[33] Y8, *End of Creation*, 432–3. Edwards's use of 'amiable', 'valuable', 'in some sense', and 'it may
be looked on', are in place to protect him from being read too strictly. See Holmes, 'Does
Edwards Use a Dispositional Ontology?' 114n50.

[34] Y23, '*Miscellanies* 1218. End of Creation, Glory of God', 150n1.

[35] *Miscellanies* 1208 is noteworthy here: 'Though it is true God's happiness is infinite, eternal,
unchangeable and independent, and so can't properly be added to, nor can he be
dependent on the creature for it, yet something seems to be supposed in the objection that
is not true.' Y23, '*Miscellanies* 1208. End of Creation, Glory of God', 138. Edwards continues
to address the concern that God cannot truly delight in the creature.

[36] Y23, '*Miscellanies* 1218. End of Creation, Glory of God', 150 – my emphasis.

[37] 'God seeks occasion for the exercise of one and the other of these attributes, by giving
exercise to beings that may be capable objects of their exercise, in the same manner and
for one common reason, viz. because it is in itself fit and suitable that these attributes of
God should be exerted and should not be eternally dormant. 'Tis true, 'tis from an excellent

Edwards at the same time emphasizes God's aseity and seeks motivation for God to create. Notably, this is not God's *being as becoming*, but God's *willing* that causes God to 'flow-out' of himself. This willing is caused by the *fit* and *suitable* desire to put his perfections into exercise. Edwards strategically avoids tying creaturely realities to God, that they somehow constitute God, and focuses the discussion instead on God's self-willing. Edwards continues to display more interest, following his emphasis seen in the Trinity, in the *personhood* of God, using that as the appropriate register for 'God-talk', rather than God's being or essence. In comparing, for instance, the eternal generation of the Son and the creation of the world, Edwards states 'that it [eternal generation] is not an arbitrary production but a necessary emanation. Creation is an arbitrary production. They are the effects of the mere will and good pleasure of God.'[38] He likewise avoids making creatures God's end by reading creation through his trinitarian grammar, orienting the concept around God's own self. As will be shown below, this orientation allows Edwards to tie creaturely glorification of God to God's own self-glorification, so that by being *for himself*, God is *for the creature*.

Continuing in *End of Creation*, Edwards appropriates the previous discussion by invoking the word 'fullness'. Fullness should be seen as God's happiness, delight and glory,[39] that which is true of God's life *in se*. Therefore, as it is with God's attributes which are dormant, finding further value in being exercised, so it is with God's fullness emanating toward creation. Edwards argues that God 'flows out' in his own life. Mirroring that reality, it is suitable and fit that God 'flow out' or 'emanate' that life to creation, since it is the highest of all goodness and therefore the very thing which should be seen, known and loved by creatures. As Edwards goes on to explain, just as God is a fountain of both light and knowledge, as well as holiness, moral excellence and beauty (in other words, the Son

---

disposition of the heart of God that God seeks occasion to exercise his goodness and bounty, and also his wisdom, justice, truth. And this, in one word, is a disposition to glorify himself according to the Scripture sense of such an expression, or a disposition to express and communicate himself *ad extra*.' Y23, '*Miscellanies* 1218. End of Creation, Glory of God', 150.

[38] Edwards, 'Jesus Christ Is the Shining Forth of the Father's Glory', in *The Glory and Honor of God: Volume 2 of the Previously Unpublished Sermons of Jonathan Edwards* (ed. Michael D. McMullen; Nashville: Broadman & Holman, 2004), 228. Edwards uses 'emanation' to refer either to the eternal generation of the Son or Spirit or for God's life *ad extra*. For Edwards, the differentiation is found in the nature of God's *being*, his emanating the Son and the Spirit as the reality of his existence, and *will*, the emanating externally to himself. Ibid., 229. As noted in the previous chapter, this was a direct attack on Clarke's position.

[39] This is a gloss on Edwards's own definition of fullness: 'signifying and comprehending all the good which is in God natural and moral, either excellence or happiness'. Y8, *End of Creation*, 433n7.

and the Spirit respectively), so also it is fitting that God would communicate this *ad extra*. Edwards emphasizes the close connection between the
ad extra communication of God's life *ad intra* and the actual inner life of
God, using the term 'multiplication' and comparing it to a stream from a
fountain. He makes this point explicit in *Miscellanies* 1082: 'This twofold
way of the Deity's flowing forth *ad extra* answers to the twofold way of the
Deity's proceeding *ad intra*, in the proceeding and generation of the Son
and the proceeding and breathing forth of the Holy Spirit; and indeed is
only a kind of second proceeding of the same persons.'[40]

Therefore, God is truly known by his economic movement, which is
an image, reiteration or multiplication of God's life *in se*. As Edwards
continues to show, God's life, as perfect and good in and of itself, is the
fullness of truth and beauty. It is a virtue that these be known by others, and
it is good in itself that they would be communicated. Edwards explains:

> Thus it is fit, since there is an infinite fountain of light and knowledge
> and understanding: and as there is an infinite fountain of holiness,
> moral excellence and beauty, so it should flow out in communicated
> holiness. And that as there is an infinite fullness of joy and happiness, so
> these should have an emanation, and become a fountain flowing out in
> abundant streams, as beams from the sun.[41]

Edwards here appropriates his favourite *natural* image of the Trinity, the
sun, to explicate God's economic communication. The beams of the sun
emanate the self-contained life of the sun, bearing both light and heat
(Son and Spirit respectively).[42] Knowledge of God without love is light
without heat.[43] It is valuable, therefore, that God would allow knowledge
of himself in other beings, as well as love *for* and delight *in* him.[44] Again,
in Edwards's words:

---

[40] Y20, '*Miscellanies* 1082. End of the Creation', 466.

[41] Y8, *End of Creation*, 433.

[42] Edwards understands God's economic movement to be a 'second proceeding' of the
immanent, thereby being the true image of it. Edwards's sun illustration, therefore, works
both ways, for economic as well as for immanent: 'As always whenever there was a sun it
shined or light proceeded from it, so always whenever there was a God the Son of God
proceeded from him or was begotten of him.' Edwards, 'Jesus Christ Is the Shining Forth
of the Father's Glory', 229.

[43] See Jonathan Edwards, *Religious Affections* (ed. John E. Smith; The Works of Jonathan
Edwards, vol. 2; New Haven: Yale University Press, 1959), 120, as one of many references.

[44] Y8, *End of Creation*, 433. Building upon this idea, Edwards would later go on to say, 'This is
agreeable to what has just been observed of God's glory being so often represented by an
effulgence, or emanation, or communication of light, from a luminary or fountain of light.
What can be thought of, that so naturally and aptly represents the emanation of the internal

Thus it appears reasonable to suppose that it was what God had respect to as an ultimate end of his creating the world, to communicate of his own infinite fullness of good; or rather it was his last end, that there might be a glorious and abundant emanation of his infinite fullness of good *ad extra*, or without himself, and the disposition to communicate himself or diffuse his own *fullness*, which we must conceive of as being originally in God as a perfection of his nature, was what moved him to create the world.[45]

Taking this paragraph and what precedes it at face value, God's end in creating the world was that God might communicate the fullness (read 'glory') which he experiences in his own inner life. Creatures are 'secondary' thoughts (consequential ultimate ends[46]), created in correspondence with this communication as 'receivers', therefore necessarily as persons (receiving communication through understanding and responding through will). Creatures are made in the image of God to be capable of true knowledge, love and happiness, which find their fulfilment in God.

1. God Creates because of Who He Is

In answering our first point of clarification, it would be a mistake to suppose, as some have, that Edwards is positing the idea that God had an eternal disposition to diffuse or emanate himself *ad extra* as part of his *being*.[47] Edwards's first point in this treatise is an affirmation of just the

---

glory of God; or the flowing forth, and abundant communication of that infinite fullness of good that is in God? Light is very often in Scripture put for comfort, joy, happiness and for good in general.' Y8, *End of Creation*, 521, and 530.

[45] Y8, *End of Creation*, 433–4. By making God's last end 'a glorious and abundant emanation of his infinite fullness of good *ad extra*', Edwards is putting new language to the traditional Reformed distinction of the *causa finalis* in creating for the glory of God. Richard A. Muller, 'Causa', in *Dictionary of Latin and Greek Theological Terms: Drawn Principally from Protestant Scholastic Theology* (Grand Rapids: Baker Academic, 1985), 61. Richard Sibbes is a representative example, 'It is God's end in all things, his own glory.' Richard Sibbes, *The Works of Richard Sibbes* (vol. 5; Edinburgh: James Nichol, 1863), 323.

[46] Notably, not subordinate ends. See Y8, *End of Creation*, 440–1, 505.

[47] Lee argues that Edwards's God is both fully actual as well as dispositional. This 'disposition' in God is to enlarge himself in creation. In Lee's words, 'The consequence of Edwards' conception of God's creation of the world as the exertion of God's original dispositional essence itself is that the world is in some sense a further actualization of God's own being .... Through God's creative act, according to Edwards, God's own happiness is "enlarged". God's self-communication in creating the world, then, in some sense aims at "the fullness and completeness of himself"'. Most of these assertions will be shown to be misguided below. For now it is enough to say that I agree with both Holmes and Crisp that Lee forces a misguided philosophical project into Edwards's theology, thereby ignoring Edwards's clear

opposite, that God is immutable, sufficient and fully complete in his own life. Furthermore, Edwards finds it obvious that 'God is above all need and *all capacity of being added to and advanced*, made better or happier in any respect.'[48] That said, it is not without justification that some have supposed such a view. Edwards affirms, at the end of the section just developed, that 'we may suppose *that a disposition in God, as an original property of his nature, to an emanation of his own infinite fullness, was what excited him to create the world; and so that the emanation was aimed at by him as a last end of creation.*'[49] Here, I address Edwards's use of the term 'disposition' as a 'property' of God's nature and immediately turn to provide clarification concerning Edwards's use of 'nature' in this context.

What are we to do with language that seems to suggest God has, as a part of his being, the 'property' and 'disposition' to create? First, I agree with both Crisp and Holmes against Lee that it can be assumed that Edwards affirmed a robustly orthodox doctrine of God characterized by immutability, simplicity and *actus purus*. In other words, Edwards was, fundamentally, a good Reformed theologian (and saw himself as such). Second, again contrary to Lee, I take Edwards's 'disposition' language to be predicated of God qua persons rather than God qua being. Having 'an original property of his nature' refers to finding it fit and suitable that his perfections are exercised. This is, we could say, just *who* God is. Edwards avoids discussing the divine essence itself outside of the personhood of God; therefore, dispositions are 'characterological' attributes of persons in reference most specifically to their will.[50] In willing to exercise his

---

statements and utilizing his unclear language to bolster his own view. In other words, Lee must ignore the tradition Edwards aligned himself with, the statements affirming simplicity, immutability and pure-act theism as well as the orthodoxy to which Edwards ascribed (see Holmes, 'Does Jonathan Edwards Use a Dispositional Ontology?' 106–7). Likewise, in assuming that God's emanation is 'an extension of God's being', Lee's project proves irrevocably inadequate. Sang Hyun Lee, 'Edwards on God and Nature', in *Edwards in Our Time: Jonathan Edwards and the Shaping of American Religion* (ed. Sang Hyun Lee and Allen C. Guelzo; Grand Rapids: Eerdmans, 1999), 22. Patricia Wilson-Kastner makes this same mistake as well (see Wilson-Kastner, 'God's Infinity and His Relationship to Creation', 312), and Beilby, with different reasons, confuses Edwards's position and believes it undermines God's aseity (see Beilby, 'Divine Aseity, Divine Freedom', 654).

[48] Y8, *End of Creation*, 445.

[49] Y8, *End of Creation*, 435.

[50] I am not asserting that Edwards cannot use 'disposition' language in other contexts, but only that here he uses it through the lens of personhood and not being. Lee's confusion over Edwards's use of disposition and the willing of God (rather than being) is clear in the following statement: 'God in God's own inner-trinitarian being is dynamic also in the sense that God remains eternally a disposition to repeat or communicate himself, although the inner-trinitarian exercise of the divine disposition is "an eternal, adequate, and infinite exercise" of that divine disposition. This can only be so because disposition is God's essence.' Lee, 'Edwards on God and Nature', 20. My criticism with Lee does not have to do

unrealized attributes and diffuse his fullness eternally, God is simply willing to be who God is (viz. a God who delights in his own perfections and finds it fit and suitable that they be exercised). Third, as provocative as this language appears, Edwards is simply reasserting what the tradition contends in affirming God's immutability, simplicity and *actus purus*: God willed to create eternally.[51] Likewise, as noted above, the traditional Reformed delineation of God's ends is that God's last end in creating was his own glory.[52] Edwards's emanation language merely repeats that claim, only now he emphasizes its suitability and fitness.

We pause here momentarily to flesh out my baldly asserted claim that Edwards's use of 'disposition', in reference to a *property* of God's *nature*, is being predicated not of his essence but of his will. First, as seen in the previous chapter, talk of the divine essence is only had through talk of persons; in other words, the divine essence has two properties, under-standing and will. If Lee's use of property and nature language holds, Edwards's trinitarian psychology falters. Second, it is unjustified to assume that Edwards's use of 'property' is necessarily metaphysical.[53] For instance, in his *Freedom of the Will*, Edwards develops what it means for a person's decisions to be truly *from* them. He states,

with his ground-breaking development of Edwards's philosophy, but how he allows that to bleed over into Edwards's theology. I have no doubt that the two are closely related (his philosophy and theology), but if we are going to allow one to govern the other, we have to allow his theology to govern his philosophy. This is the heart of my critique of Lee – Edwards was primarily a theologian, and his theological reasoning governs his thought as a whole.

[51] For example, Heidegger: 'The decree of God is the act of God, by which from eternity, according to His utterly free will, He has by an unchangeable counsel and purpose specified and resolved on the things that were to come into being outwith Himself in time, together with their causes, operations and circumstances and the manner in which they are bound to be made and to exist, for proof of his glory.' Likewise, Wollebius, 'The decree of God is the inward act of the divine will, by which from eternity He has most freely and most surely decreed concerning the things which had to be made in time.' Quoted in Heinrich Heppe, *Reformed Dogmatics* (ed. Ernst Bizer; Eugene: Wipf & Stock, 2008), 137. Heppe offers a summary: 'Since then the counsel to create the world existed in God from eternity and since the execution of this counsel is nothing else than the absolute energy of the divine will, the result is that the making of the world produced absolutely no change or completion in the being or blessedness of God.' Heppe, *Reformed Dogmatics*, 194.

[52] Muller, 'Causa', 61. Again, Richard Sibbes proves noteworthy: 'God aimeth at his own glory, and it is no pride in him, because there is none above him, whose glory he should seek. And therefore it is natural for God to do all for his own glory, as it is natural for him to be holy, because he is the first cause, and the last end, of all things. It is fit the first cause and last end of all things should have all the glory.' Richard Sibbes, *The Works of Richard Sibbes* (vol. 4; Edinburgh: James Nichol, 1863), 890.

[53] An instance of this occurs in his sermon 'Of God the Father', when, in referencing the Trinity, he states, 'Independence [used here as not-dependent] is an essential property of the divine nature.' Y25, 'Of God the Father', 147. It would be odd to assert that not-dependence is a property in a metaphysical sense.

> Because those things in our *external* actions, are most properly said to be *from* us, which are *from* our choice; and no other *external* actions but those that are from us in this sense, have the nature of blame; and they indeed, not so properly because they are *from* us, as because we are *in them*, i.e. our wills are in them; not so much because they are from some *property* of ours, as because they are our *properties*.[54]

This text assumes that external action is willed action, but it is notable that Edwards invokes the language of property to talk about character. Likewise, earlier in *Freedom of the Will*, Edwards claims that the will is a faculty, power or *property* of a person.[55] He again makes this link between the willed or characterological nature of personal properties more explicit in his work *Original Sin*, suggesting that being upright is 'used to express a character or property of moral agents'.[56] Admittedly, this usage is odd, but the usage is consistent in Edwards's thought in reference to persons.

   Third, and most importantly, Lee's assumption, as well as what seems like the most natural reading of the text, is that Edwards is using 'nature' in reference to God's essence. In light of this, it is relevant that Edwards was criticized because of his use of the word 'nature' in the *Religious Affections*, and in response composed a missive to explain his usage. His qualifications are of particular relevance:

> I confess, my skill in the English tongue does not extend so far as to discern the great impropriety of the word as I have used it. The word 'nature' is not used only to signify the essence of a thing, but is used very variously .... That *property* which is natural to anyone and is eminently his *character*, I think, is, without abuse of language or going cross to the common use of it, called his proper *nature*, though [it] is not just the same with his essence. Thus we say concerning an exceeding good-natured man, that ingenuity is his very nature.[57]

Immediately following this admission, Edwards once again refers back to his beloved image of the sun, noting the sun's nature to emit light and heat, claiming that it is clearly not the essence of the sun being communicated, only its *nature*. Lee again mistakes Edwards's talk of God's nature with his

---

[54] Y1, *Freedom of the Will*, 428.
[55] Y1, *Freedom of the Will*, 163.
[56] Jonathan Edwards, *Original Sin* (ed. Clyde A. Holbrook; The Works of Jonathan Edwards, vol. 3; New Haven: Yale University Press, 1970), 235.
[57] Y8, *True Virtue*, 639 – my emphasis.

essence and therefore assumes that God is communicating and enlarging his own being,[58] the very mistake Edwards is defending against. Therefore a disposition, as an original property of God's nature, refers to God's *willing* the *ad extra* exercise of his unexercised attributes and infinite fullness and not, as Lee suggests, that God is both fully actual as well as dispositional *in being*.[59] There are several notable gains to following this particular reading of this text. First, it allows Edwards to be what he claims to be, an orthodox Reformed theologian.[60] Second, it allows Edwards to believe what he claims to believe, namely, that God is immutable, infinite and pure act. Last, as just shown, it allows Edwards to use language consistent with his usage in other areas of his corpus.

Turning our attention more positively to Edwards's use of disposition language, he states, in *Miscellanies* 1218,

> Both these dispositions, of exerting himself and communicating himself, may be reduced to one, viz. a disposition effectually to exert himself, or to exert himself in order to an effect. That effect is the communication of himself, or himself *ad extra*, which is what is called his glory. This communication is of two sorts: the communication that consists in understanding or idea, which is summed up in the knowledge of God; and the other is in

---

[58] 'Edwards' dispositional definition of the divine being means that God is inherently a tendency toward an increase or enlargement of God's own being.' Sang Hyun Lee, *The Philosophical Theology of Jonathan Edwards* (Princeton: Princeton University Press, 1988), 184.

[59] I suggest that Lee's statement, 'God is infinitely actual, but God's essence remains as a disposition to communicate himself through more knowledge and love of beauty', would seem nonsensical to Edwards. See Y21, 'Editor's Introduction', 36–7.

[60] Janice Knight suggests that Edwards belongs to the Puritan emphasis deemed 'The Spiritual Brethren', and that this language of diffusion, emanation and God's communicative nature are standard for thinkers in this vein. See Janice Knight, *Orthodoxies in Massachusetts: Rereading American Puritanism* (Cambridge: Harvard University Press, 1994), 134–6. It should, I would think, go without saying that Edwards saw himself as a Reformed theologian, even allowing the use of the term (albeit hesitantly) 'Calvinist' to represent at least a portion of his thought (see Y1, *Freedom of the Will*, 131). The point here is not, to quote McClymond's unfortunate essay 'Hearing the Symphony', that I am involved in some kind of 'proxy war', vying to pull Edwards to my side of things. Such an accusation amounts to little more than saying that people who disagree with his own position clearly have external agendas. McClymond, furthermore, uses rhetorically charged categories and labels to dismiss competing readings rather than engaging their position. See McClymond, 'Hearing the Symphony: A Critique of Some Critics of Sang Lee's and Amy Pauw's Accounts of Jonathan Edwards' View of God', in *Jonathan Edwards as Contemporary: Essays in Honor of Sang Hyun Lee* (Festschrift Sang Hyun Lee; ed. Don Schweitzer; New York: Peter Lang, 2010), 68–92 (71–6). What is so unfortunate about this chapter is that it deviates so radically from McClymond's other work. Importantly, McClymond is correct in seeing a tendency in interpretation to try to make Edwards fit one's preconceived notions. But the works he criticizes are simply too important and too sophisticated to be painted with so broad a brush.

the will, consisting in love and joy, which may be summed up in the love and enjoyment of God. Thus that which proceeds from God *ad extra* is agreeable to the twofold subsistences which proceeds from him *ad intra*.[61]

This disposition to create is picked up by Edwards in *Miscellanies* 1208, where Edwards asserts that this disposition stems from the divine happiness which is both eternal and immutable. God is eternally inclined toward the exercise of his happiness, but as infinite happiness, he cannot add to it. God's happiness, Edwards adds, is based on the reality that God 'eternally sees and enjoys this future gratification of it as though it were present. And, indeed, all things are present to him; with him is no succession, no past and future.'[62] Therefore, God's delight *ad extra* is true delight, but it is not new to God; rather, it already is part of his infinite happiness. Edwards fails to advance this claim explicitly in the *End of Creation*, but the focus is the same: God is immutable and infinitely happy in his own inner life, and God delights in the communication of his perfections. There Edwards states explicitly,

> Nor do any of these things argue any dependence in God on the creature for happiness. Though he has real pleasure in the creature's holiness and happiness; yet this is not properly any pleasure which he receives from the creature. For these things are what he gives the creature. They are wholly and entirely from him .... God's joy is dependent on nothing besides his own act, which he exerts with an absolute and independent power.[63]

---

[61] Y23, '*Miscellanies* 1218. End of Creation, Glory of God', 153.

[62] Y23, '*Miscellanies* 1208. End of Creation, Glory of God', 138. Edwards offers an expansion of the eternality of God in *Freedom of the Will* (Y1, *Freedom of the Will*, 385–6), and *Miscellanies* 1340. 'And this immutability, being constant from eternity, implies duration without succession, is wholly mystery and seeming inconsistence.' Y23, '*Miscellanies* 1340. Reason and Revelation', 371. Edwards continues, 'Infinite understanding, which implies an understanding of all things, of all existence, past, present and future, and of all truth, and all reason and argument – this implies infinite thought and reason .... Perfect knowledge of all things, even of all the things of external sense, without any sensation or any reception of ideas from without, is inconceivably mystery. Infinite knowledge implies a perfect, comprehensive view of the whole future eternity, which seems utterly impossible .... And again, if God perfectly views an eternal succession or chain of events, then he perfectly sees every individual part of that chain, and there is no one link of it hid from his sight .... If there be an absolute immutability in God, then there never arises any new act in God or new exertion of himself – and yet there arises new effects, which seems an utter inconsistence.' Y23, '*Miscellanies* 1340. Reason and Revelation', 372. See also *Miscellanies* 679 on the same issue.

[63] Y8, *End of Creation*, 447. Edwards lofts one of his favourite arguments in rebuttal: if my view has a problem on this point, so does yours: 'If there be something that God seeks as agreeable, or grateful to him, then in the accomplishment of it he is gratified .... But then according to the argument of the objection, how can he have anything future to desire

In other words, there is no real (read 'constitutive') relation for God with his creation.[64] He states that 'these expressions plainly mean no more than that God is absolutely independent of us; that we have nothing of our own, no stock from whence we can give to God; and that no part of his happiness originates from man.'[65] God's real relations are intrinsic to himself and are therefore 'full'. God's inner life is an interpersonal fountain of knowledge and love, which cannot be added to.[66] God wills his external emanation (reiteration or multiplication of his knowledge and love), because God wills the communication of his glory as a good in itself. Therefore, God's decision to create was eternal and was based on his will (grounded in *who* God is), rather than in his being (grounded in *what* God is).[67] This claim is consistent with how the tradition addressed these issues. Holmes rightly states,

> There is a distinction made regularly in the history of Christian theology between those things that God cannot be God without doing, and those things that He merely chooses to do. The standard application of this distinction relates to God's decision to create: it is of the nature of God to beget the Son (and to spirate the Spirit); He could not be who He is without so doing. By contrast, it is merely God's good pleasure to create.

---

or seek, who is already perfectly, eternally and immutably satisfied in himself?' Y8, *End of Creation*, 448–9.

[64] 'But he has complete happiness, because he has these perfections, and can't be hindered in exercising and displaying them in their proper effects. And this surely is not thus, because he is dependent; but because he is independent on any other that should hinder him.' Y8, *End of Creation*, 447.

[65] Y8, *End of Creation*, 448.

[66] In expositing Gregory of Nyssa, Patricia Wilson-Kastner offers a summary of Gregory's view which offers some interesting overlaps with Edwards. She states, 'God did not need to obtain good for himself; he is the fullness ... of good. He could, however, create beings like him who were able to receive his own good.' Wilson-Kastner, 'God's Infinity and His Relationship to Creation', 307. Wilson-Kastner seems confused, however, about Edwards's actual position about this 'fullness' when she states, 'It would seem that Edwards is saying that a part of the divine fullness is eternally alienated from God.' Wilson-Kastner, 'God's Infinity and His Relationship to Creation', 317.

[67] Edwards, again, refuses to talk about God as *what* rather than *who*. Here, Beilby's objection is simply odd, exposing his real concern: 'Divine aseity requires that God's decision to create the world be free in a libertarian sense of the word – God possessed *power to the contrary* in his choice. While he was not and could never be "disinterested" in his decision, there was nothing – either external to him or *part of his internal nature* – that necessitated one choice or made another impossible.' Beilby, 'Divine Aseity, Divine Freedom', 656. This is exactly what Edwards finds abhorrent, that freedom necessitates being opposite of your nature, or *who you are* as a person. God is not less free because he is holy, good and loving and cannot choose to be wicked or evil.

He could have not done so, and His perfection would not have been altered or lessened in any way.[68]

God created because he willed to create, and his will is determined by who he is; or, in other words, God is free to will what the greatest good is (his 'disposition'). God's reiteration *ad extra*, therefore, is grounded upon his own infinite fullness, which, in Edwards's words, is 'what excited him to create'.[69] Edwards's concern throughout the treatise is to emphasize God's self-regard in respect to creation: 'A respect to himself or an infinite propensity to, and delight in his own glory, is that which causes him to incline to its being abundantly diffused.'[70] As already emphasized in the previous chapter, Edwards conceives of God fundamentally as *persons*. Edwards takes it to be obvious that persons exist outside of themselves through willed action (hence his appropriation of metaphysical language to talk about character and will) and not in any way through an enlargement of their being, a position Lee claims Edwards held. But this is simply not how Edwards conceived of God. Edwards's real concern is to emphatically deny that God somehow created *because of some created reality*.[71] Edwards's focus on God's self-regard, and therefore on God's self-diffusion, pushes the issues back on God's own self rather than creation. While this emphasis admittedly leads him to use terms and images that can at times be ambiguous, with a careful reading of the text, his concerns and the overall flow of his thought reveal his intentions.

III God's Intention to Create

Here we briefly turn our attention to the relationship between God's *original* ultimate end (his own glory diffused) and his consequential ultimate end. In short, once God wills to glorify himself through creaturely realities, God binds himself to this decree, willing it ultimately and allowing creatures to participate in his self-glorification. As we have seen thus far, Edwards believes it is reasonable to assume that a person who values specific attributes will value the exercise of those attributes. Furthermore,

---

[68] Holmes, *God of Grace and God of Glory*, 35.
[69] Edwards's God therefore shares nothing with the God of process theology. God is not a being who exists as becoming but is fullness itself, and fullness that wills the overflow of himself.
[70] Y8, *End of Creation*, 439.
[71] This is the content of the first objection to his view that Edwards addresses. See Y8, *End of Creation*, 445–50.

Edwards claims, by 'delighting in the expressions of his perfections ... he manifests a delight in himself; and in making these expressions of his own perfections his end, *he makes himself his end.*'[72] Therefore the ground of God's creating, as mentioned above, is his communicative inner life and desire to exercise his dormant attributes for his own glory.[73] His motivation for creating was therefore logically prior to creation in both intention and foresight.[74] In *Miscellanies* 243, Edwards develops his ongoing thoughts concerning glory, positing,

> God's glory is a good independent of the happiness of the creature; that is a good absolutely and in itself, and not only as subordinate to the creature's real good, not only because 'tis the creature's highest good .... Though it still appears to me exceedingly plain that to communicate goodness is likewise an absolute good, and what God seeks for itself, and that the very being of God's goodness necessarily supposes it; for to make happy is not goodness if it be done purely for another superior end.[75]

Edwards is carefully navigating the issues to avoid the idea that God needs the creature or that he created because of something outside of himself.[76] This concern does not, however, stop him from pushing hard on this idea, emphasizing God's life is truly interwoven with the creatures. In a careful statement, which I quote at length, Edwards states,

> *God looks on* the communication of himself, and the emanation of the infinite glory and good that are in himself to belong to the fullness and completeness of himself, *as though* he were not in his most complete and glorious state without it. Thus the church of Christ (toward whom

---

[72] Y8, *End of Creation*, 437.

[73] Cocceius states, 'The end of creation is the glory of God, i.e. the manifestation of the eminence, power and virtues of God in the creature and to the creature .... From this it follows that the goodness of the creature consists in it being a witness and evidence of the divine glory.' Quoted in Heppe, *Reformed Dogmatics*, 195.

[74] Y8, *End of Creation*, 438. In a helpful summary, Edwards states, 'This propensity in God to diffuse himself may be considered as a propensity to himself diffused, or to his own glory existing in its emanation. A respect to himself, or an infinite propensity to, and delight in his own glory, is that which causes him to incline to its being abundantly diffused, and to delight in the emanation of it.' Y8, *End of Creation*, 439. Along relatively similar lines, Voetius states, 'There are no outward impelling causes (if one may indeed use this expression of God). The divine goodness is inward; the good diffuses and communicates itself.' Quoted in Heppe, *Reformed Dogmatics*, 195.

[75] Y13, '*Miscellanies* 243. Glory of God', 358–9.

[76] In *Miscellanies* 1245, Edwards states, 'He [Jesus] being the end of all God's works *ad extra*, therefore the accomplishment of all was committed to him.' Y23, '*Miscellanies* 1245. Election', 178. Even with creation in mind God 'aims' his ends toward himself in his Son.

and in whom are the emanations of his glory and communications of his fullness) is called the fullness of Christ: *as though* he were not in his complete state without her; as Adam was in a defective state without Eve .... Indeed after the creatures are intended to be created, God may be conceived of as being moved by benevolence to these creatures, in the strictest sense, in his dealings with, and works about them.[77]

Edwards makes several key distinctions here. First, his use of 'as though' should not be ignored.[78] Second, and building upon the first, Edwards shifts from God and his own inner goodness to God's intention to create. Here God has in mind the entire history of redemption, taking it upon himself to redeem.[79] God is alpha and omega in the affair of redemption, *and once God intends to redeem*, he wagers his own faithfulness on the fulfilment of his promises.[80] In other words, God can be said to be incomplete, in a sense, because he has committed himself to redemption, but the work of redemption takes place in time and therefore is unfulfilled until the consummation of all things. It is easy to misunderstand Edwards's discussion if one neglects his initial distinction between original and consequential ultimate ends. Edwards makes it clear that God can have one *original* ultimate end, but that original ultimate end can be worked out through consequential ends, in this case, God's emanation of his fullness *to humankind*. When Edwards addresses God's delight in the creature, he does so in light of the fact that, first, God delights in his knowledge and love *ad intra*; second, that God delights in exercising this fullness *ad extra*; and third, that upon creating, God delights in communicating himself to the creature. Therefore, when Edwards states that ''tis no argument of the emptiness or deficiency of a fountain that it is inclined to overflow', it is not an issue of God's 'being

---

[77] Y8, *End of Creation*, 439–40 – my emphasis.

[78] See Holmes, 'Does Jonathan Edwards Use a Dispositional Ontology?' 114n50.

[79] Edwards claims that God's disposition to exercise his fullness is to an effect, therefore it seems that once God commits to this it would be contrary to God's nature to leave it unfulfilled. Y23, '*Miscellanies* 1218. End of Creation, Glory of God', 153.

[80] Edwards understands 'righteousness' to mean 'covenant faithfulness'. He states, 'And this further may be taken notice of here, viz. that, as was observed before, though the word righteousness be in its original and principal signification a forensic term, yet as moral terms in general were taken from courts of judgement, so the word righteousness came to express moral good in general; and particularly, God's faithfulness is often called his righteousness. And it is often found that when the Scripture speaks of God's mercy and favor and saving goodness by the name of God's righteousness, his covenant faithfulness is what is intended.' Y21, '"Controversies": Justification', 353–4. See also Y9, *History of the Work of Redemption*, 114.

as becoming', but God's bringing about his ends by communicating his knowledge and will.[81]

In anticipation of our development of redemption, and foreshadowing the following section, which highlights Edwards's trinitarian depiction of glory, I briefly address the nature and task of God's emanation *to creatures*. Edwards argues that one part of the 'fullness' that God communicates of himself is God's self-knowledge. He states, 'This knowledge in the creature is but a conformity to God. 'Tis a participation of the same: 'tis as much the same as 'tis possible for that to be, which is infinitely less in degree: as particular beams of the sun communicated, are the light and glory of the sun in part.'[82] The elect, in other words, receive and know God by participating in God's own self-knowledge. This is the external image of the procession of the Son, God's idea and knowledge, which, for the purpose of redemption, is poured forth in God's emanation of himself to the creature.[83] Therefore God is glorified as his perfections and excellencies are known and are seen.[84] By uniting the elect to God's own self-understanding,

[81] Y8, *End of Creation*, 448. Edwards navigates the objection that his scheme undermines God's immutability, sufficiency and independence of the creature by invoking God's eternality: 'For though these communications of God, these exercises, operations, effects and expressions of his glorious perfections, which God rejoices in, are in time; yet his joy in them is without beginning or change. They were always equally present in the divine mind. He beheld them with equal clearness, certainty and fullness in every respect, as he doth now. They were always equally present, as with him there is no variableness or succession .... And his view of, and joy in them is eternally, absolutely perfect, unchangeable and independent. It can't be added to or diminished by the power or will of the creature; nor is in the least dependent on anything mutable or contingent.' Y8, *End of Creation*, 448.

[82] Y8, *End of Creation*, 441.

[83] Ramsey raises the issues of the possibility of Neo-Platonism in Edwards's use of 'emanation', as does Patricia Wilson-Kastner (Wilson-Kastner, 'God's Infinity and His Relationship to Creation, 307) and Danaher (Danaher, *Trinitarian Ethics of Jonathan Edwards*, 205–11). Holmes finds this critique incredible, stating, 'My contention is that a neoplatonic reading of Edwards is simply inconceivable, if my Trinitarian reading is accepted. The Fathers, after all, avoided platonising emanationisms precisely by asserting the doctrine of the Trinity.' Holmes, *God of Grace and God of Glory*, 59. See also Y8, *End of Creation*, 433n5. I think Holmes is right to a degree, but positing a 'Neo-Platonic flavour' to Edwards's thought would not be far-fetched. Crisp claims that Edwards's view can be categorized by what he calls 'pure act panentheism'. I take Edwards's emanation language to simply draw the link between who God is *ad intra* with who he is *ad extra*. In other words, emanation serves to link the processions with the missions. This, again, puts my view at odds with Lee's, who states, 'And it is Edwards' dispositional conception of God that enables Edwards to combine the categories of emanation and teleology. The logic behind this wedding of the two usually unrelated concepts is to be traced to the idea of disposition and its ontologically productive character.' Lee, *Philosophical Theology of Jonathan Edwards*, 199. This kind of account runs against everything Edwards says about his own conception of God as pure act, simple and immutable. As Holmes notes, Lee makes the leap from 'God's own happiness is enlarged', to 'God's own life' is now enlarged, taking that to mean God's own being. Holmes, 'Does Jonathan Edwards Use a Dispositional Ontology?', 108.

[84] This concept of seeing God's excellency and glory, and its Christological orientation, is a central idea in Edwards's theology of redemption (addressed below).

Edwards suggests the elect participate in God's own self-glorification. This self-glorification is, once again, derivative of the original ultimate end of creation but is still an ultimate end, a consequential ultimate end, in God's plan of self-glorification. As should be expected, Edwards addresses God's holiness, or the procession of the Spirit, in the same way. Just as with the divine knowledge, so also the creature partakes of God's own moral excellency, which Edwards calls 'the beauty of the divine nature'.[85] Again, just as with God's self-knowledge, God allows the elect to partake of his holiness and therefore binds the creature to his own self-glorification without truly adding to it. In his own words, 'As God delights in his own beauty, he must necessarily delight in the creature's holiness; which is a conformity to, and participation of it, as truly as the brightness of a jewel, held in the sun's beams, is a participation, or derivation of the sun's brightness, though immensely less in degree.'[86]

This brightness is the creature's love to God, the work of God's Spirit within the heart of the elect (or originally Adam). Loving, for Edwards, is therefore a 'comprehension of true virtue', a participation in, and therefore conformity to, the love that God communicates from the fullness of his life. This participation leads to an experience of God's inner life itself, what Edwards calls God's happiness or fullness. Therefore, upon intending to create, God chooses to communicate himself as true knowledge, love, beauty and delight:

> God is all in all, with respect to each part of that communication of the divine fullness which is made to the creature. What is communicated is divine, or something of God: and each communication is of that nature, that the creature to whom it is made, is thereby conformed to God, and united to him; and that in proportion as the communication is greater or less. And the communication itself is no other, in the very nature of it, than that wherein the very honor, exaltation and praise of God consists.[87]

By making himself the end for which he created the world, God's plan of redemption is *from* him, *by* him and ultimately *in* him. God, in other words, is not merely the type of all things valuable, leaving everything

---

[85] Y8, *End of Creation*, 442.
[86] Y8, *End of Creation*, 442. Edwards's language here resembles Eastern Orthodox depictions of the essence/energies distinction stemming from Gregory Palamas and reading back to the Cappadocian theologians. It is not surprising, as I have already noted, that Edwards ends up developing a very similar account of *theosis*.
[87] Y8, *End of Creation*, 442.

good, beautiful and true in the world as antitype. God is the *only thing* which is truly good, beautiful and true, and everything that is so participates, in some manner, in him. The answer for fallen humanity, as will be seen below, is conformity to God through participation in his knowledge and love – *theosis.* This is how Edwards answers the objection that God, if he were truly unchangeable, infinitely happy and sufficient, would not derive pleasure from the creature's praise or happiness. God delights in the creature's happiness and praise because it is an actual instance of his own happiness, glory and delight.[88] It is also the case that God's being *for* himself is his being *for* the creature. God knows that his own life is the greatest, happiest, most infinite goodness in existence, and therefore by making this his end, he wills the creature's good, that they too might know this goodness.[89] In other words, God cannot be selfish because his own life is the storehouse of goodness, excellency, love and virtue.[90]

IV Revelation of Glory

As we have seen, in Edwards's development, God creates for his own glory. Here, I highlight Edwards's trinitarian conception of glory, which runs parallel to his idea that God iterates his own life into creation. We have already seen Edwards switch between the terms happiness, fullness,

---

[88] As Edwards notes in *Miscellanies* 679, 'So that God has a real delight in the spiritual loveliness of the saints, which delight is not a delight distinct from what he has in himself, but is to be resolved into the delight he has in himself: for he delights in his image in the creature, as he delights in his own being glorified, or as he delights in it, that his own glory shines forth. And so he hath real proper delight in the happiness of his creatures, which also is not distinct from the delight that he has in himself, for 'tis to be resolved into the delight that he has in his own goodness …. God, when he beholds his own glory shining forth in his image in the creature, and when he beholds the creature made happy from the exercises of his goodness, because these and all things are from eternity equally present with God this delight in God can't properly be said to be received from the creature, because it consists only in a delight in giving to the creature.' Y18, '*Miscellanies* 679. Goodness of God', 238.

[89] This is why God's self-motivation is not selfish. Edwards states, 'God's seeking himself in the creation of the world, in the manner which has been supposed, is so far from being inconsistent with the good of his creatures, or any possibility of being so, that it is a kind of regard to himself that inclines him to seek the good of his creature.' Y8, *End of Creation*, 452.

[90] Attaching this concept to virtue, Edwards states, 'In some sense, the most benevolent generous person in the world seeks his own happiness in doing good to others, because he places his happiness in their good. His mind is so enlarged as to take them, as it were, into himself. Thus when they are happy he feels it, he partakes with them, and is happy in their happiness.' Y8, *End of Creation*, 461. God, Edwards argues, being infinite, does not enlarge per se, but flows forth and expresses himself to creatures, 'making them to partake of him, and rejoicing in himself expressed in them, and communicated to them.' Y8, *End of Creation*, 462.

delight and glory, but here we address glory as such.[91] Edwards exposits the Hebrew word *kavod* and the Greek word *doxa*, describing a threefold overflow that parallels his account of God's end in creating: first, glory is 'used to signify what is internal, what is within the being or person, inherent in the subject'; second, it is used 'for emanation, exhibition or communication of this internal glory'; last, it is used 'for the knowledge or sense, or effect of these, in those who behold it, to whom the exhibition or communication is made; or an expression of this knowledge or sense or effect'.[92] Therefore, following the work noted above concerning Edwards's doctrine in *End of Creation*, Edwards's definition of glory maps directly onto his understanding of God's trinitarian *nature*, God's *ad extra* movement and God's redemption of creatures through participation in that glory.

Just as God's glory has a threefold 'architecture', God's glory is also trinitarian.[93] Edwards uses the terms 'fullness' and 'excellency' to describe God's glory, which we have argued is the nature of God's life as Trinity: personal beatific-delight.[94] This fullness, again, is his knowing and willing

[91] Edwards specifically asserts, in *Miscellanies* 1142, that 'there are three things called by the name of glory in Scripture: excellency, goodness and happiness.' Y20, '*Miscellanies* 1142. Glory of God', 517. Happiness is an interesting addition here and is what I refer to as delight in the inner life of God. Note the difference in Sibbes's definition: 'Glory is excellency, greatness, and goodness, with the eminency of it, so as it may be discovered.' Richard Sibbes, *The Works of Richard Sibbes* (vol. 6; Edinburgh: James Nichol, 1863), 324. Edwards's addition of happiness to the idea of glory calls out his definition of 'fullness' as deriving from the beatific life of God, and communicated to the saints through a participation in that beatific life. Edwards notes, 'Happiness is very often in Scripture called by the name of glory, or included in that name in Scripture. God's eternal glory includes his blessedness [his beatific-delight], and when we read of the glorifying of Christ, and the glory which the Father has given him, it includes his heavenly joy. And so when we read of the glory promised to or conferred on the saints, and of their being glorified, their unspeakable happiness is a main thing intended. Their joy is full of glory, and they are made happy in partaking of Christ's glory.' Y20, '*Miscellanies* 1082. End of the Creation', 466.

[92] Y8, *End of Creation*, 513.

[93] See Holmes, *God of Grace and God of Glory*, 53–5, for an explanation of why this trinitarian theme is not emphasized in *End of Creation*. Danaher emphasizes the trinitarian nature of Edwards's thought here but does so through his mistaken understanding of Edwards's trinitarian models. Danaher, *Trinitarian Ethics of Jonathan Edwards*, 210–11.

[94] Edwards emphasizes that all three persons of the Trinity have the same glory: 'Glory belongs to the Father and the Son, that they so greatly loved the world: to the Father, that he so loved the world that he gave his only begotten Son, who was all his delight, who is his infinite objective happiness; to the Son, that he so loved the world that he gave himself. But there is equal glory due to the Holy Ghost on this account, because he is the love of the Father and the Son that flows out primarily towards each, and secondarily towards the elect that Christ came to save; so that, however wonderful the love of the Father and the Son appear to be, so much the more glory belongs to the Holy Spirit, in whom subsists that wonderful and excellent love.' Y21, 'Treatise on Grace', 189. This is in reference to the economic overflow of God's glory, but this overflow is grounded in the glory known in pure act in the inner life of God (see Y21, *Discourse*, 119, 121). Likewise, 'Each of the persons of the Trinity, as they are the same God, they have the same divine essence, so they have all the same glory.' He goes on to talk about Christ's 'partaking' in the same divine glory as the Father, and

emanating forth in his inner life, fully actualized, infinite and perfect. The emanation of his glory *ad extra* is the willed image of his necessary eternal emanation *ad intra*. Edwards develops his account with a threefold participation – a participation in God's self-knowing (through the Son), holiness (through the Spirit) *and* happiness – the beatific delight of God.[95] This participation is communion with God that continues eternally, as 'an increasing knowledge *of* God, love *to* him, and joy *in* him'.[96] The creation of creatures for redemption maps onto the twofold emanation of knowledge and will and, in the person of Christ, is iterated to creatures through the union, illumination and infusion of the Spirit (where the elect come to know the 'happiness' of God). Redemption is the ground of creation, and all creation was created for God's own glorification. This is achieved in the elect by their *beholding* God and his glory. Edwards states, 'The exhibition of glory is to the view of beholders. The manifestation of glory, the emanation or effulgence of brightness, has relation to the eye. Light or brightness is a quality that has relation to the sense of seeing: we see the luminary by its light. And knowledge is often expressed in Scripture by light.'[97]

Therefore, the end for which God created the world was the glory of God.[98] God's glory is one reality, and yet it consists in a threefold movement: there is God's eternal fountain of glory *ad intra*, God's diffusion of that glory and the creature's glorifying God through participation in his knowledge and love.[99] God's glory, for the purpose of redemption and for God's end to be realized, necessitates a creaturely response. Edwards claims that 'in these things, viz. in knowing God's excellency, loving God for it, and rejoicing in it; and in the exercise and expression of these, consists

---

explains it by the description, 'i.e. in the same excellency and the same happiness, or in one word, as a partaker of the same glory'. Edwards, 'Jesus Christ Is the Shining Forth of the Father's Glory', 227.

[95] Y8, *End of Creation*, 441–2.

[96] Y8, *End of Creation*, 443 – my emphasis.

[97] Y8, *End of Creation*, 521.

[98] This also refers to damnation. One example would be: 'But God's glory requires that his displeasure be manifested against sin also in the acts and effects of it.' Edwards, 'The Glory and Honor of God Requires That His Displeasure Be Manifested', in *Glory and Honor of God*, 37.

[99] 'The emanation or communication is of the internal glory or fullness of God, as it is. Now God's internal glory, as it is in God, is either in his understanding or will. The glory or fullness of his understanding is his knowledge. The internal glory and fullness of God, which we must conceive of as having its special seat in his will, is his holiness and happiness. The whole of God's internal good or glory, is in these three things, viz. his infinite knowledge/his infinite virtue or holiness, and his infinite joy and happiness …. So that, as I said, the fullness of the Godhead is the fullness of his understanding, consisting in his knowledge, and the fullness of his will, consisting in his virtue and happiness. And therefore the external glory of God consists in the communication of these.' Y8, *End of Creation*, 528.

God's honor and praise: so that these are clearly implied in that glory of God'.[100] Since God's glory increases in the elect for eternity, through uniting the elect to himself, God's end for creation was for *this* eternal good, as a necessary consequence of being infinite goodness in himself.[101]

V The Dogmatic Task of God's End in Creating

Here I briefly attend to the dogmatic task of Edwards's doctrine just exposited. In doing so, I outline an answer to the question: what work does this doctrine do in Edwards's theology with specific reference to redemption? First, contrary to certain commentators noted above, Edwards's doctrine establishes God's aseity as the ground and foundation for his theology. *This God* is the God who engages creation as infinite fullness and whose own abundance never ceases or diminishes. Concerning aseity, Bavinck is instructive, 'But as is evident from the word "aseity", God is exclusively from himself, not in the sense of being self-caused but being from eternity to eternity *who he is*, being not becoming.'[102] For Edwards specifically, *who* God is, and what God's fullness is, must be interpreted as God's personal beatific-delight. Edwards's doctrine of God stands as the fountain of his thought and forms his theology as a whole.

Second, as I will develop more fully in the next chapter, Edwards's vision of God's end in creating establishes a trajectory for redemption. Since knowing God necessitates partaking of his self-knowing, self-loving and happiness, creatures are called to knowledge and holiness through an increasing union with him for eternity (and a sight of God which 'happifies'). Again, contra Lee, it is not that Edwards mixes metaphors of emanation and teleology, but in creating for his own glory, and creating creatures as receivers of that glory (persons), Edwards's account entails a specific teleology of union, illumination and infusion.[103] In Edwards's words, 'The image is more and more perfect, and so the good that is in the creature comes forever nearer and nearer to an identity with that which

---

[100] Y8, *End of Creation*, 529.

[101] See Y8, *End of Creation*, 535. As Edwards states early on in *Miscellanies* 247, 'And it was his inclination to communicate himself that was a prime motive of his creating the world. His own glory was the ultimate [end], himself was the end; that is, himself communicated.' Y13, '*Miscellanies* 247. Glory of God', 361.

[102] Herman Bavinck, *Reformed Dogmatics: God and Creation* (ed. John Bolt; trans. John Vriend; vol. 2; Grand Rapids: Baker Academic, 2003), 152 – my emphasis.

[103] Lee, 'Edwards on God and Nature', 22.

is in God.'[104] Likewise, 'For it will forever come nearer and nearer to that strictness and perfection of union which there is between the Father and the Son.'[105] By intending to redeem creatures, God intends to pull creatures up into his very own life.[106] This redemption entails an asymptotic increase in union for eternity, where the elect are united to God in ever-increasing unity.[107]

Third, Edwards locates his understanding of redemption within his understanding of God's self-glorification. As God is the fount of the creation, God is also the last end of creation.[108] There is emanation and there is remanation.[109] For God to be the end of his creation, and to desire true communication of his love, it is necessary that God's purposes in his creation and communication be fulfilled. Therefore, to receive this communication and respond in kind, God created persons capable of

---

[104] Y8, *End of Creation*, 443.

[105] Y8, *End of Creation*, 443.

[106] 'In this view, those elect creatures which must be looked upon as the end of all the rest of the creation, considered with respect to the whole of their eternal duration, and as such made God's end, must be viewed as being, as it were, one with God. They were respected as brought home to him, united with him, centering most perfectly in him, and as it were swallowed up in him: so that his respect to them finally coincides and becomes one and the same with respect to himself. The interest of the creature is, as it were, God's own interest, in proportion to the degree of their relation and union to God.' Y8, *End of Creation*, 443.

[107] 'As the creature's good was viewed in this manner when God made the world for it, viz. with respect to the whole of the eternal duration of it, and the eternally progressive union and communion with him; so the creature must be viewed as in infinite strict union with himself. In this view it appears that God's respect to the creature, in the whole, unites with his respect to himself. Both regards are like two lines which seem at the beginning to be separate, but aim finally to meet in one, both being directed to the same center. And as to the good of the creature itself, if viewed in its whole duration, and infinite progression, it must be viewed as infinite; and so not only being some communication of God's glory, but as coming nearer and nearer to the same thing in its infinite fullness. The nearer anything comes to infinite, the nearer it comes to an identity with God. And if any good, as viewed by God, is beheld as infinite, it can't be viewed as a distinct thing from God's own infinite glory.' Y8, *End of Creation*, 459. Patricia Wilson-Kastner, comparing Edwards to Gregory of Nyssa, quotes Gregory as saying, 'And as to the good of the creature itself, it must be viewed as infinite; and is coming nearer and nearer to the same thing in its infinite fullness. The nearer anything comes to infinite, the nearer it comes to an identity with God.' Wilson-Kastner, 'God's Infinity and His Relationship to Creation', 312.

[108] 'And when God is so often spoken of as the last as well as the first, and the end as well as the beginning, what is meant (or at least implied) is, that as he is the first efficient cause and fountain from whence all things originate, so he is the last final cause for which they are made; the final term to which they all tend in their ultimate issue.' Y8, *End of Creation*, 467.

[109] For instance, 'In the creature's knowing, esteeming, loving, rejoicing in, and praising God, the glory of God is both exhibited and acknowledged; his fullness is received and returned. Here is both an *emanation* and *remanation*. The refulgence shines upon and into the creature, and is reflected back to the luminary. The beams of glory come from God, and are something of God, and are refunded back again to their original. So that the whole is *of* God, and *in* God, and *to* God; and God is the beginning, middle and end in this affair.' Y8, *End of Creation*, 531.

affective (beatific) knowledge.[110] Redemption, therefore, should be understood within the context of God's creating for his own glory, so that God's
redeeming activity is driven by *this* self-glorification.

Last, an account of redemption must, on this view, explain how persons
come to receive and remanate God's communicative nature. As a communication of glory, the elect must behold and love, therefore mirroring
God's inner life back to him. As I show below, personhood is a person's
natural image of God, created for the purpose of receiving emanation
and responding in remanation, but this remanation entails *regeneration.*
Regeneration is the doctrine that gives an account of the elect receiving
the spiritual image of God that humanity lost in the fall. God's redeeming
activity entails participation in God's own self-knowing and self-loving.
God's own life *ad intra,* iterated to creation *ad extra,* provides the contours
for the scheme of redemption. As depicted in Figure 1 in the introduction,
God's emanation is effectual for remanation, so that redemption entails
participation, through Christ, in the beatific-delight of God.

---

[110] Lee states, 'Edwards' conceptual tools are his dispositional ontology, the *God ad intra/God ad
extra* distinction, and the idea of God's creative activity as repetition. God's creation of the
world, for Edwards, is the exercise of God's original dispositional essence.' Lee, 'Edwards on
God and Nature', 24. I find Lee's analysis faulty concerning both the divine essence as well
as the issue of repetition. God 'images' his knowledge and will (i.e. his 'nature') to creation,
not his being. This will become clear more fully in the final chapter of this volume.

Chapter 3

Heaven Is a World of Love

Thus far I have outlined Edwards's doctrine of the Trinity as personal beatific-delight, and have highlighted *this depiction* of the Trinity as the fountain and foundation of Edwards's theology. Building upon this foundation, I have addressed how *this* God communicates his inner life economically for his own glory. This economic existence is the *emanation* of God, or God's communicating his personal nature to his creation. Now, in juxtaposition, I expound the notion of *remanation,* known in its perfection in consummation. Edwards's use of emanation and remanation call to mind a pouring forth and a re-collecting, and are therefore parallel concepts. I address emanation and consummation in one section – God's creating and glorifying action – to bracket off redemption, which must be exposited *in line with* God's creating purpose and activity *in anticipation* of God's work of consummation. In this chapter I take the concepts developed in Chapter 2 and show their perfection in the consummation of all things.

In his sermon 'Heaven Is a World of Love', the final instalment in his series 'Charity and Its Fruits', Edwards tracks the theological decisions already noted in this volume in two ways: first, in addressing God's glory he commends God as the fountain of love; and second, he refuses to focus on God abstracted from his trinitarian nature. He claims,

> There dwells God the Father, who is the Father of mercies, and so the Father of love, who so loved the world that he gave his only begotten Son …. There dwells Jesus Christ, the Lamb of God, the Prince of peace and love …. There Christ dwells in both his natures, his human and divine, sitting with the Father in the same throne. There is the Holy Spirit, the spirit of divine love, in who the very essence of God, as it were, all flows out or is breathed forth in love …. There in heaven this fountain of love, this eternal three in one, is set open without any obstacle to hinder access to it.[1]

---

[1] Y8, 'Charity and Its Fruits', 369–70.

Heaven is the place where the infinite life and love of the Trinity is communicated to finite creatures without the barrier of sinful flesh inhibiting
pure sight of God.[2] The reality that heaven is a world of love is derivative
of the fact that God is a God of love. Edwards depicts this love, once again,
in a trinitarian manner: 'It [love] flows out in the first place [necessarily]
and infinitely towards his only begotten Son, being poured forth without
measure, as to an object which is infinite, and so fully adequate to God's
love in its fountain.'[3] The Son is not loved by God as a mere instance of love
but is loved infinitely and eternally as the pure act of the Godhead.

> And the Son of God is not only the infinite object of love, but he is also
> an infinite subject of it. He is not only the infinite object of the Father's
> love, but he also infinitely loves the Father. The infinite essential love of
> God is, as it were, an infinite and eternal mutual holy energy between the
> Father and the Son, a pure, holy act whereby the Deity becomes nothing
> but an infinite and unchangeable act of love, which proceeds from both
> the Father and the Son. Thus divine love has its seat in the Deity as it is
> exercised within the Deity, or in God towards himself.[4]

Edwards describes here, as we have emphasized, the personal beatific-
delight of God. The stream of love flowing fully to Christ is communicated
through Christ to all of his members. The saints and angels alike receive love
through Christ as secondary and derivative realities of God's inner-triune
love. Seeing and knowing God in this manner results in unity among the
members; or, as Edwards puts it, 'They all with one heart and one soul
… love their common Redeemer. Every heart is wedded to this spiritual
husband.'[5] God's love flows out to the body of Christ, uniting its members
in increasing union, both to himself and each member with the other. In
eternity, the elect drink from this fountain of love as persons who partake

---

[2] For Edwards, heaven is the localized presence of God's glory. 'What I shall say may be
comprised in this proposition; viz. that the God of love dwells in heaven.' Y8, 'Charity and
Its Fruits', 369. God's presence, as appropriated to his essence, is ubiquitous, but God's
glory is particularly manifested in heaven. Y8, 'Charity and Its Fruits', 369; see also Y8, *End
of Creation*, 524–5. Furthermore, heaven is the true country of God's people: 'Those that are
here upon earth are in a strange land; they are pilgrims and strangers, and are all going
hence, and heaven is their center where they all tend.' Y13, '*Miscellanies* 429. Ascension',
481. The Messiah remained only for a short time on earth because heaven was where his
full reign resides. Heaven 'is the proper land of Israel; it is their home, their resting place'.
Y13, '*Miscellanies* 429. Ascension', 480–1.
[3] Y8, 'Charity and Its Fruits', 373.
[4] Y8, 'Charity and Its Fruits', 373.
[5] Y8, 'Charity and Its Fruits', 374.

in God's own personal beatific-delight.[6] The glorified elect experience life with the Father through Christ by the uniting activity of the Spirit of love.

This is the overall picture Edwards offers of heaven, but as seen below, it is a picture that develops in several key steps, growing towards perfection and consummation. To develop an account of heaven, I offer a close reading of the *Miscellanies* material and relevant primary sources. As I show, Edwards conceives of three 'eras' of heaven that must be explicated closely. To do so, we look at heaven as such, and then the three consecutive eras of heaven, with a specific emphasis on the beatific vision.

I The Changing Realm of the Unchangeable God

In *Miscellanies* 952, a lengthy entry concerning heaven, Edwards claims, 'There is nothing in the Scripture that in the least intimates the external heaven or paradise to be unchangeable, and not capable of being perfected and exalted to higher glory.'[7] Edwards carefully demarcates God himself from where God chooses to reveal his glory. Only God is unchangeable, as Edwards emphasizes: 'It is too much honor to any created thing to suppose it to be so perfect that no occasion whatsoever, even the rewarding of the infinite merits of the infinitely beloved Son of God himself, is occasion great enough for altering it.'[8] The heaven the elect experience is therefore not static but is inherently and necessarily dynamic. However, the 'place' where God truly resides, to use problematic language from the outset, is truly unchangeable. This 'heaven' is the 'state of God's own infinite and unchangeable glory', and is above and beyond the created realms (including the created heavens).[9]

---

[6] Edwards uses the term 'infinite' at times to talk about finite creatures in heaven. When he does so, we take it to be a potential infinite rather than an actual infinite. Don Schweitzer uses this distinction as well. For his development of the idea of infinity in Edwards's writings, see Don Schweitzer, 'Jonathan Edwards' Understanding of Divine Infinity', in *Jonathan Edwards as Contemporary: Essays in Honor of Sang Hyun Lee* ed. Don Schweitzer (New York: Peter Lang, 2010), 49–65.

[7] Y20, '*Miscellanies* 952. Consummation of All Things', 213.

[8] Y20, '*Miscellanies* 952. Consummation of All Things', 213.

[9] 'The only heaven that is unalterable is the state of God's own infinite and unchangeable glory, the heaven which God dwelt in from all eternity, which is absolutely of infinite height and infinite glory, and which may metaphorically be represented as the heaven that was the eternal abode of the blessed Trinity, and of the happiness and glory they have one in another; and is an heaven that is uncreated, and the heaven from whence God infinitely stoops to behold the things done in the created paradise, and of which [we] conceive of as the infinite and unchangeable expanse of space that is above and beyond the whole universe, and encompasses the whole, is the shadow.' Y20, '*Miscellanies* 952. Consummation of All Things', 213. In his 'Blank Bible' Edwards writes, musing on Isa. 57:15, 'Eternity that God inhabits is here spoken of as something infinitely before and infinitely above the

Again, Edwards's starting assumption is the immutability and perfection of God, and, as noted in previous chapters, his inner life is his infinite glory. God created two worlds which correspond to the two orders of creatures, one for humanity and one for angels. While the upper world of the angels is incorruptible and the lower world of humanity is corruptible, both are mutable. Heaven's incorruptibility does not derive from itself but is solely based upon the divine will and grace.[10] Incorruptibility, on the one hand, is only truly predicable of God and thereby adheres derivatively to that which God upholds and wills as such. Mutability, on the other hand, is the mode of creation. Creatures exist, and will always exist, mutably. Mutability inheres both for the redeemed and the unregenerate, who are both journeying toward a 'universal change'. 'This universal change shall be at the end of the world, or immediately after the day of judgement', the regenerate being glorified and the unregenerate perishing.[11]

Both heaven and hell exist as locations of change, and it is this unique mutability which is the focus of our engagement here. In order to develop this aspect of heaven, I delineate Edwards's conception of the various 'eras' of heaven, which provides context for the beatific vision of God in glory. In this conceptualization, Edwards follows his argument in *End of Creation*: God communicates his infinite fullness to finite creatures for his own glory, which never ceases nor rests in completion. Therefore, once we understand the progressive reality of heaven, statements concerning the beatific vision in Edwards's *Miscellanies* entries that appear to contradict one another are in fact compatible.[12] In order to demonstrate this compatibility, I exposit

---

whole creation, even above the highest heavens, "the high and holy place" spoken of in the following words. It is the eternal state of his own infinite glory and blessedness in which the persons of the Trinity dwell together, infinitely above heaven, and in which they ever did dwell.' Jonathan Edwards, 'Isaiah 57:15', in *The Blank Bible* (ed. Stephen Stein; The Works of Jonathan Edwards, vol. 24; New Haven: Yale University Press, 2006), 691.

[10] Y20, '*Miscellanies* 952. Consummation of All Things', 211.

[11] Y20, '*Miscellanies* 952. Consummation of All Things', 211.

[12] Missing this point will misconstrue one's notion of the beatific vision in Edwards's thought. William Schweitzer is a good example of this mistake. In his exposition, he fails to account for the three ages of heaven that correspond to Christ's redeeming activity. Rather than recognizing the progressing nature of the beatific vision in Edwards's thought (also corresponding to Christ's redeeming activity) he either pits one age against the other or else ignores key material on the beatific entirely (most notably Edwards's sermon on Romans 2.10 (see below)). William M. Schweitzer, 'Interpreting the Harmony of Reality: Jonathan Edwards' Theology of Revelation' (unpublished doctoral dissertation, University of Edinburgh, 2008), 138–46. He, unfortunately, did not remedy this mistake in the published volume. See William M. Schweitzer, *God is a Communicative Being: Divine Communicativeness and Harmony in the Theology of Jonathan Edwards* (T&T Studies in Systematic Theology; London: T&T Clark, 2012), 131–41.

three eras in the history of heaven: (1) from creation to Christ's ascension; (2) from Christ's ascension to consummation; (3) from consummation to eternity.[13]

1. First Era: From Creation to Christ's Ascension

To understand Edwards's position on heaven we must sift his *Miscellanies* into the appropriate periods of heaven's history. A failure to demarcate these eras adequately, and therefore divide the material according to the correct age, would further muddy waters already murky due to the nature of Edwards's note material. For instance, Edwards uses the term 'heaven' broadly, but he always denotes a specific moment in that perfect but mutable realm, easily mistaken as referencing consummation alone. I will avoid this error by demarcating the periods closely, highlighting the nature of the beatific vision in each.

Robert Caldwell, whose analysis I am following closely, names this first period because Edwards never does so specifically. This period, Caldwell summarizes, is an age of probation for the angels.[14] Recall, only God is immutable, and hence even the angels, the inhabitants of the highest heavens, are subject to change, and, as we will see, sin. 'But the highest heavens in their own nature are capable of ruin, in the highest and most excellent part of it, in the head of all that part of the creation, and so of the whole creation, viz. Lucifer.'[15] In *Miscellanies* 936, Edwards explains Lucifer's fall:

But when it was revealed to him, that as high and glorious as he was, that he must be a ministering spirit to the race of mankind that he had seen newly created, that appeared so feeble, mean and despicable, so vastly inferior not only to him, the prince of the angels and head of the universe, but also to the inferior angels, and that he must be subject to one of that race that should hereafter be born, he could not bear it. This

---

[13] In so doing, I am walking through Edwards's discussion of the periods of heaven in his *Miscellanies* entries as well as tracking alongside Robert W. Caldwell's section on heaven in his book *Communion in the Spirit: The Holy Spirit as the Bond of Union in the Theology of Jonathan Edwards* (Studies in Evangelical History and Thought; Waynesboro: Paternoster, 2006), 174–84.

[14] Caldwell, *Communion in the Spirit*, 174.

[15] Y20, '*Miscellanies* 952. Consummation of All Things', 211. Edwards's use of 'highest heavens' here is unfortunate after his own delineation between 'God's heaven', which one would assume to be the highest, and heaven itself.

occasioned his fall, and now he with the other angels he drew away with him are fallen.[16]

This first period marks the probation of the angels, where some fall and some prove themselves faithful. It also demarcates the trial of the angels' obedience, either serving Christ *and* the elect in the work of redemption, or rebelling.[17] Christ, the judge of the angels, will not end their period of testing until his return (his ascension).[18] A major task of the angels prior to Christ's ascension is to minister to Christ and his church in the world as God's plan of redemption is carried out. Christ's work in the world, as an extension of his purpose in creating, is a manifestation of his glory, which the angels partake of through beholding:

> As the perfections of God are manifested to all creatures ... by the fruits of those perfections, or God's works – the wisdom of God appears by his wise works, and his power by his powerful works, his holiness and justice by his holy and just acts ... *so the glorious angels have the greatest manifestations of the glory of God by what they see in the work of men's redemption, and especially in the death and sufferings of Christ.*[19]

The importance of this last statement should not go unnoticed. Angels grow in knowledge of God through Christ's work *in the world*. In *Miscellanies* 555, Edwards reasons, 'One end of the creation of the angels, and giving them such great understanding, was that they might be fit witnesses and spectators of God's works here below, and might behold all parts of the divine scheme.'[20] The work of redemption, as the greatest of God's designs, *is revelation*. The angels, with the 'best seats in the house', watch and grow as they meditate upon God's action in the world. God saw fit, Edwards explains, to have creatures of great discernment and understanding, 'that they might behold the whole series, from the beginning to the consum-

---

[16] Y20, '*Miscellanies* 936. Fall of the Angels. Satan the Prince of the Devils', 191. It is noteworthy that the fall of the angels, and one could say with it, the fall of the world, was a response to the work of redemption. This is the beginning parallelism of the triworld vision.

[17] In *Miscellanies* 937 Edwards purports, 'Their work and service that was appointed them, that was the trial of their obedience, was to serve Christ and his elect people in this affair; and it was by obeying Christ as his servants in this affair that they actually obtained eternal life.' Y20, '*Miscellanies* 937. Angels. Elect. Their Dependence on Christ', 197.

[18] 'The Lord Jesus Christ, God-man, is the judge of the angels that gives them the reward of eternal life. They did not enjoy perfect rest till he ascended and confirmed them.' Y20, '*Miscellanies* 937. Angels. Elect. Their Dependence on Christ', 197–8.

[19] Y20, '*Miscellanies* 937. Angels. Elect. Their Dependence on Christ', 197 – my emphasis.

[20] Y18, '*Miscellanies* 555. Heaven. Separate State. Angels', 99.

mation of all things'.[21] Mortal man's imperfect perception of God's glory in the work of redemption is counteracted, so to speak, by the angels in heaven, and as will be shown below, by the glorified saints as well, who meditate *on* and glory *in* God's action in the world.

Furthermore, Edwards suggests that the elect angels grew in holiness and happiness after Satan and his angels fell, because they obtained knowledge of God and knowledge of themselves, of good and evil, and advanced in the way of humility. To this he adds, 'What they beheld of the glory of God in the face of Christ as man's Redeemer, and especially in Christ's humiliation, greatly increased their holiness and their obedience.'[22] The angels grow in holiness because of their sight of God, which is found in beholding God qua Redeemer, as God *enacts* redemption. God is known to a greater degree in his action, most specifically his redeeming action. Christ's operation with the angels, in short, mirrors Christ's work with humankind; angels are confirmed upon their initial acceptance of Christ and his work but are not rewarded eternal life until judgement.[23]

The saints, alongside the angels, attend to God's redemptive activity through Christ to grow in their knowledge of God. As revelation to the church is progressive, so is the revelation – and therefore knowledge, joy and delight – in heaven.[24] In *Miscellanies* 372, he states, 'Their joy is continually increased, as they see the purposes of God's grace unfolded in his wondrous providences towards his church.'[25] This hints at Edwards's progressive and teleological understanding of history, and the increase

---

[21] Y18, '*Miscellanies* 555. Heaven. Separate State. Angels', 99.

[22] Y20, '*Miscellanies* 940. The Elect Angels', 199.

[23] 'Man is confirmed when he first believes in Christ, but his work is not done till death, and the reward not bestowed till then.' Y20, '*Miscellanies* 947. Confirmation of the Angels', 204.

[24] 'It seems to me probable that that part of the church that is in heaven have been, from the beginning of the world, progressive in their light and in their happiness, as the church on earth has; and that much of their happiness has consisted in seeing the progressive wonderful doings of God with respect to his church here in this world.' Y13, '*Miscellanies* 421. Heaven', 478. Likewise, in *Miscellanies* 1089: 'The saints, in going out of this world and ascending into heaven, don't go out of sight of the affairs that appertain to Christ's kingdom and church here, and things appertaining to that great work of redemption that is carrying on here; but, on the contrary, go out of a state of obscurity and ascend above the mists and clouds into the bright light. And ascending to a pinnacle in the very center of light, where everything appears in clear view, the saints that are ascended to heaven have advantage to view the state of Christ's kingdom in this world, and the works of the new creation here, as much greater than they had before; as a man that ascends to the top of an high mountain has a greater advantage to view the face of the earth than he had while he was below in a deep valley or forest below, surrounded on every side with those things that impeded and limited his sight.' Y20, '*Miscellanies* 1089. The Saints in Heaven', 472.

[25] Y13, '*Miscellanies* 372. Heaven', 444.

of revelation within it.[26] The saints exponentially increase in happiness as they converse with Christ and witness his work of redemption. It is here where Edwards's trifold vision of theology comes to the forefront of his analysis. Because of Edwards's *Christological* focus of revelation, and his emphasis on the revelatory nature of Christ's work, the glorified saints and angels progress in knowledge only as Christ enacts his work of redemption on earth. As he states in *Miscellanies* 421, 'The church in heaven and the church on earth are more one people, one city, and one family than generally is imagined,'[27] and again in *Miscellanies* 529, 'Shall the royal family be kept in ignorance of the success of the affairs of the kingdom?'[28] The work of redemption, as the locus of God's work, is the organizing event of revelation, which glorified saints, angels and the elect behold to progressively grow in their knowledge of God.

In this first period, angels are in probation, awaiting their confirmation in Christ, the God-man, who will reign in heaven. The glorified saints enter the family of God and alongside the angels obtain their joy and happiness through a visual apprehension of God's perfections, work and glory. Therefore the happiness and perfecting of the saints in heaven is tied to God's work of redemption in the world; or, as Edwards says in *Miscellanies* 777, 'The church in heaven and the church on earth are so united, that the glory of the one is not advanced and perfected without the perfecting of the glory of the other.'[29] Likewise,

This renders it more probable that the happiness of heaven is PROGRESSIVE, having several PERIODS of new accession of glory and blessedness to their state ... and that the same periods that are happy and blessed periods to the church on earth, are so also to the church in heaven: as particularly, that the church in heaven had a new accession of glory when the church on earth was redeemed out of Egypt ... that again

---

[26] In *Miscellanies* 372, Edwards states '... and that their joy is increasing and will be increasing, as God gradually in his providence unveils his glory till the last day'. Y13, '*Miscellanies* 372. Heaven', 445.

[27] Y13, '*Miscellanies* 421. Heaven', 478.

[28] Y18, '*Miscellanies* 529. Heaven', 71. See also Edwards's sermon on Rev. 14:2, 'Praise, One of the Chief Employments of Heaven'. Sermon X in *The Works of President Edwards: With a Memoir of His Life* (ed. Dwight; vol. 8 (New York: G. & C. & H. Carvill, 1830), 314–15. Furthermore, 'Departed saints are doubtless of the family; the angels, they also are of the family; saints and angels are all gathered together in one in Christ (Eph. 1:10; and Col. 1:16, 20).' Y18, '*Miscellanies* 555. Heaven. Separate State. Angels', 100.

[29] Y18, '*Miscellanies* 777. Happiness of Heaven is Progressive', 432. 'For Edwards, a fundamental dynamic which courses through the history of heaven consists in the growth of its inhabitant's [*sic*] happiness, a growth which takes place visually through beholding new "accession[s] of [God's] glory and blessedness"'. Caldwell, *Communion in the Spirit*, 175.

they had another happy period of glorious advancement in the time of the establishment of the throne of David ... and again had another happy period of new accession of glory at the redemption of the church on earth out of Babylon; and that the light, and love, and glory of the church in heaven was as much advanced from the period of Christ's first coming, especially from his ascension into heaven, as of the church on earth.[30]

As I noted in my introduction, Edwards, following John Owen, delineates eras of increasing revelation in redemptive history; unlike Owen, however, Edwards runs revelation through his tri-world matrix, as noted here, heaven's parallel connection to earth. The saintly inhabitants of heaven partake of the glory of God in heaven as well as on earth. This does not diminish the beauty, glory and splendour of heaven, but it does denote the particularity of heaven's era in relation to the work of Christ. Therefore, while the glorified saints see Christ and the Father (in some capacity) in this first era, their sight is still 'clouded'.[31] It is darkened to the degree that their attention is pulled to God's working in the world. It is only after Christ is raised that the glorified saints shall see him as he is.[32] This first era of heaven is defined by a sight that is pulled toward earth, where God is revealing himself through the history of redemption. As such, this era of heaven's history always looks ahead to the completion of Christ's work and the anticipation that he will reign over them eternally.

2. Second Era: From Ascension to Consummation

If heaven is affected by Christ's work of redemption on earth, which Edwards takes as axiomatic, then how much more are the inhabitants of the upper world affected when the king returns? With continued Christocentric emphasis, Edwards claims, 'The coming of Christ, I believe, made an exceeding great addition to the happiness of the saints of the old testament who were in heaven, and especially was the day of his ascension

---

[30] Y18, '*Miscellanies* 777. Happiness of Heaven is Progressive', 431–2.
[31] In *Miscellanies* 710, Edwards explains, 'But yet the glorified souls of saints in their present state in heaven, though they can't be said properly to see as in an enigma, yet 'tis but darkly in comparison of what they will see after the resurrection.' Y18, '*Miscellanies* 710. Heaven. Separate State. Resurrection', 337.
[32] 'Yet the sight that the saints [in heaven] shall have at the resurrection is spoken of as if it were the first sight, wherein they should see him as he is.' Y18, '*Miscellanies* 710. Heaven. Separate State. Resurrection', 337.

a joyful day amongst them.'[33] Prior to the ascension, the mode of being for the inhabitants was preparatory, awaiting the arrival of the coming bride-groom.[34] But even this second era is 'between the times' for the heavenly community.[35] In *Miscellanies* 435 Edwards states, 'All things in heaven and earth and throughout the universe are in a state of preparation for the state of consummation; all the wheels are going, none of them stop, and all are moving in a direction to the last and most perfect state.'[36] Recalling the wheels within the wheels, Edwards asserts that the saints in heaven continue to experience the grand countdown to consummation, as the one great wheel continues to complete its turn.

The preparatory reality of this second era does not diminish its redemptive importance; it is the necessary penultimate turn of God's redemptive wheel. Redemption and revelation increase on earth, so too in heaven. Christ's ascending to heaven was a redemption of the fall of Lucifer, who was created to reign in heaven: 'He was the head of the whole society, the captain of the whole host.'[37] Therefore, the risen Christ, upon ascending, fills the vacancy.[38] Because of the fall of Satan, heaven, in a sense, lacked redemption. Until Jesus was raised up to be ruler of heaven, the angelic inhabitants were, as we saw in the first era, in a place of probation. Upon his return, the angels in heaven were confirmed, and their eternal status solidified. Edwards argues that Christ, upon his ascension, gave the elect angels the reward of eternal life, and the angels 'receive their fullness from him as their head and as their Lord'.[39] In this second era, then, the angels enjoy a communion with God that they did not know prior to the incar-nation or ascension.[40]

The angels' interest in the incarnation therefore equals that of the church. Christ's becoming man was also becoming *creature*. As we see

---

[33] Y13, '*Miscellanies* 372. Heaven', 444–5.

[34] Y13, '*Miscellanies* 371. Resurrection', 443. *Miscellanies* 371: 'But the more properly perfect and consummate state of God's people, of the church, will be after the resurrection; and the whole is now only a growing and preparing for that state. All things that are now done in the world are but preparations for it.' Y13, '*Miscellanies* 371. Resurrection', 443.

[35] See Y13, '*Miscellanies* 435. Heaven', 483–4.

[36] Y13, '*Miscellanies* 435. Heaven', 483.

[37] Y20, '*Miscellanies* 936. Fall of the Angels. Satan the Prince of the Devils', 191.

[38] Y20, '*Miscellanies* 936. Fall of the Angels. Satan the Prince of the Devils', 194.

[39] Y18, '*Miscellanies* 744. Confirmation of the Angels by Jesus Christ', 385.

[40] 'By this it appears that the angels at Christ's ascension received their fullness, i.e. their whole reward, all their confirmed life and eternal blessedness, from Christ as their judge .... He did not only adjudge it to them, but he gives it to them; and they possess it as united to him in a constant dependence on him, and have that more full enjoyment of God than they before had, as beholding God's glory in his face and as enjoying God in him, for he is here spoken of not only as their Lord but their head.' Y18, '*Miscellanies* 744. Confirmation of the Angels by Jesus Christ', 386.

in *End of Creation*, God has always 'designed to communicate himself to creatures, the way in which he designed to communicate himself to elect beloved creatures, *all of them*, was to unite himself to a created nature, and to become one of the creatures'.[41] Likewise, Christ's ascension 'advanced' the Old Testament saints in heaven and the angels as well as the church on earth. As stated previously, these groups are connected as one family *in* Christ. Prior to Christ's arrival, the heavenly saints and angels were in a state of infancy.[42] The age after the resurrection is therefore a 'new age' in the history of heaven, where greater glory, happiness and joy reign.[43]

Not unlike the first age, the saints and angels in heaven remain acutely aware of the work of redemption, beholding with perfect clarity Christ's kingdom on earth in all of its glory, in distinction from the saints on earth, who see only as through a glass darkly. Edwards states in *Miscellanies* 529:

> The saints in heaven are under infinitely greater advantages to take the pleasure of beholding how Christ's kingdom flourishes, than if they were here upon earth: for they can better see and understand the marvellous steps that divine wisdom takes in all that is done, and the glorious ends he accomplishes, and what opposition Satan makes, and how he is baffled and overthrown .... They will behold the glory of the divine attributes in his work of providence, infinitely more clearly than we can.[44]

Edwards is clear that the happiness of heaven 'consists very much in BEHOLDING the manifestations that God makes of himself in the WORK OF REDEMPTION'.[45] Creatures cannot have an immediate sight of God but must have their vision of God mediated through Christ. While the discussion of spiritual knowledge must wait until the next chapter, we anticipate aspects of it here. Edwards suggests that there are four signs used for obtaining mediated knowledge of other persons: (1) images or resemblances; (2) words and declaration; (3) effects (or deductions); or (4) a priori, by arguing from causes.[46]

---

[41] Y18, '*Miscellanies* 744. Confirmation of the Angels by Jesus Christ', 389 – my emphasis.

[42] Y18, '*Miscellanies* 744. Confirmation of the Angels by Jesus Christ', 390.

[43] As an instance, *Miscellanies* 710 states, 'It looks to me probable that the glory of the state of the church after the resurrection will as much exceed the present glory of the spirits of just men made perfect, as the glory of the gospel dispensation exceeds the Mosaic dispensation, or as much as the glory of the state of the church in its first or purest state of it.' Y18, '*Miscellanies* 710. Heaven. Separate State. Resurrection', 335.

[44] Y18, '*Miscellanies* 529. Heaven', 72.

[45] Y18, '*Miscellanies* 777. Happiness of Heaven is Progressive', 427.

[46] Y18, '*Miscellanies* 777. Happiness of Heaven is Progressive', 428. The saints in this second age do not yet have glorified bodies, and therefore their senses are not mediated by fleshly

Leaving aside questions concerning earthly ectypal knowledge, our focus remains on those in heaven and their role in beholding God's glory. Edwards claims, in *Miscellanies* 777, that the saints 'see and know God in heaven by his Word or speech, for there the saints are with God, and converse with God, and God converses with them by voluntary manifestations and significations of his mind'.[47] But speaking with Christ is not the sole means of knowing God, the saints 'see his glory as it is manifested in the work of redemption, which the angels desire to look into, and by which the manifold wisdom of God is made known to the angels'.[48] Because of the importance of this statement and its centrality in Edwards's thought, I quote him at length:

> So far as they see God and know him in his works (which is the principal way in which God manifests himself, and to which the manifestation of himself in his Word is subordinate: the manifestations God makes of himself in his works are the principal manifestations of his perfections, and the declarations and teaching of his Word are to lead to those; by God's declaring and teaching that he is infinitely powerful or wise, the creature believes that he is powerful and wise as he teaches, but in seeing his mighty and wise works, the effects of his power and wisdom, the creature not only hears and believes, but sees his power and wisdom: and so of his other perfections) they see and know [him] as he manifests himself in the work of redemption, which [is] the greatest and most glorious of all God's works, the work of works to which all God's works are reduced.[49]

The way God makes himself known, in short, is by Christ in his work of redemption.[50] This work of redemption is God's self-revelation in

---

organs. In discussing the senses after the resurrection, Edwards states, 'As the saints after the resurrection will have an external part, or an outward man, distinct from their souls, so it necessarily follows that they shall have external perception or sense. And doubtless then all their sense, and all the perception that they have, will be delighted and willed with happiness. Every perceptive faculty shall be an inlet of delight.' Y18, '*Miscellanies* 721. Happiness of Heaven after the Resurrection', 350.

[47] Y18, '*Miscellanies* 777. Happiness of Heaven is Progressive', 430. 'They converse with God by conversing with Christ, who speaketh the words of God.' Y18, '*Miscellanies* 777. Happiness of Heaven is Progressive', 430.

[48] Y18, '*Miscellanies* 777. Happiness of Heaven is Progressive', 430.

[49] Y18, '*Miscellanies* 777. Happiness of Heaven is Progressive', 430.

[50] 'His works at the same time are wonderful, and cannot be found out to perfection; especially the work of redemption, which is that work of God about which the science of divinity is chiefly conversant, is full of unsearchable wonders.' Y22, 'The Importance and Advantage of a Thorough Knowledge of Divine Truth', 95.

his image and is the work in which the heavenly inhabitants are very much invested. By beholding his glory, they behold God *in his works* rather than in his being, which is invisible. Importantly, Edwards claims, 'That BEATIFICAL VISION that the saints have of God in heaven, is in *beholding the manifestations* that he makes of himself in the *work of redemption*.'[51] Edwards continues by adding, the 'business and employment of the saints ... in contemplation, praise, and conversation, is mainly in contemplating the wonders of this work, in praising God for the displays of his glory and love therein, and in conversing about things appertaining to it'.[52]

Edwards's employment of the beatific vision in this context is extraordinary. He does not merely appropriate the beatific vision to Christ, God's image, but he allows it to bleed into a vision of God *through* his work of redemption. For all practical purposes, the saints in heaven are still pilgrims. They have truly 'arrived', but because of their relation to the history of redemption they are not given full access to God.[53] The heavenly realm is still intimately concerned with the rest of the family on earth, watching God's glory advance through the redemption of the church. Nonetheless, within this heavenly 'pilgrim' state, the saints still see Christ, converse with him and see his work in a purified way. Edwards does not hesitate to speak of the beatific vision in this sense as well: 'So I believe the saints in heaven are made perfectly holy and impeccable by means, viz. by the beatific vision of God in Christ in glory, by experiencing so much the happiness of holiness, its happy nature and issue, by seeing the wrath of God on wicked men, etc.'[54]

Therefore, while the beatific vision is usually parsed as the mode of knowing beyond pilgrim theology (i.e. the age of faith), for Edwards, these two 'ages' of knowing are collapsed into one another so that pilgrim theology is beatific in form, and the beatific vision is pilgrim in

---

[51] Y18, '*Miscellanies* 777. Happiness of Heaven is Progressive', 431 – my emphasis. 'The saints and angels see God by beholding the displays of his perfections, but the perfections of God are displayed and manifested chiefly by their effects. Thus the chief way wherein the wisdom of God is to be seen is in the wise acts and operations of God, and so of his power, mercy, and justice and other perfections. But these are seen, even by the angels themselves, chiefly by what God does in the work of redemption.' Y20, '*Miscellanies* 1089. The Saints in Heaven', 473.

[52] Y18, '*Miscellanies* 777. Happiness of Heaven is Progressive', 431.

[53] Interestingly, in Caldwell's explication of heaven, he offers an excursus of the beatific vision in the second period of heavenly history. Even if not a material point, it seems significant. The beatific vision, the pure vision, is certainly in the consummation of all things (exposited below). Caldwell, *Communion in the Spirit*, 179–80.

[54] Y13, '*Miscellanies* 442. Angels Confirmed', 490–1.

scope. Heaven is a progressive state and therefore is necessarily a pilgrim journey.[55]

There remains one major unfinished piece of business between humankind and the Father which must be addressed prior to the consummation of all things. While both humankind and angels have been judged upon arriving in the second age, there is still a judgement to come, and a final period whose glory surpasses all prior.[56] This balance between the 'already' nature of perfection and the 'not yet' glory of consummation is subtle in Edwards's development. It is clear that in this second age the saints will not only see Christ but also converse with him intimately as friends and siblings.[57] This conversation will be vastly more intimate than it was for those who conversed with him in his earthly ministry, because in this age of heaven the union is perfected.[58] Beyond union with the glorified Christ, the key difference between the second period and the first is the saints' relationship to God the Father. Thus, 'the saints being united to Christ, shall have a more glorious union with and enjoyment of the Father, than otherwise could be, for hereby their relation becomes much nearer'.[59] As members of the Son of God, the saints partake of his enjoyment of his Father, and there is, furthermore, 'intimate union and conversation' *with the Father*.[60] United to Christ, the saints, in their measure, see and enjoy God the Father.[61] Christ mediates, almost as a lens, the various 'beatific' realities of the heavenly life of the saints, 'for he is the head of the glorified body, and the sight of the eyes that are in the head are for the information of the whole body'.[62]

---

[55] Paul Ramsey offers three reasons explaining why Edwards understands heaven as progressive: (1) anthropological; (2) metaphysical; and (3) theological. The anthropological reality is the finitude of a creature's ideas. Edwards's anthropology demands a sanctified understanding and will truly perceiving God in his beauty, and thereby receiving that beauty in faith. By seeing God's ways, works and Christ himself in glory, the number of ideas would grow exponentially. This growth is the seedbed for holiness. The metaphysical reasoning has to do with the finitude of the creaturely state compared to the infinite reality of the fountain from which they drink. Growth is eternal and progressive because the object (more appropriately – subject) of the gaze of the elect is infinite. The last reason, what he calls the theological reason, is that God is the infinite God who glorifies himself through the communication of his fullness. Y8, 'Appendix III: Heaven is a Progressive State', 709–12. Therefore, as it is in creating the world, so it is for eternity: God glorifies himself through his creation. Caldwell offers two reasons for the saints' progression in heaven. See Caldwell, *Communion in the Spirit*, 178.

[56] See *Miscellanies* 371, 664b, 736, 742, 743, 952, and 1126.

[57] Y18, '*Miscellanies* 571. Heaven. Wisdom and Gloriousness of the Work of Redemption', 107.

[58] Y18, '*Miscellanies* 571. Heaven. Wisdom and Gloriousness of the Work of Redemption', 109.

[59] Y18, '*Miscellanies* 571. Heaven. Wisdom and Gloriousness of the Work of Redemption', 109.

[60] Y18, '*Miscellanies* 571. Heaven. Wisdom and Gloriousness of the Work of Redemption', 110.

[61] Y20, '*Miscellanies* 1089. The Saints in Heaven', 469–70.

[62] Y20, '*Miscellanies* 1089. The Saints in Heaven', 470.

This seeing, enjoying and conversing with God the Father is all done *in* Christ, which will be the case throughout eternity. But this is where this age fundamentally differs from the age to come. The saints in heaven grow in holiness by conversing with angels, Christ, and the Father and by beholding God's trinitarian work of redemption. Man is confronted by the infinite depth of God through a beatific vision of Christ, the divine God-man, both in himself and through his works. Further, as God continues to glorify himself, man is continually perfected. This last point is qualified by the fact that man is perfected *in kind*. I will not elaborate on this point here, but it is important to note the two distinctions Edwards offers: first, man's ability to grow will depend on his status in heaven, which is based upon his life on earth. Second, man is dependent upon God's revelation for growth.[63] This is relevant for the periods of the church. God has decided that a certain truncated beatific vision will be allowed prior to the consummation of all things. While the saints will grow in this vision, the glory found in it will not compare to the glory found in the final beatific vision in eternity.

In canvassing these first two eras of heaven, we can already see that 'sight' takes centre stage in Edwards's development. In the first era, the church focused its attention on God's work in the world through Christ, with particular emphasis on Christ's ministry. They beheld the glory of God as it was communicated through the history of God's redemption of the world. In the second era, this sight is given much greater depth. Not only do the saints and angels in heaven understand more, which is certainly true, but they also know God more. Just like in Edwards's development of the Trinity, redemption revolves around three poles – persons, beatific and delight. God's communication of his glory is a personal communication of his personal nature, known through sight as that which causes delight to well up in the hearts of the elect. Since God's self-knowledge is emanated and seeks remanation, this sight starts off as darkened sight (in conversion) and is ever-perfected through the eras of redemptive history. Turning

---

[63] It is enough to say, following *Miscellanies* 822, that Edwards's understanding of the 'degrees of glory' was based upon three factors (the two mentioned above act as summary): (1) the actual view of himself which God gives; (2) the particular station and circumstance God has set the believer; and (3) the degree of knowledge. The degree of knowledge, furthermore, is broken down into three things: (1) the extent and strength of the knowing faculty; (2) the degree of notional knowledge; and (3) the degree and manner in which God allows spiritual views of himself into their minds. Y18, '*Miscellanies* 822. Degrees of Glory. Perfection of Happiness', 533; see also: *Miscellanies*: 367, 403, 431, 589, 594, 681, 817, 824.

our attention to the final age of the church in heaven, we see this sight perfected.

3. Third Era: Consummation of All Things

It is clear up to this point that heaven's inhabitants grow in their capacity to receive the divine glory/beauty. Likewise, the progress of the church directly relates to the degree of glory revealed, which increases upon each movement of redemptive history. God created the world, Edwards reminds his readers, to glorify himself, 'but it was principally that he might glorify him[self] in his disposal of the world, or in the use he intended to make of it, in his providence'.[64] In fact, the work of redemption plays such an important role in his understanding of God's self-glorification that Edwards argues, 'It was the end of the creation of heaven: the preparing that blessed and glorious habitation was with an eye to this.'[65] Likewise, as we have seen, the angels were created for this end, that they might serve the Son of God, the Mediator, and, as we have seen, it was the impetus for Lucifer's fall.[66]

Furthermore, God's end for creation is that the Father might give a spouse to his Son, as Edwards comments in *Miscellanies* 702, so that the Son might have a partner in which he can pour forth his love. The bride/bridegroom metaphor is an overarching image for Edwards's conception of redemption and orients this final era of heaven as the marriage of the Lamb. 'The wedding feast is eternal; and the love and joys, the songs, entertainments and glories of the wedding never will be ended.'[67] Following in the footsteps of the 'Spiritual Brethren', Edwards focuses on the love of the groom for his bride, and the bride's basking in that love.[68] His use of *beholding, manifesting* and *seeing* calls out this reality, as we see in *Miscellanies* 702: '*Seeing* therefore that the love of God has been most *manifested* to them, it will doubtless be most enjoyed by them …. God *communicates* his love to enjoyment *by manifestation*.'[69]

The third age differs from the second in several key ways. First, Christ

---

[64] Y18, '*Miscellanies* 702. Work of Creation. Providence. Redemption', 284.

[65] Y18, '*Miscellanies* 702. Work of Creation. Providence. Redemption', 284.

[66] Y18, '*Miscellanies* 702. Work of Creation. Providence. Redemption', 284.

[67] Y18, '*Miscellanies* 702. Work of Creation. Providence. Redemption', 298. While Edwards does not end up talking about God's end being to give his Son an image to give his love to, it does serve as a helpful summary of Edwards's theology of redemption.

[68] See Janice Knight, *Orthodoxies in Massachusetts: Rereading American Puritanism* (Cambridge: Harvard University Press, 1994), 109–29.

[69] Y18, '*Miscellanies* 702. Work of Creation. Providence. Redemption', 299 – my emphasis.

hands over his representational kingdom to the Father.[70] Second, the saints and angels are fully judged and openly justified, and Christ himself is 'openly and publicly and remarkably justified'.[71] Third, the saints are perfected; Christ is glorified in a greater manner than before, and all of heaven changes.[72] Caldwell provides a helpful summary:

> Heaven in its final state commences with the resurrection and day of judgement. Afterwards, heaven shall ascend to a new level of happiness, glory, and joy as the following realities obtain: individuals in the church are finally united to their resurrection bodies, the church is no more divided between the upper and lower worlds, all receive their heavenly rewards, and Christ's bride, the church, enters into the eternal marriage-day feast of the lamb.[73]

Last, picking up on Caldwell's summary, this day is the true wedding day, the age of the wedding feast, 'and marriage is not only for this acquaintance and communion on the wedding day, but in order to it ever after .... The glory and exaltation that the Father gives Christ, will not be diminished after the day of judgement.'[74] It is this final reality that concerns us here. In *Miscellanies* 742, Edwards states,

> When the end comes ... God will be all; *the church now shall be brought nearer to God the Father*, who by his economical office sustains the dignity

---

[70] Y18, '*Miscellanies* 742. Consummation of All Things. Christ's Delivering Up the Kingdom to the Father', 373. In *Miscellanies* 742, Edwards states, 'But doubtless this representative kingdom, when the special ends of it shall be answered, shall be delivered up, and things shall return to their own primaeval original order, and every person of the Trinity, in the ultimate and eternal state of things, shall continue each one in the exercise of his own economical place and work.' Y18, '*Miscellanies* 742. Consummation of All Things. Christ's Delivering Up the Kingdom to the Father', 373. Likewise, 'When the end comes, that relation that Christ stands in to his church, as the Father's viceroy over her, shall cease, and shall be swallowed up in the relation of a vital and conjugal head, or head of influence and enjoyment, which is more natural and essential to the main ends and purposes of his union with them.' Y18, '*Miscellanies* 742. Consummation of All Things. Christ's Delivering Up the Kingdom to the Father', 374.

[71] Y18, '*Miscellanies* 664b. Wisdom of God in the Work of Redemption', 206.

[72] My focus has not been on the bodies (or lack thereof) of the saints in each age, but this is an important concept in Edwards's thought. In *Miscellanies* 233, on the 'Happiness of Heaven' he writes, 'So the glorified spiritual bodies of the saints shall be filled with pleasures of the most exquisite kind that such refined bodies are capable of; not with any pleasures that in the least tend to clog the mind, and divert from mental and spiritual pleasure and the pure joys of holiness.' Y13, '*Miscellanies* 233. Happiness of Heaven', 351, see also *Miscellanies* 263.

[73] Caldwell, *Communion in the Spirit*, 183.

[74] Y18, '*Miscellanies* 736. Consummation of All Things. Christ's Delivering Up the Kingdom to the Father', 361.

and appears as the fountain of Deity. *And her enjoyment of him shall be more direct. Christ God-man shall now no longer be instead of the Father to them,* but, as I may express it, their head of their enjoyment of God, as it were, the eye to receive the rays of divine glory and love for the whole body, and the ear to hear the sweet expressions of his love, and the mouth to taste the sweetness and feed on the delights of the enjoyment of God – the root of the whole tree planted in God to receive sap and nourishment for every branch.[75]

This period represents the fulfilment of all that was prior. Christ still mediates vision of the Father, but now, in a way not fully parsed, the vision is more direct and complete. We might make this distinction by saying that, in the ages preceding consummation, the saints had a vision of the Father *by* Christ, where in eternity they have it *with* Christ. In this sense, Edwards states, 'The church never will be *with* Christ to behold his glory in that eminent and glorious manner before, as she will then, when the marriage of the Lamb is come.'[76] A couple of *Miscellanies* later Edwards continues, 'The way in which the saints will come to an intimate full enjoyment of the Father is not by the Father's majesty ... but by their ascending to him by their union with Christ's person.'[77] Christ is still the divine mediator, and continues to act as the 'uniting point' of creature and Creator.[78] In this final age, opposed to the rest, there is no work of redemption to contemplate (not visually at least), *but now only a God who has redeemed.*[79] Each era

[75] Y18, '*Miscellanies* 742. Consummation of All Things. Christ's Delivering Up the Kingdom to the Father', 374 – my emphasis.
[76] Y18, '*Miscellanies* 736. Consummation of All Things. Christ's Delivering Up the Kingdom to the Father', 361 – my emphasis.
[77] Y18, '*Miscellanies* 742. Consummation of All Things. Christ's Delivering Up the Kingdom to the Father', 375.
[78] 'Christ's mediation between the Father and the elect will continue after the end of the world; and he will reign as a middle person between the Father and them to all eternity ... as the bond of union with the Father, and of derivation from him, and of all manner of communication and intercourse with the Father.' Y18, '*Miscellanies* 742. Consummation of All Things. Christ's Delivering Up the Kingdom to the Father', 374.
[79] Edwards ties God qua Redeemer and God qua Creator closely together. The two roles/identifiers are never far from his conception of God. Even in this final age, both Creator and Redeemer are central realities for Edwards. When Heaven is re-created by Christ, it is done so that God's creating power would be manifest to his elect. Edwards states in *Miscellanies* 952, 'The elect creatures, that are the eye and mouth of the creation, that are made to behold God's works and to give him the glory of them, did not behold the first creation. The angels did not behold the creation of heaven, that most glorious part of the creation, nor did they see the creation of themselves. And men beheld no part of God's work in producing the creation. But the time will come when God will make all things new by a new creation, wherein his power towards the whole will be much more displayed than in the first creation. When God shall effect this creation, men and angels shall see God perform it; they

in the history of heaven focuses more and more on God himself, who has become identified as the God of history, the alpha and omega of all things. For the saints to be fully glorified and perfect, they must partake of him who is glory and perfection. In *Miscellanies* 741, Edwards states, 'It seems by this to have been God's design to admit man as it were to the inmost fellowship with the deity,' claiming there is 'an eternal society or family in the Godhead in the Trinity of persons.'[80] This language of family connects to Edwards's metaphor of marriage as the picture of redemption; he states, 'It seems to be God's design to admit the church into the divine family as his son's wife.'[81] As noted in the last section, eternity is understood as an ever-increasing asymptotic union of bride and groom; the church, as bride, is united to the family of God through the love of the perfect Son.[82]

Each era of heaven focuses more fully on the Father. This last age of heaven is the perfection and redemption of God's people *in* Christ brought before the Father.[83] The saints and angels are fully justified, sanctified and glorified. Christ's role as representative of the Father is handed over, and he can enjoy his bride for an eternal wedding feast.[84] It is only after the kingdom has been handed over to the Father that he fully accepts Christ and his church and rewards them with the 'joys of their eternal wedding'.[85] Christ will now 'fully obtain, and be possessed of, all that honor and glory in himself that is the end of his administration of his delegated kingdom'.[86] Just as heaven changes in preparation for the new glory, so is Christ the subject of a new glorification.[87] Edwards explains,

shall see God produce the new heaven and new earth by his mighty power.' Y20, '*Miscellanies* 952. Consummation of All Things', 219.

[80] Y18, '*Miscellanies* 741. Happiness of Heaven', 367.

[81] Y18, '*Miscellanies* 741. Happiness of Heaven', 367.

[82] 'And 'tis to be considered that the more those divine communications increase in the creature, the more it becomes one with God: for so much the more is it united to God in love, the heart is drawn nearer and nearer to God, and the union with him becomes more firm and close: and at the same time the creature becomes more and more conformed to God. The image is more and more perfect, and so the good that is in the creature comes forever nearer and nearer to an identity with that which is in God.' Y8, *End of Creation*, 443.

[83] In *Miscellanies* 371, Edwards states, 'Then God will fully have glorified himself, and glorified his Son and his elect; then he will see that all is very good, and will rejoice in his own works, which will be the joy of all heaven. God will rest and be refreshed; and thenceforward will the inhabitants keep an eternal Sabbath, such an one as all foregoing Sabbaths were but shadows of.' Y13, '*Miscellanies* 371. Resurrection', 444.

[84] Y20, '*Miscellanies* 952. Consummation of All Things', 213.

[85] Y20, '*Miscellanies* 957. Heaven Made New After the Day of Judgement', 232.

[86] Y18, '*Miscellanies* 742. Consummation of All Things. Christ's Delivering Up the Kingdom to the Father', 376.

[87] Y20, '*Miscellanies* 957. Heaven Made New After the Day of Judgement', 232.

And from that manifestation of complacence, the Son shall be changed into the same image of complacence and love, and shall put [on] that divine glory, the glory of that infinitely sweet divine love, grace, gentleness and joy, and shall shine with this sweet light far more brightly than ever he did before; he shall be clothed with those sweet robes in a far more glorious manner than ever before .... Thus God the Father will give the Son his heart's desire .... His heart's desire was that he might express his infinite love to his elect spouse full and freely; to this end God the Father will now crown him with a crown of love, and array him in the brightest robes of love and grace as his wedding garments, as the robe in which he should embrace his dear redeemed spouse, now brought home to her everlasting rest in the house of her husband.[88]

Thus, as Christ is changed, so is heaven.[89] This was true as well with Christ's first ascension into heaven: 'It seems impossible that it should be otherwise than that all heaven should put on a new glory at the same time that Christ puts on a new glory.'[90] As Christ receives new glory, he communicates that glory to the church as his bride, and heaven will be transformed anew. 'The beams of the Son's new glory of grace and love shall advance that whole world to new glory and sweetness.'[91] Christ, as God-man, will also be 'admitted to a higher enjoyment of the Father than ever he was admitted to before, and in him the saints shall enjoy him'.[92] The saints, just as in the second age, enjoy the Father through their union with Christ, though now with much greater union and glory. In this age, 'God will make more abundant manifestations of his glory and of the glory of his Son, and will pour forth more plentifully of his Spirit, and will make answerable additions to the glory of the saints.'[93]

As we have seen, Edwards evidences a progressive understanding of the beatific vision throughout the various stages of heaven, as well as invoking a beatific form to the pilgrim existence of life on earth. While Edwards freely used the term 'beatific' (more often 'beatifical') in these ways,

---

[88] Y20, '*Miscellanies* 957. Heaven Made New After the Day of Judgement', 232.
[89] At Christ's return from judgement, all of heaven changes: 'The house shall be garnished and beautified exceedingly to make it fit for his reception in this his highest glory.' Y20, '*Miscellanies* 952. Consummation of All Things', 212. Likewise, 'In heaven, when Christ returns thither in his highest glory after the day of judgement: all heaven will as it were rejoice, and put on new life, new beauty and glory, to welcome him thither.' Y20, '*Miscellanies* 952. Consummation of All Things', 216–17.
[90] Y20, '*Miscellanies* 952. Consummation of All Things', 216.
[91] Y20, '*Miscellanies* 957. Heaven Made New After the Day of Judgement', 232.
[92] Y20, '*Miscellanies* 957. Heaven Made New After the Day of Judgement', 234.
[93] Y13, '*Miscellanies* 371. Resurrection', 444.

this third and last period can be understood as *the* beatific vision, being the fulfilment of all that has preceded, no longer seeing through a glass darkly but participating in the inner-trinitarian vision of God. Heaven is, therefore, an asymptotic increase of union and communion with God for eternity – where the sight that delights continues to delight to an ever-increasing degree. The life of mankind, we might say, comes to look more and more like the inner life of God, recognizing that this life is by grace and will always be a finite reflection of God's infinite glory.

II Edwards and the Beatific

In this section, I address Edwards's view of the beatific vision with particular focus on the theological backdrop of Reformed theology preceding Edwards.[94] To do so, I develop Edwards's view after providing a sketch of John Owen's and Francis Turretin's positions on the beatific vision. I suggest that Edwards offers a correction to what Suzanne McDonald calls the 'Reforming' of the beatific vision by John Owen, offering a truly trinitarian account (which she claims Owen lacks). In so doing, I show that Edwards's doctrine of the beatific was more than a theological 'hand wave' to the afterlife. Rather, it was a central and defining feature of his work (not to mention the underlying teleology of his vision of redemption). The beatific, we might say, is the thread which starts in Edwards's doctrine of God and is woven throughout his thought in such a way as to be one of the central defining features of his theological tapestry. The scant appearance of this doctrine in the secondary literature is a symptom of a fundamental misunderstanding of Edwards's theology – particularly his understanding of redemption.

In addressing Owen and Turretin, I briefly chart the theological issues and debates preceding Edwards, utilizing two of his favourite theological resources. This is in contrast to the main secondary text discussing Edwards and the beatific, Paul Ramsey's appendix titled, 'Heaven Is a Progressive State' in the volume on Edwards's ethical writings, which bypasses the Reformed context entirely and focuses solely on Aquinas and Dante as precursors to Edwards's position.[95] By locating Edwards's work in his more

---

[94] For a complete development of this line, see Kyle Strobel, 'Jonathan Edwards's Reformed Doctrine of the Beatific Vision', in *Jonathan Edwards and Scotland* (ed. Ken Minkema, Adriaan Neale and Kelly van Andel; Edinburgh: Dunedin Academic Press, 2011), 171–88.

[95] Ramsey's analysis fails to recognize Edwards's theological moorings, focusing instead on the gap between Edwards's task and the task of medieval theology (for instance, see Y8, 'Appendix III: Heaven is a Progressive State', 720–3). Likewise, Caldwell engages in an

immediately relevant theological context we can better understand his somewhat idiosyncratic position as part of a larger debate concerning epistemology, Christology and pneumatology.

1. John Owen: Reforming Aquinas

Suzanne McDonald, in her paper at the 'John Owen Today' conference (Cambridge, 2008), suggests that Owen reformed Aquinas's view of the beatific vision by making it specifically Christological.[96] In his work on the glory of Christ Owen states, 'That which at present I design to demonstrate is, that the beholding of the glory of Christ is one of the greatest privileges and advancements that believers are capable of in this world, or that which is to come.'[97] Owen notes several key passages for his understanding of this 'beholding', such as 2 Corinthians 3:18 – that those who behold his glory are changed or transformed into his likeness; 1 John 3.1-2 – that becoming like him is predicated on seeing him as he is; and 2 Corinthians 4:6 – that the light of the knowledge of the glory of God is seen only in the face of Jesus Christ.

Owen defines the beatific vision as an intellectual view or apprehension of God and his glory, as manifested in Christ.[98] Owen distinguishes two

---

excursus of the beatific vision when discussing the second period of heaven without any reflection on the theological discussion preceding Edwards (see Caldwell, *Communion of the Spirit*, 177–82). Schweitzer, likewise, fails to locate Edwards's discussion both within his own thought as well as the theological backdrop.

[96] I follow McDonald's analysis closely and focus on Owen's work, 'Meditations and Discourses on the Glory of Christ in His Person, Office, and Grace: with The Differences Between Faith and Sight; Applied Unto the Use of Them that Believe', in *The Works of John Owen* (ed. William H. Gould; vol. 4 (London: Johnstone and Hunter, 1850–55), 273–415. While it is not in the scope of this work to engage with Thomas, it is helpful to delineate how Owen 'reforms' him here. McDonald suggests that Owen makes two major changes to the beatific discussion. First, he changes the 'what' of the vision from the divine essence (Thomas) to Christ himself and, more specifically, his two natures. Second, he changes the 'how' of the vision by emphasizing both the intellectual (with Thomas) and the bodily (against Thomas). See Suzanne McDonald, 'Beholding the Glory of God in the Face of Jesus Christ: John Owen and the "Reforming" of the Beatific Vision' (paper delivered at the John Owen Today Conference, Westminster College, Cambridge, 2008), hereafter 'McDonald paper'. Importantly, McDonald, in suggesting that Owen provides a Christological orientation to Thomas's thought, does not deny that Thomas was Christological, but, in her words, 'In the Thomistic tradition, the emphasis seems to be upon Christ as instrumental for our participation in the beatific vision, but not upon presenting Christ as being intrinsic to the beatific vision itself.' McDonald Paper. This paper will be coming out as a chapter in the volume, *The Ashgate Research Companion to John Owen's Theology* (ed. Kelly Kapic and Mark Jones; Aldershot: Ashgate Publishing, forthcoming).

[97] John Owen, *The Glory of Christ* (ed. William H. Goold; The Works of John Owen, vol. 1; London: Banner of Truth Trust, 1965), 287.

[98] Owen, *Glory of Christ*, 240.

ways or degrees of beholding the glory of Christ: first, by faith, which is the 'sight' given in this world; and second, by sight, which is the immediate vision in eternity.[99] Owen thus, as noted above, establishes a distinctively *Christological focus* to the beatific vision, claiming that Christ and his glory are the immediate object of the elect's faith and sight.[100] Likewise, prior to glorification, 'we have no way to take into our minds any true spiritual apprehensions of the nature of immediate vision, or what it is to see the glory of Christ in heaven'.[101] Faith is the pilgrim counterpart to this immediate vision. Cultivating faith is therefore a precursor to beholding Christ's glory by sight.

Owen introduces the ideological currency in which his understanding of the beatific vision trades, stating,

> The enjoyment of God by sight is commonly called the BEATIFICAL VISION .... Howbeit, this we know, that God in his immense essence is invisible unto our corporeal eyes, and will be so to eternity; as also incomprehensible unto our minds. For nothing can perfectly comprehend that which is infinite, but what is itself infinite. *Wherefore the blessed and blessing sight which we shall have of God will be always 'in the face of Jesus Christ'.*[102]

Owen, like Edwards, follows the distinction between archetypal and ectypal knowledge of God, forcing all knowledge of God into a Christological and revelatory mode.[103] Knowledge of God on the earthly side of glory is pilgrim knowledge, mediated by the person and work of Christ.[104] Therefore, for Owen, seeing God can only be seeing Christ, because the divine essence is infinite and invisible, and therefore unable to be comprehended or beheld through sight. Owen expands on his Christological claims by noting that Christ, as the image of the invisible God, is always the face by which the Father is known by his children. In seeing the glory of Christ, the saints see the glory of the Father.[105]

---

[99] Owen, *Glory of Christ*, 288.
[100] Owen, *Glory of Christ*, 288. This distinction does not entirely separate the two for Owen. For Owen, there is a sense where sight is the perfection of faith, and therefore without faith, sight will never occur. He states, 'No man shall ever behold the glory of Christ by *sight* hereafter, who doth not in some measure behold it by *faith* here in this world. Grace is a necessary preparation for glory, and faith for sight.' Owen, *Glory of Christ*, 288.
[101] Owen, *Glory of Christ*, 290.
[102] Owen, *Glory of Christ*, 292–3 – my emphasis.
[103] The archetypal/ectypal distinction in Edwards's thought will be addressed in the following chapter.
[104] 'He, and he alone, declares, represents, and makes known, unto angels and men, the essential glory of the invisible God, his attributes and his will.' Owen, *Glory of Christ*, 294.
[105] 'Nothing is more fully and clearly revealed in the Gospel, than that unto us Jesus Christ

Yet, it was this glory that was veiled in the incarnation. Owen, invoking natural imagery, suggests that a divine person taking on flesh and the role of a servant is like the sun under a total eclipse.[106] What is provocative about the incarnation is not so much that the Word became flesh but that so few seemed to notice:

> Hence the most saw nothing of it, and the best saw it but obscurely. But in this glory that veil is taken off, whereby the whole glory of his person in itself and in the work of mediation is most illustriously manifested. When we shall immediately behold this glory, we shall see him as he is. This is that glory whereof the Father made grant unto him before the foundation of the world, and wherewith he was actually invested upon his ascension.[107]

The veil which is cast off of Christ is fundamentally his role as a servant. Owen's understanding of the glory of Christ in this passage is not 'the *essential glory* of his divine nature', but *the manifestation* of his glory in particular. Christ's person, in other words, truly manifests his glory in power, no longer veiled by his role as servant.[108] This image of Christ which acts as a veil is nonetheless the image he has left humankind, however imperfect and obscure in comparison to his real, substantial glory.[109] Owen states, 'There is a wall between him and us, which yet he standeth behind. Our present mortal state is this wall, which must be demolished before we can see him as he is. In the meantime he looketh through the *windows* of the ordinances of the Gospel.'[110]

Unlike earthly vision, which is mediated by faith through Scripture, the vision in heaven is immediate, direct and intuitive.[111] Furthermore, as

---

is "the image of the invisible God"; that he is the character of the person of the Father, so as that in seeing him we see the Father also; that we have "the light of the knowledge of the glory of God in his face alone", as hath been proved.' Owen, *Glory of Christ*, 305. For Owen, this is connected with the renewal of the image of God: 'This is that whereby the image of God is renewed in us, and we are made like unto the first-born.' Owen, *Glory of Christ*, 305.

[106] 'But this temporary eclipse being past and over, it now shines forth in its infinite lustre and beauty, which belongs unto the present exaltation of his person.' Owen, *Glory of Christ*, 344.

[107] Owen, *Glory of Christ*, 343.

[108] Edwards's view, that only after Christ hands over his representative kingdom is his glory fully known, maps onto this idea.

[109] Owen, *Glory of Christ*, 376.

[110] Owen, *Glory of Christ*, 377. Owen asserts that the difference between the Catholic Church and the Protestant on this point is that the former attempts to use man-made images to try and behold Christ, while the latter assert that Christ's glory is seen only by faith as revealed in the gospel. Owen, *Glory of Christ*, 393.

[111] Owen, *Glory of Christ*, 378.

intellectual vision, 'it is not, therefore, the mere human nature of Christ
that is the object of it, but his divine person, as that nature subsisteth
therein.'[112] There will be a new 'visive power' or 'faculty' of beholding
Christ's glory which man will not receive until heaven and without which
man could not see him as he is.[113] This new ability to see Christ does not
take away from the ability of the glorified humanity to see Christ bodily, but
the beatific vision specifically entails seeing the divine person.[114]

Owen's understanding of the beatific vision is governed by his
Christocentric focus; Christ is, and will always be, the image of the
invisible God. That being said, Owen distinguishes between beholding
Christ by faith and by sight. An immediate vision of Christ prior to
glory is withheld from the regenerate because they could not receive its
benefits. In an interesting analogy, Owen suggests that if the luminaries
in the heavenly realm (stars, moon and sun) had been collapsed into
one focused light, it would overwhelm our senses; likewise with the
revelation of Christ. The light known by pilgrims is 'distributed' light,
light through God's self-revelation in Scripture, while the beatific vision
entails a focused light which the glorified saints can behold.[115] 'In the
vision which we shall have *above*, the whole glory of Christ will be at *once*
and *always* represented to us; and we shall be enabled in one act of the
light of glory to comprehend it.'[116]

Owen offers several suggestions concerning the effects of faith and sight:
First, the vision in heaven is perfectly and absolutely transforming, while the
vision of faith in this life effects only an imperfect transformation. Further,
the immediate vision of Christ is *beatifical* and therefore gives perfect rest
and blessedness to those who partake in it. Distinguishing between glorification and sanctification, Owen claims that vision is the principle of life
in heaven while faith is the principle of life on earth, and love is the 'great
vital acting' of that principle.[117] McDonald summarizes: 'For Owen the
content of the beatific vision is primarily Jesus Christ … acknowledged by
faith now, apprehended in its fullness in eternity. Beholding the glory of
God is beholding the glory of the person of Christ in the mystery of the

---

[112] Owen, *Glory of Christ*, 379.
[113] Owen, *Glory of Christ*, 380. Owen states, 'And this sight is not an external aid, like a glass
helping the weakness of the visive faculty to see things afar off; but it is an internal power,
or an act of the internal power of our minds, wherewith they are endowed in a glorified
state.' Owen, *Glory of Christ*, 406.
[114] Owen, *Glory of Christ*, 383.
[115] Owen, *Glory of Christ*, 409.
[116] Owen, *Glory of Christ*, 410.
[117] Owen, *Glory of Christ*, 272.

union of the two natures.'[118] In other words, Christ is, and will always be, the visible image of the invisible God.

2. Francis Turretin and the Beatific

As a brief foil to the theological creativity of Owen, I highlight Francis Turretin, another of Edwards's main sources. Although I argue that Edwards follows and expands Owen, Turretin's account serves as a helpful backdrop. In a statement sounding very much like Edwards, Turretin says: 'This perfection of the intellect by the beatific vision will be followed by no less a consummation of the will by absolute holiness and by a most pure and intense love to arise from that infinite light and the celestial intuition of it.'[119]

Turretin, in volume three of his *Elenctic Theology*, addresses the concept of the beatific vision under a question concerning eternal life. Claiming that Aquinas held to a vision of Christ located in the intellect, while Scotus held to love through the will, Turretin suggests these are not mutually exclusive and must be understood as united in the beatific vision. Specifically, sight, love and joy are united in the vision of God.[120] Turretin explains: 'Sight contemplates God as the supreme good; love is carried out towards him, and is most closely united with him; and joy enjoys and acquiesces in him. Sight perfects the intellect, love the will, joy the conscience.'[121]

Turretin offers four clarifying remarks concerning whether or not a vision of God can be had with corporeal eyes. He compares a bodily vision with a spiritual one, claiming: '(1) one vision is ocular, sensible and external, another mental, intellectual and internal; (2) one is the natural of reason, another the supernatural and spiritual of faith; (3) one symbolic and enigmatic, the other intuitive and beatific; (4) one apprehensive and inadequate, the other adequate and comprehensive.'[122]

Therefore, creatures cannot see God with their bodily eyes, but by spiritual sight, which is necessarily mental and intellectual. For a vision to be spiritual,

---

[118] McDonald Paper.

[119] Francis Turretin, *Institutes of Elenctic Theology* (ed. James T. Dennison; trans. George Musgrave Giger; vol. 3; Phillipsburg: P&R, 1992), 611.

[120] Turretin, *Institutes of Elenctic Theology*, 609.

[121] Turretin, *Institutes of Elenctic Theology*, 609.

[122] Turretin, *Institutes of Elenctic Theology*, 610. It seems that Edwards could have been using this passage in his own reflection upon these verses. Edwards states, 'When that which is perfect is come, then we shall no more see by a looking glass, in an enigma, but shall see face to face, as the Apostle shows (I Cor. 13:10, 12).' Y18, '*Miscellanies* 710. Heaven. Separate State. Resurrection', 336. Edwards uses the word enigma here, a word not used often in his corpus, musing over the same passages as Turretin.

it is necessarily intellectual, supernatural, beatific and comprehensive. In contrast to Owen, who offers a Christological recasting of the beatific vision, Turretin ignores Christ's role entirely, focusing on anthropological and epistemological questions.[123] In the words of Suzanne McDonald, 'Christ is literally almost invisible throughout his entire discussion of the vision of God in glory. He is mentioned only a few times in passing, and only because references to the book of Revelation require it.'[124] Turretin therefore offers deity abstracted from the Trinity, and Christ is absent from his account entirely, while Owen offers a thoroughly Christological view.

Summary

McDonald's work on John Owen and the beatific vision has highlighted several helpful implications of Owen's view. First, Owen moves beyond the tradition (read 'Aquinas') by positing a Christological vision of the beatific, which changes both the *what* and the *how* of the vision. The 'what' is, in her words, 'the glory of God in the person of Christ, in his divinity and humanity'; and the 'how' is by both glorified *physical* sight as well as purified intellectual apprehension.[125] Owen's understanding therefore both provides greater room for the glorified human body to participate in glory and explains Christ's role in relation to glorified saints. Turretin, himself seeking to move beyond Aquinas, focuses on uniting the whole person in the vision (both intellect and will), but fails to talk about God qua Trinity, addressing anthropological questions instead of God's self-revelation in Christ. In the end his view neglects not only the bodily Christ but the bodily saint as well.[126]

McDonald helpfully highlights a critique that I pick up here in mapping Edwards's background. She notes that just as Turretin discusses the beatific

---

[123] This is not to say that Turretin failed to think theologically about Christ's role in heaven, which he does in the second volume of his work. There, just as in the third volume, Turretin fails to link Christ's bodily presence in heaven to the beatific. Beyond anthropological questions, Turretin turns to faith, hope and love, seeking to abstract to their perfection as a way to talk about the vision. Furthermore, he continues by holding the beatific in contrast with damnation. See Turretin, *Institutes of Elenctic Theology*, 609.

[124] McDonald Paper.

[125] McDonald Paper.

[126] Turretin argues that the bodily eyes will become 'spiritual as to qualities' but denies that they will be able to see God in any way. God is invisible, and therefore requires a 'mental' vision not an 'ocular' one. His reason is that while the bodily eyes will become spiritual, the addition of supernatural qualities to something raises it 'above its own natural grade' but does not raise it 'above its own species'. Therefore Turretin allows for the bodily saint, but denies the saints corporeal nature to be utilized in the vision in any way. Turretin, *Institutes of Elenctic Theology*, 611.

without Christ, Owen's discussion occurs without real reference to the Holy Spirit. In her words,

> We don't just need a christological revolution in our thinking about the beatific vision. We need to be clear that the Holy Spirit, just as now, will be the one by whom we are enabled to behold the glory of God in the face of Jesus Christ, and the Holy Spirit, then as now will be the one who transforms and sustains our lives in glory, just as he anticipates that in our lives now. We need a fully Trinitarian account of the beatific vision.[127]

3. A Happifying Sight: Jonathan Edwards and the Beatific

McDonald's desire to see a truly trinitarian and Reformed account of the beatific vision is realized in the work of Jonathan Edwards, who utilizes and expands the insights of Owen and Turretin. In order to explicate this doctrine, I will focus on Edwards's interpretation of two main texts, Matthew 5:8 and Romans 2:10, while using other sermons and notes to round out the exposition. These texts build upon the insights found above, with a specific focus on the third period of heaven.[128]

In 1722, at the very beginning of his New York pastorate, Edwards preached a sermon on Mt. 16:26.[129] In talking about dwelling with God in heaven, he states, 'The Beatifical Vision of God: *that* is the tip of happiness! To see a God of infinite glory and majesty face to face, to see him as he is, and to know him as we are known.'[130] Later in the sermon he claims that the vision is 'of Jehovah himself, the Eternal Three in One God, blessed forevermore'.[131] This is Edwards's first preached reflections on the beatific. In it, we see a desire to accomplish what both Owen and Turretin failed to

---

[127] McDonald Paper.

[128] It has been suggested to me that Edwards changed his position after giving his sermon on Rom. 2:10 to Owen's position in *Miscellanies* 777. This is a misunderstanding of Edwards's claim in *Miscellanies* 777. There Edwards claims that 'no creature can thus have an immediate sight of God, but only Jesus Christ, who is in the bosom of God: for no creature can have such an immediate view of another created spirit, for if they could they could search the heart and try the reins'. Y18, '*Miscellanies* 777. Happiness of Heaven is Progressive', 428. As will be shown, this is precisely what Edwards *does not* say in his account of seeing God. The saints' sight of God is always mediated by Christ, one could say *through* Christ, and it is never simply seeing, but seeing *pro nobis*. Likewise, it is impossible for a finite Spirit to 'try the reins' of an infinite Spirit.

[129] Jonathan Edwards, 'The Value of Salvation', in *Sermons and Discourses, 1720–1723* (ed. Wilson H. Kimnach; The Works of Jonathan Edwards, vol. 10; New Haven: Yale University Press, 1992), 311.

[130] Y10, 'The Value of Salvation', 324.

[131] Y10, 'The Value of Salvation', 331.

achieve – a trinitarian conception of glorified sight. In these early accounts, however brief, Edwards seems to follow Turretin more closely than Owen, failing to mention Christ's mediating role entirely.[132]

In 1742, the issue of the beatific again arises for Edwards, this time in a vastly different context. Edwards published his 'Some Thoughts Concerning the Present Revival of Religion in New-England' (hereafter *Some Thoughts*), stating:

> I have observed or been informed of … such views of the glory of the divine perfections, and Christ's excellencies, that the soul in the meantime has been as it were perfectly overwhelmed, and swallowed up with light and love and a sweet solace, rest and joy of soul … in that clear and lively view or sense of the infinite beauty and amiableness of Christ's person, and the heavenly sweetness of his excellent and transcendent love …. The soul dwelt on high, and was lost in God, and seemed almost to leave the body; dwelling in a pure delight that fed and satisfied the soul; … that it seemed to the person as though soul and body would, as it were of themselves, of necessity mount up, leave the earth and ascend thither.[133]

While Edwards does not give the name 'beatific' to this detailed rapture of ecstasy, later in the discourse, Edwards references the 'beatifical' to describe these kinds of experiences. Likewise, several years earlier, in his 'A Faithful Narrative of the Surprising Work of God' (hereafter *Faithful Narrative*), he writes of a woman who 'gave me an account of the sense she once had, from day to day, of the glory of Christ, and of God in his various attributes, that it seemed to me she dwelt for days together in a kind of beatific vision of God'.[134] Importantly for Edwards's mature position, he goes on to state that she 'seemed to have, as I thought, as immediate an intercourse with him as a child with a father', and 'she often expressed a sense of the glory of God appearing in the trees, and growth

---

[132] I am not suggesting that Edwards was self-consciously orienting his own view to the positions of Owen and Turretin. Edwards owned and knew the thought of these thinkers well; therefore my claim is that Edwards was working within a doctrinal discussion which had these kinds of contours. It may very well be that Edwards had Turretin and Owen on his desk when he was working, but that kind of claim is not necessary for what I argue here. For discussion on Edwards's use of Turretin see Y26, 'General Index', 349–50; 466–7, and for Owen see Y26, 'Reformed (Calvinist) Divinity', 53–4, 455.

[133] Jonathan Edwards, *Some Thoughts Concerning the Revival*, in *The Great Awakening* (ed. C. C. Goen; The Works of Jonathan Edwards, vol. 4 (New Haven: Yale University Press, 1972), 332–3.

[134] Y4, *A Faithful Narrative*, 195.

in the fields, and other works of God's hands.'[135] In these texts, not only does the concept of beatific break forth from heaven into the day-to-day reality of the world, but the beatific orients and saturates piety.[136] This experience of the beatific, as we have seen, parallels the second age of heaven, where the saints watch from 'above' and see perfectly, juxtaposed with the saints on earth, who watch from below, seeing imperfectly but still nonetheless beatifically.

3.3.3.1 Exposition of Mtt. 5:8

In 1730 Edwards preached on Mt. 5:8 and explicated two doctrines: (1) 'It is a thing truly happifying to the soul of men to see God'; and (2) 'The having a pure heart is the certain and only way to come to the blessedness of seeing God.'[137] In this sermon Edwards develops two key concerns of the beatific vision: first, the nature of spiritual knowledge; and second, how that knowledge relates to the spiritual circumstances and experience of the person.

In offering his exposition of the first doctrine, Edwards engages what is meant by seeing God. Edwards follows Owen and Turretin in claiming that since God is invisible he cannot be seen with bodily eyes. Following Owen further, he states that the saints will see God's glory in Christ with their eyes in heaven. This is a distinct move away from his initial thoughts, which seemed to remove Christ from the vision altogether. Edwards, again following both Owen and Turretin, suggests that God is only seen by the intellect, claiming, 'God is a spiritual being, and he is beheld with the understanding.'[138] Edwards suggests that the soul has powers of sight to apprehend spiritual objects without use of the senses and that this sight is superior to sight with bodily senses. This is important in light of our background work: Edwards follows Owen's analysis against Turretin's anaemic Christology. McDonald helpfully summarizes Owen's inclination:

---

[135] Y4, *A Faithful Narrative*, 195.

[136] In 1733 Edwards stated, 'With respect to light and knowledge, we should labor to be continually growing in knowledge of God and Christ, and divine things, clear views of the gloriousness and excellency of divine things, that we come nearer and nearer to the beatific vision.' Y17, 'The True Christian's Life a Journey Towards Heaven', 434–5. Importantly, in revisions for repreaching this sermon in Boston in October of 1753, Edwards changes the last part of the sentence to '... clear views of the glory of God, the beauty of Christ and excellency of divine things, that we come nearer and nearer to the beatific vision.' Y17, 'The True Christian's Life a Journey Towards Heaven', 434–5.

[137] Y17, 'The Pure in Heart Blessed', 61.

[138] Y17, 'The Pure in Heart Blessed', 63.

Owen emphatically turns aside from any approach that rejects the place of physical sight in relation to the beatific vision because of his single-minded christological focus. He agrees that intellectual apprehension *is* primary, but even the reason for this is christological. It is not because of an overarching theory of the relationship of knowledge and immateriality, but because the beatific vision is about beholding the glory of Christ. That means the fullest possible intellectual apprehension of the hypostatic union.[139]

Edwards thus follows Owen's insistence on the role of Christ, but he refuses to limit the beatific to that reality alone.

Seeing God, for Edwards, is not having an apprehension by hearsay (testimony), by speculative reasoning, or even having an immediate apprehension of God that does not 'happify' (which the demons undoubtedly have). Seeing God *is*, Edwards emphasizes: (1) having a direct and immediate *sense* of God's glory and excellency; and (2) a *certain* understanding of his love and a *certain* apprehension of his presence.[140] His use of 'certain' highlights that the vision must achieve its effect – it is happifying – for one to truly *see* God. The result is that each age of redemptive history can have a greater and deepening 'sight' of God, even though no one has a pure and immediate sight of God until the consummation of all things. The focus here is not a vision of God as such, but a vision of God's glory, a knowledge of his love and a sense of his presence. Here, as we will see in the next chapter, Edwards ties his understanding of redemption, in all ages, to the beatific. Knowing God, for Edwards, is partaking in his self-knowledge of beatific-delight. God's beatific self-knowledge serves as the archetype of all other knowledge. To know God is to behold and delight in him *beatifically*.

In the first sense of seeing God, Edwards emphasizes that one cannot have a view of God by 'ratiocination'. There must accompany a certain *sense* of seeing God, of coming to see his 'amiable and glorious holiness'.[141] Therefore, one could come to understand that God is merciful without actually having an immediate view of his mercifulness. The mind must have a real sense of the excellency and beauty of God to truly *see* God. Likewise, there must be a specific understanding of God's love in any apprehension of his presence. Edwards explains, 'He that sees God, he don't only see him as present by his essence; for so he is present with all, both godly and

[139] McDonald Paper.
[140] Y17, 'The Pure in Heart Blessed', 64.
[141] Y17, 'The Pure in Heart Blessed', 64.

ungodly. But he is more especially present with those whom he loves.'[142] In other words, there is a general understanding of God's presence, and there is God's presence *pro nobis*. God must be seen, not abstractly, but who he is *for us*, and, importantly, what that means *for us*. It is not without justification to distinguish these two types of presence as essential and personal. God is omniscient, we would say, *essentially*, but present with the elect *personally*.

Therefore, for Edwards, the main difference between seeing God on earth compared to in heaven is the difference between a mediated sight through the gospel as through a glass darkly on earth and a certain kind of immediate sight in heaven (a sight which 'deepens' through each era of heaven). Edwards admits a kind of immediacy on earth, in that the sight is not dependent upon ratiocination, and it is still immediate sight of God in Christ as enlightened by the Spirit.[143] In eternity the saints will behold Christ with bodily eyes and will also behold God with intellectual sight. Interestingly, what this intellectual faculty of sight beholds is the divine excellency and love of God. Edwards explains that 'their souls will see the spiritual nature of God itself immediately. They shall behold his attributes and disposition towards them more immediately.'[144] True knowledge of God, therefore, entails seeing God personally (who he is) rather than essentially (what he is). This distinction follows the contours of Edwards's work on the Trinity, where Edwards parses God's *quiddity* in terms of persons rather than essence. Therefore, knowing God entails entering into his life of personal beatific-delight through his own self-revealing in Christ.

In seeing God, believers participate in God's revelatory emanation, receiving God's glory and finding it 'happifying'.[145] As the Father beholds his perfect image, love and delight proceed from their mutual beholding. Furthermore, the love of the elect is enraptured as it beholds this love: 'The love of so glorious a Being is infinitely valuable, and the discoveries of it are capable of ravishing the soul above all other loves.'[146] Edwards goes on to say that this vision of God is 'man's true happiness: that is, not only his pleasure, but his perfection and true excellency'.[147] The vision of God that humanity partakes in prior to glorification is what sanctifies; understanding

[112] Y17, 'The Pure in Heart Blessed', 64.
[113] This will be developed in the next chapter.
[114] Y17, 'The Pure in Heart Blessed', 66.
[115] 'Intellectual pleasure consists in beholding of spiritual excellencies and beauties; but the glorious excellency and beauty of God, they are far the greatest. God's excellence is the supreme excellence; when the understanding of the reasonable creature dwells here, it dwells at the fountain and swims in a boundless and bottomless ocean.' Y17, 'The Pure in Heart Blessed', 67.
[116] Y17, 'The Pure in Heart Blessed', 67.
[117] Y17, 'The Pure in Heart Blessed', 68.

and will move together in knowledge and love in beholding the goodness and beauty of God. Believers partake, in finite and imperfect ways, in the life that the triune members enjoy infinitely, perfectly and eternally.[148] 'And when it [the soul] actually exercises delight in God, it is its most noble and exalted exercise that it's capable of.'[149]

Likewise, Edwards exhorts his hearers that 'we have the glorious attributes and perfections of God declared to us; the glory of God in the face of Jesus Christ is discovered in the gospel which we enjoy'.[150] Importantly for our later observations, Edwards links the earthly vision of the elect with their vision in heaven:

> The knowledge which believers have of God and his glory as appearing in the face of Christ is the imperfect beginning of this heavenly sight; 'tis an earnest of it. 'Tis the dawning of the heavenly light; and this beginning must ever more recede, or a perfect vision of God in heaven cannot be obtained. And all those that have these beginnings, they shall obtain the perfection also.[151]

3.3.3.2 Exposition of Romans 2:10

In 1735, between the New York pastorate and his writing an apologetic for the revivals, Edwards devoted a sermon to the idea of the beatific, in which he claimed 'to give a description of the consummate and eternal glory and blessedness of the saints', showing first its nature and wherein it consists, and second, its circumstances.[152] The text Edwards chose for this task was Romans 2:10. This text is therefore the major source concerning Edwards's view of the third period of heaven, and it is here where Edwards focuses his attention foremost on what the beatific life of eternity shall entail.[153]

---

[148] Therefore, God communicates his inner life to man, allowing man's finitude to be filled out of the abundance of God's plenitude.

[149] Y17, 'The Pure in Heart Blessed', 68.

[150] Y17, 'The Pure in Heart Blessed', 74–5.

[151] Y17, 'The Pure in Heart Blessed', 75. Richard Muller notes, 'Although considered soteriologically or teleologically the *theologia beatorum* appears as the end result of progress in faith, the Protestant orthodox tend to discuss it first, before the discussion of the *theologia viatorum*.' Richard A. Muller, *Prolegomena to Theology* (Post-Reformation Reformed Dogmatics, vol. 1; Grand Rapids: Baker Academic, 2nd edn, 2003), 259. Therefore, I keep this discussion distinct from those questions until the next chapter, where I address the issue of spiritual knowledge more fully.

[152] JEC, Unpublished Sermon, Rom. 2:10, #373 [L. 31r.]. For our purposes here, I only address the first point, and do not exposit the circumstances of the vision.

[153] By failing to address the most important text on the beatific vision in Edwards's thought,

Edwards navigates his initial point through six advancing steps of glory, starting with the glory of heaven itself and moving through the glory of bodies, souls and society to Christ, his fifth point. Here, Edwards focuses on seeing and conversing with Christ, the penultimate moment prior to engaging the beatific vision specifically. In this fifth point, possibly 'channeling' Owen, Edwards offers a Christological orientation to creaturely sight in heaven, arguing that the saints in heaven will both see and converse with Christ in a twofold sense. This twofold seeing of Christ maps on to the twofold nature of sight in humankind. First, 'they shall see him as appearing in his glorified human nature with their bodily eyes';[154] and second, 'they shall see him with the eye of the soul'.[155] In this latter sight, the glorified will come to understand Christ's mediatorial role, the eternal covenant of redemption between the Father and the Son, Christ's love to them before the foundation of the world, the mystery of the incarnation, the glorious way of salvation by Christ and a full understanding of the infinite wisdom of God in contriving the way of salvation.[156] At first glance, Edwards seems to be following Owen, but Edwards does not label this description as 'beatific', but simply as 'seeing' and 'conversing' with Christ,[157] which is, as noted above, a step prior to the full-fledged beatific vision.[158]

It is when he turns to discuss the 'eye of the soul' that Edwards first addresses the beatific vision. In seeing the divine nature, the elect will 'behold that bright and perfect image of God that the Father beheld and was infinitely happy in beholding from all eternity'.[159] This sight includes Christ, but it is a spiritual sight, thereby beholding the love, beauty and excellency of Christ.[160] In describing this vision, Edwards reminds his hearers, "Tis not in beholding any form or visible representation or shape or color or shining light that the highest happiness of the soul consists, but 'tis in seeing God who is a spirit spiritually with the eye of the soul.'[161]

Schweitzer provides a truncated depiction of the beatific vision. Schweitzer, 'Interpreting the Harmony of Reality', 138–46.

[154] JEC, Unpublished Sermon, Rom. 2:10, #373 [L. 37v.].

[155] JEC, Unpublished Sermon, Rom. 2:10, #373 [L. 38r.].

[156] JEC, Unpublished Sermon, Rom. 2:10, #373 [L. 38r.].

[157] It is relevant to this discussion that Edwards has a place for glorified bodily sight in heaven. Though he does not put this kind of sight within the beatific, it is still an important piece for him.

[158] According to my development above, this is clearly an aspect of the beatific vision, even if it is not integral to the *final* beatific vision.

[159] Unpublished Sermon, Rom. 2:10, #373 [L. 39r.].

[160] 'The sight of Christ which has already been spoken of is not here to be excluded because he is a divine person. The sight of him in his divine nature therefore belongs to the beatifical vision.' JEC, Unpublished Sermon, Rom. 2:10, #373 [L. 41r.].

[161] JEC, Unpublished Sermon, Rom. 2:10, #373 [L. 41v.].

In his sixth point, which is our focus here, Edwards baldly states, 'The saints in heaven see God ... not only see that glorious city ... and the glorified body of Christ, but they shall see God himself.'[162] Within this sixth point, Edwards provides another six issues which he believes need to be developed to exposit the vision adequately. In order to accomplish this, Edwards provides an exposition of (1) the faculty that is the immediate subject of the vision; (2) the nature of the act of the vision *as seeing*; (3) the object; (4) the manner; (5) the means; and (6) the effects of the vision.

Edwards begins, again, by affirming that God cannot be seen with bodily sight but must be seen with the eye of the soul.[163] Through further exposition of the 'eye of the soul', Edwards states, 'The soul has in itself those powers whereby 'tis sufficiently capable of apprehending spiritual objects without looking through the window of the outward senses. The soul is capable of [seeing][164] God more immediately and more certainly and more fully and gloriously than the eye of the body is.'[165] Therefore, this 'intellectual' sight, this sight of the soul, is immediate: 'They shall see God as we immediately behold the sun after it is risen above the horizon, and no cloud or vapour in the heavens to hinder its light.'[166] Edwards's use of 'immediate' contrasts with ratiocination – not needing argumentation for clarity – as we behold the beauty of a sunset and know its beauty *immediately*. This navigates Edwards's concern in *Miscellanies* 777, that an unmediated sight could somehow 'search the heart and try the reins' of God himself, an activity only Christ has with the Father. Creaturely sight of God is always mediated by Christ, but the sight itself, the sight had through that mediation, is immediate. Edwards explains that this sight is perfect, if only perfect 'in its kind':

> It shall not be a comprehensive sight because 'tis impossible that a finite mind should comprehend God, but yet it shall be perfect in its kind. It shall be perfectly certain without any doubt or possibility of doubt. There shall be such a view of God in his being and in his power and holiness

---

[162] JEC, Unpublished Sermon, Rom. 2:10, #373 [L. 41r.].

[163] Edwards follows both Owen and Turretin by invoking God's invisibility, but he also utilizes angelology. He reasons that angels must have a sight of God, and being without a body, a pure sight of God must not depend upon a body.

[164] JEC, Unpublished Sermon, Rom. 2:10, #373 [L. 42v.]. The transcription has 'being' rather than 'seeing', but the context provides the obvious clue.

[165] JEC, Unpublished Sermon, Rom. 2:10, #373 [L. 42v.–L. 43r.]. Edwards also says that 'the soul is capable of apprehending God in a thousand times more perfect and glorious manner than the eye of the body is.' Ibid., [L. 42r.].

[166] JEC, Unpublished Sermon, Rom. 2:10, #373 [L. 43r.].

and goodness and love and all sufficiency that shall be attended with an intuitive certainty without any mixture of unbelief.[167]

In focusing his attention on Christ as both the object and mediator of the vision, Edwards clearly follows Owen's concerns, emphasizing the role of Christ as intrinsic to the vision itself. One sees Christ through one's eyes in his glorified body, which is the highest and most excellent bodily sight, and he is seen through an eye of the soul in his divine nature.

After addressing the faculty and the nature of sight, Edwards continues by offering a twofold analysis of the vision with respect to its object: first, the saints shall see everything in God that tends to excite and inflame love; and second, they shall see everything in him that gratifies love. Regarding the latter, Edwards asserts,

> This very manifestation that God will make of himself that will cause the beatifical vision will be an act of love in God. It will be from the exceeding love of God to them that he will give them this vision which will add an immense sweetness to it .... They shall see that he is their Father and that they are his children. They shall see God gloriously present with them; God with them and God in them and they in God .... Therefore *they shall see God as their own God*, when they behold this transcendent glory.[168]

The vision is had *in* an act of love. It could be this reality that Edwards was describing in the *Faithful Narrative* when discussing the woman who had 'immediate intercourse' with God, as a child with a father. This sight of God is not of an object abstracted from the concern of the saints but is a sight of God's very love *to them*, a vision of God *pro nobis*.[169] Musing upon this future reality, Edwards preaches that the saints will 'not only have a sight of the glorious attributes of God's goodness and mercy in their beatific vision of God, but they will be sensible of the exceeding greatness of the fruits of it; the greatness of the benefits that he has bestowed'.[170] Just as the inner-trinitarian life is one of personal beatific-delight, so too is participation within that life a participation *as a person* who delights beatifically in God.

---

[167] JEC, Unpublished Sermon, Rom. 2:10, #373 [L. 43r.–L.43v.].
[168] JEC, Unpublished Sermon, Rom. 2:10, #373 [L. 44r.–L.44v.] – my emphasis.
[169] Edwards states that 'when they see the beauty of God's holiness they shall see it *as their own* for them to enjoy forever. When they see the boundless ocean of God's goodness and grace *they shall see it to be all theirs*.' JEC, Unpublished Sermon, Rom. 2:10, #373 [L. 44r.] – my emphasis.
[170] JEC, Unpublished Sermon, Rev. 14:2, #344 (under Proposition II point 2).

Edwards continues by turning his attention to the *manner* in which the glorified shall see God through having communion with Christ:

> The saints shall enjoy God *as partaking with Christ of his enjoyment of God*, for they are united to him and are glorified and made happy in the enjoyment of God *as his members* .... They being in Christ *shall partake of the love of God the Father to Christ*, and as the son knows the Father so they shall *partake with him in his sight of God*, as being as it were parts of him as he is in the bosom of the Father.[171]

At some point after his earliest mention of the beatific vision as seeing Jehovah himself, Edwards orients the vision Christologically around *seeing Christ* as well as partaking in Christ's own sight of the Father.[172] In *Miscellanies* 1089, Edwards addresses the nature of the mystical body of Christ, shedding light on the reality of the saints' participation in the Father's love to Christ:

> For he is the head of the glorified body, and the sight of the eyes that are in the head are for the information of the whole body. And what he enjoys they enjoy. They are with him in his honor and advancement. They are with him in his pleasures; they are with him in his enjoyment of the Father's love, and the love wherewith the Father loves him is in them, and he in them [John 17:22].[173]

In this way, Edwards's vision goes beyond Owen's Christological orientation, making Christ both the object and the manner by which the vision of God is obtained. Looking back at his sermon on Romans 2.10, Edwards adds, 'They being in Christ shall partake of the love of God the Father to Christ, and as the Son knows the Father, so they shall partake with him in his sight of God, as being, as it were, parts of him.'[174] The saints enter into

---

[171] JEC, Unpublished Sermon, Rom. 2:10, #373 [L. 44v.] – my emphasis.

[172] In the mid-1730s, Edwards also preached a sermon on the excellency of Christ which might explain this partaking. There Edwards explains, 'For Christ being united to the human nature, we have advantage for a more free and full enjoyment of him, than we could have had if he had remained only in the divine nature. So again, we being united to a divine person, as his members, can have a more intimate union and intercourse with God the Father, who is only in the divine nature, than otherwise could be.' Jonathan Edwards, 'The Excellency of Christ', in *Sermons and Discourses, 1734–1738* (ed. M. X. Lesser; The Works of Jonathan Edwards, vol. 19; New Haven: Yale University Press, 2001), 593.

[173] Though this text is addressing the second period of heaven, its description holds true for the third period, but would be a greater fulfilment. Y20, '*Miscellanies* 1089. The Saints in Heaven', 470.

[174] JEC, Unpublished Sermon, Rom. 2:10, #373 [L. 44v].

God's existence of personal beatific-delight through their mystical union with Christ. Christ still mediates the vision of the Father, but the saints participate through their union to Christ's person in the inner-triune love that makes up God's life. Here, Edwards has come to view the beatific vision as a partaking in the personal relations existing within the trinitarian life of God. While Edwards has provided a strong Christological orientation to the vision, McDonald's question still remains: where is the Spirit?[175] Edwards does indeed provide a reply.

Following on the heels of *manner*, Edwards addresses the *means* by which God grants this vision to his saints, stating that the means by which God grants this vision to his saints is the Holy Ghost. 'By the Holy Ghost a spiritual sight of God is given in his world, so 'tis the same Holy Spirit by which a beatifical vision is given of God in Heaven.'[176] In Heaven, the saints are as dependent upon God as on earth for grace, holiness and light. Therefore, Edwards says that 'they shall have this beatifical vision of God because they will be full of God, filled with the Holy Spirit of God'.[177] It is hard to know how this 'because' functions here, but several things are clear based on his analysis: first, this vision is an 'intellectual' or 'spiritual' vision and is therefore attained by the work of the Spirit in the heart/soul of the glorified. Second, the beatific vision is effectual; the effect of the vision is tied to whether or not one is glorified by the vision. It is not surprising, then, that Edwards immediately addresses the effect of the vision after arguing for the necessity of the Spirit. Last, Edwards describes how the believer is drawn into the inner life of the Trinity through Christ, and the means by which this occurs is the work of the Spirit, the same Spirit who is the bond of union/love in the inner life of God. As noted above, God's manifestation of himself to the saints is 'an act of love in God', which we have noted is the Holy Spirit. God, in an act of love for his redeemed saints, binds them to his life through his overflowing love for them in Christ, the same love which he pours infinitely upon his Son.

Edwards's final point addresses the effects of the vision. He states that 'the soul hereby shall be inflamed with love'.[178] Furthermore, 'the soul

---

[175] We have already seen that God manifests himself *in* love, which is in fact the Spirit.

[176] JEC, Unpublished Sermon, Rom. 2:10, #373 [L. 45r.]. Importantly, Edwards ties the vision by the Spirit in the world with the vision in heaven. Edwards does not need to posit, with Owen, new 'visive faculties', turning instead to pneumatology.

[177] JEC, Unpublished Sermon, Rom. 2:10, #373 [L. 45r.].

[178] JEC, Unpublished Sermon, Rom. 2:10, #373 [L. 45r.]. In 1747 Edwards preached a funeral sermon for David Brainerd looking at 2 Cor. 5.8. There, he states: 'None sees God the Father immediately, who is "the King eternal, immortal, invisible": Christ is the "image of that invisible God", by which he is seen by all elect creatures. "The only begotten Son that is in the bosom of the Father, he hath declared him", and manifested him. "None has ever

shall not be an inactive spectator but shall be most active, shall be in the most ardent exercise of love towards the object seen. The soul shall be, as it were, all eye to behold, and yet all act to love';[179] the effect of this, Edwards says elsewhere, is 'happifying',[180] and following the God who exists in 'pure act', the soul is 'most active'.[181] Edwards emphasizes here that the human person is fully realized, with a properly functioning understanding and a perfectly oriented will. The understanding beholds without hindrance and loves without pride, 'adoring at God's feet and yet embraced in the arms of his love'.[182] The soul will be perfectly satisfied in every way, because it does not just receive the effects of God, but God himself: 'God will communicate and, as it were, *pour forth himself* into the soul.'[183]

Edwards, as we have seen, incorporated Owen's Christological focus of sight in heaven. But Edwards tempers Owen's suggestion by focusing not on the hypostatic union but rather on participation in the inner-trinitarian vision of love. In so doing, he focuses the beatific upon seeing God *pro nobis*, seeing God as he who unites believers to his own life. Edwards's view also fills the lacuna McDonald lamented concerning Owen's normally robust pneumatology, absent in his account of the beatific vision. By placing the vision in the context of the triune life, Edwards incorporates his understanding of the beatific nature of the Trinity *ad intra*, and his vision of the believer's participation within that life. It is within the person of Christ, the true mediator between God and humanity, that believers can now see and be seen, as they know and are known.

---

immediately seen the Father, but the Son"; and none else sees the Father any other way, than by "the Son's revealing him". And in heaven, the spirits of just men made perfect do see him as he is. They behold his glory. They see the glory of his divine nature, consisting in all the glory of the Godhead, the beauty of all his perfections; his great majesty, almighty power, his infinite wisdom, holiness and grace, and they see the beauty of his glorified human nature, and the glory which the Father hath given him, as God-man and Mediator .... And as they see the unspeakable riches and glory of the attribute of God's grace, so they most clearly behold and understand Christ's eternal and unmeasurable dying love to them in particular. And in short they see everything in Christ that tends to kindle and enflame love, and everything that tends to gratify love, and everything that tends to satisfy them.' Y25, 'True Saints are Present with the Lord', 230.

[179] JEC, Unpublished Sermon, Rom. 2:10, #373 [L. 45v.].
[180] Y17, 'The Pure in Heart Blessed', 63.
[181] In his sermon 'Serving God in Heaven', Edwards states that 'every faculty of the soul will be employed and exercised, and will be employed in vastly more lively, more exalted exercises than they are now, though without any labor or weariness'. Y17, 'Serving God in Heaven', 259.
[182] JEC, Unpublished Sermon, Rom. 2:10, #373 [L. 45v.].
[183] JEC, Unpublished Sermon, Rom. 2:10, #373 [L. 46r.] – my emphasis.

Conclusion

God's end in creating the world is to glorify himself. To do so, he creates a spouse for Christ to love as his perfect image, and he reveals himself to her so that she can partake of God's own life. God's end in creating for his own glory orients redemption toward receiving the elect into his own life to partake in his beatific-delight. God reveals himself in heaven through Christ, and this revelation is constituted by Christ's bodily presence as well as the display of his work in creation unto consummation. In consummation, the elect participate in Christ's own vision of the Father. Prior to consummation, the work of redemption is a Christological revelation to the creature, visible through sanctified/glorified eyes, whether through a glass darkly on earth or seen clearly in heaven. *Remanation*, therefore, just like emanation, is always Christologically mediated – highlighted by the metaphor of the church as bride and Christ as groom – with consummation depicted as an eternal wedding day.

Our focus on Edwards's doctrines of heaven and the beatific vision has sought to highlight the teleology of his theology. The end of the elect is oriented toward a vision of God, whose life is defined by infinite beauty, delight and communion. What is most relevant is that Edwards's theology of redemption, as seen through the *End of Creation* and the progression of heaven, is both pilgrim as well as beatific. In this sense, Edwards's vision of redemption is asymptotic in form. The saints in this life experience an ever-increasing, ever-deepening and ever-expanding love, union and delight in God for eternity. This reality, God's emanation *for the purpose of* remanation, serves as the guiding plumb line for the following chapters, in which we will look at spiritual knowledge, regeneration and religious affection. If, as we have seen, God's inner life of beatific-delight is the glory of his own personal nature that he communicates to his creation, how does the overflow of that glory, which culminates in the beatific vision just described, order and direct redemption? What, in other words, is the inauguration of this sight that culminates in the full beatific vision in eternity? How is the obtaining of that sight the impetus for remanating God's glory back to him through fallen creaturely reality? These questions will help guide the following analysis of key doctrines of redemption as we consider them in light of our heuristic key.

Interlude: The Heuristic Key

It proves instructive to pause momentarily for some reflection on what has preceded and what will follow. If we think of the movement of this volume as a three-act play, this interlude calls our attention to the context, characters and plot line this story has developed thus far. Only grasping what has gone before will we truly understand what lies ahead. Without the first two acts of the play, which, respectively, introduce the characters and give them depth, context and meaning (read: doctrine of God), and then develop the plot further (read: doctrines of creation and consummation), the third act will inevitably appear shallow and confused. Such is the history of interpretation of Edwards's theology. The loose ends found throughout Edwards's corpus are rarely tied together because the first two acts of the play are either ignored or made to follow other imagined plot lines. Inevitably, these loose ends never fully find resolution. In this interlude, I develop a terse statement of our heuristic key (the first two acts), mined from Edwards's thought and developed along a trinitarian trajectory. This heuristic key, I have argued, orders Edwards's theology, and by this framework all things hold together.

As I have emphasized in the first three chapters, God, as the sovereign creator and redeemer, is the God of personal beatific-delight. My heuristic key entails a 'top-down' reading of Edwards's theology, with the trinitarian God as the ontological and organizing principle of his thought. The three central categories – person, beatific and delight – appropriated to Father, Son and Spirit respectively, make a tight three-cord thread which is woven from the inner life of God through to creation and consummation. *This God of personal beatific-delight redeems persons by revealing himself beatifically and glorifying himself in the creature's delightful response.* In creating for his own glory, God binds creaturely realities to his self-glorification, wherein he unites creatures to his Son by his Spirit for true participation in the divine life of beatific-delight.

The scope of Edwards's theological project, therefore, articulates God's movement 'from glory to glory'. Glory in its eternal existence is God's personal life of beatific-delight. As a communicative being, God communicates this glory to his creation and seeks a return – emanation and remanation, as we have seen. Eternity is an ever-increasing asymptotic increase in union and communion, where the glorified creature participates through Christ in the inner life of God. Glory has returned to its fountain because God made creatures such that they could receive emanation and remanate glory back to God. Or, in Edwards's summary, "'From glory to glory", that is, changed from the glory of God, from a sight of his glory, "to glory", to a glory in ourselves like it.'[1] This is, in short, the structure of emanation and remanation, or, as I have termed it, God's beatific self-glorification. This is the engine that drives the wheels of redemption, each following a specific cycle until all ends when *the* wheel of history returns to God in judgement.

This account serves as an interpretative scheme, what we could call 'God's beatific self-glorification', by pinpointing theology proper, God's end in creation and consummation as grounding and organizing principles of Edwards's theology. Ultimately, God's trinitarian nature determines Edwards's entire theology, in which God's end in creating and consummating serves as second-order architecture to delineate how *this* God relates to his creatures. Reading Edwards the 'right-way-round', therefore, is reading Edwards according to his theological and specifically Reformed genius. As a Reformed theologian, Edwards's trinitarian thought grounds his theology and locates creation and consummation within the redemptive movement of the triune God. To put this another way, God's persons and his work in redemption function to orient doctrinal questions accordingly. This 'key' locates doctrines such that every question finds its answer in the God of redemption. This, I suggest, is the proper way to read Edwards. To demonstrate the interpretative power of this heuristic key, I turn our attention to creaturely reception of emanation and the turn to remanation by applying our key to spiritual knowledge, regeneration and religious affection. It would be a mistake, I should note, to see these three doctrines as simply case studies. Rather, these are extensions of the interpretative architecture developed in the first two sections. To foreshadow how this plot finds resolution, and to affirm the interpretative power of my scheme, is to do the same thing – namely, show how personhood, beatific-delight and glory are the structuring principles of Edwards's theology. These are the central features of my heuristic key – the schematic for Edwards's theology – such that Edwards's development of doctrine should follow these contours.

[1] Y15, '89. 2 Corinthians 3:17-18', 76.

Section 3

Redemption as Remanation

'A man, when he is converted, he begins that work that he is not only to spend all his life in, but to spend his eternity in.'[1]

'The love of Christ another way tends to sweeten and endear all his virtues and excellencies, viz. as his love has brought him into such a relation to us as our friend, our elder brother, our Lord, our head and spiritual husband, our Redeemer, and hath brought us into so strict an union with him that our souls are his beloved bride. Yea, we are the members of his body, his flesh and his bone (Ephesians 5:30).'[2]

'But the holiness of Christians is merely and entirely a reflection of God's light, or communications of God's righteousness, and not one jot of it is owing to ourselves. 'Tis wholly a creature of God's, a new creature; 'tis Christ within us.'[3]

[1] Y17, 'Serving God in Heaven', 260.
[2] Y16, 'To Lady Mary Pepperrell', 418.
[3] Y13, *Miscellanies 66. Righteousness*, 236.

Chapter 4

Spiritual Knowledge

In framing the themes of redemption, we have thus far focused on God's inner life, God's purpose in creating and his work of consummation. This development, I have suggested, provides the necessary dogmatic machinery for understanding Edwards's doctrines of redemption.[1] Instead of offering a comprehensive analysis of redemption, I address spiritual knowledge, regeneration and religious affection as three essential moments on the turn from emanation to remanation, where God pulls creatures within his own self-glorification. These three moments serve as occasions to apply and extend my overarching heuristic proposal. If our previous analysis stands, it should afford new insight into aspects of Edwards's thought that have been neglected, misunderstood or underdeveloped. In what follows, I highlight the interpretative gains of our account by examining three topics often left muddy in other nonsystematic analyses. I suggest that a distinctively dogmatic account of the sort advanced here, focusing on the triune God's immanent life and willed economic mission to create, sustain and redeem, provides the necessary context for investigating underdeveloped doctrines (spiritual knowledge), for correcting misinterpretation (regeneration) and for integrating with Edwards's overarching theological task (religious affection).

---

[1] A thoroughly robust analysis of redemption would have to consider the person and work of Christ in his mediation, as well as questions concerning Edwards's covenant schema and issues related to the Spirit's work (some of which will be addressed below). Noteworthy contributions to these areas are: Craig Biehl, *The Infinite Merit of Christ: The Glory of Christ's Obedience in the Theology of Jonathan Edwards* (Jackson: Reformed Academic Press, 2009); Robert W. Jenson, *America's Theologian: A Recommendation of Jonathan Edwards* (Oxford: Oxford University Press, 1988), 111–22; Jenson, 'Christology', in *The Princeton Companion to Jonathan Edwards* (ed. Sang Hyun Lee; Princeton: Princeton University Press, 2005), 72–86; Robert W. Caldwell, *Communion in the Spirit: The Holy Spirit as the Bond of Union in the Theology of Jonathan Edwards* (Studies in Evangelical History and Thought; Waynesboro: Paternoster, 2006), 55–86, and, most impressively, Seng-Kong Tan, 'Trinitarian Action in the Incarnation', in *Jonathan Edwards as Contemporary: Essays in Honor of Sang Hyun Lee* (ed. Don Schweitzer; New York, Peter Lang, 2010), 127–50.

While the chapters below are specific applications of our interpretative scheme, it would be misguided to assume that they are three hermetically sealed categories. In fact, this section will broadly sketch three integrated doctrines, explicating Edwards's comment noted above, that conversion inaugurates the work of *eternal* life. The kind of redemption Edwards envisages, in other words, entails a *new kind of sight*, spiritual sight made possible by the regeneration of the elect, which in turn enables a Godward movement of the soul in understanding and will. This movement, known as religious affection, will be shown to mirror the processions of Word and Spirit in God's own life as knowledge and love in redeemed humanity. In applying my heuristic to *these* doctrinal issues, I sketch a rough account of how God redeems the elect through his self-glorifying beatific-delight, and expand my interpretative key to include 'anchor points' in redemption. This account, in brief, is that God's inner life of personal beatific-delight is the archetype which emanates economically through the Son and the Spirit, the Son as God's perfect understanding and the Spirit as his love/delight, which together provide truly *beatific* knowledge (knowledge in the mode of seeing God affectionately). Unable to obtain this sight through natural capacities, God regenerates the elect by uniting them to Christ, illuminating God's beauty and infusing his *Holy* Spirit. Able to see clearly, though still clouded by sin, the regenerate mirror God's own processions of understanding and will by seeing God and pouring forth in affection.

It is my contention that spiritual knowledge in Edwards's thought must be explored through this larger dogmatic account. In what follows, I ground Edwards's understanding of spiritual knowledge in his theology in three ways. First, I show that spiritual knowledge is substantiated by the beatific. The beatific thread in Edwards's thought starts in God's inner life and is woven through the work of redemption toward consummation, where it finds its fulfilment in eternity. Second, in my previous analysis I developed God's movement toward the creature as well as his completion of that movement, emanation and remanation respectively. This context provides the theological moorings for spiritual knowledge and the redemption of fallen creatures. In this sense, the economic life of God entails the Son as both the image and mediator of revelation, as well as the Spirit who illuminates Christ, infuses grace and unites the believer to Christ. Last, while I frame redemption broadly, and spiritual knowledge specifically, with creation and consummation, it is further necessary to emphasize the role consummation plays in proleptically orienting spiritual knowledge.[2]

[2] I do not address the nature of the mind and imagination in Edwards's thought, as important

By way of contrast, Edwards commentators have tended to focus on Locke when questions arise concerning Edwards's epistemology.[3] Likewise, in addressing spiritual knowledge directly, Miklos Veto and Michael McClymond follow Miller's *philosophical* inclination, now read as Neo-Platonic tendencies.[4] Far from simply poaching Neo-Platonic categories, Edwards, I argue, puts his trinitarian theology to work in grounding the task, means and goal of redemption in *who God is*. In an important statement, Edwards integrates spiritual knowledge with God's beatific self-glorification:

> How good is God, that he has created man for this very end, to make him happy in the enjoyment of himself, the Almighty, who was happy from the days of eternity in himself, in the beholding of his own infinite beauty: the Father in the beholding and love of his Son, his perfect and most excellent image, the brightness of his own glory; and the Son in the love and enjoyment of the Father. And God needed no more, could accede no more. ... 'Twas not that he might be made more happy himself, but that [he] might make something else happy; *that he might make them blessed in the beholding of his excellency, and might this way glorify himself.*[5]

Edwards depicts God's life as the mutual beholding of infinite beauty. God created humanity that another being might partake in God's goodness and delight. This beatific-delight, as I developed in the first chapter and traced into creation and consummation, provides the theological setting for talking about Edwards's understanding of spiritual knowledge. To

as those themes are. My focus here is on the broader-level theological moves which will ground his other material. This is particularly relevant for the material on the mind which is often both early as well as solely relegated to the notes. For helpful discussions, see Sang Hyun Lee, 'Jonathan Edwards' Theory of the Imagination', *The Michigan Academician*, no. 23 (1972), 233–41; Lee, *The Philosophical Theology of Jonathan Edwards* (Princeton: Princeton University Press, 1988), 115–69. See also Stephen H. Daniel, *The Philosophy of Jonathan Edwards: A Study in Divine Semiotics* (Bloomington: Indiana University Press, 1994), 88, 93–9; and Y6, 'Editor's Introduction', 111–36.

[3] I agree with Helm that Edwards borrowed from Locke but never became 'Lockean' in any meaningful way. See Paul Helm, 'John Locke and Jonathan Edwards: A Reconsideration', *Journal of the History of Ideas* 7, no. 1 (1969), 51–61 (51). The shape of Edwards's account, in other words, is based on the Reformed theology handed him, while his appropriation took on Lockean characteristics (new simple idea, meaning, etc.). These are, of course, not irrelevant. For an important point about Edwards's later critiques of Locke's epistemology, see Robert E. Brown, 'Edwards, Locke, and the Bible', *Journal of Religion* 79 (1999), 361–84 and Y6, 'Editor's Introduction', 111–36.

[4] Michael J. McClymond, *Encounters with God: An Approach to the Theology of Jonathan Edwards* (Oxford: Oxford University Press, 1998), 25–6; Miklos Veto, 'Spiritual Knowledge According to Jonathan Edwards', *Calvin Theological Journal* 31 (1996), 161–81.

[5] Y14, 'Nothing Upon Earth Can Represent the Glories of Heaven', 153 – my emphasis.

illuminate the major movements of his account, I first turn to Edwards's exposition of Mt. 5:8, using that to highlight his concerns. Second, in keeping with my emphasis that Edwards was fundamentally a good *Reformed* theologian, my interpretative lens on spiritual knowledge is the Reformed orthodox distinction between archetypal and ectypal knowledge, whose contours he creatively traces.[6] The purpose of this backdrop is not to provide an expansive account but to offer a systematic reconstruction within the context of Edwards's own theological milieu and to show how his development of God's knowledge as personal beatific-delight forms all creaturely (spiritual) knowledge. The remainder of this chapter addresses his Christological orientation, the affective dimension of knowledge and the heavenly directed nature of spiritual knowledge *as sight.*

I Seeing God: The Beatified Pilgrim

In providing a sketch of Edwards's position at the outset, I outline Edwards's move to collapse the pilgrim and beatific into one mode of knowing, forcing all spiritual knowledge into a pilgrim-beatific form, which I alluded to in the section on heaven. To do so, I return to key elements of Edwards's sermon on Matthew 5.8, which I analyzed in the section on his understanding of the beatific vision.[7] Edwards's exposition initially addresses the concept of seeing God, noting first that God is not seen with bodily eyes. In his words, '[True] blessedness of the soul don't enter in at that door.'[8] God is invisible, therefore seeing God 'implies a seeing God glorious and seeing him gracious, a seeing the light of his countenance both as it is understood of the effulgence of his glory and the manifestation of his favor and love'.[9] To buttress his assertions, Edwards turns to exegetical matters. First, Moses saw God's goodness, which is not visible itself but is a spiritual reality. Likewise, Edwards interprets the transfiguration as an outward manifestation of an inward beauty. While the disciples

---

[6] McClymond notes the archetype and ectype but does so through Neo-Platonic participation. See McClymond, *Encounters with God*, 25–6; and Veto, *Spiritual Knowledge*, 161–81. As should be clear, I think this is a mistake. It would be naive, however, to deny that Edwards employs Neo-Platonic contours to his thought. On my view, though, these contours are read through his Reformed theology and do not orient the account itself. In other words, I believe that the term 'Neo-Platonic' becomes a very easy way to put Edwards into a tradition but that this is not the tradition Edwards is closest to. The turn to philosophy comes too quickly and ends up providing an overly reductionistic portrayal of Edwards's thought.

[7] Y17, 'The Pure in Heart Blessed', 59–86.

[8] Y17, 'The Pure in Heart Blessed', 61.

[9] Y17, 'The Pure in Heart Blessed', 65.

saw Jesus with bodily eyes, it was still the spiritual sight that grasped the real *spiritual* reality. He points to John 1.14 as well, that the Word was made flesh and was full of 'grace and truth'. Again, the incarnate Christ was seen with bodily eyes, but grace and truth were not; these realities are discerned spiritually, with the eye of the soul.[10]

Advancing his exegetical insights, Edwards suggests that the sight of God is an intellectual sight: 'God is a spiritual being, and he is beheld with the understanding. The soul has in itself those powers whereby it is capable of apprehending objects, and especially spiritual objects.'[11] Here Edwards spells out his understanding of seeing God most clearly: 'But to see God is this: it is to have an immediate and certain understanding of God's glorious excellency and love.'[12] This sight is immediate, Edwards explains, 'to distinguish from a mere acknowledging that God is glorious and excellent by ratiocination, which is a more indirect and mediate way of apprehending things than intuitive knowledge'.[13] Sight of God, in other words, is revealed sight and cannot be had by mere speculation. Furthermore, *seeing* God truly entails affection – creaturely sight of God mirrors the archetype of God's own life of seeing himself and delighting – therefore, seeing God is that which is 'truly happifying to the soul'.[14] Edwards admits that the vision prior to heaven entails mediation through the gospel (as in a glass darkly), but this still entails true sight directly imparted to the soul.[15] While the sight in heaven is 'especially' called seeing God, its earthly counterpart is the dawning of that light; it is the same light mediated through the gospel.[16]

Faith and sight, rather than being contraries, are for Edwards united in a spiritual register. Spiritual knowledge is the merging of the beatific vision, a happifying sight, with a spiritual sense of the soul, what Edwards calls the 'sense of the heart' given in regeneration. Therefore, pilgrim creaturely

---

[10] Y17, 'The Pure in Heart Blessed', 62–3. John Owen makes the same observation, positing faith as the 'sight' by which the disciples saw Jesus as grace and truth. John Owen, *The Glory of Christ* (ed. William H. Goold; The Works of John Owen, vol. 1; London: Banner of Truth Trust, 1965), 289.

[11] Y17, 'The Pure in Heart Blessed', 63. He continues by stating, 'There is a more perfect way of perception than by the eyes of the body. We are so accustomed and habituated to depend upon our senses, and our intellectual powers are so neglected and disused, that we are ready to conceive that seeing things with the bodily eyes is the most perfect way of apprehending them. But it is not so; the eye of the soul is vastly nobler than the eye of the body.' Y17, 'The Pure in Heart Blessed', 63.

[12] Y17, 'The Pure in Heart Blessed', 64.

[13] Y17, 'The Pure in Heart Blessed', 64. Notice that Edwards's use of 'immediate' here follows his typical usage of 'not mediate'. Here, this point is stated explicitly, as he contrasts this immediate knowledge with ratiocination.

[14] Y17, 'The Pure in Heart Blessed', 64.

[15] Y17, 'The Pure in Heart Blessed', 65.

[16] Y17, 'The Pure in Heart Blessed', 65.

existence is quickened by a mediated sight of God, which continues on the same trajectory through life and death, when it is had immediately (with clear views, though still mediated Christologically) in heaven. In other words, seeing God on earth *is a species* of the saints' sight of God in heaven. This sight of God is not, as noted in the last chapter, a vision of God as if he were an unrelated object. Quite the opposite in fact. The saints see God *pro nobis*: 'He is graciously present with them, and when they see him they see him and know him to be so. They have an understanding of his love *to them*; they see him from love manifesting himself *to them*.'[17] The blessed sight of God is not beautiful because it is *pro nobis*, but it is beautiful and it is *pro nobis*. This sight is not purposeless, but purposeful; it is happifying. 'He that has a blessed-making sight of God, he not only has a view of God's glory and excellency, but he views it as having a propriety in it. They also see God's love to them; they receive the testimonies and manifestations of that.'[18]

In summary, Edwards expands the category of the beatific to include the person and work of Christ. In his words, 'the principal discoveries of God's mind and will to mankind were reserved to be given by Jesus Christ, his own Son and the Redeemer of men, who is the light of the world.'[19] This light, known in both his person and work, is had by both saints in heaven (with clear views) and saints on earth (through a glass darkly). As known by faith, this sight is imperfect, but it is truly seen spiritually, necessitating a work of the Spirit in regeneration (illumination). As a sight of God, a true sight, it is beatific and therefore 'happifying', or, as we will say here, affectionate – inclining the affections to God. To see God affectionately is to know him, not as an object, but as a subject, and therefore we know him personally (i.e. in his truth, beauty and love).

As I have noted in my previous analysis, God's triune life is religious affection in pure act – God sees himself and flows forth in infinite affection to himself – and this serves as the archetype for creaturely knowledge of God. Furthermore, God creates the world for self-glorification, and the means by which he self-glorifies is by allowing creaturely participation in his self-knowing and self-willing. In other words, God's personal beatific-delight is had by other *persons*, who receive spiritual sight through their understanding and who delight through their wills. In doing so, God is glorified, there is emanation – communication of God's 'nature' through vision and regeneration – and there is remanation – God receiving glory through creaturely participation. As spiritual sight (entailing participation), it is only through

---

[17] Y17, 'The Pure in Heart Blessed', 64 – my emphasis.
[18] Y17, 'The Pure in Heart Blessed', 64.
[19] Y17, 'The Pure in Heart Blessed', 59.

grace and regeneration that the elect come to have affectionate knowledge of God. This affectionate knowledge of God does not undermine, but in fact upholds, the creature as a rational creature. In Edwards's words,

> But in this kind of delight in seeing of God, the understanding approves of it. It is a thing most agreeable to reason that the soul should delight itself in this, and the more reason is in exercise, the more it approves of it; so that when it is enjoyed, it is with inward peace and a sweet tranquility of soul. There is nothing in human nature that is opposite to it, but everything agrees and consents to it.[20]

In order to flesh out this account, as noted above, I highlight Edwards's use of the archetypal/ectypal distinction against a broad Reformed backdrop and further detail Edwards's development of spiritual knowledge as pilgrim-beatific.

II Reformed Backdrop: Archetypal and Ectypal

Michael Horton rightly claims, 'This distinction between archetypal and ectypal knowledge is the epistemological corollary of the Creator-creature distinction.'[21] All infinite knowledge maps on to the archetypal, while all finite knowledge dispenses into different categories of ectypal. Along these lines, John Owen, in his own discussion concerning the nature of theology, states,

> Therefore, as that attribute of God by which He comprehends Himself and all of His perfections is an infinite attribute, it can be entered into by no other being. ... We will say, then, that this attribute of absolute Godhead, to know 'first-truths' in knowing, comprehending and loving itself, may not improperly be called 'archetypal theology'.[22]

---

[20] Y17, 'The Pure in Heart Blessed', 67.

[21] Michael Scott Horton, *Lord and Servant: A Covenant Christology* (Louisville: Westminster John Knox Press, 2005), 17. Likewise, Muller states, 'Revelation, given in a finite and understandable form, must truly rest on the eternal truth of God: this is the fundamental message and intention of the distinction between archetypal and ectypal theology.' Richard A. Muller, *Prolegomena to Theology* (Post-Reformation Reformed Dogmatics, vol. 1; Grand Rapids: Baker Academic, 2nd edn, 2003), 229.

[22] John Owen, *Biblical Theology, or, the Nature, Origin, Development, and Study of Theological Truth, in Six Books: In Which Are Examined the Origins and Progress of Both True and False Religious Worship, and the Most Notable Declensions and Revivals of the Church, from the Very Beginning of the World*, (Morgan: Soli Deo Gloria Publications, 1994), 15.

While this distinction does, in an epistemological register, uphold the Creator-creature distinction, its purpose is to bracket the theological task within and under God's self-revelation, thereby making theological knowledge relational knowledge.[23] Ectypal theology is most often distributed into three modes of creaturely knowing: union, which is the knowledge available to Christ; vision, the knowledge had by the beatified; and revelation, which is knowledge functioning within a pilgrim or viator mode.[24] As Muller explains, 'This substantially singular theology, as known infinitely and absolutely by the divine subject, God, is archetypal; as known finitely and relatively by the creaturely subject, ectypal.'[25]

Turretin likewise acknowledges a threefold division of theology (where theology is taken as ectypal): natural, supernatural and beatific, explaining, 'the first from the light of reason, the second from the light of faith, and third from the light of glory'.[26] The first is natural theology and as such belongs to all humankind. The second is a subgenus of persons who make up the church, the elect, and the third are those elect participating in the beatific vision in heaven.[27] Holding Edwards against this backdrop highlights both the similarity and difference between Edwards and his Reformed predecessors.

---

[23] As noted by Asselt, 'As will become clear, the importance of this distinction is that it serves to clarify the idea that the Reformed conception of Christian theology is fundamentally a relational enterprise, determined by and determinative of the divine-human relationship.' Willem J. van Asselt, 'The Fundamental Meaning of Theology: Archetypal and Ectypal Theology in Seventeenth-Century Reformed Thought', *Westminster Theological Journal* 64, no. 2 (2002), 320–37 (325).

[24] See Sebastian Rehnman, *Divine Discourse: The Theological Methodology of John Owen* (Texts and Studies in Reformation and Post-Reformation Thought; Grand Rapids: Baker Academic, 2002), 57; Asselt, 'Fundamental Meaning of Theology', 331; Muller, *Prolegomena to Theology*, 230, 235. Rehnman states, concerning these categories, 'A similar concise rehearsal is found in Mastricht, Turretin, Coccejus, Baxter, and Braunius.' Rehnman, *Divine Discourse*, 57. Further, Rehnman notes, 'Ectypal theology can be distinguished according to its causality, which is either of nature or above nature; supernatural or revealed ectypal theology is subdivided according to the subject. The latter is in descending order either of Jesus Christ, of angels, or of men. Human ectypal theology can be further distinguished into that of pilgrims or of the blessed, and the theology of pilgrims is further subdivided into *ante lapsum* and *post lapsum*.' Rehnman, *Divine Discourse*, 63.

[25] Muller, *Prolegomena to Theology*, 230.

[26] Turretin, *Institutes of Elenctic Theology* (ed. James T. Dennison; trans. George Musgrave Giger; vol. 1; Phillipsburg: P&R, 1992), 5.

[27] For Turretin on archetypal and ectypal, see Martin I. Klauber, 'Francis Turretin on Biblical Accommodation: Loyal Calvinist or Reformed Scholastic?', *Westminster Theological Journal* 55 (1993), 74–86; Timothy Ross Phillips, 'Francis Turretin's Idea of Theology' (unpublished doctoral dissertation, Vanderbilt University, 1986), 121–35; Richard A. Muller, 'Scholasticism Protestant and Catholic: Francis Turretin on the Object and Principles of Theology', *Church History* 55, no. 2 (1986), 193–206.

III Edwards's Use of the Archetypal/Ectypal Distinction

Turning our attention to Edwards, we find that here the careful exposition of the triune God in Chapter 1 is put to work. God is who he is as Trinity. Edwards's God is the God of personal beatific-delight. Archetypal theology, on Edwards's view, is the Father gazing upon his Son in perfect and infinite self-knowing, spirating happiness that is unchanging, eternal and pure act. The Son in his procession is God's self-understanding, and the Spirit pours forth as love, the bond of union within the inner life of God. Ectypal theology is based on this pattern of trinitarian knowing that mirrors the processions of understanding and willing in creaturely existence, pressing ectypal knowledge into a visual and affectionate mold. As seen above, for emanation to return as remanation, God must communicate *himself* to persons – those with understanding and will – who must receive this communication through understanding and must respond affectionately through the will, thereby mirroring God's own life. This is not without precedent in the tradition:

> In Cocceius' view, moreover, the *theologia archetypa* is an inward trinitarian knowing, the Father knowing the Son, the Son knowing the Father, and the Spirit searching out the deep things of God – a cognitive parallel with Cocceius' doctrine of the *pactum salutis*. Cocceius' definition of archetypal theology also coincides with his insistence that theology is a practical discipline oriented toward the goal of salvation.[28]

Edwards makes a similar move but adapts it at key points according to his doctrine of the Trinity. The *theologia archetypa* entails an inward trinitarian knowing, but it is more correctly a trinitarian experience of beatific glory. The material parallel for Edwards, similarly, is God's economic movement to redeem through God's self-understanding revealed in his Son and the union, illumination and infusion of the Spirit in the elect. For Edwards, elect creatures mirror the inner-trinitarian seeing with sanctified vision, inclining them to the glory of God through spiritual apprehension. True knowledge of God is *personal* – known through seeing and experiencing God – and is necessarily affectionate. Therefore, taking God's life *ad intra* as the fountainhead, coupled with the horizon of consummation as the channel to which Edwards's theology of redemption flows, one might assume that categories of beatific and progressive growth take precedence

---

[28] Muller, *Prolegomena to Theology*, 234.

in Edwards's understanding of spiritual knowledge, which has been our continued emphasis.

Therefore, our attending to Edwards's understanding of spiritual knowledge must take place, as here, within a beatific register. Edwards clearly follows his Reformed predecessors in positing the beatific vision in heaven. However, it is not accurate, I claim, on Edwards's view, to argue that sight somehow replaces faith. While it is standard to pit faith and sight against one another as mutually exclusive realities,[29] or as the defining features of pilgrim and glorified existence respectively, Edwards refused to follow suit.[30] Edwards pulls the pilgrim nature of earthly existence into

[29] John Owen states, 'There are, therefore, two ways or degrees of beholding the glory of Christ, which are constantly distinguished in the Scripture. The one is by *faith*, in this world – which is "the evidence of things not seen"; the other is by *sight*, or immediate vision in eternity, 2 Cor. V. 7, "We walk by faith, and not by sight."' Owen, *Glory of Christ*, 288. Interestingly, Owen does use vision language to develop his understanding of faith. It is not as strong as Edwards's usage, but could be the place Edwards discovered it. There is a tradition to see faith as a kind of seeing which Edwards seems to be radicalizing here. Richard Sibbes is a noteworthy example: 'A weak sight here by faith changeth us; but a strong sight, when we shall see face to face, perfectly changeth us.' Richard Sibbes, *The Works of Richard Sibbes* (vol. 4; Edinburgh: James Nichol, 1863), 290.

[30] Paul Ramsey makes the same observation (see Y8, 'Appendix III: Heaven is a Progressive State', 716). In 1734, Edwards preached that 'faith shall cease in vision, and hope in fruition, but love never faileth'. JEC, Unpublished Sermon, Rev. 14:2, #344. If this is Edwards's final position, then the consummation of all things is the only 'era' where faith and sight become mutually exclusive. However, Edwards is clearly addressing 1 Cor. 13:8 in the immediate context, where prophecies, tongues and knowledge will fail, but love will last forever. Later in the 1730s, Edwards makes the same claim, saying, 'When other things shall fail by death, when faith shall cease and be turned into vision, and hope shall cease and be turned into fruition in heaven, love shall not cease but only be perfected. That love which in this world is but a spark shall in heaven be blown up to a flame.' Jonathan Edwards, 'The Spirit of the True Saints Is a Spirit of Divine Love', in *The Glory and Honor of God: Volume 2 of the Previously Unpublished Sermons of Jonathan Edwards* (ed. Michael D. McMullen; Nashville: Broadman & Holman, 2004), 314. In contrast, when Edwards preached his sermon series 'Charity and Its Fruit' in 1738, he had clearly moved beyond his earlier position to state, 'Saving faith and hope have love as an ingredient in them and as the essence of them.' Y8, 'Charity and Its Fruits', 355. By putting love at the essence of faith and hope, there is a real sense that it is impossible for them to cease. This makes reasonable sense with faith, which Edwards ties to 'closing' with Christ, but it is hard to know what this could mean for hope. It could be that Edwards is reiterating his distinction from sermon 10, 'Grace Tends to Holy Practice', by delineating saving and common faith and hope. The faith that ceases then would be common faith rather than saving. Y8, 'Charity and Its Fruits', 299. Take for instance his comment in sermon 14, 'Divine Love Alone Lasts Eternally': 'Though when wicked men die, who have had common enlightenings and motions of the Spirit, their gifts shall eternally cease, and their common temporary faith which they have had, which has had no divine love as an ingredient in it and to be the soul of it shall cease.' Y8, 'Charity and Its Fruits', 359. At first glance, Edwards seems to contradict this a few pages later when he claims that 'faith fails' (Y8, 'Charity and Its Fruits', 362), but this is in reference to the miraculous gifts given in the early church. Tyron Edwards must have realized the seeming contradiction and deleted 'and faith fails' in his edition. Y8, 'Charity and Its Fruits', 362n8. Later in the sermon still, Edwards suggests, 'If ever you arrive at heaven, faith and love must be the wings which must carry you there.' Y8, 'Charity and Its Fruits', 397. Commenting on this passage, Ramsey

the heavenly realm, making heaven a progressive state of existence, and extends the beatific vision of eternity back into Christian existence; it is, in fact, already the reality of the regenerate, who have the 'sense of the heart', the sanctified vision of the redeemed. Therefore, here, I briefly exposit Edwards's use of these distinctions, focusing our attention on his merging of the pilgrim with the beatific.

Edwards, admittedly, refrains from using the language of archetypal and ectypal, but he clearly assumes the categories themselves. As we have seen, in God's inner life the Son *actually is* God's understanding, thereby providing the archetype.[31] Knowledge of God, therefore, exists archetypally as the Father contemplating his own understanding affectionately. The way Edwards epistemologically orients creaturely knowledge of God, and God's self-knowledge, is with the language of sight.[32] As I have shown, in Edwards's depiction of the Trinity, God's life entails a mutual beatific gazing between the Father and Son. Likewise, it is fitting that Christ would take on the prophetical (revelatory) office in the economy, because he is God's actual wisdom and omniscience, therefore Jesus's role for creaturely knowledge is revelation.[33]

According to Edwards's trinitarian theology, the archetypal/ectypal distinction focuses all knowledge of God *Christologically*, which, in turn, emphasizes its revealed character. Following the Reformed distinction of Christ's human knowledge as by union, Edwards, states in *Miscellanies* 777,

> Jesus Christ is admitted to know God immediately; but the knowledge of all other creatures in heaven and earth is by means, or by manifestations or signs held forth. And Jesus Christ, who alone sees immediately, [is] the grand medium of the knowledge of all others; they know no otherwise

notes, 'Apparently Edwards does not join those who hold that faith disappears in sight and hope in realization, while only charity lasts eternally.' Y8, 'Editor's Introduction', 103.

[31] As we see below, it is not simply knowledge that is the archetype, but the corresponding procession of the Spirit as the love/happiness of God. All true knowledge of God takes on this affective form.

[32] In the *Religious Affections*, Edwards makes the following claim about the importance of knowledge: 'Knowledge is the key that first opens the hard heart and enlarges the affections, and so opens the way for men into the kingdom of heaven.' Y2, *Religious Affections*, 266.

[33] See JEC, Unpublished Sermon, Deut. 18:18, #743. Also, Edwards links God's glory being revealed in Jesus and his prophetic office in JEC, Unpublished Sermon, 2 Cor. 3:18, #72. Furthermore, 'We can give reasons for it [revelation of Christ] now it is revealed, and it seems so rational, that one would think the light of nature sufficient to discover it. ... For all that philosophy and human wisdom could do, it was the gospel that first taught the world wherein mankind's true blessedness consisted, and told them the way to come to it.' Y17, 'The Pure in Heart Blessed', 74; see also Y22, 'The Importance and Advantage of a Thorough Knowledge of Divine Truth', 85–6.

than by the exhibitions held forth in and by him, as the Scripture is express.[34]

Christ's immediate ectypal knowledge of God is revealed to the elect through Christ's person and work. Edwards develops a clear archetypal/ ectypal distinction, utilizing his demarcation of union and beatific.[35] Admittedly, Edwards does not use the language of pilgrim or viator very often, although in *Miscellanies* 435 he claims that the church's earthly state is viatory and itinerary. Furthermore, Edwards freely uses journey language to exposit the Christian life, which is simply a gloss on 'pilgrim'. Edwards's avoidance of the technical archetypal/ectypal terminology could very well be accounted for because of the polemical nature of his texts, but in any case, the theological substance remains intact.

Importantly, for Edwards, ectypal knowledge mirrors the knowledge of other persons. Personal knowledge is either essential (spiritual, bodily, etc.) or characterological (good, faithful, etc.), with the characterological aspect necessitating revelation (a *self*-revealing through word and deed). As I have already noted, *Miscellanies* 777 expounds upon the idea of revealed knowledge by positing four distinct signs by which a 'spiritual being' can be manifested to another: (1) images or resemblances; (2) words and declarations; (3) effects (through deductions) and; (4) a priori. Edwards expands:

'Tis in these ways only that we see and know one another's souls or minds: either by that image and resemblance there is in the body, and its air and motions of the sense and affections, and motions of the mind; or by words or voluntary significations we make to each other, of what we are conscious of in our own minds, by voice, writing, or other signs; or from the effects we see of each other's thoughts, choice, sense and exercises of mind in our actions and works; and as we may argue something about each other a priori.[36]

Here, Edwards's first move is to put knowledge of God in the same overall category of *knowing other minds*. This is a corollary to my emphasis on God qua persons relating to creatures qua persons. As I emphasize below, coming to know God is only possible through the first two signs – images and words. Believers, therefore, only come to know God *in Christ*, the

---

[34] Y18, '*Miscellanies* 777. Happiness of Heaven is Progressive', 428.
[35] In his explanation, Christ 'sees' immediately, suggesting that Christ's knowledge by union is also oriented beatifically.
[36] Y18, '*Miscellanies* 777. Happiness of Heaven is Progressive', 429.

internal image and word of God who put on flesh and revealed himself to creatures. Furthermore, knowing God entails knowing a real (intrinsic) attribute of God's nature, namely, his own image, and not a relational (extrinsic) attribute which can be deduced or known a priori. Knowing God, for Edwards, entails knowledge of a personal being. A philosopher who deduces that God is eternal, for instance, cannot be said to actually know God even though her conclusions were true. Spiritual knowledge of God tracks along the same contours as the real/relational distinction, which is a further instance of Edwards's concern to talk about God in terms of trinitarian *personhood* rather than an abstracted divine essence.

Here, however, Edwards orders the focus of his discussion of spiritual knowledge by what it means to know another being, *without actually becoming that being.* Earlier in *Miscellanies* 777, Edwards states that if there is immediate (not mediated) view of any mind by another, then the consciousnesses merge into one; there would be union of the persons and a loss of identity.[37] Edwards asserts that only God can have true *immediate* knowledge of other minds, as part of the distinction between Creator and creature, and is therefore unobtainable by creatures. Edwards poses a twofold safety for what could be deemed 'epistemological union': first, that spiritual beings come to know other spiritual beings *as persons* through self-revelation (by images or words), and therefore a type of mediation; second, the infinite/finite distinction, where the finite can never fully comprehend the infinite and therefore could not fully collapse into a God, who has all knowledge before his mind at all times.

1. Sanctified Sight

True knowledge of God, according to Edwards, is revealed knowledge that takes the form of the archetype in its corresponding ectypal mode as *sanctified sight.* It is, in other words, not sight through natural means, but supernatural, revealed in Christ by the Spirit. Prior to addressing the Christological mediation of creaturely knowledge, I focus on the form of pilgrim knowledge as pilgrim-*beatific* knowledge.[38] As I have already empha-sized, Edwards conjoins the pilgrim and beatific into one progressive

---

[37] This serves to explain how Christ could have two understandings and two wills and yet a singular consciousness grounding a singular identity.

[38] In *The Religious Affections*, Edwards states, 'And besides the things that have been already mentioned, there arises from this sense of spiritual beauty, all true experimental knowledge of religion; which is of itself, as it were, a new world of knowledge.' Y2, *Religious Affections*, 275.

state, connecting the Christological mediation of the elect on earth to its fulfilment in heaven. It is not surprising, then, to find that knowledge of God by both the saints in heaven as well as the saints on earth (prior to the consummation) is by Christ's work of redemption. Again, in *Miscellanies* 777, Edwards states, 'Hence that BEATIFICAL VISION that the saints have of God in heaven, is in beholding the manifestations that he makes of himself in the work of redemption. ... *All other ways of knowing God are by seeing him in Christ the Redeemer.*'[39] God manifests himself through Christ's work of redemption and through Christ the redeemer, as is emphasized below. Therefore, while the saints in heaven have a 'bird's-eye view' of redemption, the saints on earth see through a glass darkly.[40] However darkly their sight might be, it is still sight. Faith and sight are not mutually exclusive for Edwards, and here we see that pilgrim theology is not hermetically sealed from the beatific reality of heaven but, in Christ, participates in it.[41] Spirit-indwelled believers have a sanctified sight – a vision of divine things through Christ – and it is this which orients the saint's life to God.

By contrast, Trueman's comments concerning Owen are valuable,

The distinction between the two forms of knowledge is not in their object, which in both cases is God as he has revealed himself, but in their respective modes of knowledge: for the former, the *viatores*, the mode is faith, while the latter, the *possessors* see God face to face, and Owen, like other Puritans, drew on the medieval scholastic tradition in order to make this point clear.[42]

Edwards's 'radicalization' of the tradition was not in the object of knowledge but the mode of knowledge, a mode which mirrors the teleological 'ascension' of the saints to a pure sight of God. The earthly sight is clouded, but that does not negate its status as sight.[43] Instead of posing two distinct kinds of

---

[39] Y18, '*Miscellanies* 777. Happiness of Heaven is Progressive', 431 – my emphasis.

[40] In *Miscellanies* 1089 Edwards states, 'And ascending to a pinnacle in the very center of light, where everything appears in clear view, the saints that are ascended to heaven have advantage to view the state of Christ's kingdom in this world.' Y20, '*Miscellanies* 1089. The Saints in Heaven', 471.

[41] It seems likely that Edwards's neglect of pilgrim or viatory language could be explained by his merging the beatific and the pilgrim. The emphasis, therefore, is on heaven as a progressive state.

[42] Trueman, *Claims of Truth: John Owen's Trinitarian Theology* (Carlisle: Paternoster, 1998), 55–6. Admittedly, Edwards's 'radicalization' may be just a re-emphasis on one specific aspect of this distinction. That said, I still think the use of the term 'radical' is justified.

[43] 'The gospel is as a reflecting glass that refracts the glory of Christ as the light of the Sun is reflected from a looking glass, and as 'tis represented in a perspective glass or a glass through which we behold Christ as philosophers view the stars through glasses that they

knowledge, Edwards casts all knowledge of God in terms of sight. Nowhere is this more apparent than in Edwards's sermon on Revelation 14.2. There, after discussing the continual praise of the saints in heaven because of their clear sight of God, he turns his attention to the saints on earth, stating,

> But here they see but as in a glass darkly; they have only now and then a little glimpse of God's excellency. … Now the saints see the glory of God but by a reflected light, as we in the night see the light of the sun reflected from the moon, but in heaven they shall directly behold the Sun of Righteousness, and shall look full upon him when shining in all his glory.[44]

The distinction between direct and reflected light is an important one,[45] in that it ties together earthy and heavenly sight even as it distinguishes them.[46] This is how Edwards can say, 'The knowledge which believers have of God and his glory appearing in the face of Christ is the *imperfect beginning* of this heavenly sight.'[47] Faith and sight find solace in the pilgrim-beatific.[48] Edwards takes it to be axiomatic that

> the Scripture is ignorant of any such faith in Christ of the operation of God, that is not founded in a spiritual sight of Christ. That believing on Christ, which accompanies a title to everlasting life, is a seeing the Son,

can't distinctly see with their naked eyes.' JEC, Unpublished Sermon, 2 Cor. 3:18, #72 [L. 20v.]. See also JEC, Unpublished Sermon, Rom. 2:10, #373.

[44] JEC, Unpublished Sermon, Rev. 14:2, #344 (under Proposition II point 1). Later in this sermon, Edwards offers his congregation direction by stating, 'Though you have not an immediate vision of God, as they have, may [you] yet have a clear spiritual sight of him, and that you may know more of God, and have frequent discoveries of him made to you.'

[45] Edwards again links heavenly life with earthly: 'The knowledge which the saints have of God's beauty and glory in this world, and those holy affections that arise from it, *are of the same nature and kind with what the saints are the subjects of in heaven, differing only in degree and circumstances*: what God gives them here, is a foretaste of heavenly happiness, and an earnest of their future inheritance.' Y2, *Religious Affections*, 133 – my emphasis.

[46] Edwards draws this same distinction in his funeral sermon for Brainerd: 'Now the saints, while in the body, see something of Christ's glory and love; as we, in the dawning of the morning, see something of the reflected light of the sun mingled with darkness: but when separated from the body, they see their glorious and loving Redeemer, as we see the sun when risen, and showing his whole disk above the horizon, by his direct beams, in a clear hemisphere, and with perfect day.' Y25, 'True Saints, When Absent from the Body, Are Present with the Lord', 230. The difference is in purity and directness of sight, not in what is being viewed.

[47] Y17, 'The Pure in Heart Blessed', 75 – my emphasis. He goes on to talk about the saints on earth having the 'beginnings' of the perfect sight in heaven.

[48] In his unpublished sermon on 2 Cor. 3:18, Edwards states, 'I don't say that all believers have an exceedingly clear sight of Christ. There is a great difference in the degrees of clearness; they may have a true sight of Christ and yet they may see him but darkly (1 Cor. 13:12), but if they have but a glimpse of his true excellency it makes him appear lovely above all.' JEC, Unpublished Sermon, 2 Cor. 3:18, #72 [L. 16v.].

and believing on him, John 6:40. True faith in Christ is never exercised, any further than persons behold 'as in a glass, the glory of the Lord', and have 'the knowledge of the glory of God in the face of Jesus Christ' (II Cor. 3:18 and 4:6).[49]

By tying together the heavenly sight with a kind of seeing on earth, Edwards can make claims such as the following, from his work *A Faithful Narrative*, 'It seemed to me she dwelt for days together in a kind of beatific vision of God; and seemed to have, as I thought, as immediate an intercourse with him as a child with a father.'[50] Likewise, in his sermon on Romans 2:10, Edwards claims,

> Yet God sometimes is pleased to remove the veil to draw the curtain and give the saints sweet views, sometimes, that is, as it were a window or gap opened in Heaven and Christ shows himself through the lattice. They sometimes have … sweet light breaking forth from above into the soul, and God and the Redeemer sometimes comes to them and makes friendly visits to them and manifests himself to them.[51]

Edwards's praise of his wife's piety is well attested, and his depiction of her experience in his *Some Thoughts Concerning the Revival* note that she had been 'swallowed up with light and love and a sweet solace, rest and joy of soul … more than once continuing for five or six hours together … *in that clear and lively view* or sense of the infinite beauty and amiableness of Christ's person.'[52] He continues to highlight that there was 'a constant stream of sweet light, at the same time the soul all flowing out in love to him; so that there seemed to be a constant flowing and reflowing from heart to heart'.[53] Edwards's use of light, as I will show more fully below,

---

[49] Y2, *Religious Affections*, 175–6.
[50] Y4, *A Faithful Narrative*, 195. He goes on to note that 'she often expressed a sense of the glory of God appearing in the trees, and growth of the fields, and other works of God's hands'. Y4, *A Faithful Narrative*, 195.
[51] JEC, Unpublished Sermon, Rom. 2:10, #373.
[52] Y4, *Some Thoughts Concerning the Revival*, 332 – my emphasis. While Catholic theologians can talk of the beatific vision in preglorified humanity, Edwards's emphasis is slightly different. It is still beatific, in his estimation, but it is focused Christologically in such a manner as to mirror Owen's understanding of the vision in eternity. What is more interesting than the fact that the beatific has made its way into the pilgrim mode, I suggest, is the fact that it is the only mode available for personal knowledge of God (i.e. knowing Christ in any form is, itself, an aspect of the beatific).
[53] Y4, *Some Thoughts Concerning the Revival*, 332. The trinitarian imagery here is unmistakable, as well as the correlation between emanation and remanation with the human heart flowing and reflowing.

is a gloss on Christ himself, seen through the enlightening work of the Spirit, and while 'clear' views are rare, all knowledge takes on the form of this sight.

These ecstatic circumstances, of course, are not the norm for day-to-day life.[54] Nonetheless, by being in Christ, Edwards allows for 'the lattice to be opened and God revealed', which is in fact what the moment of conversion truly is. Although all of life might not be lived in ecstasy, the believer is still affected by the reality of God in nature, Scripture and with others as a type of *seeing God himself*. God's self-revelation pervades the mundane. Along these lines, he claims that 'the soul is spiritually sensible of God as being present with it and manifesting and communicating himself'.[55] Edwards also claims that there is 'substance' in the peace and pleasure spiritual sensibility brings: 'This pleasure is not as mere shadow as earthly pleasures are, but 'tis substance' and that 'those pleasures don't defile the soul but purify it . . . don't deform ... but beautify it'. Further, the pleasures 'leave something more of God, more of a divine disposition and temper ... they do, as it were, cause the soul to shine as Moses' face did when he had been conversing with God in the mountain'.[56]

Therefore, for Edwards, regenerate existence is defined by a sanctified spiritual sight that is one *in kind* with the sight of the saints in heaven. Coming to know God is had through apprehension, and unlike his development of the four signs manifesting other beings, a sight of God is only available through images and words. In a clarifying statement, Edwards claims,

Hence that BEATIFICAL VISION that the saints have of God in heaven, is in beholding the manifestations that he makes of himself in the work of redemption: for that arguing of the being and perfections of God that may be a priori, don't seem to be called seeing God in Scripture, but only that which is by [the] manifestations God makes of himself in his Son.[57]

---

[54] 'As the feebleness of grace and prevalence of corruption, obscures the object; so it enfeebles the sight; it darkens the sight as to all spiritual objects, of which grace is one. Sin is like some distempers of the eyes, that make things to appear of different colors from those which properly belong to them, and like many other distempers, that put the mouth out of taste, so as to disenable from distinguishing good and wholesome food from bad, but everything tastes bitter.' Y2, *Religious Affections*, 195.

[55] JEC, Unpublished Sermon, Rom. 2:10, #373.

[56] JEC, Unpublished Sermon, Rom. 2:10, #373.

[57] Y18, '*Miscellanies* 777. Happiness of Heaven is Progressive', 431. The same is true for pilgrim theology. In *End of Creation*, Edwards states, 'And if it be thus fit that God should have a supreme regard to himself, then it is fit that this supreme regard should appear, in those things by which he makes himself known, or by his word and works; i.e. in what he says, and in what he does. ... And if it was God's intention, as there is great reason to think

Jonathan Edwards's Theology

Seeing God, to use our distinction from above, is seeing him personally rather than essentially. In other words, knowing God through his relational attributes is knowing *about* him, while knowing God through his real attributes is knowing him truly – *seeing* him. Again, in his sermon on Mt. 5.8, Edwards reiterates the impossibility of an apprehension of God from mere hearsay or speculative reasoning, claiming that this 'is not that beatific, happifying sight of God', connecting the sight of God here with a truly beatific sight.[58] Therefore, Edwards can say that the business of the saints is found in 'contemplating the wonders of this work, in praising God for the displays of his glory and love therein'.[59] One can come to know *about* God abstracted through effects and a priori reasoning, but sanctified existence depends upon knowing God personally, which is only had by knowing him in Christ.[60] By gazing upon images (e.g. the work of redemption) and words (e.g. Scripture), man can see the beauty and excellency of Christ and therefore see the moral and spiritual reality of who God is (if and only if they know sensibly).[61] Knowledge of God in Christ is an affective knowledge had through God's revealing *himself* personally to the creature.

2. A Christologically Mediated Vision

Edwards, as we have seen, follows the broad contours of his Reformed background, interpreting ectypal knowledge through his trinitarian

it was, that his works should exhibit an image of himself their author, that it might brightly appear by his works what manner of being he is, and afford a proper representation of his divine excellencies, and especially his moral excellence, consisting in the disposition of his heart; then 'tis reasonable to suppose that his works are so wrought as to show this supreme respect to himself wherein his moral excellency does primarily consist.' Y8, *End of Creation*, 422.

[58] Y17, 'The Pure in Heart Blessed', 63.

[59] Y18, '*Miscellanies* 777. Happiness of Heaven is Progressive', 431.

[60] This concept runs deep in Edwards's thought. In a sermon on Jas 2.19, Edwards states, 'A sight of the greatness of God in his attributes, may overwhelm men, and be more than they can endure; but the enmity and opposition of the heart, may remain in its full strength, and will remain inflexible; whereas, one glimpse of the moral and spiritual glory of God, and supreme amiableness of Jesus Christ, shining into the heart, overcomes and abolishes this opposition, and inclines the soul to Christ, as it were, by an omnipotent power: so that now, not only the understanding, but the will, and the whole soul receives and embraces the Savior.' Y25, 'True Grace', 635–6. This is the redemption of a person to persons, rather than persons to an object, or objects to persons.

[61] In *The Religious Affections*, Edwards states, 'Spiritually to understand the Scripture, is to have the eyes of the mind opened, to behold the wonderful spiritual excellency of the glorious things contained in the true meaning of it, and that always were contained in it, ever since it was written; to behold the amiable and bright manifestations of the divine perfections, and of the excellency and sufficiency of Christ.' Y2, *Religious Affections*, 280–1. For spiritual knowledge mediated through Scripture, see Brown, *Jonathan Edwards and the Bible* (Bloomington: Indiana University Press, 2002), 41–56.

theology. Knowledge of God in the ectype finds its form and content governed by God's own personal beatific-delight and therefore necessitates an affectionate, personal response. In order to flesh out Edwards's understanding of Christologically mediated knowledge, I briefly develop his explication of Christ as the visual manifestation of the invisible God. In a sermon on James 2:19, Edwards claims, 'The sight of the glory of God, in the face of Jesus Christ, works true supreme love to God: this is a sight of the proper foundation of supreme love to God, viz. the supreme loveliness of his nature.'[62] The glory of God is truly revealed in the image of the Son through the Spirit's 'ordinary' work in the soul. As ectypal knowledge, founded on the beatific archetype, the elect must behold Christ and 'incline' to him with affection. Along these same lines, using a passage frequently invoked in discussions concerning the beatific, he states:

> The sense of divine beauty, is the first thing in the actual change made in the soul, in true conversion, and is the foundation of everything else belonging to that change; as is evident by those words of the Apostle, II Cor. 3:18, 'But we all with open face, beholding as in a glass, the glory of the Lord, are changed into the same image, from glory to glory, even as by the Spirit of the Lord.[63]

Christ is the mediator who stands between fallen creatures and God and therefore serves as the image of the invisible God, the revelation of the Father to the creation.[64] Edwards, in a sermon on 2 Peter 1:19, states, 'As the natural world is all enlightened with the light of the sun, so is the church of God and the whole spiritual world by Jesus Christ.'[65] Therefore, all spiritual knowledge functions *Christologically*. For Edwards, Christ's knowledge of

---

[62] Y25, 'True Grace', 636.
[63] Y25, 'True Grace', 636. Also: 'Indeed the first act of the Spirit of God, or the first that this divine temper exerts itself in, is in spiritual understanding, or in the sense of the mind, its perception of glory and excellency, etc. in the ideas it has of divine things; and this is before any proper acts of the will. Indeed, the inclination of the soul is as immediately exercised in that sense of the mind which is called spiritual understanding, as the intellect. For it is not only the mere presence of ideas in the mind, but it is the mind's sense of their excellency, glory and delightfulness.' Y13, '*Miscellanies* 397. Conversion. Spiritual Knowledge', 463.
[64] In *The Religious Affections*, Edwards notes, 'By this sense of the moral beauty of divine things [spiritual knowledge], is understood the sufficiency of Christ as a mediator: for 'tis only by the discovery of the beauty of the moral perfection of Christ, that the believer is let into the knowledge of the excellency of his person, so as to know anything more of it than the devils do: and 'tis only by the knowledge of the excellency of Christ's person, that any know his sufficiency as a mediator. ... 'Tis by seeing the excellency of Christ's person, that the saints are made sensible of the preciousness of his blood, and its sufficiency to atone for sin.' Y2, *Religious Affections*, 273.
[65] Y19, 'Light in a Dark World, A Dark Heart', 731.

God, had through pneumatological union, functions as perfect creaturely knowledge of God; all other ectypal knowledge functions by the Spirit's illumination *of* Christ through union *to* Christ. This kind of Christological emphasis is not without precedent. Van Asselt, in his discussion of Junius, states:

> What is particularly interesting in Junius's discussion of ectypal theology is that the discussion of the subdivisions of ectypal theology *in subiecto* is dominated by an unmistakable christological emphasis. The christo-logical framework of ectypal theology is expressed by Junius's saying that the theology of union in Christ is the principle of the two other forms of ectypal theology: the theology of vision and that of revelation. Whereas archetypal theology is the *matrix* of all forms of theology, the theology of union is the mother (*mater*) of the two other forms of ectypal theology, i.e. the theology of vision and revealed theology.[66]

In Edwards we find a Christological emphasis as well as the uniting of vision and revelation within the believer's union with Christ. Following Christ's knowledge by union, the regenerate's knowledge of God is by union *with* Christ and illumination *of* Christ. Van Asselt states, 'Both forms of theology, therefore, Christ has sanctified in his Person.' For Edwards, pilgrim and beatific theology are pulled into one knowing in Christ. The saints' have knowledge of God, as ectypal knowledge, by illumination and union with Christ, where the believer participates in a kind of beatific pilgrimage *in* Christ.[67]

Christ is therefore both the object and perfection of pilgrim-beatific knowledge. Just as the Spirit mediates the knowledge of Christ to the elect in union, so the Spirit mediates between the Logos and the human nature: 'Christ taught the things of God as of his own knowledge ... without a revelation', and yet 'the knowledge of divine things that the human nature had was by the Spirit of God, *by his inspiration and revelation*: for he taught and did the business of the great prophet of God by the Spirit'.[68] Christ's

---

[66] Asselt, 'Fundamental Meaning of Theology', 332.

[67] Asselt's summary of Junius and the later orthodox can be said of Edwards as well: 'Their use of the archetypal-ectypal distinction, and the crucial significance of the theology of union in its relation to the two other forms of ectypal theology is a means of developing an understanding of the principles and task of theology which is determined by a strong trini-tarian and christological – and, *mutatis mutandis*, a pneumatological – framework.' Asselt, 'Fundamental Meaning of Theology', 334–5. The idea of a pilgrimage in Christ is, I would suggest, standard Reformed Christology.

[68] Y18, '*Miscellanies* 766. Incarnation of the Son of God', 413 – my emphasis. Edwards navigates this seeming contradiction through his understanding of union and conveyance. 'For

two natures, Edwards poses, are bound together in the Spirit, making the human Jesus one person with the Logos through identity of consciousness.[69] By uniting to the human nature through the Spirit, Christ paves the way for the elect. In his sermon, 'The Excellency of Christ', Edwards states, 'We being united to a divine person, as his members, can have a more intimate union and intercourse with God the Father, who is only in the divine nature, than otherwise could be.'[70] Therefore, 'We being members of the Son, are partakers in our measure, of the Father's love to the Son, and complacence in him.'[71] Robert Caldwell notes, 'This union, this "something really in them, and between them", entitles them to partake of the divine life in a way similar to the way the divine Son partakes of the inner-trinitarian life.'[72] His focus here is ontological, but for our purposes, this is true in one qualified sense: the person of Christ partakes in the knowledge of the divine life through union with the Logos by the Spirit, while the elect partake in the knowledge of God by union with Jesus through his Spirit.[73]

Knowledge of God, therefore, is always mediated *Christologically* through a *pneumatologically* achieved union. By being in Christ, the elect partake in Christ's benefits of truly knowing, and in this sense *seeing*, the divine and consequently experiencing transformation through a sight of his glory. In Edwards's words, 'We, by being in Christ a divine person, do as it were ascend up to God, through the infinite distance, and have hereby advantage for the full enjoyment of him also.'[74] Space restrictions limit

those works of the divine power were his own no otherwise than as they were the works of the divine Logos, united to the human nature, or to the human understanding and will.' Y18, '*Miscellanies* 766. Incarnation of the Son of God', 412. Edwards invokes the Spirit as the bond of union to explain the Spirit's work of 'conveyance' between the divine and human natures. Therefore, while it is the Spirit's 'motion' that causes the action of the man Jesus, this 'motion' is 'of his divine person, the person of the Logos, conveying and uniting the divine understanding and will, and so of the divine nature with the human.' Y18, '*Miscellanies* 766. Incarnation of the Son of God', 412–13.

[69] "Tis not [just] any communion of understanding and will that makes the same person, but the communion of understanding is such that there is the same consciousness.' Y13, '*Miscellanies* 487. Incarnation of the Son of God', 529.

[70] Y19, 'The Excellency of Christ', 593.

[71] Y19, 'The Excellency of Christ', 593.

[72] Caldwell, *Communion in the Spirit*, 132.

[73] My focus here is on relations as such. There is certainly a difference in the type of union being invoked. In other words, the union between Jesus and the Logos is not the same type as believers to Christ.

[74] Y19, 'The Excellency of Christ', 594. Julie Canlis's study of ascent and ascension in Calvin is enlightening here. Note the parallel emphasis with Edwards: 'For Calvin, humanity's ascent is solely a participation in Jesus, whose bidirectional mission summarizes soteriology: "The situation would surely have been hopeless had the very majesty of God not descended to us, since it was not in our power to ascend to him" (II.12.I). Here Calvin uses "ascent" to denote the intended "direction", or *telos*, of humanity. It is a word that summarizes the call

our exploration of Christological themes, but it is enough to say that Edwards's understanding of the incarnation as spiritual union provides the theological framework for his understanding of the excellency of Christ – where the life and work of Christ reveal God's goodness, excellency and will.[75] Jesus has 'sweet conjunction' of excellencies through union with the Spirit, and the elect come to view these through the Spirit's illumination. Therefore, when Edwards preached evangelistic sermons, such as the one titled 'The Excellency of Christ', he portrayed Christ in his excellencies because the unregenerate needed to *see* Christ's excellency for salvation. As he states in his sermon on Hebrews 1:3,

> The manifestation of the glory of God in the person of Christ is, as it were, accommodated to our apprehensions. The brightness is suited to our eyes. We can't look upon the glory of God immediately; our eyes will be dazzled. But Christ being a person who is come to us in our nature has, as it were, softened the light of God's glory and accommodated to our view.[76]

Later in the same sermon, he refers to this sight of Christ's excellency, particularly his infinite power and humility 'joined together', as 'ravishing'.[77] This is the very theme of Edwards's sermon on Christ's excellency, that Christ's infinite highness and lowness would come together in one person. Edwards the preacher, therefore, often reads more like Edwards the poet, or, to use appropriate visual imagery, Edwards the painter.[78] This is further

---

to creatures to be in communion with God; as such, it encapsulates the Christian life.' Julie Canlis, *Calvin's Ladder: A Spiritual Theology of Ascent and Ascension* (Grand Rapids: Eerdmans, 2010), 123–4.

[75] I disagree with Ramsey, McClenahan and Williamson in that I do not believe 'excellency' or specifically the sermon 'The Excellency of Christ' is an adequate lens through which to view Edwards's Christology. An attempt to do so is anaemic and proves to be a misuse of the sermon. It also ignores Edwards's clear following of Owen's pneumatologically robust Christology. See *Miscellanies* 513, 624, 709, 764b, 766, 958, 1043; Notes on Scripture, #476; #130, and #285.

[76] Edwards, 'Jesus Christ Is the Shining Forth of the Father's Glory', in *The Glory and Honor of God: Volume 2 of the Previously Unpublished Sermons of Jonathan Edwards* (ed. Michael D. McMullen; Nashville: Broadman & Holman, 2004), 233.

[77] JEC, Unpublished Sermon, 2 Cor. 3:18, #72 [L. 18r.].

[78] James Carse notes the centrality of visual language in Edwards: 'As we shall see, the concept of visibility runs straight through the whole of Edwards's thought. It is the thesis of this book that when we understand what Edwards has comprehended under the term "visibility" we shall have located the vital center of his thought.' James P. Carse, *Jonathan Edwards and the Visibility of God* (New York: Scribner, 1967), 27. Likewise, 'Therefore, one often has the impression that he is painting a verbal picture of Christ.' Ibid., 100. However, it is my thesis that Carse fails to achieve his end, and in many ways, this work is an attempt to locate Edwards's visibility language within a broader theological matrix.

illustrated by the aesthetic nature of this vision. Edwards states, 'Spiritual understanding consists primarily in a sense of that spiritual beauty,' and likewise, 'There is nothing pertaining to divine things besides the beauty of their moral excellency, and those properties and qualities of divine things which this beauty is the foundation of.'[79]

Edwards's understanding of the visual nature of Christ's excellency and the visual component to salvation is driven by his pneumatologically robust Christology, his aesthetic notion of excellency (as the conjunction of the highness and lowness) and the Spirit's illumination of the elect. This is why Edwards can claim, 'This *Spirit* of Christ is the immediate instructor of the souls of men in spiritual knowledge and understanding,' as well as, immediately following, '*Christ* is the great teacher.'[80] He goes on to compare Christ to the sun and the Spirit to the rays of light emanating from the sun, stating, 'The Spirit of Christ is as the rays, as the very light itself. The Sun don't enlighten us immediately, but by his beams. 'Tis Christ's face that shines into the heart, but 'tis the Spirit of Christ are the rays by which it shines into them'; and furthermore, "Tis Christ only that makes men like to himself by his own Spirit, and he doth in this way by giving a sight of himself by revealing himself to the soul.'[81] Just as the beatific sight in glory is conveyed by the Spirit, so also pilgrim sight of Christ is a *Spirit*ual sight, flowing forth from the Spirit's uniting and illuminating work, oriented to Christ, the image of the invisible God and mediator between the Father and humanity.

3. Modes of Knowing

The focus of this section has been the Christological orientation of ectypal theology, but this orientation is only fully understood in relation to the trinitarian archetype. God's inner-trinitarian knowing is *beatific*; it happifies. Therefore, true knowledge of God is modeled on both processions of Son *and* Spirit – true vision *and* love. In order to elucidate creaturely knowledge, therefore, it is necessary to highlight Edwards's

---

[79] Y2, *Religious Affections*, 272.
[80] JEC, Unpublished Sermon, 2 Cor. 3:18, #72 [L. 2r.].
[81] JEC, Unpublished Sermon, 2 Cor. 3:18, #72 [L. 3r.]. He continues, "Tis the Spirit of Jesus Christ that makes like to Jesus Christ. ... True believers have a likeness of the glory and excellency of Jesus Christ upon their souls and that the sight they have of the glory of Christ changes them into this likeness; they have a transforming sight of the Glory of Christ. But in this doctrine we are taught that this is done by the Spirit of that person whose glory is seen.' JEC, Unpublished Sermon, 2 Cor. 3:18, #72 [L. 3r.].

distinction between speculative and sensible understanding.[82] The former refers to a person's capacity for reasoning or speculation, knowledge attainable through analytic reasoning, while the latter Edwards refers to as 'the sense of the heart', and depends upon revelation, union and illumination.[83] In other words, on the one hand, speculative knowledge of God is natural theology, or knowledge concerning *deity* abstractly considered. Sensible knowledge, on the other hand, delineates supernatural theology, knowledge *of God*, what we have called the pilgrim-beatific. On Edwards's view, sensible knowledge is necessary for salvation; it requires a sense of the heart, or in his words:

> The former [speculative understanding] includes all that understanding that is without any proper ideal apprehension or view, or all understanding of mental things of either faculty that is only by signs, and also all ideal views of things that are merely intellectual ... is mere speculative knowledge, whether it be an ideal apprehension of them, or no. But all that understanding of things that does consist in or involve such a sense or feeling, is not merely speculative but sensible knowledge; so is all ideal apprehension of beauty and deformity, or loveliness and hatefulness ... and the idea of all the affections of the mind, and all their motions and exercises, and all ideal views of dignity or excellency of any kind.[84]

After dividing knowledge into the categories of speculative and sensible, Edwards proceeds to offer a twofold delineation of sensible knowledge. He first addresses the way sensible knowledge is obtained. Again, offering two distinct categories, Edwards suggests that there is (1) a natural sensible knowledge that people have, allowing them a natural knowledge of beauty and deformity, pleasure and sorrow, and excellency and hatefulness. This knowledge is only of the natural realm and has no import for spiritual realities. Furthermore, (2) Edwards posits a sense of the heart derived from (and only from) an immediate influence of the Spirit of God working on

---

[82] Edwards makes a similar distinction in *The Religious Affections*, more specifically looking at the spiritual component in relation to the speculative. 'The Apostle seems to make a distinction between mere speculative knowledge of the things of religion, and spiritual knowledge, in calling that the form of knowledge, and of the truth; "which has the form of knowledge, and of the truth in the law" (Romans 2:20). The latter is often represented by relishing, smelling, or tasting.' Y2, *Religious Affections*, 272–3.

[83] Edwards states, 'This sight of the glory of Christ don't so much consist in the imagination that it should seem to them as if they saw a visible shape or as if they saw a light with their bodily eyes ... but it consists in the inward sense of the heart.' JEC, Unpublished Sermon, 2 Cor. 3:18, #72 [L. 16v.–L. 17r.].

[84] Y18, *Miscellanies* 782. Ideas. Sense of the Heart', 459.

the heart, impressing a sense of spiritual things on the minds of the elect.[85] The sense of spiritual things given by the Spirit is what Edwards calls the 'ordinary work of the Spirit of God in the hearts of men'.[86]

Edwards develops the sense of the heart both to help correct the notion that this vision of God is natural and to emphasize that saving knowledge of God is by grace alone.[87] On Edwards's account, the sense of the heart is the architecture necessary for beatific pilgrim knowledge. To exposit the life of faith through a visual trope, even when 'visual' is used in a spiritual sense, doctrinal work is needed to buttress that endeavour, which Edwards achieves through invoking this sense. The sense of the heart serves to demarcate natural versus supernatural theology – it delineates ectypal knowledge – and is therefore an epistemological corollary to positing pilgrim-beatific knowledge.[88] As we saw in the previous chapter, Edwards understands the soul to have the capability of spiritual sight, a sight that allows the saint to *experience* God himself by partaking in God's own self-experience. The sense of the heart is the *sense* of this experience; it is beholding the beauty of God and delighting in him.[89]

Since archetypal knowledge is affectionate knowledge, it is mediated to creatures Christologically and conveyed by the uniting and illuminating work of the Spirit. God reveals himself to the creature through the mode of participation – participation in his own understanding and delighting in

---

[85] Y18, '*Miscellanies* 782. Ideas. Sense of the Heart', 461. It is important to note that Edwards does not believe the sense of the heart provides new propositional knowledge. In *The Religious Affections* Edwards states, "Tis also evident that spiritual knowledge does not consist in any new doctrinal explanation of any part of the Scripture; for still, this is but doctrinal knowledge, or the knowledge of propositions; the doctrinal explaining of any part of Scripture, is only giving us to understand, what are the propositions contained or taught in that part of Scripture.' Y2, *Religious Affections*, 278.

[86] Y18, '*Miscellanies* 782. Ideas. Sense of the Heart', 462.

[87] Edwards's use of the word 'taste' is used of the sense of the heart as well, with the hope that the sense of taste could push again the idea of bodily sight. He also uses it, I believe, because it offers the idea of *texture* and *inclination*. The sight Edwards proposes is not a neutral vision but, like beauty, will draw the soul out toward it (see Y2, *Religious Affections*, 283–5). Edwards's use of 'palate' pushes toward aesthetic implications. It could also be that Edwards adopted Augustine's understanding in *The Confessions* of 'sight' as something of a meta-category for all of the senses. Augustine, *The Confessions* (ed. John E. Rotelle, O.S.A.; trans. Maria Boulding, O.S.B.; The Works of Saint Augustine: A Translation for the 21st Century; New York: New City Press, 1990), 273.

[88] I am tempted to say 'anthropological corollary', but this is not exactly right.

[89] Likewise, Morris notes, 'The Immediacy of God in "the sense of the heart" is only a particular application of this general epistemological position. Here, where God acts not upon man's mind through the external structures of nature, but internally within the mind of man by His spirit, the true nature and union of outer world and inner mind, are revealed as one in the new simple idea of the divine.' William S. Morris, 'The Genius of Jonathan Edwards', in *Reinterpretation in American Church History* (ed. Jerald C. Brauer; Chicago: University of Chicago Press, 1968), 335.

his own delight – thereby allowing creaturely knowledge and love of God through his own self-knowledge and self-love. Furthermore, the excellency of Christ, the beauty of God, is *seen* and thereby *known* through words (e.g. Scripture[90]) and images (e.g. God's work of redemption through Christ), because God reveals his truth through Word and Image, and the Spirit illuminates *him* immediately to the heart of the believer. God, in other words, is known immediately through these mediating realities, through the work of the Spirit, who provides this earthly counterpart to the heavenly beatific vision.

4. A Heavenward Journey

As noted thus far, Edwards offers a Christologically mediated revelation through vision, a sanctified sight where the heavenly has saturated earthly realities and a mode of knowing which necessitates sensible or affective knowledge. By failing to make a clean break between pilgrim and beatific knowledge, opting instead for incremental advancement of purity (of sight) and union with Christ, Edwards casts the Christian life as a journey or pilgrimage specifically toward heaven. After focusing on the *beatific* nature of the vision, we now turn to all knowledge of God as *pilgrim* knowledge. In the previous chapter I noted that heaven is a progressive state, and here I note that it is a pilgrimage started in conversion. The progressive nature of the heavenly vision, in other words, is a continuation of the same vision had on earth.

When preaching on Hebrews 11:13–14 in 1733 (and again in 1753), Edwards articulates his doctrine as follows: 'This life ought so to be spent by us, as to be only a journey towards heaven.'[91] Most of this sermon is exactly what one would expect from a generation catechized on *The Pilgrim's Progress*, but it serves to highlight an important piece of Edwards's theology. Heaven is not merely an isolated future realm but is a destination connected to the journey made on earth – the difference is not in kind but in degree – they are, as it were, different places along the same path. That this is the case is evinced by his practical guidance in the sermon, proposing that the way to heaven entails living a heavenly kind of life on

---

[90] In *Miscellanies* 126, Edwards states, 'Hence we learn, in what sense the Word of God is said to be written in the hearts of believers. There is that disposition of the mind, that when it comes to be put forth into action, raises such a series and succession of thoughts, as sweetly corresponds and harmonizes with the expressions of God's Word.' Y13, '*Miscellanies* 126. Spiritual Understanding of the Scriptures', 290.

[91] Y17, 'The True Christian's Life a Journey Towards Heaven', 429–46.

earth, which means imitating the saints who are in heaven as they love, serve and praise God.[92] Or, as Edwards explicitly states, 'We ought to be continually growing in holiness and, in that respect, coming nearer and nearer to heaven.'[93]

One's *nearness* to heaven – more meaningful than one's nearness to death – comes in incremental advancement on the path of the beatified pilgrim.[94] Again, Edwards states clearly that believers should grow in 'clear views of the gloriousness and excellency of divine things, that we come nearer and nearer to the beatific vision'.[95] Edwards's use here of 'beatific vision' is a gloss for the perfection of the beatific vision in consummation, while spiritual sight leading up to it is a type of this vision. But, as we have seen, the revelatory nature of the work of redemption makes it a part of the beatific vision, even for saints in heaven. Likewise, Edwards continues, sounding more like a mystic than a Reformed pastor, 'We should labor to [be continually growing] in divine love, that this may be an increasing flame in our hearts, till our hearts ascend wholly in this flame.'[96]

While union, knowledge and our glorifying of God are imperfect in the earthly realm, heaven knows their perfection, thereby grounding the teleological horizon of the saints' pilgrimage. Notably, perfection in heaven does not eliminate the pilgrim nature of heavenly existence itself; as we saw in the previous chapter, growth and perfection are not contradictory for finite beings. In earthly existence, Edwards states, 'These [earthly pleasures] are but shadows; but God is the substance. These are but scattered beams; but God is the sun. These are but streams; but God is the fountain. These are but drops; but God is the ocean.'[97] All of these images imply a true connection with God himself and therefore connect heaven and earthly existence. This connection frames the issue of redemption, allowing us to posit a robustly theological view of the sense of the heart, spiritual knowledge and the pilgrim-beatific reality of the Christian life. Toward this end, Edwards muses on the gift of a sight of Christ:

[92] Y17, 'The True Christian's Life a Journey Towards Heaven', 433.
[93] Y17, 'The True Christian's Life a Journey Towards Heaven', 434.
[94] Again, Edwards crosses the bounds of the earthly life and glory by positing that there truly is 'religion' on both sides of the chasm: 'There is doubtless true religion in heaven, and true religion in its utmost purity and perfection. But according to the Scripture representation of the heavenly state, the religion of heaven consists chiefly in holy and mighty love and joy, and the expression of these in most fervent and exalted praises.' Y2, '*Religious Affections*', 113. Likewise, Edwards uses the image of singing a song to convey that believers on earth must learn the song they will continue to sing for eternity. See Y22, 'They Sing a New Song', 227–44.
[95] Y17, 'The True Christian's Life a Journey Towards Heaven', 434–5.
[96] Y17, 'The True Christian's Life a Journey Towards Heaven', 435.
[97] Y17, 'The True Christian's Life a Journey Towards Heaven', 438.

'Tis something from heaven, is of a heavenly nature, and tends to heaven. And those that have it, however they may now wander in a wilderness, or be tossed to and fro on a tempestuous ocean, shall be increased, and perfected, and the souls of the saints, all be transformed into a bright and pure flame, and they shall shine forth as the sun, in the kingdom of their Father.[98]

By refusing to posit a category distinction between faith and sight, Edwards draws a strong line of continuity between God's work in creation for his own glory and the creatures receiving that glory; a kind of relation that will develop incrementally to eternity. There is emanation, Edwards argues, and there is remanation. Commenting on John Owen, Sebastian Rehnman offers helpful insights fitting for Edwards as well:

Humans enjoy the clear vision of divine things in heaven, communicated by Christ through his Spirit, and since the mode implies a clear vision or intuitive knowledge ... it is the theology of the elect *in patria*. This idea shows the adherence to what Harnack called 'Areopagite theology', which doctrine of God as all in all through emanation, gave direction to the goal of theology. For all things must be merged in the unity of the knowledge of God, and through this vision the soul is liberated and united with God.[99]

Likewise, for Edwards, there is emanation and there is remanation, or there is vision of glory, beholding that glory and delighting in it. God's work of redemption in the world is a mirror image of God's life in eternity, beholding his infinite beauty and holiness with happiness flowing forth. In seeking to make the elect happy, Edwards is convinced that God offers a view of himself. As a theologian, therefore, it is his trinitarian theology he turns to for his architecture of redemption rather than Neo-Platonism or Locke.[100] The journey of the pilgrim-beatific just exposed serves to orient our discussion of regeneration and religious affection. As we turn our attention to the two following application points, the question we should ask concerning redemption is, *how can these things be?*

---

[98] Y25, 'True Grace', 640.
[99] Sebastian Rehnman, *Divine Discourse: The Theological Methodology of John Owen* (Texts and Studies in Reformation and Post-Reformation Thought; Grand Rapids: Baker Academic, 2002), 69–70.
[100] It might be said that Locke and Neo-Platonism provided Edwards with a grammar from which to colour his trinitarian thought.

Chapter 5

Regeneration

The material developed thus far – the Trinity as personal beatific-delight, God's working for his own glory toward a consummation of vision and participation, and the necessity for true *spiritual* knowledge – is put to work in this section to expound on the question of regeneration. In applying our heuristic key, I utilize the material on spiritual knowledge to highlight the contours of pilgrim existence. In mapping Edwards's goals, purpose and direction, I answer the question: what is God's work that allows the elect to partake in the pilgrim-beatific life? Our task, therefore, is to address how the elect partake in God's self-glorification, which is at one and the same time the elect's journey of increasing holiness. I hold this account up against John Owen's, one of Edwards's favourite commentators, as well as Michael McClenahan, who uses Owen in an attempt to interpret Edwards. In contrast, I argue that Edwards departs from Owen at the very point McClenahan invokes, using my development of Edwards's theology to navigate the discussion. My development addresses the regenerating work of the Spirit – illumination and infusion – focusing specifically on the nature of God's work of grace to redeem *persons*.[1]

In God's work of regeneration, the person becomes wholly something new.[2] This is represented by Edwards in *Miscellanies* 241, concerning regeneration: 'It may be in the new birth as it is in the first birth.'[3] In comparing the new or 'spiritual' generation with the old or 'natural' generation, Edwards follows Van Mastricht, Owen and Turretin, who argue that

---

[1] Union could be added here but because of space restrictions is not. Salvation, for Edwards, necessitates union, by the Spirit, to Christ. Union, with illumination and infusion, are truly one movement of the Spirit composed of three acts. I treat these all here under regeneration because this is what Edwards tended to do. The elect are 'created anew', according to Edwards, and this work necessitates union, illumination and infusion. Y3, *Original Sin*, 361–9.

[2] See Y21, 'Treatise on Grace', 159–61.

[3] Y13, '*Miscellanies* 241. Regeneration', 357.

regeneration is the first act (or principle) rather than the habitual exercise of that principle.[4] Van Mastricht states:

> For as by natural generation a man receives neither the habits nor acts of reasoning, speaking, or writing, but only the power, which under proper circumstances, in due time, comes forth in act, so also, in regeneration, there is not bestowed upon the elect any faith, hope, love, repentance, etc., either as to habit or act, but the power only of performing these exercises is bestowed, by which the regenerate person does not as yet actually believe or repent, but only is capacitated thereto.[5]

The point is that regeneration provides not a new life but a new nature. The Spirit of God works his own nature (viz. divine love) in the heart, creating, as I addressed briefly in the previous chapter, sensible knowledge (a sense of the heart) of divine things.[6] Likewise, in the _Religious Affections_, Edwards uses, as he often does, the metaphor of taste to talk about this new sense. As a way of contrasting natural affection with spiritual, he compares two men, one who does not have the sense of taste and one who does, both of whom love honey. The first man loves honey because of its colour, the second because of its taste.[7] The second man has the excellency and sweetness of honey as the _foundation_ for his love, and that foundation is entirely distinct from what the first man can claim to have.[8] Likewise, the man who has true spiritual knowledge has

---

[1] John Owen, _The Holy Spirit_ (ed. William H. Goold; The Works of John Owen, vol. 3; London: Banner of Truth, 1966), 307; Francis Turretin, _Institutes of Elenctic Theology_ (ed. James T. Dennison; trans. George Musgrave Giger; vol. 2; Phillipsburg: P&R, 1992), 531; Peter van Mastricht, _A Treatise on Regeneration_ (Morgan: Soli Deo Gloria Publications, 2002), 26. So also, Sibbes, 'So the heart is the whole inward man. He not only enlightens the understanding, but infuseth grace into the will and affections, into the whole inward man. ... Therefore God doth not only open the understanding to conceive, but he opens the will to close with and to embrace that that [_sic_] is good. . . . You see then, here _is the opening of the heart before there is attending_. Before there can be any attending and applying of the mind, the mind must be sanctified and strengthened. The soul must be sanctified before it can attend.' Richard Sibbes, _The Works of Richard Sibbes_ (vol. 6; Edinburgh: James Nichol, 1863), 525.

[5] Mastricht, _A Treatise on Regeneration_, 26.

[6] This may seem to contradict my previous point that regeneration entails the first principle and not the continued exercise of that principle. By working divine love in the heart of the believer, the Spirit is not generating the believer's love, but is uniting them in love to the Son. The first principle entails, we might say, embracing the love of God as God's love for me.

[7] Y2, _Religious Affections_, 208–10. The example of tasting honey is used, not only by Edwards, but also by Shepard and Charnock before him. See Brad Walton, _Jonathan Edwards, Religious Affections, and the Puritan Analysis of True Piety, Spiritual Sensation, and Heart Religion_ (Studies in American Religion; Lewiston: The Edwin Mellen Press, 2002), 197.

[8] In his sermon on Rev. 14:2, Edwards states, 'The beginnings of future things are in this world. The seed must be sown here; the foundation must be laid in this world. Here is laid

a divine *taste* or *sense* of God, knowing God's excellency and glory with sensible knowledge rather than simply speculative. As Edwards claims in the *Religious Affections*, 'A spiritual application of an invitation or offer of the gospel consists in giving the soul a spiritual sense or relish of the holy and divine blessings offered.'[9] As I have emphasized, ectypal knowledge entails affectionate knowledge, built on the archetype of God beholding and relishing his own self and therefore cast into the mould of God's beatific delight. Furthermore, I have suggested that this emphasis is grounded in his focus on God as persons, necessitating a personal response by creatures and putting them on the path of *the* beatified pilgrim – Christ.

The Spirit's enlightening work gives the believer a sense or taste of God's excellency and glory, thereby allowing her to receive God's revelation of himself in Christ, to know God's love infused into her heart and to partake in the beatific-delight of God himself.[10] Edwards refers to this in his sermon 'The Threefold Work of the Holy Ghost' when he states, 'The Holy Spirit, when he enters, he lets in that divine light that discovers truth, and makes it appear as truth and shows the way of salvation, which appears and makes itself known by its own intrinsic evidence, which it carries with it.'[11] The believer knows, *sensibly*, with their heart (their inclining mind), that God is holy, lovely and true.

In brief, such are the contours of this section. The purpose of the following is not to offer a robust account of illumination or infusion but to exposit these in light of our interpretative scheme – God's beatific self-glorification – setting regeneration alongside spiritual knowledge on the continuum of emanation and remanation. Doing so will further outline, in broad strokes, Edwards's theology of redemption, as well as provide further justification for beatific self-glorification as an interpretative framework for Edwards's thought. Furthermore, this account will continue to help

---

the foundation of future misery, and of future happiness.' JEC, Unpublished Sermon, Rev. 14:2, #344 (under Application section II point 2). Likewise, using similar language, Mastricht states, 'This spiritual life, as conveyed in regeneration, is very imperfect, being only the first act or principle of spiritual life, and only the seeds of spiritual graces, which gradually, like the seeds of vegetables, grow up into the stalk, blossoms, and fruit. Hence the regenerate, merely as such, are called newborn babes.' Mastricht, *A Treatise on Regeneration*, 30.

[9] Y2, *Religious Affections*, 225.

[10] This emphasis on the Spirit providing a taste or sense was standard in the Puritan material leading up to Edwards. See Walton, *Jonathan Edwards*, 197–206.

[11] Y14, 'The Threefold Work of the Holy Ghost', 407. Following this quote, Edwards states, 'The whole soul accords and consents to it; all prevailing opposition ceases. The heart that before opposed, now yields; it opposes no longer, but entirely closes with it and adheres to it with the inclination and affection.' Y14, 'The Threefold Work of the Holy Ghost', 409; see also Y21, 'Treatise on Grace', 159, 174.

organize Edwards's vision of redemption, thereby helping inform religious affection, our last application point.

I The Spirit's Work: Illumination

As I have extensively shown, the work of redemption for Edwards requires that the elect *see God* through a glass darkly. Edwards, following the Reformed tradition, addresses the Spirit's work of illumination, infusion, regeneration and conversion,[12] which are, for him, logical delineations of one event. To focus our discussion, I advance regeneration as illumination and infusion, thereby following the Spirit's work in the souls of the saints. The key text that will serve as a guide for illumination is Edwards's sermon 'A Divine and Supernatural Light' (hereafter *Divine Light*). While our discussion differentiates these two interconnected realities, it is important to note that they are two effects of one act of the Spirit and therefore cannot truly be abstracted from one another.[13]

In *Divine Light*, Edwards follows Owen, Mastricht and Turretin in emphasizing the *immediacy* of the Spirit's work in the soul. This account pushes against the idea of 'moral suasion', that God somehow works externally to coax the unregenerate to regenerate.[14] For Edwards, this is impossible.

---

[12] See Turretin, *Institutes of Elenctic Theology*, vol. 2, 522–3; Owen, *The Holy Spirit*, 231, 320.

[13] Edwards's soteriology is organized by the economic activity of Son and Spirit and not by an individual theological locus (e.g. justification by faith). One of the reasons why commentators differ so radically and fail to follow the logic of Edwards's account is because they miss this point. See Kyle Strobel, 'By Word and Spirit: Jonathan Edwards on Redemption, Justification, and Regeneration', in *Jonathan Edwards and Justification* (ed. Josh Moody; Wheaton: Crossway, 2012), 45–69.

[14] Edwards follows Mastricht, who states, 'This [regeneration], certainly, is not a moral act, exercised in offering and inviting, as is the case with the external call, but it is a physical act, powerfully infusing spiritual life into the soul.' Mastricht, *A Treatise on Regeneration*, 17. See also Y21, 'Editor's Introduction', 41; Y21, 'Treatise on Grace', 165; Y21, 'Efficacious Grace, Book I', 202, 207–8, 218. Edwards sounds remarkably close to Mastricht when he states that 'nothing will be produced but only an improvement and new modification of those principles that are exercised. Therefore it follows that saving grace in the heart, can't be produced in man by mere exercise of what perfections he has in him already, though never so much assisted by moral suasion, and never so much assisted in the exercise of his natural principles, unless there be something more than all this, viz. an immediate infusion or operation of the Divine Being upon the soul.' Y21, 'Treatise on Grace', 165. Also, in his sermon on Jn 3.3, Edwards states, 'The change of man from a sinner to a saint is not a moral, but a physical change.' Y17, 'Born Again', 187. Edwards states in his 'Efficacious Grace, Book I', 'If the Spirit of God does anything at all besides moral suasion, his grace is efficacious'; as well as, 'to deny any physical influence at all of the Spirit of God on the will, but only MORAL SUASION ... is to deny that the Spirit of God does anything at all.' Y21, 'Efficacious Grace, Book I', 202, 207; see also Turretin, *Institutes of Elenctic Theology*, vol. 2, 524. Edwards, Mastricht and Turretin all seem to be arguing toward the same end. Turretin goes on to

Regeneration entails a new creation, a new nature, and not merely an additional power added to the faculties. *Seeing* God, in other words, and thereby knowing him, is not an act of ratiocination. In his *Treatise on Grace*, Edwards summarizes well,

> Therefore, it follows that saving grace in the heart, can't be produced in man by mere exercise of what perfections he has in him already, though never so much assisted by moral suasion, and never so much assisted in the exercise of his natural principles, unless there be something more than all this, viz. an immediate infusion or operation of the Divine Being upon the soul. Grace must be the immediate work of God, and properly a production of his almighty power on the soul.[15]

Highlighting the nature of spiritual and divine light, Edwards begins *Divine Light* by addressing what it is not, three aspects of which I highlight here. First, he draws a distinction between common and special illumination, which parallels the distinction between common and saving grace.[16] In both instances, the Spirit is the one working illumination and grace, but the Spirit's 'common' working has no saving influence and is merely external. The Spirit's work of special illumination and saving grace, however, include the Spirit's further work of infusion in the being of the elect, ministering

---

use the term 'hyperphysically' when talking about infusion, and he seems concerned that 'physical' might be linked with 'natural'.

[15] Y21, 'Treatise on Grace', 165. Edwards emphasizes the polemical nature of his use of 'immediacy': 'Therefore so many schemes have been drawn to exclude, or extenuate, or remove at a great distance, any influence of the Divine Being in the hearts of men, such as the scheme of the Pelagians, the Socinians, etc.' Y21, 'Treatise on Grace', 177. Edwards explains his usage in *Divine Light*, saying, 'When it is said that this light is given immediately by God, and not obtained by natural means, hereby is intended, that 'tis given by God without making use of any means that operate by their own power, or a natural force. God makes use of means; but 'tis not as mediate causes to produce this effect.' Y17, 'A Divine and Supernatural Light', 416. McClenahan argues that Edwards's use of 'Immediacy' is a technical theological term, used specifically in reference to Tillotson, who attempted to argue that faith was attributed to the Spirit's work, but not immediately persuading people of the truth. See Michael McClenahan, 'Jonathan Edwards's Doctrine of Justification in the Period up to the First Great Awakening' (unpublished doctoral dissertation, University of Oxford, 2006), 287. To Edwards, Tillotson's claim is that God only acts on people in the same manner as the devil. Edwards spent considerable time throughout his life undercutting just those kinds of assertions. McClenahan seems correct about the polemical piece, and there is little doubt that Edwards would utilize this with his polemics in mind, but this term is widely used in this context so must not be seen as simply Edwards's polemics (see Turretin, *Institutes of Elenctic Theology*, vol. 2, 526, 529–30, for an example). Cherry argues similarly as McClenahan, minus the Arminian polemical piece. Conrad Cherry, *The Theology of Jonathan Edwards: A Reappraisal* (Bloomington: Indiana University Press, 1990), 44–55.

[16] See Y17, 'A Divine and Supernatural Light', 410.

by his own nature, namely, as the *Holy* Spirit. In the first instance, the Spirit assists, but in the second the Spirit 'exists in the soul habitually'.[17] Second, Edwards argues that this light does not consist in an impression on the imagination, as if it were seen with bodily eyes, stating, "Tis no imagination or idea of an outward light or glory, or any beauty of form or countenance, or a visible luster or brightness of any object.'[18] These ideas of imagination may accompany the spiritual light, but they are not constitutive of it. The spiritual and divine light is a *spiritual* reality that is seen *spiritually* (just as in heaven). This frames his third point, that this light does not offer new truths or propositions. Rather, this light gives a 'due apprehension of those things that are taught in the Word of God'.[19]

    The Spirit's gifting of divine light illumines the elect to see God's beauty, excellency and holiness; it does not offer secret knowledge.[20] The divine light is 'a true sense of the divine excellency of the things revealed in the Word of God, and a conviction of the truth and reality of them, thence arising'.[21] It truly enlightens what is already visible so that the elect see and experience the invisible realities. This special illumination of the Spirit of God results in a saving conviction of the gospel because it is a sight of the excellency and glory of God. Illumination, as noted above, inseparable from infusion, actually changes the nature of the creature. Turretin argues similarly, claiming that man 'cannot properly understand and will in the sphere of morals unless renewed by supernatural dispositions and habits'.[22] Edwards's understanding of God's excellency and glory functions in the moral register of God's being, utilizing illumination and infusion as regeneration to correlate the creature to this reality. Again, tracing the contours of our essence/person distinction, to truly see God, one must not only see his natural attributes (greatness, strength, etc.) but must also see his moral attributes (holiness, glory, etc.) – *who* he is rather than *what*. This sight is accomplished in two ways: First, illumination offers, '[a] true sense of the

[17] Y17, 'A Divine and Supernatural Light', 411.
[18] Y17, 'A Divine and Supernatural Light', 412.
[19] Y17, 'A Divine and Supernatural Light', 412. Likewise, see Owen, *The Holy Spirit*, 234–40. One familiar with Edwards's writings can't help but remember Edwards's 'Personal Narrative', where he describes his experience of hating the doctrine of sovereignty shift to delighting in it. After that experience, he states, 'The doctrine of God's sovereignty has very often appeared, an exceeding pleasant, bright and sweet doctrine to me: and absolute sovereignty is what I love to ascribe to God.' Y16, 'Personal Narrative', 792.
[20] Edwards's fourth point concerns affections, and how not every affecting sight of God derives from the spiritual and divine light. See Y17, 'A Divine and Supernatural Light', 412–13.
[21] Y17, 'A Divine and Supernatural Light', 413.
[22] Turretin, *Institutes of Elenctic Theology*, vol. 2, 523.

divine and superlative excellency of the things of religion'.[23] This light, in other words, illumines revelation so as to reveal the excellency of God in Christ and his working of redemption. Furthermore, this light illumines in such a way, or, better, illumines such a subject, that it provides a *sense* of *his* excellency and glory. Edwards continues, 'He that is spiritually enlightened truly apprehends and sees it, or has a sense of it. He don't merely rationally believe that God is glorious, but he has a sense of the gloriousness of God in his heart.'[24] Knowledge of God entails a sense of God's glory as true beauty, therefore Edwards invokes his delineation between speculative or notional knowledge and a 'sensible' knowledge, or as here, a sense of the heart.[25]

As we have seen, for Edwards, knowledge of God is *affective* knowledge, and therefore true knowledge of God must be sensible knowledge, knowledge which inclines.[26] All ectypal knowledge is formed by the archetype of God's self-knowing and self-loving. A mere rational knowledge cannot suffice because God is not a divine mind pondering equations but has affectionate self-knowledge – the Father gazing upon the Son and emanating love, happiness and delight. True knowledge of God, to be saving knowledge, is not merely knowing things about God, even true things, but gazing upon God and having one's heart moved in love. Edwards asserts, 'When the heart is sensible of the beauty and amiableness of a thing, it necessarily feels pleasure in the apprehension.'[27] This assertion proves important for

---

[23] Y17, 'A Divine and Supernatural Light', 413.

[24] Y17, 'A Divine and Supernatural Light', 413. Note how Edwards ties this spiritual light to the love of God: 'Hence we learn the distinguishing nature of true spiritual light, that it brings divine love into the heart with it. When a person is converted, then the day dawns and the daystar arises in his heart. There is a beam of divine light let into the soul, but this light always brings love into the heart. The soul the same moment that 'tis filled with spiritual light 'tis also filled with divine love. The heart immediately goes out after God and the Lord Jesus Christ. ... When light and love go together, they show the truth of one another, they evidence the divinity of each.' Jonathan Edwards, 'The Spirit of the True Saints Is a Spirit of Divine Love', in *The Glory and Honor of God: Volume 2 of the Previously Unpublished Sermons of Jonathan Edwards* (ed. Michael D. McMullen; Nashville: Broadman & Holman, 2004), 312.

[25] Owen navigates the same claim by stating, 'There is a wide difference between the mind's receiving doctrines *notionally*, and its receiving the things taught in them *really*.' Owen, *The Holy Spirit*, 260. Mastricht likewise claims that the regenerate 'know spiritual objects not only speculatively as true, but practically as good'. Mastricht, *A Treatise on Regeneration*, 22, see also 42 for how practical knowledge affects the will.

[26] In his *Treatise on Grace*, Edwards claims, 'So that that holy, divine principle, which we have observed does radically and essentially consist in divine love, is no other than a communication and participation of that same infinite divine love, which is God, and in which the Godhead is eternally breathed forth and subsists in the third person in the blessed Trinity.' Y21, 'Treatise on Grace', 194.

[27] Y17, 'A Divine and Supernatural Light', 414.

understanding God's work of redemption and will be emphasized in our discussion of religious affections.

Furthermore, illumination convicts the believer of the truth both indirectly and directly: indirectly, by removing hindrances and prejudices and by sanctifying the reason, and directly, by *immediately* containing within it conviction of the truth. Therefore, the Spirit's indirect work enables the elect to see clearly: 'The ideas themselves that otherwise are dim, and obscure, are by this means impressed with the greater strength, and have a light cast upon them; so that the mind can better judge of them.'[28] Likewise, the Spirit's direct work immediately convinces of the truth because the excellency is divine excellency.[29] In illuminating creatures this way, Edwards asserts, God deals with people according to their nature, as rational creatures, making use of human faculties, or, as I have emphasized, as *persons*.[30] God does not ignore or bypass the faculties but utilizes them. In Edwards's words, 'The natural faculties are the subject of this light: and they are the subject in such a manner, that they are not merely passive, but active in it; and acts and exercises of man's understanding are concerned and made use of in it.'[31] The Spirit's work, therefore, truly enlightens, allowing the person to receive and respond rightly. Edwards explains,

> God in letting in this light into the soul, deals with man according to his nature, or as a rational creature; and makes use of his human faculties. But yet this light is not the less immediately from God for that; though the faculties are made use of, 'tis as the subject and not as the cause; and that acting of the faculties in it, is not the cause, but is either implied in the thing itself (in the light that is imparted), or is the consequence of it. As the use that we make of our eyes in beholding various objects, when the sun arises, is not the cause of the light that discovers those objects to us.[32]

This last phrase is as important as it is convoluted. Edwards continually employs the image of the sun to describe both the Trinity itself and the

[28] Y17, 'A Divine and Supernatural Light', 415.
[29] Y17, 'A Divine and Supernatural Light', 415. For a similar dissection of the issues, see Mastricht, *A Treatise on Regeneration*, 22–3, and Owen *The Holy Spirit*, 266–7. Owen claims that there is a twofold impotency in man, a natural and a moral, which can only be 'cured' through an immediate operation of the Spirit of God in illumination.
[30] This is, again, standard: See Owen, *The Holy Spirit*, 221–8, 238–40, 261–2; Mastricht, *A Treatise on Regeneration*, 22–6; Turretin, *Institutes of Elenctic Theology*, vol. 2, 522–3.
[31] Y17, 'A Divine and Supernatural Light', 416.
[32] Y17, 'A Divine and Supernatural Light', 416.

work of illumination by the Spirit, as I will show more fully below. Here, the force of his statement is that divine light does not bypass the understanding but allows it to see correctly, just as the sun's light illuminates objects for the eye to behold. Far from being anti-intellectual, or somehow undermining the understanding, Edwards posits this beholding of divine beauty as the highest intellectual enterprise.[33] Therefore, God's illuminating work, coupled with the infusion of the Spirit into the elect, allows the elect to *see* rightly and therefore be sanctified into God's image.[34] Edwards closes out his sermon by noting, 'This light is such as effectually influences the inclination, and changes the nature of the soul. It assimilates the nature of the divine nature, and changes the soul into an image of the same glory that is beheld.'[35] The sanctifying effect of this knowledge is that it will, in Edwards's words, 'wean from the world, and raise the inclination to heavenly things'.[36] This light is effectual because it is Christ's calling of the soul to himself, and his call does not return unfulfilled.[37] Again, in Edwards's words,

> This light, and this only, will bring the soul to a saving close with Christ. It conforms the heart to the gospel, mortifies its enmity and opposition against the scheme of salvation therein revealed: it causes the heart to embrace the joyful tidings, and entirely to adhere to, and acquiesce in the revelation of Christ as our Savior; it causes the whole soul to accord and symphonize with it, admitting it with entire credit and respect, cleaving to it with full inclination and affection. And it effectually disposes the soul to give up itself entirely to Christ.[38]

[33] See Y17, 'The Pure in Heart Blessed', 67.
[34] This work, as noted above, simply is the work of regeneration. This is seen in the strength of the language Edwards uses to talk about it: 'This light is such as effectually influences the inclination, and changes the nature of the soul. It assimilates the nature to the divine nature, and changes the soul into an image of the same glory that is beheld. ... This light, and this only, will bring the soul to a saving close with Christ.' Y17, 'A Divine and Supernatural Light', 424. Likewise, Edwards claims, 'I would observe that it must needs be that conversion is wrought at once. That knowledge, that reformation and conviction that is preparatory to conversion may be gradual, and the work of grace after conversion may be gradually carried on; yet that work of grace upon the soul whereby a person is brought out of a state of total corruption and depravity into a state of grace, to an interest in Christ, and to be actually a child of God, is in a moment.' Y21, 'Treatise on Grace', 161. Furthermore, Edwards uses new birth, regeneration, calling and 'opening the eyes of the blind' synonymously with conversion. See Y21, 'Treatise on Grace', 160–1.
[35] Y17, 'A Divine and Supernatural Light', 424.
[36] Y17, 'A Divine and Supernatural Light', 424.
[37] Y21, 'Treatise on Grace', 162.
[38] Y17, 'A Divine and Supernatural Light', 424.

1. The Effect of Illumination on the Soul

The divine and supernatural light *causes* a sense of the heart because it illumines, from within, the excellency, glory and holiness of God in Christ. The sense of the heart is an effect of the Spirit, infused into the elect, illuminating the glory, holiness and excellency of Christ to the believer so that their apprehension of these things leads to understanding God and being inclined toward him. Both the regenerate and the unregenerate have a sense of the heart: the regenerate have a sense of the heart concerning God and his self-revelation and the unregenerate a sense of the heart toward self-love and evil.[39] Edwards, possibly for clarity and consistency, focuses his use of 'sense of the heart' on sensible knowledge *of God*, a usage I follow here. *This* sense of the heart is a corollary of illumination and is the means by which God orders the soul for the Spirit's habitation. This becomes clear when Edwards invokes the doctrine of illumination and glosses the material typically addressed by the sense of the heart with the idea of 'receiving':

> One glimpse of the moral and spiritual glory of God, and supreme amiableness of Jesus Christ, shining into the heart, overcomes and abolishes this opposition, and inclines the soul to Christ, as it were, by an omnipotent power: so that now, not only the understanding, but the will, and the whole soul *receives* and *embraces* the Savior. This is most certainly the discovery, which is the first internal *foundation* of a saving faith in Christ.[40]

Edwards can gloss his 'sense of the heart' by speaking of the understanding and will *receiving* and *embracing* God's revelation in Christ. But how are we to understand his use of 'foundation' here? Notably, the discovery itself is the foundation of saving faith. In light of my analysis, it is fitting to say that the spiritual sense is a taste because it is the dawning of glory in the soul, a glory that orders the soul according to a principle of love by the infusion of the Spirit. In *Religious Affections*, Edwards covers the same material by stating,

---

[39] This is seen in *Miscellanies* 732, where Edwards states, 'The mind of a natural man is capable of a sense of the heart of natural [evil], or of those things that are terrible to nature. ... For the mind of man, without any supernatural principle, is in like manner capable of two things, viz. (1) of a conviction of the judgments by reasons that evince the truth of the things of religious, that respect natural good; and (2) of a sense of heart of natural good.' Y18, '*Miscellanies* 732. Common Illumination', 358.

[40] Y25, 'True Grace', 635–6 – my emphasis.

This new spiritual sense, and the new dispositions that attend it, are no new faculties, but are new principles of nature. I use the word 'principles', for want of a word of a more determinate signification. By a principle of nature in this place, I mean that *foundation which is laid in nature*, either old or new, for any particular manner or kind of exercise of the faculties of the soul … so that to exert the faculties in that kind of exercises, may be said to be his nature. So this new spiritual sense is not a new faculty of understanding, but it is a new *foundation laid in the nature* of the soul, for a new kind of exercises of the same faculty of understanding. So that new holy disposition of heart that attends this new sense, is not a new faculty of will, but a *foundation laid in the nature* of the soul, for a new kind of exercises of the same faculty of will.[41]

This sense, Edwards claims, is an entirely new *perception* or *sensation* of the mind, and he links it to Locke's idea of a 'new simple idea'.[42] Therefore, the foundation laid in the nature of the elect is simply the impression made on the soul by the perception and sensation of pilgrim-beatific glory; it is the light of God's holiness, beauty and glory dawning in the soul and awakening it to the reality of God. In *True Virtue*, Edwards uses similar language to talk about the natural affection between members of the opposite sex, claiming that 'there is a *foundation laid in nature* for kind affections between the sexes.'[43] This foundation is a *natural* ordering of the soul which grounds perception and inclination toward the opposite sex. By

---

[41] Y2, *Religious Affections*, 206 – my emphasis. Walton helpfully notes, 'As in Edwards, so in his predecessors, the notion of a spiritual sensation provides the basis for discussing regeneration in sensual and aesthetic terms. Hence appear innumerable references to "seeing" and "tasting" the divine attributes, to experiencing, "relishing", "delighting" in the "beauty" of God, and to valuing God's "beauty" as it is in itself, without reference to self-love. Several authors, including Sibbes, Goodwin and Owen, consider the "affective" knowledge of God, derived from the "experience" of divine realities mediated through spiritual sensation, as one of the fundamental signs, if not *the* fundamental sign, of true grace.' Walton, *Jonathan Edwards*, 137. Walton's purpose is to show continuity between Edwards and his predecessors, while I have focused on exposing how Edwards coheres within his own work rather than the tradition. Nonetheless, Walton's point is helpful. Edwards, as emphasized repeatedly in this thesis, is a Reformed theologian who worked creatively in the tradition handed him.

[42] Y2, *Religious Affection*, 205. Walton makes an important point concerning Edwards's use of the term 'new simple idea': 'It will be noted how similar van Mastricht's term for a perception, *intelligentia simplex*, is to Locke's term, "simple idea". It is also to be noted that van Mastricht, like Edwards, but unlike Locke, understands perception to be essentially volitional.' Walton, *Jonathan Edwards*, 201. We agree with Walton's further assessment that 'a comparative review of *Religious Affections* and "Miscellany 782" with Locke's *Essay* will show that, with regard to the ideas developed in these two Edwardsian works, there are more differences than similarities between the Calvinist and the empiricist'. Walton, *Jonathan Edwards*, 206

[43] Y8, *True Virtue*, 604 – my emphasis.

the Spirit working his grace in the heart of a person, she is truly affected *super*naturally to God; the faculties are rightly ordered, thereby having a right foundation.[44] The foundation, therefore, laid in the nature of the regenerate, is the effect on the soul by the presence of the Spirit as light and holiness. It is the *taste* of divine beauty provided by illumination.[45] As I will emphasize below, grace working in the soul is not its own principle or habit but is the Spirit acting as a principle there. The soul welcomes this action because it has been ordered accordingly; fleshly self-love no longer reigns in the will, but love of God reorders the soul to receive his grace.[46] The work of regeneration, as illumination and infusion, is completed simultaneously, only allowing for logical and not temporal delineations.

5.1.1.1 Owen and Illumination

It will prove instructive to provide a sketch of Owen's statements concerning this same issue. Owen, like Edwards, claims that the mind 'is renewed by grace, or brought into another habitude and frame, by the implantation of a ruling, guiding, spiritual light in it'.[47] Owen, like Edwards, focuses on the light entering the soul and the necessity of the heart's being the object of change. Owen uses the idea of a 'practical principle' in the heart that plays the same role as Edwards's 'sensible' knowledge. Likewise, Owen sets up a similar issue to Edwards, claiming, 'The true nature of saving illumination consists in this, that it gives the mind such a direct intuitive insight and prospect into spiritual things as that, in their own spiritual nature, they suit, please, and satisfy it, so that it is transformed into them, cast into the mould of them, and rests in them.'[48]

Therefore, the question for Owen, just as for Edwards, becomes, what change happens to allow for this new spiritual understanding? This is

---

[44] My distinction is that Edwards uses the term 'foundation' more for the effect of the Spirit's presence than the Spirit himself. The Spirit's illumination provides a 'taste' of glory, and that taste, with the presence of the Spirit in the soul, helps to order the believer to beauty rather than destruction.

[45] Y25, 'True Grace', 636.

[46] Man is returned, in a sense, to his situation pre-Fall, with certain differences noted below. Edwards states, in *Miscellanies* 471: 'But in the sanctifying work of the Holy Ghost, not only remaining principles are assisted to do their work to a greater degree, but those principles are restored that were utterly destroyed by the fall; [so that] the mind habitually exerts those acts that the dominion of sin had made the soul wholly destitute of, as much as a dead body is destitute of vital acts.' Y13, '*Miscellanies* 471. Spirit's Operation', 513.

[47] Owen, *The Holy Spirit*, 252. Earlier in the same work, Owen claims, 'Spiritual darkness is in and upon all men, until God, by an almighty and effectual work of the Spirit, shine into them, or create light in them.' Owen, *The Holy Spirit*, 246.

[48] Owen, *The Holy Spirit*, 238.

where Owen invokes language Edwards refuses, which offers a plausible reason why Edwards is so adamant that his 'sense of the heart' is not a new faculty in the soul. Owen argues that God 'is said to give us a *new faculty*, because of the utter disability of our minds naturally to receive them [perceptions of spiritual things]'.[49] Likewise, in parallel with his new 'visive faculty' provided to the elect in heaven, Owen again claims that upon regeneration the elect are given a 'visive faculty' to discern and see spiritually.[50] The work this new faculty does for Owen is almost identical, mutatis mutandis, to the work Edwards's pneumatology does for him, and Owen's understanding of illumination, just as for Edwards, gives a 'new nature' and inclines the person to 'evangelical obedience'.[51] Likewise, the light, in revealing these mysteries, 'lay[s] them as the foundation for faith and obedience. It inlays them in the mind, and thereby conforms the whole soul unto them.'[52]

While Edwards turns to his trinitarian resources to link the infused principles of grace, love and holiness to the Spirit's work *ad intra*, and therefore *ad extra* in his mission to sanctify, Owen abstracts principles and dispositions of grace and invokes the language of 'faculties'. Edwards, committed to his trinitarian psychology of a being with understanding and will, refuses new faculties because the regenerate would be, in a sense, other than human persons. Edwards's trinitarian thought has resources of its own to address this issue, highlighted by his use of the sun's light and heat as a depiction of the economic life of God. Both Owen and Edwards, therefore, can make the point that, in Owen's words, 'this consists in a new, spiritual, supernatural, vital principle or habit of grace, infused into the soul, the mind, will and affection, by the power

---

[49] Owen, *The Holy Spirit*, 252 – my emphasis. I am unsure how Owen holds this view with his statement that 'there is an eye in the understanding of man, – that is, the natural power and ability that is in it to discern spiritual things'. Owen, *The Holy Spirit*, 332. And likewise, 'The grace, therefore, here asserted in the giving of an understanding is the causing of our natural understandings to understand savingly.' Owen, *The Holy Spirit*, 331. A possible explanation is developed when he delineates a '*twofold capacity* or *ability*' of receiving, knowing, or understanding spiritual things in the mind of man'. First, a natural power in man, whereby he uses his natural faculties for notional knowledge. God's giving understanding therefore necessitates renovation by grace. Second, man has a 'power' in the mind to discern spiritual objects, necessitating the 'visive faculty', that is both supernatural and spiritual. In his words, 'Wherefore, between the natural capacity of the mind and the act of spiritual discerning there must be an interposition of an effectual work of the Holy Ghost enabling it thereunto.' Owen, *The Holy Spirit*, 262.

[50] Owen, *The Holy Spirit*, 246: 'There was no creature that has a visive faculty; there was darkness subjectively in all.'

[51] See Owen, *The Holy Spirit*, 278–9.

[52] Owen, *The Holy Spirit*, 279.

of the Holy Spirit',[53] and mean very different things. For Owen, this infusing is exactly as he says, while for Edwards, the Spirit infuses *himself* into the soul of the believer, *functioning* there as a principle of life and holiness. Owen, furthermore, speaks of the Spirit's *creating* the new saving light of illumination, whereas for Edwards, the Spirit is that light.[54] Just as knowledge entails participation in Christ, God's self-understanding, so also regeneration, as being made holy, necessitates participation in the *Holy* Spirit as the divine principle of love, grace and holiness. Edwards, in conceiving of eternity as participation in the inner life of God, orients redemption around partaking in God's *own* personal beatific-delight, rather than around abstracted principles of grace.

5.1.1.2 Foundation in the Soul and the Holy Spirit

Before moving on, I briefly engage the debate concerning the function of the Holy Spirit within the elect and the foundation laid in the nature of the soul. Michael McClenahan argues that Edwards distinguishes the indwelling of the Holy Spirit from the new foundation that is laid in the soul.[55] I have made a similar assumption here.[56] McClenahan, however, moves beyond this to argue that grace can exist outside of the Spirit, claiming that Edwards's view is identical to Owen's: 'It is clear that these new principles of nature are infused habits of grace, which provide a new foundation for gracious acts,' and he conceives of these as *from* the

---

[53] Owen, *The Holy Spirit*, 329. Likewise, 'The principle itself infused into us, created in us, is called the "new man"'. Owen, *The Holy Spirit*, 221. Furthermore, he states, 'In the circumcision of our hearts, wherein the flesh, with the lusts, affections, and deeds thereof, is crucified by the Spirit, he takes from them their enmity, carnal prejudices, and depraved inclinations, really though not absolutely and perfectly; and instead of them he fills us with *holy spiritual love, joy, fear, and delight*, not changing the being of our affections, but sanctifying and guiding them by the principle of saving light and knowledge before described.' Owen, *The Holy Spirit*, 335.

[54] It might be better to say that the Spirit is the means by which the light, namely Christ, enters the soul, but separating those here does not seem helpful.

[55] McClenahan, 'Jonathan Edwards's Doctrine of Justification', 294–5.

[56] It has been popular as of late to talk about Lombard's view of uncreated grace and Aquinas's view of uncreated and created grace (see Anri Morimoto, *Jonathan Edwards and the Catholic Vision of Salvation* (University Park: Pennsylvania State University Press, 1995), 41–50; Sang Hyun Lee, 'Grace and Justification by Faith Alone', in *The Princeton Companion to Jonathan Edwards* (ed. Sang Hyun Lee; Princeton: Princeton University Press, 2005), 131–2; Gerald R. McDermott, 'Jonathan Edwards on Justification by Faith – More Protestant or Catholic', *Pro Ecclesia: A Journal of Catholic and Evangelical Theology* 27, no. 1 (2008), 92–111; John J. Bombaro, 'Jonathan Edwards's Vision of Salvation', *Westminster Theological Journal* 65 (2003), 45–67. I will avoid this language in my analysis because I find it relatively unhelpful and foreign to Edwards. If pushed on placing Edwards on this continuum somewhere, I would have to agree with Bombaro, against Morimoto, that Edwards only allows for 'uncreated' grace at work in man, namely, the Spirit of God.

Spirit but not the Spirit functioning as a principle of grace himself.[57]
McClenahan here fails to do justice to Edwards's trinitarian theology, his
depiction of spiritual knowledge or his ubiquitous depiction of the Spirit *as
the* principle of grace. Instead, he confuses the issues and claims, 'The light
is not the indwelling Spirit or a new faculty created in the soul, but is the
effect of the Spirit's renovation on human understanding.'[58] McClenahan,
not recognizing their logical demarcations, collapses the discussion of the
new foundation laid in the soul, illumination and infusion into one. But
Edwards is clear on this issue: the Spirit is infused as a habit of grace that
orders the soul as God's love, and it is nonsensical to posit an 'infused habit
of grace' other than or outside of the Spirit.[59] In contrasting my claim with
McClenahan's, I highlight the interpretative gains of my dogmatic account.

In his analysis of the issues, McClenahan attempts to dispose of Cherry
and Waddington's view that the Spirit functions as a habit of grace, simply
by invoking Owen, but he fails to recognize that it is exactly at this point
where Edwards's pneumatology advances beyond Owen's own.[60] Edwards's
trinitarian theology either possesses resources that Owen's does not or else
Owen simply fails to utilize trinitarian insights here. This is why Edwards,
instead of invoking a new faculty – or, as McClenahan has it, gracious dispositions and habits beyond the Spirit – claims, 'I suppose there is no other
principle of grace in the soul than the very Holy Ghost dwelling in the soul
and acting there as a vital principle.'[61] Edwards continues to emphasize that
further acts of grace in the soul are created only by the Spirit's work *as a
principle*, just as he does in the inner life of God. Further, in his *Treatise on
Grace*, Edwards distances himself from the view that one ought 'to speak
of a habit of grace *as a natural disposition to act grace*, as begotten in the
soul by the first communication of divine light, and as the natural and

[57] McClenahan, 296. McClenahan assumes that if he can show that Edwards's use of 'immediately' does not undermine the use of holy principles which are not the Spirit himself,
then his point follows. It does not. McClenahan never moves beyond showing that his
point is possible. In the end, Edwards's positive statements linking the Holy Spirit to the
grace infused in the soul and the trinitarian theology that gives the term 'grace' meaning,
undermine his efforts. Terms like 'grace' and 'holiness' have no meaning outside of the
Spirit.
[58] McClenahan, 'Jonathan Edwards's Doctrine of Justification', 296 – my emphasis.
[59] This is presumably Edwards's assumption when, in *Religious Affections*, he baldly states, 'The
Spirit is no revelation of any fact by immediate suggestion, but is grace itself in the soul.'
Y2, '*Religious Affections*', 234.
[60] See Cherry, *Theology of Jonathan Edwards*, 42, Jeffrey C. Waddington, 'Jonathan Edwards's
"Ambiguous and Somewhat Precarious" Doctrine of Justification', *Westminster Theological
Journal* 66 (2004), 352–72 (367). McClenahan attempted to make the same move with Lee,
once again invoking Owen. See McClenahan, 'Jonathan Edwards's Doctrine of Justification',
286.
[61] Y21, 'Treatise on Grace', 196.

necessary consequence of the first light, it seems in some respects to carry a wrong idea with it'.[62] Along these lines Caldwell states, 'The central role the Spirit plays in regeneration is not unlike his role within the Trinity. ... Edwards conceived the entire scope of redemption to be, in one sense, an "externalization" of the Trinity, the Trinity turned "inside-out" '.[63] While McClenahan is correct to note the difference between the foundation laid in the soul by the illuminating work of the Spirit and the Spirit himself, by ignoring how Edwards puts his pneumatological insights to work, he fails to understand that the Spirit acts as a habit of grace upholding the soul by *being the very love of God itself dwelling there.*

McClenahan's critique stems from a misunderstanding of what I have been emphasizing here, namely, that God treats people as *people*; or, with Owen and Mastricht, that God treats people as rational creatures.[64] McClenahan's allergy to Edwards's position derives from his belief that it necessarily undermines the integrity of the human person, as if the Spirit would overpower the faculties rather than free them from their bondage.[65] It is difficult to see why this critique must hold.[66] Edwards's position affirms, time and again, that God treats persons as *rational* creatures, which is why he has a robust understanding of illumination that does not bypass the faculties but 'enlightens' them. The Spirit's illuminating work is not merely a work done at the outset of the Christian life but *is integral to the work of sanctification itself.* The Spirit's direct effect on the soul allows the regenerate to apprehend the beatific-glory of God, and that work, as seen in *Divine Light,* clarifies/sanctifies understanding and inclines the will to God. As Edwards stated in his notebook on 'Efficacious Grace',

---

[62] Y21, 'Treatise on Grace', 196 – my emphasis. 'Natural' here should be read as 'apart from the Spirit'.

[63] Robert W. Caldwell, *Communion in the Spirit: The Holy Spirit as the Bond of Union in the Theology of Jonathan Edwards* (Studies in Evangelical History and Thought; Waynesboro: Paternoster, 2006), 102.

[64] See Owen, *The Holy Spirit*, 250–2; Mastricht, *A Treatise on Regeneration*, 11; Turretin, *Institutes of Elenctic Theology*, vol. 2, 524.

[65] Reflecting on the Holy Spirit as a disposition in the soul, McClenahan states, 'If this is in fact Edwards's view, it is very difficult to see how he can retain the integrity of the human person.' McClenahan, 'Jonathan Edwards's Doctrine of Justification', 294.

[66] As Scripture attests, 'Where the Spirit of the Lord is, there is freedom' (ESV). Interestingly, Edwards ties the freedom in the Spirit to both sight and adoption into God's life. See Y15, '89. 2 Corinthians 3:17–18', 76, and Y15, '196. Galatians 5:18', 115. Furthermore, it is hard to see why McClenahan believes his view would salvage this. If he is correct, that invoking the Spirit as a principle of grace in the heart would somehow undermine personhood, then grace acting in the heart as a principle would do this just the same. There is no functional difference between the Spirit working grace in the heart and the Spirit functioning in the heart as a principle of grace. The point Edwards wants to emphasize is that grace, apart from the Spirit, cannot exist.

We are not merely passive in it [efficacious grace], nor yet does God do some and we do the rest, but God does all and we do all. God produces all and we act all. For that is what he produces, our own acts. God is the only proper author and fountain; we only are the proper actors. We are in different respects wholly passive and wholly active.[67]

In this sense, the illumination of the Spirit, as an indwelling principle of grace, disposes the soul to freely will God. In his sermon 'The Pleasantness of Religion', Edwards states that 'in the religious man, all the powers are of one consent, and there is peace among them, and they all concur in the same thing'.[68] This only occurs as the Spirit dwelling in man holds his soul in order, enlightening the glory, holiness and beauty of God in Christ.[69] Furthermore, in *Charity and Its Fruits*, Edwards states,

But when the Spirit by his ordinary influences bestows saving grace, he therein imparts himself to the soul in his own holy nature; that nature on account of which he is so often called in Scripture the Holy Ghost, or the Holy Spirit. By his producing this effect the Spirit becomes an indwelling vital principle in the soul, and the subject becomes a spiritual being, denominated so from the Spirit of God which dwells in him. ... Yea, grace is as it were the holy nature of the Spirit of God imparted to the soul.[70]

It may seem ambiguous that the Holy Spirit imparts grace, or his 'holy nature', to the soul in infusion. Furthermore, Edwards may be seen to muddy the waters in claiming that true grace in the heart is 'the preciousness of the heart, by which it becomes precious or excellent; by which the very soul itself becomes a precious jewel'.[71] At first glance, one might believe that this points to McClenahan's view – the Spirit must make the soul into a 'precious jewel' by infusing 'habits of grace'. But this would be a misguided conclusion. In a letter to an unnamed correspondent

---

[67] Y21, 'Efficacious Grace, Book III', 251. In his 'Blank Bible', Edwards states, concerning Rom. 8:1–4, 'The Spirit dwelling in believers as a principle of life and action, or as the Spirit that they walk after, delivers them from the power of sin over them.' Y24, 'Romans 8:1–4', 1009.

[68] Y14, 'The Pleasantness of Religion', 107.

[69] Edwards also has an idea of the Spirit acting as the uniting action of one's own being, so that a person has union within themselves. See Y8, *True Virtue*, 589–90, and William J. Danaher, *The Trinitarian Ethics of Jonathan Edwards* (Columbia Series in Reformed Theology; Louisville: Westminster John Knox, 2004), 58.

[70] Y8, 'Charity and Its Fruits', 158.

[71] Y8, 'Charity and Its Fruits', 158.

concerning issues raised in *Religious Affections*, Edwards states that the Holy Spirit has holiness as a part of his nature in two respects. First, his beauty and glory can be understood as his nature, similarly to the way 'brightness' may be said to be the nature of the sun. Second, the Spirit's 'proper character' is in respect to his office and work, where the elect are his concern.[72] Again, as noted previously, he invokes the image of light and heat being the nature of the sun, but here he claims that getting a 'sun tan' does not communicate the essence of the sun. Likewise, 'A diamond or crystal that is held forth in the sun's beams may properly be said to have some of the sun's brightness communicated to it; for though it hasn't the same individual brightness with that which is inherent in the sun ... yet it is something of the same nature.'[73]

Again, as I have been emphasizing, the focus of Edwards's trinitarian thought is not on essence language, therefore, not the Holy *Spirit*, but focuses on persons and natures, or *Holy* Spirit. Here Edwards is concerned to show how grace functions in the heart by invoking *theosis* as his governing image of redemption.[74] In short, the Spirit's immediate work of grace on the soul can be compared to the sun sending forth its rays and enlightening humanity. This enlightening is the ordering of the soul according to the illumination of the Spirit, or, as shown above, the foundation laid in nature for the reception of divine things. This foundation, which is the *result* of the Spirit's illumination and infusion, holds the soul in place so that it can be 'bright'.[75]

Therefore, McClenahan's concern to protect creaturely integrity is unwarranted. The elect become holy because the *Holy* Spirit is infused in them, renovating their souls. Holiness, in other words, takes on both a

---

[72] Y8, 'Unpublished Letter on Assurance and Participation in the Divine Nature', 639.

[73] Y8, 'Unpublished Letter on Assurance and Participation in the Divine Nature', 640.

[74] Note how closely Edwards's language is to Basil's: 'Shining upon those that are cleansed from every spot, He makes them spiritual by fellowship with Himself. Just as when a sunbeam falls on bright and transparent bodies, they themselves become brilliant too, and shed forth a fresh brightness from themselves, so souls wherein the Spirit dwells, illuminated by the Spirit, themselves become spiritual, and send forth their grace to others.' Basil, *The Treatise De Spiritu Sancto, The Nine Homilies of the Hexaemeron and the Letters of Saint Basil the Great* (A Select Library of Nicene and Post-Nicene Fathers of the Christian Church, vol. 8; Grand Rapids: Eerdmans, 1978), 15. For more on *theosis* and its background, both ancient and in context, see Michael McClymond, 'Salvation as Divinization: Jonathan Edwards, Gregory Palamas and the Theological Uses of Neoplatonism', in *Jonathan Edwards: Philosophical Theologian* (ed. Paul Helm and Oliver Crisp; Aldershot: Ashgate, 2003), 139–60, and Kyle Strobel, 'Jonathan Edwards and the Polemics of *Theosis*', *Harvard Theological Review*, 105:3 (July 2012): 259–79.

[75] Edwards believed that Adam and Eve had the Holy Spirit infused into their souls in such a way that would uphold the order of the soul and allow them to be free (see *Miscellanies* 301). The infusion of the Spirit in regeneration parallels this original righteousness this way.

metaphysical and a functional definition for Edwards.[76] A person is holy in their being because *holiness itself* is infused there as the *Holy* Spirit. Likewise, a person is functionally holy because they reflect God's glory back to him by apprehending his glory and being inclined toward him in joy. This is what Edwards undoubtedly means when he states, 'That intelligent being whose will is *truly right and lovely*, he is morally good or excellent,'[77] as well as, 'Truly gracious affections, *they are built elsewhere:* they have their *foundation out of self*, in God and Jesus Christ.'[78] Edwards equates moral goodness/ excellency with holiness, and these are *seen* in the moral realm.[79] Creaturely holiness is a mirror image of God's inner life as personal beatific-delight, as Edwards states, 'Holiness in man, is but the image of God's holiness.'[80] Therefore, he can say, 'There are no works of God that are so high and divine, and above the powers of nature, and out of the reach of the power of all creatures, as those works of his Spirit, whereby he forms the creature in his own image, and makes it to be a partaker of the divine nature.'[81]

This does not, *contra* McClenahan, undermine the rational nature of persons but rather allows them to function as *spiritual* beings. The Spirit's infusion as a principle of 'life and action' allows the regenerate to *see* and *will* rightly, thereby maintaining their status as rational creatures.[82] This is why Edwards's depiction of the soul as a jewel, and his 'other' image

---

[76] This is my language, but I take it to be an accurate portrayal of Edwards's points in his sermon on Rev. 3:20: 'There are two ways that the holiness of Christ may be ours – by being ours to behold and enjoy and ours to have communicated to us for us to be partakers of.' Jonathan Edwards, *The Blessing of God: Previously Unpublished Sermons of Jonathan Edwards* (ed. Michael D. McMullen; Nashville: Broadman & Holman, 2003), 366. Likewise, *Miscellanies* 66 states, 'But the holiness of Christians is merely and entirely a reflection of God's light, or communications of God's righteousness, and not one jot of it is owing to ourselves. 'Tis wholly a creature of God's, a new creature; 'tis Christ within us.' Y13, '*Miscellanies* 66. Righteousness', 236.

[77] Y2, *Religious Affections*, 255 – my emphasis.

[78] Y2, *Religious Affections*, 253 – my emphasis.

[79] 'This moral excellency of an intelligent being, when it is true and real, and not only external, or merely seeming and counterfeit, is holiness. Therefore holiness comprehends all the true moral excellency of intelligent beings: there is no other true virtue, but real holiness.' Y2, *Religious Affections*, 255.

[80] Y2, *Religious Affections*, 256. Edwards makes a similar move in 'Charity and Its Fruits' with the 'spiritual image of God'. See Y8, 'Charity and Its Fruits', 159, and Y1, *Freedom of the Will*, 166. The key in the latter is that persons can have the spiritual image of God only by having the Spirit of God, which was what Adam and Eve were once endowed with.

[81] Y2, *Religious Affections*, 158.

[82] Edwards's use of 'principle' is important here. In reference to the Spirit's functioning as a 'principle of life and action', Edwards is simply restating the point I am making, viz. that the Spirit functions as the gracious disposition in the heart. This is, I believe, what Edwards is referencing when he states, 'But man, when he is changed from a sinner to a saint, has new principles of perception and action, principles that are entirely diverse and not arising merely from [a] new disposition of the old, as contracted habits and those changes that are wrought by education do.' Y17, 'Born Again', 187.

of the Trinity as the sun emanating light and heat, are so important. The jewel takes on the light and heat of the sun and itself becomes something of a 'little sun'. Edwards states, 'When the Sun of Righteousness shines upon the soul of the Godly man he communicates his light and heat so to him that there is as it were a little sun, a living principle of light and heat, kindled up in the soul *that is the exact image of the sun.*'[83] Edwards's trinitarian theology of God's emanation that effects remanation thus drives his account of the unregenerate being made regenerate. This account, as I have shown, orders soteriology according to a robust model of *theosis*, a model that goes hand in hand with the beatific for Edwards. Edwards's trinitarian theology, as we have seen, pushes away from discussions of the divine essence to focus on the divine persons. In redemption, likewise, the divine persons possess in their divine nature the capacity for creaturely participation. Edwards often quotes 2 Peter 1.4, that believers are 'partakers of the divine nature', when parsing out this reality. God's self-glorification through creatures entails vision and participation in the divine nature through the Son and by the Holy Spirit. Illumination addresses the need for a vision of God, and infusion addresses the reality of participation.[84]

II The Spirit's Work: Infusion

As I have just emphasized, the Spirit enters the soul of the unregenerate and in one act sanctifies the soul.[85] In doing so, the Spirit infuses himself into the being of the elect, acting there 'habitually'. The Spirit acts according to his personal nature as the *Holy* Spirit, thus functioning in the regenerate as a principle of holiness and love. This is why, as evidenced above, it is impossible to address the issue of illumination without also discussing infusion. Therefore, to round out our discussion of regeneration, it is necessary to address the Spirit's infusion into the soul in the act of regeneration. Infusion is, in Edwards's words, the Spirit acting as supernatural love and holiness, affecting the soul supernaturally, so that these principles 'are caused to exist in the soul habitually, and according to such a stated constitution or law, that lays such a foundation for exercises in a

---

[83] JEC, Unpublished Sermon, Mt. 25:1-12, #451 [L. 11r.] – my emphasis. The point that the image of God functions in man as it does in the Godhead is emphasized below.
[84] Again, union is assumed here.
[85] There have been many who have stumbled over Edwards's use of sanctification in reference to regeneration, but this was standard terminology in his day. For one such instance, see Owen, *The Holy Spirit*, 223.

continued course, as is called a principle of nature'.[86] These works, again, do not impede the work of the faculties but allow them to function fully: 'Not only are remaining principles assisted to do their work more freely and fully, but those principles are restored that were utterly destroyed by the fall.'[87] These 'principles', Edwards explains, are the Holy Spirit himself, whose presence orders the soul for remanation, an ordering that serves as the 'foundation' for future activity. Importantly, without the Spirit, persons would fall back into themselves, but by the grace of God, as we will discuss below, they will not.

In the *Religious Affections*, Edwards asks,

> What is it that is the beginning or earnest of eternal life in the soul, but spiritual life? And what is that but grace? The inheritance that Christ has purchased for the elect, *is the Spirit of God* ... in his vital indwelling in the heart, exerting and communicating himself there, in his own proper, holy or divine nature: and this is *the sum total* of the inheritance that Christ purchased for the elect.[88]

Christ's work of atonement 'purchases' the Spirit for the elect, and this purchase is the sum total of the inheritance endowed to man, not, with McClenahan, other supernatural principles infused in the soul. This reception of grace, what Edwards calls the 'vital indwelling', is the work of the Spirit to regenerate and sanctify. Edwards explains, 'By his producing this effect the Spirit becomes an indwelling vital principle in the soul, and the subject becomes a spiritual being, denominated so from the Spirit of God which dwells in him and of whose nature he is a partaker [II Pet. 1:4].'[89] Edwards holds this 'vital indwelling' in contrast to the common work of the Spirit, in which the subject of the work never actually partakes of the Spirit's nature (love, rather than, for example, power). Edwards compares the common work to garments someone wears that never become part of one's being but are only external appendages. In contrast, the 'vital indwelling' imparts holiness, and allows the believer to live a gracious and heavenly life.[90] The believer actually *becomes* holy, because grace works in the heart as a principle of action. Likewise, 'The nature of a principle of

---

[86] Y17, 'A Divine and Supernatural Light', 411.
[87] Y17, 'A Divine and Supernatural Light', 411.
[88] Y2, *Religious Affections*, 236 – my emphasis.
[89] Y8, 'Charity and Its Fruits', 158.
[90] Y8, 'Charity and Its Fruits', 159.

grace', Edwards claims in *Charity and Its Fruits* 'is to be a principle of life, or a vital principle.'[91]

1. The Spirit Functioning as Principle of Grace

Based on his ambiguous use of the term 'principle', it is important here to address Edwards's usage more broadly. In *Charity and Its Fruits*, Edwards provides his most transparent discussion of the nature of principles, arguing, 'It is the definition of grace that it is a principle of holy action,' and then proceeding to engage the nature of these 'principles'.[92] This discussion, importantly, occurs in the sermon 'Grace Tends to Holy Practice' and is therefore oriented around how a 'principle' of grace leads to action. Along these lines, Edwards states,

> The word 'principle' is relative; it relates to something of which it is a principle. Principles and acts are correlates which necessarily have respect one to the other. Thus the meaning of a principle of life is a principle of life which acts. So when we speak of a principle of under-standing we mean a principle whence flow acts of understanding. ... And a principle of love is a principle whence flow acts of love. So when we say a principle of grace we mean a principle whence flow gracious actions.[93]

A principle, in other words, *does something*; it produces an effect in the soul, whether grace, understanding, life, sin or hatred.[94] Therefore, Edwards states, a principle of grace within man functions as a fountain flowing into a stream.[95] According to Edwards, grace can never be anything but the Spirit of God, *who is* the holiness, love and will of God.[96] Edwards wants to undermine any notion of grace that construes it as anything other than the Spirit, because participation in the divine nature always functions in a personal register. As noted above, the Spirit is what Christ purchased for

---

[91] Y8, 'Charity and Its Fruits', 299.

[92] Y8, 'Charity and Its Fruits', 298.

[93] Y8, 'Charity and Its Fruits', 298.

[94] Edwards states, 'So by a principle of sin is meant a principle whence flow acts of sin. A principle of hatred is a principle whence flow acts of hatred. And a principle of love is a principle whence flow acts of love.' Y8:, 'Charity and Its Fruits', 298.

[95] Y8, 'Charity and Its Fruits', 298. This is where McClenahan's misconstrual of Edwards is so apparent.

[96] Likewise, Edwards claims, 'What is grace but a principle of holiness? or a holy principle in the heart?' This holiness is nothing else but the Spirit. Y8, 'Charity and Its Fruits', 298.

the elect, and in *Charity and Its Fruits*, Edwards uses grace and Spirit synony-mously, what Edwards calls the *sum total* of Christ's purchase.[97]

In light of this depiction of the term 'principle', it makes sense that Edwards's anthropology assumes two *principles* of nature.[98] First, humanity has *natural* principles of nature which are the 'inferior' principles, that are 'those natural appetites and passions, which belong to the nature of man, in which his love to his own liberty, honor and pleasure, were exercised: these when alone, and left to themselves, are what the Scriptures sometimes call *flesh*'.[99] In the fall, the 'superior' principles, the *spiritual* principles, were removed, and humanity's fallenness is a result of the reign of the flesh (not having the superior principles to govern the inferior).[100] Second, what Edwards calls the 'superior' principles are humanity's truly *spiritual nature*, where holiness and righteousness reside. Importantly for Edwards, these spiritual principles are 'summarily comprehended in divine love'.[101] When people had these principles in their hearts, they were 'ordered' rightly; 'all things were in excellent order, peace and beautiful harmony, and in their proper and perfect state'.[102] Therefore, 'superior principles' in the heart can be condensed by 'love', and love is, according to Edwards's trinitarian theology, the Holy Spirit. Likewise, in *Charity and Its Fruits*, one of Edwards's main arguments is that all virtues can be encapsu-lated by love.[103] To make believers holy, therefore, God implants love

---

[97] Y8, 'Charity and Its Fruits', 295–6.

[98] Edwards also states, 'The nature of man consists in principles of perception and principles of action. The human nature whereby man differs from a beast or a tree consists in principles. Man's faculties are principles; the natural appetites are principles; a love of pleasure, and aversion to pain, and a love of honor are principles.' Y17, 'Born Again', 187.

[99] Y3, *Original Sin*, 381.

[100] These 'superior principles' are the Spirit himself. Edwards, in 'Charity and Its Fruits', says, 'Man in his first estate had the Holy Spirit, but he lost it; [it was thrown] away.' Y8, 'Charity and Its Fruits', 354.

[101] Y3, *Original Sin*, 381.

[102] Y3, *Original Sin*, 381.

[103] 'The graces of Christianity are all from the Spirit of God sent forth into the heart, and dwelling there as an holy principle and divine nature. And therefore all graces are only the different ways of acting of the same divine nature, as there may be different reflections of the light of the sun. But it is all the same kind of light originally, because it all comes from the same fountain, the same body of light.' Y8, 'Charity and Its Fruits', 332. Likewise, 'This doctrine, and what has been said under it, may in some measure show us how this is; for by this we learn that all the graces of Christianity are infused in this, inasmuch as all are concatenated; when one is infused, all are infused; there is not one grace wanting. A [convert] at the same moment that he is become such is possessed of all holy principles, all gracious dispositions.' Y8, 'Charity and Its Fruits', 334.

itself in their being, his own love, to function there as a principle and foundation for virtue.[104]

In sinning and breaking the covenant, the superior principles, *being the Holy Spirit himself,* evacuated the heart, leaving fleshliness to reign.[105] In Edwards's words,

> It would have been utterly improper in itself, and inconsistent with the covenant and constitution God had established, that God should still maintain communion with man, and continue, by his friendly, gracious vital influences, to dwell with him and in him, after he was become a rebel, and had incurred God's wrath and curse. Therefore immediately the superior divine principles wholly ceased; so light ceases in a room, when the candle is withdrawn: and thus man was left in a state of darkness, woeful corruption and ruin; nothing but flesh, without spirit.[106]

Edwards is driven to undercut our ability to will love to God, refusing to allow people the capability to grasp God through the use of inferior principles. In his *Treatise on Grace,* just as in his sermon *God Glorified,* Edwards distinguishes the grounding of the regenerates' love to God with the unregenerates' love. Self-love functions in both the believer and the unbeliever based solely on the reality that both are human (having a will equals loving what you love).[107] But on Edwards's view, 'The main ground of true love to God is the excellency of his own nature,'[108] which can only be obtained through the working of the Spirit in both illumination and infusion. Therefore, with divine love living in the hearts of the saints, the saints have a 'new principle of nature' united to their faculties.[109] They are

---

[104] 'The Spirit of God is a spirit of love. And therefore when the Spirit of God enters into the soul, love enters. God is love, and he who has God dwelling in him by his Spirit will have love dwelling in him. The nature of the Holy Spirit is love; and it is by communicating himself, or his own nature, that the hearts of the saints are filled with love or charity.' Y8, 'Charity and Its Fruits', 132.

[105] 'Another reason why what the godly have is more abiding than what false Christians have is that they embrace religion of free choice. False Christians are not religious of free choice; they don't choose God and Christ and the ways of holiness for their own sakes and of inclination to those things in themselves considered but always for some by ends. Selflove is the highest principle that a false Christian acts from. He ... [either acts] ... by fear or from an aim of the praise of men or from a self-righteous principle hoping to commend himself to God by his own Righteousness.' JEC, Unpublished Sermon, Mt. 25:1-12, #451 [L. 15r.].

[106] Y3, *Original Sin*, 382.

[107] Y8, *True Virtue*, 575–6.

[108] Y21, 'Treatise on Grace', 175.

[109] Y21, 'Treatise on Grace', 194. In his sermon on Jn 3.3, Edwards states, 'But man, when he is changed from a sinner to a saint, has new principles of perception and action, principles that are entirely diverse and not arising merely from [a] new disposition of the old, as

'partakers of the divine nature' in that they participate in God's own love, or in other words, are partakers of God's holiness 'not only as they partake of holiness that God gives, *but partake of that holiness by which he himself is holy*'.[110] Salvation, broadly speaking, is not primarily about forgiveness or even holiness (abstractly considered). Salvation is oriented by creaturely participation in God's own life. That life is the life of the Father and Son gazing upon one another in love and existing in the communion of love. We have seen that the perfection of the beatific vision in heaven is a participation in the Son's vision of the Father, so likewise is salvation a participation in the Sonship of the Son: 'We shall in a sort be partakers of his [Christ's] relation to the Father or his communion with him in his Sonship. We shall not only be the sons of God by regeneration but a kind of participation of the Sonship of the eternal Son.'[111] Furthermore,

They have spiritual excellency and joy by a kind of participation of God. They are made excellent by a communication of God's excellency: God put his own beauty, i.e. his beautiful likeness, upon their souls. ... The saints hath spiritual joy and pleasure by a kind of effusion of God on the soul. ... The saints have both their spiritual excellency and blessedness by the gift of the Holy Ghost, or Spirit of God, and his dwelling in them. *They are not only caused by the Holy Ghost, but are in the Holy Ghost as their principle. The Holy Spirit becoming an inhabitant is a vital principle in the soul.*[112]

Holiness, just like knowledge, is obtained by participation in God's self-giving, in this case the *Holy* Spirit. The superior faculties once again reign in God's chosen. Edwards states, 'Indeed, the first exercise of grace in the

---

contracted habits and those changes that are wrought by education do.' Y17, 'Born Again', 187.

[110] Y21, 'Treatise on Grace', 195 – my emphasis.

[111] Edwards, *Blessing of God*, 177. Furthermore, Edwards states, 'For there is doubtless an infinite intimacy between the Father and the Son. ... And saints being in him, shall, in their measure and manner, partake with him in it, and the blessedness of it.' Y19, 'The Excellency of Christ', 593.

[112] Y17, 'God Glorified in Man's Dependence', 208 – my emphasis. See also Y8, 'Charity and Its Fruits', 132. Schafer comments that 'God therefore takes real delight in the good principles and acts of the saints: not because there is "merit" in them (that is really beside the point), but because the love wherewith they love him is simply his own love reflected and returned to him. It is not, therefore, by the doctrine of imputed righteousness that Edwards prefers to safe-guard human dependence and divine glory; rather, it is by the doctrine of "infused grace"'. Thomas A. Schafer, 'Jonathan Edwards and Justification by Faith', *Church History* 20, no. 4 (1951), 55–67 (62–3).

first light has a tendency to future acts, as from an abiding principle by grace and by the covenant of God, but not by any natural force.'[113]
The Holy Spirit's inhabitation is divine love wrought in the heart of the elect, from which and by which they can truly love God, not based on some benefit received, or hoped to be received, from God.[114] Redemption, again, entails a true partaking in God's nature – who is love, beauty, holiness and grace. Quite simply, Edwards states,

> That holy, divine principle, which we have observed does radically and essentially consist in divine love, is no other than a communication and participation of that same infinite divine love, which is God, and in which the Godhead is eternally breathed forth and subsists in the third person in the blessed Trinity. So that true saving grace is no other than that very love of God; that is, God, in one of the persons of the Trinity, uniting himself to the soul of a creature as a vital principle, dwelling there and exerting himself by the faculties of the soul of man, in his own proper nature, after the manner of a principle of nature.[115]

2. Grace as God's Nature Infused in the Soul

As we have seen, the Spirit functions in the elect as a new 'principle', conveying his nature to the regenerate. Here, I briefly focus my attention on Edwards's use of the term 'nature' and its import in the discussion. Edwards found it important in light of some confusion over the word 'nature' to highlight that he was not suggesting that the Spirit communicated his essence but that he communicated his nature, namely, his holiness.[116] The saints are not 'Godded with God', or 'Christed with Christ', Edwards adamantly proclaimed.[117] The Spirit's economic work,

---

[113] Y21, 'Treatise on Grace', 196.
[114] Y21, 'Treatise on Grace', 175.
[115] 21, 'Treatise on Grace', 194. This is central to Edwards's understanding of the virtuous life. By infusing *love itself* into the person, Edwards has provided the foundation for *every* virtue, which is his argument in 'Charity and Its Fruits'. There, he states, 'The graces of Christianity are all from the Spirit of Christ sent forth into the heart, and dwelling there as an holy principle and divine nature. And therefore all graces are only the different ways of acting of the same divine nature, as there may be different reflections of the light of the sun. But it is all the same kind of light originally, because it all comes from the same fountain, the same body of light. Grace in the soul is the Holy Ghost acting in the soul, and there communicating his own holy nature.' Y8, 'Charity and Its Fruits', 332.
[116] See Y16, '66. To an Unknown Correspondent', 202.
[117] Y8, *True Virtue*, 633; also Y2, *Religious Affections*, 203. For the polemical background of the phrase 'Neither Godded with God nor Christed with Christ', see Strobel, 'Jonathan Edwards and the Polemics of *Theosis*'.

in other words, is to communicate his holiness and love (nature), just as the Son's work is to communicate his understanding and image. But equally disconcerting as the Spirit communicating his essence is the idea that the Spirit only communicates externally, as he does with the unredeemed (or, more horrifying to Edwards, as the devil does to humanity).[118] Edwards thus highlights the Spirit's nature by saying, 'It communicates and exerts itself in the soul in those acts which are its proper, natural and essential acts in itself *ad intra*, or within the Deity from all eternity.'[119] The Spirit, as divine love and holiness, functions as divine love and holiness in the soul of the believer. But this is not just a communication of an abstract idea or virtue; it is a personal communication of God himself. Robert Caldwell summarizes this well, 'The saint's faculties of knowing and loving are actually enabled by the Spirit to know and love God in a way similar to the way that God eternally knows and loves himself.'[120] To redeem the elect, God provides his own self-knowledge and self-love, that they may partake of his personal beatific-delight. In distinguishing in this way between the divine essence and nature in his trinitarian theology, however provocatively, Edwards manages to rediscover, mutatis mutandis, Gregory Palamas's distinction between the divine essence and energies.[121]

By parsing the Spirit's work this way, Edwards shows himself to share the Reformed concern for focusing on grace as fully *gifted* from God, in this case, as the indwelling Spirit, and not something that belongs to the redeemed.[122] So although this grace is infused, it remains united to the

[118] Edwards's concerns are clear: 'According to Dr. Whitby's notion of the assistance of the Spirit, the Spirit of God does nothing in the hearts or minds of men beyond the power of the Devil, nothing but what the devil can [do] and nothing showing any greater power in any respect than the devil shows and exercises in his temptations. For he supposes that all the Spirit of God does is to bring moral maxims and inducements to mind, and to set 'em before the understanding, etc.' Y21, '"Controversies" Notebook: Efficacious Grace', 294.
[119] Y13, '*Miscellanies* 471. Spirit's Operation', 513.
[120] Caldwell, *Communion in the Spirit*, 103.
[121] See McClymond, 'Salvation as Divinization'.
[122] It is important to keep distinct the Spirit's work of infusion, leading to holiness, with union, leading to justification. Muller highlights this: 'The Protestant scholastics deny that gratia infusa or gratia inhaerens, inhering grace, is the basis of justification. Rather gratia infusa is the result of regeneratio and the basis of sanctification, the source of all the good works of believers. The orthodox, in the main, avoid language of a habitus gratiae and prefer the term gratia inhaerens or gratia cooperans to the term gratia infusa in order to retain in their formulations the Reformers' teaching concerning grace as a power of God or a divine favour (favour Dei or gratuitus favor Dei) that never belongs to man as an aspect of human nature but is always graciously given.' Richard A. Muller, 'Gratia Infusa', in *Dictionary of Latin and Greek Theological Terms: Drawn Principally from Protestant Scholastic Theology* (Grand Rapids: Baker Academic, 1985), 131.

believer through covenant fidelity rather than metaphysical necessity.[123] In doing so, Edwards reiterates the major movements and concerns of his forebears, utilizing a robust doctrine of the Trinity and the triune economic workings to orient and inform redemption. Edwards makes this emphasis clear in his *Treatise on Grace* when he states,

> But all succeeding acts of grace, must be as immediately and to all intents and purposes, as much from the immediate acting of the Spirit of God on the soul as the first. ... Indeed, the Spirit of God, united to human faculties, acts very much after the manner of a natural principle or habit, so that one act makes way for another, and as it were settles the soul in a disposition to holy acts; but that it does so is by *grace* and *covenant*, and not from any natural necessity.[124]

Edwards maintains the fundamental *givenness* of grace because infusion is not infusion of a principle other than the Spirit. In light of this givenness, Edwards could easily have said with Calvin, 'Accordingly, whatever good things are in us are the fruits of his grace; and without him our gifts are darkness of mind and perversity of heart.'[125]

Edwards's description of the Spirit's work as 'immediate' is an attempt to undercut the methods Arminians had used to restrict God's activity *to the kind of activity* that God works externally, as though God deals with redeemed man as if he were still only 'natural'.[126] Edwards follows Van Mastricht, who states, 'This [regeneration], certainly, is not a moral act, exercised in offering and inviting, as is the case with the external call, but it is a physical act, powerfully infusing spiritual life into the soul.'[127] Edwards follows Van

---

[123] Therefore, to balance the reality of infusion, Edwards refers to the consistency of the Spirit's work in the soul as both grace and covenant. Grace, because the Spirit is grace, and covenant, because that grace depends solely on the freedom of God, but it is the freedom of a covenant-faithful God. See Y8, 'Charity and Its Fruits', 346–8, for Edwards's explanation, in seven reasons, why God does not let grace be overthrown in the soul.

[124] Y21, 'Treatise on Grace', 196–7 – my emphasis.

[125] John Calvin, *Institutes of the Christian Religion* (ed. John T. McNeill; trans. Ford Lewis Battles; vol. 1; Louisville: Westminster John Knox, 1960), 3.1.3 (541).

[126] Edwards picks this up in his *Treatise on Grace* when he states, 'The Spirit of God may operate and produce effects upon the minds of natural men that have no grace, as he does when he assists natural conscience and convictions of sin and danger. ... But he communicates holiness in his own proper nature only, in those holy effects in the hearts of the saints.' Y21, 'Treatise on Grace', 192.

[127] Mastricht, *A Treatise on Regeneration*, 17. See Y21, 'Editor's Introduction', 41, Y21, 'Charity and Its Fruits', 165, 202, 207–8, 218. Edwards sounds remarkably close to Mastricht when he states that 'nothing will be produced but only an improvement and new modification of those principles that are exercised. Therefore it follows that saving grace in the heart, can't be produced in man by mere exercise of what perfections he has in him already, though never so much assisted by moral suasion, and never so much assisted in the exercise of his

Mastricht's use of 'physical' against Turretin, who claims, 'It is not simply physical because it is concerned with a moral faculty which ought to be moved in a way appropriate to its nature; nor is it simply ethical, as if God acted only objectively and used mild suasion.'[128] Other than terminology, this is Edwards's exact point. God works to redeem the elect as persons, and therefore according to their understanding and willing, and yet he does so *physically* (through infusion rather than persuasion). By revealing his true excellency to them, and infusing love itself into their being, the elect are able to 'close' with Christ in faith.

Conclusion

In 'The Pure in Heart Blessed', Edwards claims that the intellect, as the most noble faculty of man, is active in redemption because by it persons perceive beauty and excellency, and the will is active as it inclines toward or away from God. In order to redeem a person qua person, God both illumines and infuses: illumines so that the elect can truly see and taste that the Lord is good, and infuses so that they have grace functioning in them as a disposition to future acts. Conversion, for Edwards, entails God's action on the soul, allowing a person to 'taste and see that the Lord is good'. Other 'schemes of divinity', as Edwards puts it, derogate God's glory at just this point, undermining God as the alpha and omega in this affair.[129] The problem Edwards and the Reformed sought to address is the

natural principles, unless there be something more than all this, viz. an immediate infusion or operation of the Divine Being upon the soul.' Y21, 'Charity and Its Fruits', 165. Also, in his sermon on Jn 3:3, Edwards states, 'The change of man from a sinner to a saint is not a moral, but a physical change.' Y17, 'Born Again', 187. Edwards states in his 'Efficacious Grace, Book I' that 'if the Spirit of God does anything at all besides moral suasion, his grace is efficacious'; as well as, 'to deny any physical influence at all of the Spirit of God on the will, but only MORAL SUASION, moral causes … [and] show how that this is to deny that the Spirit of God does anything at all.' Y21, 'Efficacious Grace, Book I', 202, 207.
[128] Turretin, *Institutes of Elenctic Theology*, vol. 2, 524. Edwards, Mastricht and Turretin all seem to be arguing toward the same end. Turretin goes on to use the term 'hyperphysically' when talking about infusion, and seems concerned that 'physical' might be linked with 'natural'.
[129] Y17, 'God Glorified in Man's Dependence', 212. Edwards, in his 'Treatise on Grace' states, 'And so God is himself the portion and purchased inheritance of his people. Thus God is the Alpha and Omega in this affair of redemption.' Y21, 'Treatise on Grace', 191. This is a frequent assertion of Edwards and seems to be something of a 'filter' for his working with other views of redemption. In his 'Efficacious Grace, Book III', Edwards states, in a way which is representative of how he regards this issue, 'Their scheme naturally and by necessary consequences leads men to take all the GLORY of all spiritual good (which is immensely the chief, most important and excellent thing in the whole creation) to ourselves, as much as if we, with regard to these effects, were the supreme, the first cause,

redemption of persons qua persons.[130] This entails allowing their faculties
to function according to who God truly is, or, as noted above, to *see* him
through Christ, the image of the invisible God.[131] Walton, in his study on
the background to Edwards's *Religious Affections*, summarizes the language
used and the purposes behind the Puritan arguments for how God
redeems people as such, stating,

> The theory that the 'new creature' was a new 'spring', 'seed', or
> 'principle' of spiritual life, specifically affecting the fundamental 'incli-
> nation', 'bent', 'propensity', 'disposition', or 'bias' underlying individual
> acts of affectivity and perception, elegantly explained how God could
> succeed in converting the 'whole man, mind, will and affections' without
> directly altering any faculty separately from another.[132]

The solution was to lay in the soul a new foundation, or, for Edwards, to
expose the person to the beauty, glory and holiness of God so that the
soul was reordered to divine things. This work of redemption, through
illumination, infusion and union, places the believer on the pilgrim's path
of beatific glory – true participation in God's self-glorification. God is the
underlying cause and answer for redemption, redemption that is mediated
to humanity through Christ by the uniting and illuminating work of the
Spirit, who is the very love of God. Union, illumination and infusion
therefore provide creaturely participation in God's own life. Again we find
that Edwards emphasizes personhood as he seeks to delineate an account
of regeneration that upholds the person as such (hence his continued
focus on God's dealing with humanity as rational creatures). The beatific,
furthermore, is central to this account, as it takes a real illumination of God
to orient the elect to God's own self and therefore participate in God's own
life. Affection, one of the key terms from the heuristic key will be addressed
in the following chapter, as I look at Edwards's most famous work, *Religious
Affections*.

The purpose of this section on regeneration has been to explicate
the work of God in the soul, allowing the elect to participate in God's

---

self-existent and independent and absolutely sovereign disposers.' Y21, 'Efficacious Grace,
Book III', 290.

[130] This was the main point of attack by the Arminians, who claimed that the Reformed view
of redemption undermined personhood.

[131] Or, in Edwards's words, 'We have the glorious attributes and perfections of God declared to
us; the glory of God in the face of Jesus Christ is discovered in the gospel which we enjoy.'
Y17', The Pure in Heart Blessed', 74–5.

[132] Walton, *Jonathan Edwards*, 188.

self-glorification.[133] We have shown that illumination and infusion are God's work to reveal himself to the believer, that he may partake in true spiritual knowledge. Spiritual knowledge, as developed in the first section, finds its form in the archetype of God's inner life, and therefore redemption necessitates regeneration – God sending his understanding and love to reveal and regenerate. Humankind does not possess the 'principles' to know or enjoy God in the first birth; therefore God offers a new birth: 'the principles of spiritual life, or spiritual understanding, inclination, and action: these principles are absolutely necessary in man in order to his serving and glorifying God'.[134] We turn now to address these principles in action, to the end of glorifying God.

---

[133] I have taken my heuristic key another direction in a chapter addressing Edwards's doctrines of regeneration and justification. The insights here are expanded upon in that chapter. See Strobel, 'By Word and Spirit'.

[134] Y17, 'Born Again', 191.

Chapter 6

Religious Affection as Remanation unto Glory

The purpose of this chapter is not to provide a full-blown analysis of religious affection, but rather to exposit affection as Edwards's doctrine that explains how God's communicative emanation returns in remanation. As the third point of application, and the third moment on the continuum of emanation to remanation, this chapter on affection rounds out our broad sketch of how God redeems the elect in Edwards's thought. Affection is intimately connected with spiritual knowledge and regeneration and provides the affective dimension of the ectypal knowledge Edwards posits. The regenerate truly see God in Christ illumined and respond in affection. This action of beholding and delighting is the creaturely correspondence to God's processions of understanding and will as the archetype. Creaturely affection, if experienced in true *religious* affection, mirrors the life of God within a person's own being, and she necessarily participates in God's act of self-glorification.

While the majority of Edwards scholars have detailed the historical, spiritual and practical issues inherent to his affectional theorizing, I will, with few others, focus on expounding Edwards's account of affections *theologically*. This exposition will, I propose, provide the requisite context for explaining why affection grasped Edwards's unwavering attention. Brad Walton and others have gone to great lengths to show that Edwards contributed to the affection discussion by systematizing his forebears. I emphasize here, in contrast, his theological insights noted above, arguing that God's beatific self-glorification finds its outworking in religious affection. Specifically, God's life as personal beatific-delight finds its anthropological parallel in religious affection, and affection, through the Spirit's work of union, illumination and infusion, is the locus of God's self-glorification through the creature. Furthermore, affection is the motor which propels the regenerate on the path of the beatified pilgrim and therefore is the means by which God enacts his reign in the world.

Walton, in his seminal work, *Jonathan Edwards, Religious Affections and the Puritan Analysis of True Piety, Spiritual Sensation and Heart Religion*, has argued persuasively that Edwards's insights concerning religious affection were not so much new as much as a systematization of the content provided to him by his Puritan forebears.[1] As seen throughout this volume, Edwards was a creative thinker working within a broadly Reformed/Puritan framework, and most of his provocative conclusions are creative reworkings of the theology handed down to him, specifically, as we have seen, in his doctrine of the Trinity, God's end in creating, the archetypal and ectypal distinctions, regeneration and the spiritual sense. In the same way, Edwards's work on religious affection follows the contours provided by the likes of Owen, Ames, Sibbes, etc., leaving Edwards to develop these ideas in his own theology. Therefore, I am not concerned with Edwards's treatise *Religious Affections* as such but instead religious affection as an aspect of God's work of redemption. To do so, I highlight how Edwards's understanding of religious affection mirrors his understanding of the inner-triune life of God and orients the believer on the path toward heaven (where existence will be 'all flame'). Religious affection, furthermore, is the anthropological reality of seeing and knowing God *sensibly*, being brought into existence by the Spirit's illumination and infusion into the heart of the believer. By integrating the beatific into the pilgrim, this is truly a theology of glory; its focus is not *imitatio Christi* but *imitatio Dei*.[2] God's personal beatific-delight, in other words, is the animating factor that shapes the work of redemption and is itself infinite religious affection.

---

[1] 'It is arguably the special accomplishment of Edwards that he organized, for the first time since Augustine, Bernard, William of St. Thierry and William Ames, and in a manner perhaps more exhaustive than any of them, a systematization of traditional heart-language into a thorough, clearly defined and fairly coherent analysis of religious interiority.' Brad Walton, *Jonathan Edwards, Religious Affections, and the Puritan Analysis of True Piety, Spiritual Sensation, and Heart Religion* (Studies in American Religion; Lewiston: The Edwin Mellen Press, 2002), 181.

[2] It is noteworthy that Edwards does make use of the imitation of Christ, but it is imitation in affection toward divine things. See Y2, *Religious Affections*, 111–12. Edwards has a short series of early notes (around 1728–1729) on 'Christ's Example' (see Y21, 'Christ's Example', 511–19), but these are not fully developed into his thought; he also offers some thoughts on imitation of Christ in *Original Sin*, see Y3, *Original Sin*, 199, but this idea does not play a large role in his overall thought. Studebaker helpfully notes, 'Edwards' teaching that the human soul is the image of the Trinity suggests a hermeneutical principle of reciprocity: as the soul reflects the Trinity, so the Trinity reflects the soul.' Steven M. Studebaker, *Jonathan Edwards' Social Augustinian Trinitarianism in Historical and Contemporary Perspectives* (Gorgias Studies in Philosophy and Theology; Piscataway: Gorgias Press, 2008), 166.

I Religious Affection

In accordance with the qualifications outlined above, I briefly address the nature of religious affections prior to locating them within Edwards's theology of redemption. It is here where I delineate more carefully how Edwards's anthropology mirrors the inner-triune life of God, a reflection based on God's own beatific-delight. Religious affection marks the movement of the soul in remanation as a response to the emanating revelation of God, in other words, creaturely correspondence to the triune processions revealed in their missions. Recalling Edwards's depiction of reality as wheels within wheels, in which each creature is its own wheel within a great system of wheels, the understanding is the first half-turn of emanation, and the will is the next half-turn upward, in remanation unto glory. In Edwards's words,

> The whole universe, including all creatures animate and inanimate, in all its actings, proceedings, revolutions, and entire series of events, should proceed from a regard and with a view to *God*, as the supreme and last end of all: that every wheel, both great and small, in all its rotations, should move with a constant invariable regard to him as the ultimate end of all; as perfectly and uniformly as if the whole system were animated and directed by one common soul.[3]

These rotations that regard God as the supreme end are the rotations of true religion. In the first section of his *Religious Affections*, Edwards develops his doctrine that 'true religion, in great part, consists in holy affections'.[4] It may appear contradictory, if not simply counterintuitive, that Edwards would use 1 Peter 1.8 as the launching point for a work built upon the idea of *seeing* God, which claims, 'Whom having not seen, ye love: in whom, though now ye see him not, yet believing, ye rejoice with joy unspeakable, and full of glory.' Edwards is quick to emphasize that the seeing in this verse refers to bodily sight, and that the Christians 'saw him [Jesus] spiritually, whom the world saw not, and whom they themselves had never seen with bodily eyes'.[5] Later, importantly, Edwards lists a series of doctrines too often preached without caution or explanation, one of which was that Christians

---

[3] Y8, *End of Creation*, 424–5.
[4] Y2, *Religious Affections*, 95.
[5] Y2, *Religious Affections*, 94. 'For though sight be more noble than any of the other external senses; yet this spiritual sense which has been spoken of, is infinitely more noble than that, or any other principle of discerning that a man naturally has, and the object of this sense infinitely greater and more important.' Y2, *Religious Affections*, 275.

should live by faith and not sight. There he re-emphasizes the necessity and
reality of spiritual sight, noting the possibility for error in emphasizing faith
to the detriment of *spiritual* sight:

> The Scripture is ignorant of any such faith in Christ of the operation of
> God, that is not founded in a spiritual sight of Christ. That believing on
> Christ, which accompanies a title to everlasting life, is a seeing the Son,
> and believing on him, John 6:40. True faith in Christ is never exercised,
> any further than persons behold 'as in a glass, the glory of the Lord', and
> have 'the knowledge of the glory of God in the face of Jesus Christ' (II
> Cor. 3:18 and 4:6).[6]

At the outset, however, Edwards does not seem overly concerned with the
issue of sight, but glory. Edwards claims that according to 1 Peter 1.8 this
'joy unspeakable' is 'glorified joy', a joy that knows true glory on the earthly
side of perfection. It is this glorified joy that concerns us most fully here
and helps to ground Edwards's work in his overall scheme of redemption.
His final preliminary statement prior to stating his doctrine grounds our
discussion:

> In rejoicing with this joy, their minds were filled, as it were, with a glorious
> brightness, and their natures exalted and perfected: it was a most worthy,
> noble rejoicing, that did not corrupt and debase the mind, as many
> carnal joys do; but did greatly beautify and dignify it: *it was a prelibation
> of the joy of heaven*, that raised their minds to a degree of heavenly bless-
> edness: it filled their minds with the light of God's glory, and made 'em
> themselves to shine with some communication of that glory.[7]

Looking specifically at the nature of religious affection in Edwards's
thought entails, first, recalling Edwards's anthropology, and second,
focusing attention on how that anthropology functions in affection, or, as
Edwards wanted to emphasize, true religion. Initially, therefore, Edwards
evinces what Walton refers to as a 'bipartite psychology', where the human
soul has two 'faculties', the understanding and the will, as has already been
emphasized. We recall that the understanding, on the one hand, is that by

---

[6] Y2, *Religious Affections*, 175–6. This is in contrast to the first time Edwards preached on 1
Pet. 1:8, early in his career, in 1729. There, Edwards draws a harder distinction between the
'eye of faith' and sight in heaven, which he eliminates for his explication of the verse in the
Religious Affections.
[7] Y2, *Religious Affections*, 95 – my emphasis.

which the soul is capable of perception and speculation; the will, on the other hand, is that by which the soul inclines toward or away from what is perceived or considered. Further, Edwards claims that the mind, with regard to the faculty of the will, is called the heart.[8] Walton helpfully summarizes Edwards's view of the heart:

> Thus, 'heart' refers not only to volition and affection, but also to sensation, or perception, that is, to the understanding as simultaneously apprehending and as responding affectively to what it apprehends. In other words, the 'heart' has both a volitional-affective dimension, and also a cognitive dimension.[9]

Edwards's baldly stated declaration concerning religious affections is that they are 'no other, than the more vigorous and sensible exercises of the inclination and will of the soul'.[10] Affections do not categorize movements of the soul that are slightly above 'indifference', what Edwards classifies as 'wouldlings'. On the contrary, affections delineate only 'vigorous' and 'sensible' movements of the soul. Importantly, Edwards does not give the affections existence separate from the understanding and the will. As already noted, Edwards does not fit into what is classically understood as 'faculty psychology'; the faculties of which Edwards makes use do not have their own being but are only used to call out 'movements' of the soul. Therefore it is the soul that understands and the soul that inclines, or, better, it is the person who understands and the person who wills.[11]

Affections do not call out a distinct movement of the soul apart from willing but are simply a kind of willing. In Edwards's words, 'The will, and the affections of the soul, are not two faculties; the affections are not essentially distinct from the will, nor do they differ from the mere actings of the will and inclination of the soul, but only in the liveliness and sensibleness of exercise.'[12] The will simply is affection, but when discussing religious

---

[8] Walton's point is instructive: 'That the mind is termed "heart" *with regard* to the exercises of the inclination, means simply that the heart refers to the mind as inclinational, as when, in any of its activities, its volitional-affective dimension is engaged. ... What it does not include, as far as Edwards is concerned, is purely theoretical, or 'notional', acts of the understanding.' Walton, *Jonathan Edwards, Religious Affections, and the Puritan Analysis of True Piety*, 151.

[9] Walton, *Jonathan Edwards, Religious Affections, and the Puritan Analysis of True Piety*, 153.

[10] Y2, *Religious Affections*, 96.

[11] 'As 'tis the soul only that has ideas, so 'tis the soul only that is pleased or displeased with its ideas. As 'tis the soul only that thinks, so 'tis the soul only that loves or hates, rejoices or is grieved at what it thinks of.' Y2, *Religious Affections*, 98. Edwards's use of soul here seems to function as a personal spiritual subject.

[12] Y2, *Religious Affections*, 97.

affection, what Edwards is really emphasizing is the *vigorous* affection of
the will arising from spiritual realities. The issue is one of 'degree' and
'manner', *as well as* object. The degree of the affections has to do with the
degree of inclination someone has to a specific thing, and the greater the
inclination, for or against, the more likely that there is bodily affect (as
was experienced in the revivals). This movement of the soul in religious
affection is based upon, if they are truly *religious* affections, revelation of
God, seen through spiritual sight and efficaciously applied to the heart by
the Spirit of God. Understanding through perception and the subsequent
willing are so interwoven in Edwards's thought that he rarely distinguishes
between the terms 'sense', 'perception' and 'sensation' when referring to
either the *act* of perception or the sense *impression* on the mind.[13]

Therefore, for Edwards, religious affections are a composite reaction
of understanding and will, vigorously effected by a spiritual sight of
God. Importantly, Edwards does not allow for affections to exist outside
the understanding, even though they are a kind of willing. A person
understands and is inclined toward or away from the object of their
understanding (apprehension), and thereby experiences affection. True
religious affections must entail knowledge (understanding) of God and
love (willing) to God. Because this knowledge is not speculative (merely
notional), but entails apprehension by the sense of the heart, it must necessarily be a dual movement of the soul in understanding (reception) and
willing (inclination).[14]

Thus far my emphasis has been on religious *affections*, but now I turn
to *religious* affections. Edwards assumes at the outset that his definition of
affections makes it clear that true religion must consist in them. If religion
does not consist in a vigorous willing of the soul, are we to say that the
religion God requires entails weak and lifeless inclination? Edwards refuses
to believe so. In a revealing point, Edwards states,

> If we ben't in good earnest in religion, and our wills and inclinations
> be not strongly exercised, we are nothing. The things of religion are so

---

[13] Walton, *Jonathan Edwards, Religious Affections, and the Puritan Analysis of True Piety*, 155.
Walton makes this point and then notes, 'It is not always clear, when Edwards is talking
about the "new creature" of perception or sense, whether he is referring to the new ability,
or act, or perceiving and sensing, or the new mental content resulting from the act. The
advantage of adopting the Lockean term "simple idea", is that it unambiguously refers to
the mental content, rather than to the mental act. However, Edwards does not confine
himself to this term.' Walton, *Jonathan Edwards, Religious Affections, and the Puritan Analysis
of True Piety*, 155–6.

[14] See Y2, *Religious Affections*, 101, 272.

great, that there can be no suitableness in the exercises of our hearts, to their nature and importance, unless they be lively and powerful. In nothing, is vigor in the actings of our inclinations so requisite, as in religion; and in nothing is lukewarmness so odious. True religion is evermore a powerful thing; and the power of it appears, in the first place, in the inward exercise of it in the heart, where is the principal and original seat of it.[15]

The Spirit's work in the heart, as discussed above, is the driving force of the affections. The Spirit is, Edwards claims, 'a powerful holy affection', and upon receiving the Spirit with his sanctifying and saving work, the elect are thereby baptized with fire. The Spirit's procession in the Godhead is, as it were, God's own affection. Fittingly, the effect of the Spirit's work in the hearts of the saints follows suit, vigorously inclining them to the goodness, beauty and love of God.

Admittedly, grace is had by degrees. Therefore, some of the elect are mere "babes in Christ"' while others are more mature; but by being saved, the elect necessarily, and by definition, have the Spirit infused into their being, and therefore have godliness in their hearts.[16] Edwards, again exposing his assumptions, claims that everyone who has godliness in their hearts, therefore any true Christian, 'has his inclinations and heart exercised towards God and divine things, with such strength and vigor, that these holy exercises do prevail in him above all carnal or natural affections, and are effectual to overcome them'.[17] This is not to say that religious affections are pure grace but instead are always mixed with 'nature' this side of glory.[18]

---

[15] Y2, *Religious Affections*, 100.

[16] Sin is the culprit for grace not reigning fully in man. In his sermon series the 'Wise and Foolish Virgins', Edwards claims that there is still a 'body and fountain of sin' in the hearts of the regenerate, that there is 'but a little grace' there and that corruption prevails until grace defeats it. Furthermore, not one lust is completely destroyed in conversion, and the regenerate have as many natural principles in their hearts as the unregenerate. Therefore, there are 'two contrary principles struggling one with another in the heart of a godly man like Jacob and Esau in Rebekah's womb'. Likewise, Edwards claims that a certain kind of dryness or darkness can descend on the life of the Christian, but this is simply 'grace sleeping'.

[17] Y2, *Religious Affections*, 100.

[18] Y2, *Religious Affections*, 118. 'For undoubtedly, there is much affection in the true saints which is not spiritual: their religious affections are often mixed; all is not from grace, but much from nature.' Y2, *Religious Affections*, 118. Likewise, later Edwards claims that there is a twofold defect in the saint who is low in grace: First, a defect in object. This is not an essential defect but because grace is small a defect in degree. Second, there is, in Edwards's words, 'a defect in the eye'. Sin blinds a person so that they cannot see as they ought. Y2, *Religious Affections*, 194–5; see Y2, *Religious Affections*, 266, for how grace enables sight. 'Here the faculties [of the soul] are benumbed and stupefied and clogged with flesh and sin; but there they will be as 'a flame of fire; [Heb. 1:7].' Y17, 'Serving God in Heaven', 260.

As a fundamentally *practical* thing, religion entails action. Therefore, it makes sense that true religion is concerned with affections because God, in creating persons, has made affections the 'spring' of their actions. As religion is concerned with the practical realities of persons who are being redeemed and therefore following the way of redemption, it is concerned with affections. 'Take away all love and hatred, all hope and fear, all anger, zeal and affectionate desire', Edwards prods, 'and the world would be, in a great measure, motionless and dead.'[19] Edwards spells out the practical nature of religion (and, in actuality, all of life) and then follows his anthropology by noting that unless affections are reoriented toward God, persons cannot be truly religious. This is the difference between those who hear about God's greatness, mercy, holiness, goodness, etc., without affection, and those who hear and are affected.

Once again, Edwards compares religion on earth with religion in heaven: 'There is doubtless true religion in heaven, and true religion in its utmost purity and perfection. ... The religion of heaven consists chiefly in holy and mighty love and joy, and the expression of these in most fervent and exalted praises.'[20] Notably, Edwards focuses this beatifically:

> Will any say, that the saints in heaven, in beholding the face of their Father, and the glory of their Redeemer, and contemplating his wonderful words, and particularly his laying down his life for them, have their hearts nothing moved and affected, by all which they behold or consider? ... That principle of true religion which is in them, is a communication of the religion of heaven; their grace is the dawn of glory; and God fits them for that world by conforming them to it.[21]

Edwards compares this observation with the 1 Peter text to note that religion in heaven consists of the same thing as religion on earth, referring to the love and joy of the saints here as the 'beginning and dawning of the light, life, and blessedness of heaven'.[22] Edwards believes that since heaven is the place where religion is perfected, we should learn of religion by focusing our attention on heaven rather than on earth, highlighting

---

[19] Y2, *Religious Affections*, 101.
[20] Y2, *Religious Affections*, 113.
[21] Y2, *Religious Affections*, 114.
[22] Y2, *Religious Affections*, 113. 'The knowledge which the saints have of God's beauty and glory in this world, and those holy affections that arise from it, are of the same nature and kind with what the saints are the subjects of in heaven, differing only in degree and circumstances: what God gives them here, is a foretaste of heavenly happiness, and an earnest of their future inheritance.' Y2, *Religious Affections*, 133.

the importance of grounding doctrines of redemption proleptically in consummation. Since the saints are 'strangers' on earth, and properly citizens of heaven, religion must take on the nature of heaven *in nuce*.[23]

Religious affections, therefore, are the elect's harmonious participation in the self-glorification of God. In closing with Christ in faith, the elect are in harmony with Christ, as seen above, because Christ's own love (and work of love) binds them to himself.[24] As the regenerate see through a glass darkly, their sight develops exponentially to be in greater agreement with reality through harmony with God in Christ.[25] God's beauty and holiness demands a certain kind of creaturely response, a response made possible by a sense of the heart.[26] Sanctified response to God implies understanding and willing God as such, resulting in religious affections, which become the engine for deeper longing, contemplating and meditating upon his beauty. This affirmation is why Edwards states, 'The end of the doctrines and precepts of Christianity, is to bring about this sweet harmony between the soul and Jesus Christ.'[27]

II Religious Affection within Edwards's Theology

In light of my brief analysis of religious affections, I now address the interpretative gains provided by translating religious affection through the grammar of God's beatific self-glorification. This is where my detailed development of the Trinity, God's purpose in creation, the ages of heaven and God's work to redeem the creature converge in one movement of

---

[23] Y2, *Religious Affections*, 114. Edwards, again invoking the image of the sun, notes that where there is light (understanding) there must be heat (affections), to claim that 'if the great things of religion are rightly understood, they will affect the heart'. Y2, *Religious Affections*, 120. The reason offered as to why some people are not affected is blindness. It is here where Edwards offers his attack on those who 'cry down all religious affections', claiming that while there may be affections without true religion, there is no true religion, no real seeing of God, without them. Y2, *Religious Affections*, 121.

[24] See Y13, '*Miscellanies* 416. Justification', 476. Edwards, in talking about the union known by faith, states, 'There is an entire yielding to it, and closing with it; adhering to it with the belief, with the inclination and affection. ... Faith is no other than that harmony in the soul towards Christ.' Y19, 'The Sweet Harmony of Christ', 448.

[25] 'But when they are converted, their souls are brought into an harmonious agreement with Christ in this respect.' Y19, 'The Sweet Harmony of Christ', 440.

[26] 'I cannot think but that, if man was made to love God and delight in him, he was made to do it worthily and proportionately, in a due proportion to the excellency of the object and the capacity of the agent; seeing God doth all things according to the exactest harmony.' Y13, '*Miscellanies* 99. Future State', 268. Likewise, Edwards states, 'So the temper and behaviour of the true Christian towards Christ is answerable to his nature and state.' Y19, 'The Sweet Harmony of Christ', 445.

[27] Y19, 'The Sweet Harmony of Christ', 447.

remanation. As Edwards's eschatological vision entailed revival as the Spirit-empowered engine of God's reconciling work, so in religious affection do we see revival in miniature, revival at its most foundational.

Initially, therefore, the regenerate, through participation in God's self-revelation, must correspond to the Godhead in understanding and willing God himself. As noted above, religious affection concerns the sense of the heart, or *sensible* knowledge, and not mere speculation, because it traces the contours of how God knows himself.[28] In describing this knowledge in the *Religious Affections*, Edwards states, 'The heart is the proper subject of it, or the soul as a being that not only beholds, but has inclination, and is pleased or displeased.'[29] As God the Father beholds his Son, happiness and love emanate between them as the Spirit, so also the elect behold God, in Christ; this too is inclinational – it causes love, joy and happiness to emanate between them by the Spirit, uniting them to Christ. Edwards claims that by the sense of the heart, 'the mind don't only speculate and behold, but relishes and feels'.[30] Walton expounds on this quotation, noting that Edwards uses 'mind' as a broad synonym for soul. Speculative knowledge, in other words, fails to fully actualize the soul, but the mind as both beholding and relishing, both understanding and willing, is the mind functioning toward its full and proper end.

In this sense, God's processions of understanding and willing function, mutatis mutandis, as the image of the truly religious soul in humanity: humanity actualized.[31] As noted in the section on heaven, Edwards claims,

---

[28] In *Miscellanies* 782, Edwards offers a twofold division concerning sensible knowledge. '*First* respects the ways we come by it. (1) There is that which is purely natural, either such as men's minds come to be impressed with by the object that are about them, by the laws of nature: as when they behold anything that is beautiful or deformed. ... (2) That sense of things which we don't receive without some immediate influence of the Spirit, of impressing a sense of things that do concern our greatest interest on our minds.' Second, 'The other distribution that may be made of the kinds of sensible knowledge is according to the different nature of the objects of it, into a sense of things with respect to the natural good or evil that is in them, or that they relate to, or a sense of them with respect to spiritual good or evil. By spiritual good I mean all true moral good, all real moral beauty and excellency, and all those acts of the will, or that sense of the heart, that relates to it.' Y18, '*Miscellanies* 782. Ideas. Sense of the Heart', 461–2.

[29] Y2, *Religious Affections*, 272. Owen states, 'The *subject* spoken of in these promises is the *heart*. And the heart in the Scripture is taken for the whole rational soul, not absolutely, but as all the faculties of the soul are one common principle of all our moral operations.' Owen, *The Holy Spirit* (ed. William H. Goold; The Works of John Owen, vol. 3; London: Banner of Truth Trust, 1966), 326.

[30] Y2, *Religious Affections*, 272.

[31] Studebaker makes a similar observation but highlights Edwards's relationship to the tradition. 'His teaching is not unlike Augustine's and Aquinas' notion that the human soul finds its highest image of God when it knows and loves its creator through the aid of grace.' Studebaker, *Jonathan Edwards' Social Augustinian Trinitarianism*, 141.

'The soul shall not be an inactive spectator but shall be *most active*, shall be in the most ardent exercise of love toward the object seen. The soul shall be, as it were, all eye to behold, and yet all act to love,'[32] the effect of which, Edwards says, is 'happifying'.[33] Likewise, Edwards states, 'Every faculty of the soul will be employed and exercised, and will be employed in vastly more lively, more exalted exercises than they are now, though without any labor or weariness.'[34] In his sermon 'Serving God in Heaven', Edwards states, 'They [the saints] shall *perpetually* behold God's glory and *perpetually* enjoy his love.[35] But they shall not remain in a state of inactivity, merely receiving from God; but they return to him and shall enjoy him in a way of serving and glorifying him.'[36] Edwards's use of *perpetually* here should not go unnoticed. For Edwards, creatures qua persons mirror God's processions *and* the proceedings themselves.[37] The teleology of the regenerate, therefore, is to mirror, mutatis mutandis, God's processions in pure act.

Before moving on it is important to unpack what 'mutatis mutandis' is doing here. God's pure actuality is without potential. The regenerate, as finite creatures responding to an infinite God, will be fully actualized according to their nature, but will also increase in knowledge and love eternally. In heaven the glorified saints are like containers that are always full but whose capacity is always growing. There is never an occasion without perpetual act, in other words, but as the act is realized according to one's potential, potential itself increases. This is how Edwards is

---

[32] JEC, Unpublished Sermon, Rom. 2:10, #373 [L. 45v.] – my emphasis.
[33] Y17, 'The Pure in Heart Blessed', 63.
[34] Y17, 'Serving God in Heaven', 259.
[35] Y17, 'Serving God in Heaven', 251–61.
[36] Y17, 'Serving God in Heaven', 259 – my emphasis. Furthermore, this act, mirroring God's pure action in his own life, is called *rest.*
[37] There is precedent for this kind of move in Aquinas, according to the interpretation of D. Juvenal Merriell, who argues: 'For Aquinas the act of intellect entails the action of the object upon the mind that produces a likeness of the object in the mind. ... In contrast, the act of the will moves in the opposite direction, starting from the concept in the mind and being drawn outward to the object itself. This outward-directed impulse is what Aquinas identifies as the love that proceeds in the act of will – a thing that is very different from the inner word that is a likeness of the object reproduced within the mind. Thus, in God, as in man, there are two distinct interior processions belonging to the acts of intellect and will and resulting in two entities: word and love' (127). Likewise, he states, 'The capacity to participate in the dynamic life of the Trinity is rooted in man's nature, but it is only when the mind is actively engaged in knowing and willing that the two processions actually occur in man's mind.' (128) Furthermore, 'Thus, the indwelling of the Trinity is basically the graced presence of God to the mind's faculties of intellect and will in a way that makes the intellect participate in the divine procession of the Word and the will participate in the divine procession of love' (137). D. Juvenal Merriell, 'Trinitarian Anthropology', in *The Theology of Thomas Aquinas* (ed. Rik Van Nieuwenhove and Joseph Peter Wawrykow; Notre Dame: University of Notre Dame Press, 2005), 127–8, 137. Stephen Studebaker notes this similarity as well. Studebaker, *Jonathan Edwards' Social Augustinian Trinitarianism,* 140–2.

able to state, 'Created spirits come nearer to [God], *or more imitate* [God], the greater they are in the powers and faculties.' Therefore, my use of 'mutatis mutandis' calls out Edwards's use of the infinite/finite distinction, highlighting the elect's ever-increasing potential and fulfilment but increasing eternally according to their nature. The regenerate do not merely mirror the subsistences of the Godhead, but in knowing God affectionately, the elect must reflect the *proceeding* of the subsistences in their own understanding and willing. God's perpetual gazing upon beauty and eternal flowing out toward that beauty must be realized, mutatis mutandis, in the life of the elect.[38]

Once again, Edwards's use of the sun as the 'other' image of the Trinity helps to explicate this aspect of his thought most fully.[39] This image is not in competition with personal beatific-delight but helps to both illustrate God's diffusiveness and highlight the interconnected but distinct missions of the Son (light) and Spirit (heat). In the *Religious Affections*, Edwards claims, 'But the soul of a saint receives light from the Sun of Righteousness, in such a manner, that its nature is changed, and it becomes properly a luminous thing: not only does the sun shine in the saints, but they also become little suns, partaking of the nature of the fountain of their light.'[40] God's glory, as it were, shines down upon the world and either enlightens or scorches.[41] Fallen humanity is doomed to be scorched by the beams of glory because, as fallen, they do not have the spiritual aspect of God's image. The Spirit, once infused, awakens humanity to God and sets in motion the interplay of reception and affection, opening 'a new world to its view'.[42] Spiritual understanding, consisting in a sense of the heart,

---

[38] This point is not simply 'academic'. Edwards's final sign in his *Religious Affections* points to the idea that religious affection needs to persevere. The Christian life may have stumbles and backsliding, but it will ultimately prevail. This sign points to the reality I am noting here.

[39] Edwards mentions this image in his *Discourse*, and he used the image in a sermon on Jas 1:17, with the doctrine: 'God is the Father of Lights'. See *The Blessing of God*, 343–57. In *Miscellanies* 931, he states that 'the sun is the greatest image of God [of] any inanimate creature in the whole universe (or at least it is so to us), in these two things, viz. as a fountain of light and life and refreshment, and also in being a consuming fire, an immense fountain as it were of infinitely fierce and burning heat.' Y20, '*Miscellanies* 931. Hell Torments. Conflagration', 180.

[40] Y2, *Religious Affections*, 343.

[41] This is Edwards's main point in his sermon on Mal. 4:1-2. Y22, 'Christ the Spiritual Sun', 50–64.

[42] Y2, *Religious Affections*, 273. In *God Glorified*, Edwards states, 'God puts his own beauty, i.e. his beautiful likeness, upon their souls. They are made "partakers of the divine nature", or moral image of God (II Pet. 1:4). They are holy by being made "partakers of God's holiness" (Heb. 12:10). The saints are beautiful and blessed by a communication of God's holiness and joy as the moon and planets are bright by the sun's light. The saint hath spiritual joy and pleasure by a kind of effusion of God on the soul. In these things the redeemed have

is a united movement of the soul where understanding and will function together according to the degree of light given.[43] In his sermon 'Honey from the Rock', Edwards claims that the Spirit's infusion renews the image of God, so that 'man is raised to the heavenly life, so that he is enabled to live to God and to perform those actions that are for God's glory and for his own true happiness'.[44] There is a dynamism in the image of God for Edwards, one that will increase *toward* perfection in this age and then increase *in* perfection in the age to come.[45]

The soul of the regenerate, mirroring the divine essence 'flowing forth' affectionately as the Spirit, itself 'flows forth' to God.[46] Just as the Father's love is poured forth fully on the Son, and Jesus's love 'flows out' to the church in heaven, the saints are, 'united with one mind to *breathe forth* their whole souls in love to their eternal Father, and to Jesus Christ'.[47] Further, in *Religious Affections*, Edwards discusses the soul as being 'carried out', toward its object.[48] Edwards reasons that 'if religious affections in men here below, are but of the same nature and kind with theirs [in heaven], the higher they are, and the nearer they are to theirs in degree, the better.'[49] Categorizing Edwards's trinitarian thought as 'personal beatific-delight' is another way of stating that his model of the Trinity is God experiencing

communion with God; that is, they partake with him and of him.' Y17, 'God Glorified in Man's Dependence', 208.

[43] See Y2, *Religious Affections*, 272.

[44] Y17, 'Honey from the Rock', 136.

[45] See Y19, 'Striving After Perfection', 698, for Edwards's use of 'perfection' of the image in heaven.

[46] As persons, creatures correspond to the infinite persons of God, and correspond because they have understanding and will as God has. Therefore, Edwards can state, 'The difference [between God and man] is no contrariety, but what naturally results from his greatness and nothing else, such as created spirits come nearer to, or more imitate, the greater they are in the powers and faculties. So that if we should suppose the faculties of a created spirit to be enlarged infinitely, there would be the Deity to all intents and purposes, the same simplicity, immutability, etc.' Y13, '135. Deity', 295 – my emphasis.

[47] Y8, 'Charity and Its Fruits', 374 – my emphasis. In 'Heaven is a World of Love', Edwards states, 'And love flows out from him towards all the inhabitants of heaven. It flows out in the first place necessarily and infinitely towards his only begotten Son, being poured forth without measure, as to an object which is infinite, and so fully adequate to God's love in its fountain. Infinite love is infinitely exercised towards him. The fountain does not only send forth large streams towards this object as it does to every other, but the very fountain itself wholly and altogether goes out towards him.' Y8, 'Charity and Its Fruits', 373 Likewise, Edwards understands religious affections to flow forth from the fountain of love as well. He states, 'As from true divine love flow all Christian affections, so from a counterfeit love in like manner, naturally flow other false affections. In both cases, love is the fountain, and the other affections are the streams. The various faculties, principles and affections of the human nature, are as it were many channels from one fountain.' Y2, *Religious Affections*, 150–1.

[48] See Y2, *Religious Affections*, 96, 98.

[49] Y2, *Religious Affections*, 130.

religious affections in pure act. It is the entire 'trinitarian narrative' that serves as the model for life *coram deo*.[50]

As saints pilgrimage through this world, God's revelation and increasing union diminishes the personal void between creatures and their creator. Being made holy is an eternal event that begins in conversion. Therefore, emanation and remanation occurs even in heaven: saints beholding God's glory and participating in his love and delight, returning glory to him without the great 'distance' known on earth.[51] There the redeemed are fully actualized, *perpetually* receiving and returning God's glory. Likewise, as quoted at the outset of this section, Edwards explains that conversion *begins* the work in which the saints will spend eternity. Glorification is the perfection of what is known in regeneration (illumination, infusion and union), by providing *the* object of glory unhindered. Edwards explains this in *Religious Affections*, where he reasons that the saints in heaven have higher affections simply because their sight is clearer, more in accord with the truth.[52] In 'Heaven Is a World of Love', Edwards utilizes the image of the sun once more, positing that 'the soul which only had a little spark of divine love in it in this world shall be, as it were, wholly turned into love; and be like the sun, not having a spot in it, but being wholly a bright, ardent flame'.[53]

Religious affection, in Edwards's theology, grounds the life of the believer in the triune God of glory and orients the believer on the path of heaven, where an ever-increasing participation in God's own life continues on for eternity. Affection marks the anthropological correspondence of the saints to the God who is both alpha and omega. Furthermore, the remaining component of our heuristic key is that affection is God's *self*-glorification. God's economic movement to redeem was to self-glorify *through* creaturely realities. In religious affection, God's creation purposes are substantiated in the life of the regenerate. God *self*-glorifies because, like the sun reflecting its light off of the moon, God's emanation returns in remanation

---

[50] Danaher, based on his bifurcated understanding of Edwards's doctrine of the Trinity, fails to see how this is the case, stating, 'A fuller depiction of the affections follows, however, when we view Edwards's project in the *Religious Affections* from the perspective of his psychological and social analogies.' William J. Danaher, *The Trinitarian Ethics of Jonathan Edwards* (Columbia Series in Reformed Theology; Louisville: Westminster John Knox, 2004), 118.

[51] The use of 'distance' here calls out the reality in Edwards's thought that an increase of sight follows an increase of union. Edwards's understanding of heaven entails an increasing union to eternity, which therefore entails increasing sight, knowledge and love. The elect's 'distance' on earth is based on the reality of sin, flesh and seeing through a glass darkly. See Y25, 'True Saints and Present with the Lord', 231: 'But while the saints are in the body, there is much remaining distance between Christ and them.'

[52] Y2, *Religious Affections*, 130.

[53] Y8, 'Charity and Its Fruits', 374–5.

through an apprehension of his light (Christ) and a return of his heat (Spirit). The saints' object in the beatific corresponds with the Father's, both gazing upon the Son, and their delight is the same – the *Holy* Spirit of God. In an early *Miscellanies* entry, Edwards muses on this reality, claiming that here we have an image of the Trinity in the act of redemption itself, 'wherein Christ is the everlasting father, and believers are his seed, and the Holy Spirit, or Comforter, is the third person in Christ, being his delight and love flowing out towards the church'.[54] As Christ takes the position of the Father, so the church takes the position of Christ – knowing as they are known and loving as they are loved. Furthermore, Edwards continues, 'In believers the Spirit and delight of God, being communicated unto them, flows out toward the Lord Jesus Christ.'[55] Religious affection is the point where God's communication returns to him through creaturely delight; it is his self-glorification, as his emanation is effective for remanation.

Our explication of God's beatific-delight, the nature of persons and God's creating for his own glory sheds much light on this scheme of redemption. Edwards's account takes seriously the redemption of persons as such and utilizes the trinitarian participation in beatific-delight as a model. With the spiritual and supernatural governing the natural, believers grow in an experiential knowledge of God that inclines the heart toward him as the good, the true and the beautiful. The processions are the archetype of what human persons experience ectypally in *creaturely* correspondence in glorification and in impure and inhibited act in sanctification. Religious affections function as the corollary to true knowledge of God, because knowledge of God functions in an affective register, a register God personifies in his inner life. Therefore, Edwards can say that the saints '*know experimentally* what true religion is, in the internal exercises of it; yet these are what they can neither feel, nor see, in the heart of another'.[56] Religion is truly experiential and affective, because knowledge of God by his self-revelation is knowledge of God through sight with a sense of the heart. Building upon our discussion of spiritual knowledge, regeneration and the sense of the heart above, we see that creatures are made to behold rightly, which necessitates beholding God as the fundamental good, beauty and holiness. Therefore, it makes sense that Edwards would state,

If it was God's intention, as there is great reason to think it was, that his works should exhibit an image of himself their author, that it might

[54] Y13, '*Miscellanies* 104. End of the Creation', 273.
[55] Y13, '*Miscellanies* 104. End of the Creation', 273–4.
[56] Y2, *Religious Affections*, 181 – my emphasis.

brightly appear by his works what manner of being he is, and afford a proper representation of his divine excellencies, and especially his *moral* excellence, consisting in the *disposition of his heart*.[57]

Through God's word and works the elect come to know God's heart with their hearts. This communication does not emanate without purpose, and its purpose does not go unfulfilled; God's flowing out in emanation finds its return in remanation through creaturely spiritual vision and affection. This is a trinitarian affair and was God's very purpose in creating.

As I developed in the section on heaven, knowledge of God advances in various stages in glory, tracking in parallel with God's work of redemption, as itself revelation, in the world. As God reveals himself more fully, his elect and his angels respond in understanding and loving, poured forth as worship and praise. By eliminating the pilgrim and beatific divide, Edwards makes way for a greater correspondence between the saints in heaven and the saints on earth. The affections are not mere emotional responses to God's goodness but are responses of journeying on the pilgrim's path of glory, the same path they will walk for eternity.[58] The religious affections act as the point where emanation turns back as remanation. They are the spiritual effects of the Spirit of God at work in the believer, illuminating the divine so that they truly do share in the beatific experience of the saints in heaven, however limited that sight is. Religious affections call out, as it were, proper functioning within God's creation, when the creature functions harmoniously with the agreement of the good, true and beautiful. In Edwards's mind, it is the supernatural effect of having the Spirit of God dwelling in the heart 'as a principle of new nature, or as a divine supernatural spring of life and action' that the saints become beautiful in their correspondence with pure beauty itself – a correspondence that entails an ever-increasing *personal* union in the *personal* beatific-delight of God.[59]

---

[57] Y8, *End of Creation*, 422.

[58] John E. Smith notes that 'Edwards's aim is to show not only that the two are not incompatible [inward experiences and practice], but that it is a mistake to regard them as entirely distinct.' John E. Smith, *Jonathan Edwards: Puritan, Preacher, Philosopher* (Outstanding Christian Thinkers; Notre Dame: University of Notre Dame Press, 1992), 54.

[59] Y2, *Religious Affections*, 200. Edwards emphasizes the kind of work the Spirit undertakes is qualitatively different from his work on the unregenerate. See Y2, *Religious Affections*, 202–39.

Conclusion

My goal in this volume has been to demonstrate that Jonathan Edwards's theology has an internal coherence, forged in the context of his trinitarian theology and exposition of God's nature as persons in beatific-delight. Edwards's trinitarian analysis, coupled with his focus on God's act of self-glorification through creation to consummation, served as a heuristic key to interpret various doctrines of redemption. All created reality, furthermore, is constituted of wheels within wheels, whose end, known or unknown, is to glorify their Creator. The turn of the great wheel of time rolls out in emanation and returns to its creator in remanation. I sought justification for my interpretative scheme at three application points – spiritual knowledge, regeneration and religious affection – each of which advanced my argument by expositing, in broad strokes, creaturely ectypal knowledge under God's life as archetype. Exposition of these doctrines highlights the interpretative gains of my account and makes a case for the centrality of certain dogmatic threads apparent in Edwards's work. In the secondary literature, commentators on Edwards often emphasize but do not systematize these various 'threads', such as visual imagery, personhood/person language, affection and spiritual knowledge. By explaining these emphases through Edwards's own trinitarian theology, I locate Edwards in an international scene of eighteenth-century Reformed, systematic and trinitarian theology. Therefore, in brief, I recapitulate the flow of my argument before turning to readdress the success of this endeavour in light of criticism and highlight further areas of exploration to round out this account.

Recapitulation

In the first chapter, to ground this project, I exposited Edwards's doctrine of the Trinity and suggested that Edwards's theology must be understood from the top down. Edwards's theology finds its inner logic in an explication of *this* God and *this God's* movement in Word and Spirit to redeem. To do so, I offered detailed discussion of the polemical and textual issues and argued for an evolution in Edwards's trinitarian thought. Building upon that account, I considered Edwards's *Discourse*, addressing the divine essence and persons, the divine idea, love, and perichoresis, concluding that his mature position is found in the *Discourse* (though not in well-polished form).

Edwards's mature position on the Trinity, I suggested, is best understood as personal beatific-delight (or, possibly, divine religious affection in pure act). The triune God of the Bible is the God who gazes upon his own perfect idea/image and flows forth in love and delight because that image is perfect, true and beautiful. This development focuses on God as both personal and persons, using personhood to delineate the real (intrinsic) properties of the divine essence, as well as relegating attributes typically conceived as intrinsic to extrinsic or 'relational' status (for more on this issue, see the appendix and the end of this volume). By failing to recognize the overarching composite image that organizes the *Discourse*, as well as the ideological shift in Edwards's account, contemporary commentators frequently misconstrue his position, his take on the attributes and the relation of the divine essence to the divine persons.

The second constitutive element of my heuristic proposal focused on God's economic work, placing the acts of creation and consummation in parallel. Using Edwards's trinitarian narrative as the ideological moorings, I detailed an account of the beatific God of glory, who wills to self-glorify through creaturely realities, and I framed this account with a teleological orientation of the beatific reality of heaven. The consummation of all things unfolds the beatific self-glorification of God through creaturely participation in God's own personal beatific-delight for all eternity.

In focusing our attention on God's creative activity, I evinced that Edwards maintained his commitment to God's aseity as both foundational and central to his theological task. I provided a reading of Edwards's *End of Creation* (Chapter 2) that attended to its theological backdrop, flow of the argument and idiosyncratic terminology, clarifying language which has caused much confusion and misinterpretation of his thought (language that is used consistently within his corpus). I concluded that Edwards affirms his Reformed background, asserting that God creates for his own glory, as his only original end, and achieves his ultimate end of self-glorification through creaturely realities.

In parallel to God's creating activity, I offered a sketch of heaven (Chapter 3), whose eras track with Christ's redeeming movements. Again, located under his trinitarian thought, Edwards's account of heaven focuses on apprehending God in beatific glory as the *summum bonum* of creaturely reality. As a Christologically mediated vision whose material content is *spiritual*, beatific realities are woven through Christ's person and work as redeemer. Each era of heaven provides an increase in revelation through Christ's work of redemption in the world/mediating work in heaven. The consummation of this work entails a marriage union between the elect and

Christ, united through the Spirit as the bond of love. Heaven progresses as an eternal wedding day, celebrating God's redemption of the lost, who increasingly participate in a vision of God who is now known and seen as Redeemer.

While the second section focused our attention on the grand wheel of creation and its orientation to eternity, the third section addressed the reality of the wheel's downturn for the purpose of an upturn – emanation received and given back in remanation. In doing so, I parsed Edwards's view of spiritual knowledge, regeneration and religious affection as essential moments on the wheel's movement toward consummation (Chapters 4 through 6 respectively). Serving as application points for my interpretation as well as 'anchor points' for Edwards's theology of redemption, these three doctrines further justify the interpretation I provided in the preceding analysis.

The first application of my interpretative scheme addressed spiritual knowledge. As knowledge of God, of *this* God, all spiritual knowledge is pushed into the form of beatific-delight. Furthermore, I outlined Edwards's move, understood proleptically from consummation, to collapse the traditionally sealed categories of faith and sight – the pilgrim and the beatific – into one another. Therefore, pilgrim existence is a darkened beatific sight, and heaven is a progressive state, or, in other words, a pilgrim journey of ongoing fulfilment and increase. As knowledge of God, knowledge that is both apprehension and affection, spiritual knowledge is participation within God's self-understanding and self-loving, obtained only through the economic working of the Son and Spirit.

The second application was to develop God's action in the economy that allows for this pilgrim-beatific spiritual knowledge. Looking at the Spirit's work of regeneration, I detailed illumination and infusion as the twofold work of the Spirit imparting a vision of God in Christ and the infusion of holiness to respond in affection. I developed this account in contrast to Owen and McClenahan, arguing against the latter for his failure to consider Edwards's broader theological commitments, suggesting that Edwards departs from Owen to posit the Spirit as an infused principle in the soul of the regenerate.

I then utilized both spiritual knowledge and regeneration to address religious affection in my third application. It is here where God's beatific self-glorification is shown to have provided the grammar and *telos* of Edwards's theology. Religious affection, I argued, is the result of true knowledge of God. Since all spiritual knowledge of God takes on a beatific form, because it is knowledge of *this* God of personal beatific-delight, *affection* is the necessary result. This creaturely response to emanation with remanation finds its moorings in the inner life of God, who both apprehends himself and emanates in love. The image of God in creatures takes on this dynamic quality, finding its perfection in eternity, where there is a *perpetual* beholding and *perpetual* love.

Stepping back from this recapitulation, it becomes clear that the contours navigated in this volume were nothing short of 'true religion'. True Religion, an idea at the forefront of Edwards's imagination, is simply God's beatific self-glorification. In other words, my heuristic key is the nature of true religion in Edwards's thought. True religion is perfected in heaven, as it is the perfection of the pilgrimage inaugurated on earth. Ultimately, of course, true religion is simply the ectype of the trinitarian archetype. God's own life of personal beatific-delight is 'true religion' in pure act, because true religion, like God's own life, is oriented to God himself. As we have seen, Edwards claims that 'true religion, in great part, consists in holy affections'.[60] These affections are a partaking of the divine nature in union and communion and necessitate a beatific envisioning. Holy affections are modelled after the inner life of God. True religion, in other words, is Edwards's own gloss on the heuristic key outlined here.

Evaluation

In order to provide an evaluation of what I have offered as a 'reinterpretation' of Edwards's theology, I turn to five criteria developed by Michael McClymond for identifying an adequate account of Edwards's theology.[61] Using McClymond's criteria is important because he is a representative of the 'Lee school', even as he has his distinctive emphases, and gives these criteria with the specific purpose of defending both Lee and Amy Plantinga Pauw. In other words, McClymond is helpful for evaluation because he represents the position I have argued against in this work. If my methodology passes the test of his criteria, it serves as a telling, albeit unlikely,

---

[60] Y2, *Religious Affections*, 95.
[61] My focus in the overview of McClymond's points is his chapter in *Jonathan Edwards as Contemporary*, but I note the parallel discussion in his co-written volume with Gerald McDermott in the footnotes, *The Theology of Jonathan Edwards*. Michael J. McClymond and Gerald R. McDermott, *The Theology of Jonathan Edwards* (Oxford: Oxford University Press, 2012). It seems that McClymond and McDermott's five points, which they claim should all be 'heard at once' like a symphony, are actually kept separate because they do not fully locate them in the doctrine of God. As I try to show, all of Edwards's theology is wrapped up in God and his works. Even soteriology is primarily concerned with God, as Word and Spirit. God is the primary harmony that people are called in to.

recommendation. Admittedly, evaluating one's own work can be difficult, but McClymond's focal points are at the heart of my entire analysis. That said, I turn now to McClymond's five themes.

First, McClymond argues that *trinitarian communication* is the first key to Edwards's thought. A proper reading of Edwards's theology must focus on the divine communication as reflected in the *Discourse* and *End of Creation* (my Chapters 1 and 2 respectively), and this communication must form Edwards's soteriology.[62] Second, one must adequately emphasize *creaturely participation*. 'God is the sort of God with whom creatures can participate', McClymond claims.[63] This work of participation is the economic work of God to transmit divine knowledge through the Son and divine love and happiness through the Spirit.[64] Third, McClymond develops an account of Edwards's '*voluntarist (or affectionalist) necessitarianism*'. This theme focuses on the Godward motion of redemption, that salvation is 'immediately' from God, as well as the notion that salvation entails an 'affectionalist' anthropology and soteriology.[65] Fourth, McClymond suggest a *dispositional soteriology*, claiming that 'God chiefly looks not to outward actions but to inward dispositions' and that 'dispositions precede actions'.[66] Edwards's soteriology demands an account of the affections and God's action to form and influence them. The last criterion is what McClymond refers to as a *harmonious constitutionalism*. This, he explains, means, 'In Edwards' thinking, salvation is less like a chain of beads than like a net in which each part of the net holds the rest in place.'[67]

---

[62] McClymond and McDermott, *The Theology of Jonathan Edwards*, 5. William Schweitzer attempts to make this point the whole of his interpretive reading. I have already criticized Schweitzer's view of the beatific vision, noting that he fails to grasp the breadth of what Edwards is doing. Something similar could be said with his interpretive model as well. It is not wrong, per se, it is simply too narrow. His failure to grasp the breadth of what Edwards is doing with the beatific vision is evidence for this.

[63] Michael J. McClymond, 'Hearing the Symphony': A Critique of Some Critics of Sang Lee's and Amy Pauw's Accounts of Jonathan Edwards' View of God', in *Jonathan Edwards as Contemporary: Essays in Honor of Sang Hyun Lee* (Festschrift Sang Hyun Lee; New York: Peter Lang, 2010), 68–92, (80).

[64] McClymond, 'Hearing the Symphony', 80. McClymond and McDermott, *The Theology of Jonathan Edwards*, 5.

[65] McClymond, 'Hearing the Symphony', 80. Interestingly, McClymond's third point in his volume with McDermott is 'necessitarian dispositionalism', which takes Lee's development of a dispositional ontology in Edwards's thought and applies it at the core of Edwards's theology. It is curious that McClymond does not follow suit in his own chapter. McClymond and McDermott, *The Theology of Jonathan Edwards*, 5.

[66] McClymond, 'Hearing the Symphony', 81. In his volume with McDermott, the fourth emphasis is 'theocentric voluntarism', that there is a 'divine priority in all reality'. McClymond and McDermott, *The Theology of Jonathan Edwards*, 6.

[67] McClymond, 'Hearing the Symphony', 81. This is the same as the volume with McDermott. McClymond and McDermott, *The Theology of Jonathan Edwards*, 6. The focus here, in my mind, is misguided. The Reformed genius of Edwards's soteriology is not that it is 'less like

230 Jonathan Edwards's Theology

It is noteworthy that McClymond's five criteria, mutatis mutandis, serve
to highlight exactly what I have done in this volume. Importantly, I have
argued that these exact areas are either neglected or misconstrued by those
in the 'Lee school', the broad school of thought with which McClymond
identifies himself. In one summarizing comment, McClymond points to
the advantage of Lee's and Pauw's reading of Edwards by claiming that
they 'have captured Edwards' expansive vision of God's outflowing and
overflowing love in creation and redemption, and the elect creatures'
genuine participation in the life, love, happiness, blessedness, and glory of
the Holy Trinity'.[68] If my argument stands, McClymond's criteria bolster
my argument and adds further validation for my methodology, even as my
argument directly contrasts his own interpretative school. Furthermore,
I have been able to integrate these five elements into a distinctively
Reformed vision of theology that fits neatly (though creatively) in the
theological moorings of the high orthodox period of Reformed theology.
Rather than advancing philosophical theories and frameworks as interpretative lenses, I have described a *theological* interpretative key from Edwards's
own self-proclaimed emphases and commitments, utilizing his doctrine of
God, the doctrine that consumed his mind and heart, as the fountain of
his thought.[69]

Along with these five major aspects of Edwards's theology, McClymond
attacks the critics of Lee and Pauw.[70] First, he suggests that these critics
function with a preconceived interpretative grid from which to judge
Edwards's theology and that, in contrast, Lee and Pauw develop theirs
from the text up.[71] In other words, Lee's and Pauw's views derive from a
close reading of the primary texts.[72] Second, he suggests that an adequate

---

a chain of beads than like a net', but that it is organized by Word and Spirit. McClymond
and McDermott still seem stuck in the framework they are trying to critique, and miss how
Edwards reorganizes theology around the doctrine of God. See Strobel, 'By Word and Spirit'.
[68] McClymond, 'Hearing the Symphony', 70.
[69] Importantly, McClymond and McDermott not only agree that Edwards's doctrine of the
Trinity should be the fountain of his thought, they also seem to agree that creation and
consummation should act as second-order scaffolding for interpreting Edwards. 'Like *End
of Creation*, which moves from creation to consummation, Edwards's unwritten *A History of
the Work of Redemption* was to be bracketed on either side by God's eternity,' McClymond
and McDermott, *The Theology of Jonathan Edwards*, 184. The question is, I suppose, whose
doctrine of the Trinity is one using?
[70] See my review of this volume for some more focused critiques of McClymond's argument
and approach. Kyle Strobel, 'Review of *Jonathan Edwards as Contemporary: Essays in Honor of
Sang Hyun Lee*', *Themelios* 36:3 (November 2011).
[71] McClymond fails to address the fact that two of the three main interpreters he criticizes,
Holmes and Studebaker, make this same criticism of both Lee and Pauw respectively.
McClymond's essay is far from persuasive, reading more like a rant than an actual argument.
[72] McClymond, 'Hearing the Symphony', 72–3. As is shown in my analysis, this claim is not

methodology puts Edwards in conversation with his own theological forebears, specifically seventeenth- and eighteenth-century Calvinism.[73] Third, he argues that the critics have failed to take seriously the role of Edwards's biblical exegesis.[74] Last, McClymond suggests that derivation from Lee and Pauw is nothing short of a 'proxy war', in which interpreters are seeking to 'win' Edwards to their side of orthodoxy.[75]

Leaving aside the legitimacy of McClymond's analysis, it is important to note that my analysis does not fall victim *to any* of McClymond's points of contention, nor does it fail to address the key themes he argues for.[76] Rather, what I have provided is an account *of these very issues* from the texts up. Rather than arguing based on presupposed interpretative models, I have spent focused energy throughout this volume on the nature of specific texts, arguing that Lee in particular, can at times fail to weigh texts appropriately. Furthermore, through my analysis of the *Discourse* and the *End of Creation*, I have shown how interpreters, Lee and Pauw among them, have failed to let Edwards speak for himself, reading their own interpretative schemes into Edwards's work (McClymond's very criticism of their critics). Throughout this analysis, I have both contrasted and paralleled Edwards with his theological forebears, and my argumentation and development of an interpretative key is based on Edwards's own claims and theological tradition. Furthermore McClymond's criteria support my ordering of Edwards's theocentricity, creation and consummation, as well as the use of the triune life *in se* and in the economy to form Edwards's soteriology. Through a specifically theological approach, I have determined from within the confines of his own construction that Edwards believed himself to be working creatively within Reformed and Puritan thought.[77] Even

actually substantiated on a close reading of the primary text, particularly when those texts are weighed appropriately.

[73] McClymond, 'Hearing the Symphony', 73.
[74] McClymond, 'Hearing the Symphony', 75.
[75] It is hard to know if this comment is even worth responding to. McClymond seems to posit it as a way to avoid actually engaging the argumentation of Holmes and Studebaker. When he does engage the arguments, his own rebuttal is similar to this claim – he merely accuses them of reading their own ideologies into Edwards. I am not entirely sure if McClymond has understood Holmes or Studebaker, and, in light of his analysis, it is clear he is functioning with incredibly outdated information. For instance, in criticizing Studebaker for claiming that there is not substantial difference between Eastern and Western trinitarian thought in the early church fathers, McClymond claims that Studebaker's analysis 'flies in the face' of patristic scholarship. To substantiate his claim, McClymond only offers Zizioulas. In doing so, McClymond shows himself to be completely ignorant of patristic scholarship on these claims (e.g. Lewis Ayres, Michel René Barnes, Richard Cross, Mary Clark, etc.).
[76] Admittedly, my emphasis was not on Edwards's exegesis, but it was also not 'ignored'.
[77] The flow of my argument reverses the order of this, where I make my observations that Edwards's thought is distinctively Reformed and Puritan. Against McClymond's claim that critics of Lee and Pauw are involved in some sort of 'proxy war' to prove that Edwards

as he appropriated philosophical insights from his contemporaries, the construction of Edwards's theology fits directly within the ideological moorings of the high orthodox period of the Reformed faith.

In the end, McClymond makes a point that may be more central to his criticism: Lee's position 'is a more coherent and elegant explanation of Edwards' theology than any competing viewpoint that has been offered thus far'.[78] In this sense, he is right. Other interpretative schemes have often failed at the exact point that Lee's and Pauw's thrive – cohesion, coherence and elegance. What I suggest here is that my analysis accounts for all of these concerns with more justice to Edwards's thought, development and texts, and that it provides the coherence and elegance other interpretative models have lacked. This coherence and elegance, contrary to Lee's, starts with Edwards's development of God and ends with God and his elect participating in eternal beatific-delight. The focus on personhood, beatific and delight and the harmony obtained through participation in the life of God provides an elegance, cohesion and coherence, I suggest, not found in other accounts. That said, my focus in this volume was to articulate an interpretative scheme for Edwards's theological task and not to give a robust account of his doctrines of redemption. Applying this task further, particularly to the doctrines of *theosis* and justification by faith, would, I believe, further substantiate my claims, and further establish the beauty and harmony of this account.[79]

To close, let me point out some of the directions necessary for my analysis to take. First, in light of my polemical engagement with Lee, it is necessary for this account to be held against Lee's major philosophical analysis. In other words, even though in my account I have sought to undo some of Lee's analysis, what I have not done is address the validity of his philosophical insights of Edwards's ontology (except in reference to God himself).[80] Second, because my analysis is a broad interpretative

---

is *their* Edwards, I had no such illusion when I studied Edwards. Although wrong about Holmes and Studebaker, to some degree (Studebaker does seem to really want Edwards to be Augustinian), he is right about many of the dissertations that are written about Edwards. I have no horse in the Edwards race – whether he came out a heretic or the perfect example of theological reasoning. What I found in Edwards was a thinker working creatively within the Reformed/Puritan framework that articulates a robust *catholic* theology (in a similar way, I would argue, as John Owen).

[78] McClymond, 'Hearing the Symphony', 70.

[79] I have attempted to do this in a variety of ways. See Strobel, 'By Word and Spirit', and Strobel, 'Jonathan Edwards's Polemics of *Theosis*', *Harvard Theological Review* 105:3 (July 2012): 259–79.

[80] As of the final edits of this volume, I have become aware of John Bombaro's monograph on Edwards's vision of reality. It strikes me that his analysis, mutatis mutandis, shares remarkable parallels with my own. The key difference is that his approach is philosophical

key, there is more detailed work to do in Edwards's trinitarian thought, specifically looking at the immanent/economic relationship.[81] Third, the interpretative key developed here needs to be utilized to address key areas of specific soteriological loci. Last, aspects of Edwards's thought such as his aesthetics, doctrine of revelation, eschatology, etc. could be read through this model and provide deeper insight into the coherence and interrelation of Edwards's theology. As I (and others) pick up this task, I suggest that this account will prove both coherent and elegant and, more importantly, will adequately place Edwards within his self-confessed theological allegiances.

and mine theological. See John J. Bombaro, *Jonathan Edwards's Vision of Reality: The Relationship of God to the World, Redemption History, and the Reprobate* (Princeton Theological Monograph Series; Eugene: Wiph & Stock, 2012).

[81] Seng-Kong Tan's development of Edwards on the incarnation is an excellent example of what I am thinking here. See Seng-Kong Tan, 'Trinitarian Action in the Incarnation', in *Jonathan Edwards as Contemporary: Essays in Honor of Sang Hyun Lee* (ed. Don Schweitzer; New York, Peter Lang, 2010), 127–50.

Appendix: Divine Attributes and Essence

It proves instructive to build on my exposition of the divine essence and persons, as developed by Edwards, and triangulate the position exposited above with the interpretation of Oliver Crisp and Stephen Holmes. This triangulation seeks greater clarity on the issue of the divine attributes and their predication in the Godhead specifically. I will forge a via media between Crisp and Holmes, suggesting a third option based on my development of these issues in the first chapter. In short, the crux of the debate rests on interpreting Edwards's use of *real* and *relational* properties, and how those properties relate to the divine essence and persons. As I have shown, and argue here, God's real attributes for Edwards are those attributes which are intrinsic to God, or, in other words, God without reference to anything else. Relational attributes, however, are extrinsic to God; they are, in Edwards's terms, modal or circumstantial. While intrinsic and extrinsic attributes are standard delineations, Edwards's explication of 'real' and 'relational' attributes is somewhat idiosyncratic.

Setting up the debate, Holmes states, 'The residue of a common "essence" which was so pervasive in Western theological discourse is wholly absent, and Edwards claims to be unable to think of "any rational meaning" behind the standard language that describes the essence.'[1] Holmes goes on to add, 'Edwards makes a striking move: the Father's perfections are only and precisely the Son and the Spirit.'[2] And again, 'There is, then, in Edwards a move to subsume the doctrine of the divine perfections under the doctrine of the Trinity.'[3] And here Holmes addresses the fundamental issue of our debate, 'Given that the patristic doctrine never intended to suggest three centres of knowledge and will in its language of Three Persons, the question becomes one of appropriation and perichoresis. Edwards is essentially seeking to appropriate different perfections of

---

[1] Stephen Holmes, *God of Grace and God of Glory: An Account of the Theology of Jonathan Edwards* (Grand Rapids: Eerdmans, 2001), 69.
[2] Holmes, *God of Grace and God of Glory*, 69.
[3] Holmes, *God of Grace and God of Glory*, 70.

the divine *phusis* to particular *hypostases*.'[4] In other words, 'the perfections of God are truly the being of God' itself. The classic attributes are appropriated (in Holmes's words, a 'radical extension of the doctrine of appropriation')[5] under each of the persons. In response to Holmes, Crisp states, 'It is true that Edwards is locating in the persons of the Trinity perfections that have traditionally been thought to refer to the essence of God, and this is a radical move',[6] adding, 'but the absence of specific reference to the divine essence in this particular section of the *Essay on the Trinity* should not be taken to mean that Edwards has no place for a divine essence in his doctrine of the Trinity'.[7]

Crisp offers two differing ways to demarcate commentary on this issue: first, the 'Edwardsian Trinitarian Thesis', and second, the 'Strong Edwardsian Trinitarian Thesis'. The 'Edwardsian Trinitarian Thesis' states that 'everything that is in God is God, and this must be understood of real attributes (which pertain to one of the persons of the Trinity), not of modalities (such as immutability)'.[8] And then the 'Strong Edwardsian Trinitarian Thesis' states that 'everything that is in God is God, and this must be understood of *and exhausted by* "real" attributes ("real" in the Edwardsian sense, meaning attributes which pertain to one of the persons of the Trinity), not of modalities (meaning relational properties shared between the divine persons, such as immutability)'.[9]

Crisp offers an extended critique of Holmes:

Edwards's point is surely that the perfections of God refer to the real attributes of God (Father, Son and Holy Spirit), but that the relations of existence (e.g. eternity, immutability, and so on) do not. Such relations are, we might say, merely relations God has. They do not 'pick out' or distinguish distinct divine persons. In which case, all Edwards means, contrary to Holmes, is something like the Edwardsian Trinitarian Thesis, the weaker of the two theses just given. And this is compatible with a doctrine of the divine essence. For the Edwardsian Trinitarian thesis is

---

[4] Holmes, *God of Grace and God of Glory*, 71.

[5] I agree with Holmes's assessment, although I wonder if it would be more appropriate to say that Edwards breaks with a traditional understanding of appropriation, since the Son actually is the understanding, and the Spirit actually is the will, therefore moving into the realm of identity.

[6] Crisp, 'Jonathan Edwards's God: Trinity, Individuation, and Divine Simplicity', *Engaging the Doctrine of God: Contemporary Protestant Perspectives* (ed. Bruce McCormack; Grand Rapids: Baker Academic, 2008), 83–103 (97).

[7] Crisp, 'Jonathan Edwards's God', 97.

[8] Crisp, 'Jonathan Edwards's God', 97.

[9] Crisp, 'Jonathan Edwards's God', 97.

commensurate with the belief that there are 'real' attributes that 'pick out', as it were, the real distinctions in God, that is, the divine persons of the Godhead, whereas other divine attributes which are 'mere modes or relations' pertain to the divine essence, shared between the divine persons.[10]

This exposition helps provide the landscape of the debate. Holmes's position, according to Crisp, ignores the divine essence, which Crisp believes Edwards maintains. Holmes's view, which Crisp believes is best portrayed by the 'Strong Edwardsian Trinitarian Thesis', subsumes the attributes typically applied to the divine essence under the divine persons and identifies those only as God's intrinsic attributes. Danaher, as a third voice in the discussion, provides another way of reading Edwards's material. He suggests that 'the attributes of God such as infiniteness, eternity, or immutability do not, as Augustine holds, apply to God substance-wise, but conform to the relations within a single personality'.[11] He goes on to add that 'all predications of the divine intelligence and will or power resolve into the triadic relation where "the sum of God's understanding consists in His having an idea of Himself" and "in His Loving Himself"'.[12] In understanding the divine attributes to be focused solely upon God's triune relations, Danaher seems to stand with Holmes in denying that these attributes may be predicable of the 'divine essence' per se, unless, as Crisp points out, Danaher means 'divine essence' when he states that the attributes belong to a 'single personality'.[13] In any case, Danaher is clear that the classic attributes do not, on his reading of Edwards, apply to the 'substance' of God.

I believe these views all miss the mark. As I have shown, Edwards's major area of development in his thought on the Trinity was his under-standing of the divine essence. In his 'final' analysis, he states: 'In order to clear up this matter, let it be considered, that the whole divine essence is supposed truly and properly to subsist in each of these three – viz. God, and his understanding, and love.'[14] In this statement, Edwards affirms that the divine essence exists, and it is what is *in* the divine persons. Likewise though, Edwards denies that God's immutability can somehow be identified

---

[10] Crisp, 'Jonathan Edwards's God', 98.
[11] William J. Danaher, *The Trinitarian Ethics of Jonathan Edwards* (Columbia Series in Reformed Theology; Louisville: Westminster John Knox, 2004), 31.
[12] Danaher, *Trinitarian Ethics of Jonathan Edwards*, 31.
[13] Crisp, 'Jonathan Edwards's God', 95–96n32.
[14] Y21, *Discourse on the Trinity*, 133.

as God, accepting as axiomatic that what is *intrinsically* predicated of God is God, and yet desires to say that God *is* immutable (which he never shows any desire to deny). Edwards's 'real' versus 'relational' attributes are the solution he offers to this problem.

Edwards's proposed solution is born out of his desire to allow the classic attributes to be predicated of God and yet to deny that God somehow *is* immutability, eternality and so on.[15] Edwards clearly follows Turretin's answer to the question, 'Can the divine attributes be really distinguished from the divine essence? We deny against the Socinians.'[16] Edwards's solution is to divide the discussion into things that are 'real' in God, and are truly predicable *of* him essentially (intrinsic), from those things that are true of his 'mode' or in 'relation' to him (extrinsic).[17] In doing so, Edwards does what Holmes suggests, showing that understanding, wisdom and omniscience are really just the same as God's idea and are therefore identical with the Son.[18] Likewise, God's power, will and love are identical with the Holy Spirit, as with God's holiness, justice, mercy, goodness and grace.[19] Edwards lumps together the remaining attributes by saying, 'But as for all those other things – of extent, duration, being with or without change, ability to do – they are not distinct real things, *even in created spirits*, but only mere modes and relations.'[20] Edwards is likely using 'mode' here as he uses 'modal' earlier on in the *Discourse*: 'If there be any difference it is merely modal, and circumstantial.'[21] If 'mode' can be understood as 'circumstantial', which seems likely, then Edwards is invoking a distinction he turns to elsewhere in his writings.[22] Edwards establishes the relationship between relative (the other word he uses for 'mode') and circumstantial

[15] In his sermon on Heb. 1.3, Edwards states, "Tis as natural to God to subsist in three persons as 'tis to be wise and to be holy as to be omnipresent and unchangeable.' Edwards, 'Jesus Christ Is the Shining Forth of the Father's Glory', in *The Glory and Honor of God: Volume 2 of the Previously Unpublished Sermons of Jonathan Edwards* (ed. Michael D. McMullen; Nashville: Broadman & Holman, 2004), 228–9. This is only to say that Edwards does not deny God's immutability, authority and eternality, etc., but affirms that they are in a different category of predication for him than what he calls 'real' attributes.

[16] Francis Turretin, *Institutes of Elenctic Theology* (ed. James T. Dennison; trans. George Musgrave Giger; vol. 1; Phillipsburg: P&R, 1992), 187.

[17] This first move is not controversial. All Edwards is doing is affirming the Reformed orthodox view that there is truly an attribute that the individual persons have that cannot be predicated of the divine essence as such. His view differs in that he does not make the attribute about procession but about personhood (See Richard A. Muller, *The Triunity of God* (Post-Reformation Reformed Dogmatics, vol. 4; Grand Rapids: Baker Academic, 2nd edn, 2003), 171, 186–94.

[18] Y21, *Discourse on the Trinity*, 131.

[19] Y21, *Discourse on the Trinity*, 131.

[20] Y21, *Discourse on the Trinity*, 132 – my emphasis.

[21] Y21, *Discourse on the Trinity*, 114.

[22] See Y1, *Freedom of the Will*, 165–6, 311.

in a note on Eph. 1:19-22, which, more importantly, also uses the 'real' distinction in contrast:

> In the work that was wrought, and the alteration made in exalting Christ from the depth of his humiliation to his height of glory, two things are to be considered, viz. the relative and circumstantial change, *or change of Christ's circumstances*, and the real change made in the human nature. ... This real change made in Christ in his resurrection and exaltation is an unspeakably greater power than the work of creation.[23]

Here, the relative distinction is a change of circumstances, entailing a circumstantial or relational/modal change. Therefore, 'duration' is circumstantial because it calls out what is true of God's circumstance in relation to creation, specifically his relation to time.

Furthermore, Edwards's use of 'created spirits' here is not unimportant. In speaking this way, Edwards is, on my view, using 'spirit' here the way he suggests in *Miscellanies* 396, namely, to signify the divine essence as such, or in this case, he is speaking of created 'spirits' qua spiritual substance (or, in other words, persons or angelic beings). As modes and relations, relative attributes are true of God but not intrinsic to God. Since real attributes call out distinct, real 'properties' of the divine essence, delineated by personhood, all other attributes are seen as extrinsic to God as the God of personal beatific-delight.

Therefore, relational attributes are not intrinsically predicated of God, but are true of God nonetheless. In this sense, Holmes is on the right track by arguing that the perfections of God are reconceived in light of God's trinitarian being, but he is mistaken in assuming that the divine essence has fallen out of the discussion.[24] Furthermore, I would qualify Holmes's point by claiming that Edwards interprets real attributes through personhood, thereby putting the emphasis on the *personhood* of the trinitarian being.

---

[23] Y15, '502. Ephesians 1:19-22', 600 – my emphasis.

[24] I believe Edwards maintains divine-essence language in talking about God's 'stuff', his *quiddity*. Edwards made this point in his sermon on Rom. 2:10 in 1735: "Tis not in beholding any form or visible representation or shape or color or shining light that the highest happiness of the soul consists, but 'tis *in seeing God who is a spirit spiritually* with the eye of the soul.' JEC, Unpublished sermon Rom. 2:10, #373 – my emphasis. God's nature as spirit does not change for Edwards on my view; God is composed of spiritual substance. Richard Muller notes, quoting Leigh, 'Thus, "God in respect of his nature is a *Spirit*, that is, a substance or essence altogether incorporeal: this the Scripture expressly witnesseth, John 4:24; 2 Cor. 3:17."' Likewise, 'Thus, spirituality indicates, first and foremost, that God "is not a body" and does not consist in "various parts, extended one ... beyond another."' Richard A. Muller, *The Divine Essence and Attributes* (Post-Reformation Reformed Dogmatics, vol. 3; Grand Rapids: Baker Academic, 2nd edn, 2003), 300.

Following the thrust of my argument concerning Edwards's view of the Trinity, I believe Edwards is addressing the attributes *by genus*. In order to avoid a category fallacy, Edwards must only allow attributes of persons (viz. those things that can be predicated of a person as essential to their being qua persons) to be truly predicable as intrinsic to God. Personal predicates, on the one hand, are those things that truly constitute personal being. Relative attributes, on the other hand, are attributes true of God qua deity but not God qua persons and therefore are relegated to what is true of an infinite, perfect and eternal spirit (but, contra Crisp, not entailing intrinsic predication). Edwards subsumes all the attributes under the persons of the Godhead that are naturally subsumed under attributes of understanding and will, but all other attributes are relational attributes and are not true 'properties' of the divine essence. Therefore, with Holmes, I hold to the 'Strong Edwardsian Trinitarian Thesis', contra Crisp, who would affirm the 'Edwardsian Trinitarian Thesis'.[25]

Looking more specifically at the issue of the predication of real attributes, I believe both Crisp and Holmes mistake Edwards's emphasis. Crisp states, 'According to Edwards, there are relational properties that are not "real" because they do not pick out one of the distinct persons of the trinity.'[26] Crisp takes 'relational' attributes to be 'attributes shared in the divine essence between the three divine persons'.[27] Crisp finds Edwards's view (according to his interpretation) problematic because he compares Edwards's use of 'relative' attributes to the tradition, which parses these in terms of relations like 'begottenness', lamenting the fact that Edwards's view, in his mind, fails to allow for these kinds of relative distinctions.[28] But

[25] Crisp wants to talk about the relations among the various persons, although I do not believe Edwards's 'modes' and 'relations' can be relegated to these. The question of eternality, for instance, would not seem to be a relation among the persons. In the fragment, 'On the Equality of the Persons of the Trinity', Edwards does address the relation of the individual glories each member has in relation to the work of redemption: 'And to apply a distinct glory to the Father, Son and Spirit in that sense, don't at all infer an application of proper distinct perfections or attributes, and so a distinct essence: for if we call those relations [of glory] attributes, as the use of words is arbitrary, yet to apply distinct attributes in this sense in no wise implies an applying of a distinct essence, for personal relations are not the divine essence.' Y21, *Discourse on the Trinity*, 146.

[26] Crisp, 'Jonathan Edwards's God', 99.

[27] Crisp, 'Jonathan Edwards's God', 100.

[28] As highlighted above, it is noteworthy that Edwards tends not to use 'relative' attributes like begottenness. Edwards instead focuses on personal attributes, like understanding and will, to make 'real' distinctions. This is what Edwards does in his sermon on Heb. 1:3, when discussing Christ's proceeding: 'He is the shining forth of the Father's glory in himself in his eternal proceeding from the Father, or which is the same thing he eternally proceeds from the Father as the shining forth of his glory. ... But he is so in himself by virtue of his personal properties.' Edwards, 'Jesus Christ Is the Shining Forth of the Father's Glory', in *The Glory and Honor of God: Volume 2 of the Previously Unpublished Sermons of Jonathan Edwards*

this criticism both fails to do justice to the force of Edwards's account and neglects that Edwards's polemical opponents used relative attributes of this sort to argue for a subordination of the Son and Spirit under the Father.[29] Edwards's point is not simply that these attributes cannot be predicated of one of the persons of God but that it is meaningless to say that *any person* qua person could have these attributes 'predicated' of them. This is why it is so important that Edwards is not only talking about God but also adds 'created spirits' in the discussion. In other words, 'real' properties are those properties that are properly predicated of persons as such. In these terms, Edwards is treating these 'modes' and 'relations' like Cambridge Properties (the property of distance between a person and Cambridge University) or some other kind of extrinsic property. Edwards needs to be taken seriously when he states that 'they are not distinct real things, even in created spirits, but only mere modes and relations'.[30] Furthermore, Edwards lists 'being with or without change' as a relational attribute, showing that he understands these as relations to realities or concepts extrinsic to God (e.g. time, change, etc.). In doing so, Edwards does not reject Turretin's statement that 'the attributes of God cannot really differ from his essence' but refocuses the discussion based on *what God essentially is*, namely, persons.[31]

(ed. Michael D. McMullen; Nashville: Broadman & Holman, 2004), 226. While this is odd, I do not think it is completely beyond the bounds of what theologians in both the East and the West were doing. Edwards can retain the kind of relative attributes Crisp is looking for (e.g. 'begottenness'), but these are now pushed up a level to persons, as they exist in the perichoretic union. These relative attributes were invoked to distinguish the persons, and they can still do that on Edwards's account. Edwards's use of the psychological categories distinguishes the hypostases of the divine essence, and then their perichoretic nature grounds the individual personhood. In this sense, Edwards can use two different sets of relative attributes to distinguish the persons. Richard Cross notes that, for Gregory of Nyssa, 'What really accounts for divine unity ... is the persons' unity of *activity* – a unity of a kind not found in creatures.' Richard Cross, 'Two Models of the Trinity?' *Heythrop Journal* 43 (2002), 289. In a similar fashion, we might argue that the first level of distinction among the persons for Edwards is grounded in his psychological attributes, but that these are united in perichoresis, and that perichoretic union establishes the second ground of distinction of begotten and spirated. The first ground is communicable to creatures through participation, whereas the second is not.

[29] Clarke states, 'The reason why the Son in the New Testament is sometimes stiled [*sic*] God, is not so much upon account of his metaphysical substance, how divine soever; as of his relative attributes and divine authority over us.' Samuel Clarke, *The Scripture-Doctrine of the Trinity: In Three Parts* (London: Printed for James Knapton, 1712), 296. Clarke uses relative attributes to subordinate the Son in an attempt to develop a monarchian account of the Trinity. See Clarke, *Scripture-Doctrine of the Trinity*, 280–2, 296–7, 359, and Thomas C. Pfizenmaier, *The Trinitarian Theology of Dr. Samuel Clarke (1675–1729): Context, Sources, and Controversy* (New York: Brill, 1997), 118.

[30] Y21, *Discourse on the Trinity*, 132.

[31] Francis Turretin, *Institutes of Elenctic Theology* (ed. James T. Dennison; trans. George Musgrave Giger; vol. 1; Phillipsburg: P&R, 1992), 188. It is noteworthy that Turretin states,

By contrast, Crisp details his view of Edwards's relational attributes: 'Those [attributes] that do not refer to one of the divine persons in particular ... are retained as part of the divine essence.'[32] Here, Crisp fails to follow the logic behind Edwards's real/relational distinction. The divine essence indicates God's *quiddity*; the 'spiritual stuff', whether ideal or 'spiritual substance'. But, for Edwards, the only thing that can be predicated of the divine essence is the persons of the Trinity in their subsistence as personal properties (God's essential 'whatness' is persons).[33] Edwards is clear about this. Relational attributes are not intrinsically predicable, whether of the persons or of the divine essence, in created or uncreated persons, but are truly *relational*.[34] Likewise, Crisp attempts to circumvent his own criticism by revising Edwards's statement; he says, 'It means there are certain attributes usually thought to be shared in the divine life, such as love or wisdom, that are, according to Edwards, peculiar to only one divine person.'[35] Again, 'Edwards's concern is to ensure that those attributes that belong to the Father, Son or Spirit are applied to those persons, not the divine essence, and that the attributes that simply speak of God's existence should be retained in the divine essence.'[36] By forcing Edwards into a distinction between the persons and essence, a distinction Edwards refuses to make, Crisp finds his views untenable.

'Whatever is in God essential and absolute is God himself (such are the divine attributes, power, wisdom, justice, etc.). But whatever is in God personal, relative and modal may not immediately in every way be identified with the divine essence.' Turretin, *Institutes of Elenctic Theology*, 278. Edwards takes the attributes Turretin notes and uses them to talk about attributes in God that are unexercised and focuses instead on personal attributes that are real and therefore only what is true of God himself.

[32] Crisp, 'Jonathan Edwards's God', 99. Crisp's move is not without precedent. Edwards does seem to talk about, for instance, omnipotence, in terms of the divine essence, but as I read him, this is simply his distinction between God's being and God's nature. Relative attributes, in other words, can be seen as appropriated to the divine essence but not predicated essentially.

[33] To re-emphasize, I am not denying that Edwards could talk about God's *quiddity* as spiritual substance. On the contrary, I am arguing that, for Edwards, that is not theologically interesting and is beyond comprehension or analysis.

[34] Edwards is not interested in talking about the divine essence as such. According to Richard Muller, this follows Mastricht, who believed that 'the conception we have of the divine essence is, first and foremost, negative rather than positive'. Muller, *Divine Essence and Attributes*, 235.

[35] Crisp, 'Jonathan Edwards's God', 101.

[36] Crisp, 'Jonathan Edwards's God', 101.

Conclusion

Richard Muller, quoting Leigh, states that 'the attributes of God are his perfections, which declare what sort [of being] he is'.[37] I believe that Edwards grasped this concept and, turning it around, claimed that God is persons – that is fundamentally *what he is*. Therefore his perfections must proclaim that fact. Edwards reorients the discussion of the divine attributes based on what can be said *about* God qua persons and therefore reorients the attribute discussion into real intrinsic attributes of personhood (understanding or will) and relational/extrinsic attributes. If attributes are 'real', then they are aspects of his psychology (understanding or will as subsistences) and therefore of a divine person, but if they are relational attributes, they are still 'true' about God, but not intrinsically proper.

Determining the validity of this kind of account of attribution is for another place. The emphasis of Edwards's doctrine is that God's life is the very nature of God himself, or that God is the God of personal beatific-delight. Richard Muller states, 'In Cocceius' words, very simply, "the life of God is to understand and to will." It is, in other words, a self-sufficient spiritual existence that is its own origin and its own fruition and that is therefore capable of being the foundation and source of all other life.'[38] Edwards grasped this reality of 'God's life' and applied it wholesale to his understanding of the doctrine of the Trinity, using it to ground his depiction of redemption and his development of the divine attributes. To do so robustly, Edwards utilizes a psychological analogy within a broader picture of God in beatific-delight, addressing the heterodox notions in his day that one essence necessarily implies one person. Edwards argues against such a notion, and his own view suggests something quite different – that one essence can easily imply *three* persons! This view recalibrated his understanding of divine attributes and the divine essence, and solidified his understanding of how God redeems.[39]

---

[37] Muller, *Divine Essence and Attributes*, 213.

[38] Muller, *The Divine Essence and Attributes*, 374.

[39] Edwards's notion seems to be idiosyncratic but certainly not outside the bounds of Reformed orthodoxy. Edwards's discussion falls solidly within the contours of the debates concerning the divine essence, attributes and predication.

Bibliography

Primary Sources

Yale Critical Edition (Numerical)

Edwards, Jonathan. *Freedom of the Will* (ed. Paul Ramsey; The Works of Jonathan Edwards, vol. 1; New Haven: Yale University Press, 1957).

—*The Religious Affections* (ed. Perry Miller; The Works of Jonathan Edwards, vol. 2; New Haven: Yale University Press, 1957).

—*Original Sin* (ed. Clyde A. Holbrook; The Works of Jonathan Edwards, vol. 3; New Haven: Yale University Press, 1970).

—*The Great Awakening* (ed. C. C. Goen; The Works of Jonathan Edwards, vol. 4; New Haven: Yale University Press, 1972).

—*Apocalyptic Writings* (ed. Stephen J. Stein; The Works of Jonathan Edwards, vol. 5; New Haven: Yale University Press, 1977).

—*Scientific and Philosophical Writings* (ed. Wallace E. Anderson; The Works of Jonathan Edwards, vol. 6; New Haven: Yale University Press, 1980).

—*Ethical Writings* (ed. Paul Ramsey; The Works of Jonathan Edwards, vol. 8; New Haven: Yale University Press, 1989).

—*A History of the Work of Redemption* (ed. John Frederick Wilson; The Works of Jonathan Edwards, vol. 9; New Haven: Yale University Press, 1989).

—*Sermons and Discourses, 1720–1723* (ed. Wilson H. Kimnach; The Works of Jonathan Edwards, vol. 10; New Haven: Yale University Press, 1992).

—*Typological Writings* (ed. Wallace E. Anderson and David H. Watters; The Works of Jonathan Edwards, vol. 11; New Haven: Yale University Press, 1993).

—*The 'Miscellanies': A-500* (ed. Thomas A Schafer; The Works of Jonathan Edwards, vol. 13; New Haven: Yale University Press, 1996).

—*Sermons and Discourses, 1723–1729* (ed. Kenneth P. Minkema; The Works of Jonathan Edwards, vol. 14; New Haven: Yale University Press, 1997).

—*Notes on Scripture* (ed. Stephen J. Stein; The Works of Jonathan Edwards, vol. 15; New Haven: Yale University Press, 1998).

—*Letters and Personal Writings* (ed. George S. Claghorn; The Works of Jonathan Edwards, vol. 16; New Haven: Yale University Press, 1998).

—*Sermons and Discourses, 1730–1733* (ed. Mark R. Valeri; The Works of Jonathan Edwards, vol. 17; New Haven: Yale University Press, 1999).

—*The 'Miscellanies': Entry Nos. 501–832* (ed. Ava Chamberlain; The Works of Jonathan Edwards, vol. 18; New Haven: Yale University Press, 2000).

—*Sermons and Discourses, 1734–1738* (ed. M. X. Lesser; The Works of Jonathan Edwards, vol. 19; New Haven: Yale University Press, 2001).

—*The 'Miscellanies': Entry Nos. 833–1152* (ed. Amy Plantinga Pauw; The Works of Jonathan Edwards, vol. 20; New Haven: Yale University Press, 2002).

—*Writings on the Trinity, Grace, and Faith* (ed. Sang Hyun Lee; The Works of Jonathan Edwards, vol. 21; New Haven: Yale University Press, 2003).

—*Sermons and Discourses, 1739–1742* (ed. Harry S. Stout and Nathan O. Hatch; The Works of Jonathan Edwards, vol. 22; New Haven: Yale University Press, 2003).
—*The 'Miscellanies': Entry Nos. 1153–1320* (ed. Douglas A. Sweeney; The Works of Jonathan Edwards, vol. 23; New Haven: Yale University Press, 2004).
—*The 'Blank Bible'* (ed. Stephen J. Stein; The Works of Jonathan Edwards, vol. 24; New Haven: Yale University Press, 2006).
—*Sermons and Discourses, 1743–1758* (ed. Wilson H. Kimnach; The Works of Jonathan Edwards, vol. 25; New Haven: Yale University Press, 2006).
—*Catalogues of Books* (ed. Peter Johannes Thuesen; The Works of Jonathan Edwards, vol. 26; New Haven: Yale University Press, 2008).

Previously Unpublished Sermon Volumes

—*The Blessing of God: Previously Unpublished Sermons of Jonathan Edwards* (ed. Michael D. McMullen; Nashville: Broadman & Holman, 2003).
—*The Glory and Honor of God: Volume 2 of the Previously Unpublished Sermons of Jonathan Edwards* (ed. Michael D. McMullen; Nashville: Broadman & Holman, 2004).

Sermon Transcriptions (*Chronological*)

[last accessed May 1, 2012]
—Transcription 72, 2 Corinthians 3:18 Sermon, Spring, 1728. Jonathan Edwards Center. Yale University, New Haven, CT. For web reference: http://edwards.yale.edu/archive?path=aHR0cDovL2Vkd2FyZHMueWFsZS5lZHUvY2dpLWJpbi9uZXdwaGlsby9nZXRvYmplY3QucGw/Yy40MToxNC53amVuLjcyMjc0Ny43MjI3Tk=#nlink42.
—Transcription 321, Hebrews 1:3 Sermon, April, 1734. Jonathan Edwards Center. Yale University, New Haven, CT. For web reference: http://edwards.yale.edu/archive?path=aHR0cDovL2Vkd2FyZHMueWFsZS5lZHUvY2dpLWJpbi9uZXdwaGlsby9nZXRvYmplY3QucGw/Yy40NzoxMS53amVuLVv.
—Transcription 344, Revelation 14:2 Sermon, November, 1734. Jonathan Edwards Center. Yale University, New Haven, CT. For web reference: http://edwards.yale.edu/archive?path=aHR0cDovL2Vkd2FyZHMueWFsZS5lZHUvY2dpLWJpbi9uZXdwaGlsby9nZXRvYmplY3QucGw/Yy40NzozNi53amVuVv.
—Transcription 373, Romans 2:10 Sermon, December, 1735. Jonathan Edwards Center. Yale University, New Haven, CT. For web reference: http://edwards.yale.edu/archive?path=aHR0cDovL2Vkd2FyZHMueWFsZS5lZHUvY2dpLWJpbi9uZXdwaGlsby9nZXRvYmplY3QucGw/Yy40ODoyNi53amVuVv.
—Transcription 451, Matthew 25:1–12 Sermon, December, 1737. Jonathan Edwards Center. Yale University, New Haven, CT. For web reference: http://edwards.yale.edu/archive?path=aHR0cDovL2Vkd2FyZHMueWFsZS5lZHUvY2dpLWJpbi9uZXdwaGlsby9nZXRvYmplY3QucGw/Yy41MDoyOS53amVuVv.
—Transcription 743, Deuteronomy 18:18 Sermon, June, 1744 (repreached March 1755). Jonathan Edwards Center. Yale University, New Haven, CT. For web reference: http://edwards.yale.edu/archive?path=aHR0cDovL2Vkd2FyZHMueWFsZS5lZHUvY2dpLWJpbi9uZXdwaGlsby9nZXRvYmplY3QucGw/Yy42MDozLndqqZW8=.

Secondary Sources

Asselt, Willem J. van, 'The Fundamental Meaning of Theology: Archetypal and Ectypal Theology in Seventeenth-Century Reformed Thought', *Westminster Theological Journal* 64, no. 2 (2002), 320–37.

Augustine, *The Confessions* (trans. Maria Boulding, O.S.B.; The Works of Saint Augustine: A Translation for the 21st Century; New York: New City Press, 1990).

—*The Trinity* (ed. John E. Rotelle, O.S.A.; trans. Edmund Hill, O.P.; The Works of Saint Augustine: A Translation for the 21st Century; New York: New City Press, 1991).

Barth, Karl, *Church Dogmatics: The Doctrine of The Word of God* (ed. G. W. Bromiley and T. F. Torrance; vol. I/1; New York: T&T Clark International, 2004).

Bavinck, Herman, *Reformed Dogmatics: God and Creation* (ed. John Bolt and John Vriend; vol. 2; Grand Rapids: Baker Academic, 2003).

Beilby, James, 'Divine Aseity, Divine Freedom: A Conceptual Problem for Edwardsian-Calvinism', *Journal of the Evangelical Theological Society* 47, no. 4 (2004), 647–58.

Biehl, Craig, *The Infinite Merit of Christ: The Glory of Christ's Obedience in the Theology of Jonathan Edwards* (Jackson: Reformed Academic Press, 2009).

Bombaro, John J., *Jonathan Edwards's Vision of Reality: The Relationship of God to the World, Redemption History, and the Reprobate* (Princeton Theological Monograph Series; Eugene: Wiph & Stock, 2012).

—'Jonathan Edwards's Vision of Salvation', *Westminster Theological Journal* 65 (2003), 45–67.

Brown, Robert E., 'Edwards, Locke, and the Bible', *The Journal of Religion* 79 (1999), 361–84.

—*Jonathan Edwards and the Bible* (Bloomington: Indiana University Press, 2002).

Caldwell, Robert W., *Communion in the Spirit: The Holy Spirit as the Bond of Union in the Theology of Jonathan Edwards* (Studies in Evangelical History and Thought; Waynesboro: Paternoster, 2006).

Calvin, John, *Institutes of the Christian Religion* (ed. John T. McNeill; trans. Ford Lewis Battles; 2 vols.; Louisville: Westminster John Knox, 1960).

Canlis, Julie, *Calvin's Ladder: A Spiritual Theology of Ascent and Ascension* (Grand Rapids: Eerdmans, 2010).

Carse, James P., *Jonathan Edwards and the Visibility of God* (New York: Scribner, 1967).

Cherry, Conrad, *The Theology of Jonathan Edwards: A Reappraisal* (Bloomington: Indiana University Press, 1990).

Clarke, Samuel, *The Scripture-Doctrine of the Trinity: In Three Parts* (London: Printed for James Knapton, 1712).

Crisp, Oliver, 'Jonathan Edwards's God: Trinity, Individuation, and Divine Simplicity', in McCormack (ed.), *Engaging the Doctrine of God*, 83–103.

—'Jonathan Edwards on Divine Simplicity', *Religious Studies* 39, no. 1 (2003), 23–41.

—*Jonathan Edwards on God and Creation* (Oxford: Oxford University Press, forthcoming).

—'Jonathan Edwards's Ontology: A Critique of Sang Hyun Lee's Dispositional Account of Edwardsian Metaphysics', *Religious Studies* 46, no. 1 (2010), 1–20.

—'Jonathan Edwards on the Divine Nature', *Journal of Reformed Theology* 3, no. 2 (2009), 175–201.

Cross, Richard, 'Two Models of the Trinity?', *Heythrop Journal* 43, no. 3 (2002), 275–94.

Danaher, William J., *The Trinitarian Ethics of Jonathan Edwards* (Columbia Series in Reformed Theology; Louisville: Westminster John Knox, 2004).

Daniel, Stephen H., *The Philosophy of Jonathan Edwards: A Study in Divine Semiotics* (Bloomington: Indiana University Press, 1994).

Helm, Paul, 'John Locke and Jonathan Edwards: A Reconsideration', *Journal of the History of Ideas* 7, no. 1 (1969), 51–61.

—'Edwards on the Trinity' (paper delivered at the Edwards Tercentenary Conference, Princeton Theological Seminary, 2003).

—'The Human Self and the Divine Trinity', in Schweitzer (ed.), *Jonathan Edwards as Contemporary*, 93–106.

Heppe, Heinrich, *Reformed Dogmatics* (ed. Ernst Bizer; Eugene: Wipf & Stock, 2008).

Holmes, Stephen. *God of Grace and God of Glory: An Account of the Theology of Jonathan Edwards* (Grand Rapids: Eerdmans, 2001).

—'Does Jonathan Edwards Use a Dispositional Ontology? A Response to Sang Hyun Lee', in *Jonathan Edwards: Philosophical Theologian* (ed. Oliver Crisp and Paul Helm; Aldershot: Ashgate, 2004), 99–114.

—'"Something Much Too Plain to Say": Towards a Defence of the Doctrine of Divine Simplicity', *Neue Zeitschrift für Systematische Theologie und Religionsphilosophie* 43, no. 1 (2001), 137–54.

Horton, Michael Scott, *Lord and Servant: A Covenant Christology* (Louisville: Westminster John Knox Press, 2005).

Jenson, Robert W., *America's Theologian: A Recommendation of Jonathan Edwards* (Oxford: Oxford University Press, 1988).

—'Christology', in *The Princeton Companion to Jonathan Edwards* (ed. Sang Hyun Lee; Princeton: Princeton University Press, 2005), 72–86.

Klauber, Martin I., 'Francis Turretin on Biblical Accommodation: Loyal Calvinist or Reformed Scholastic?', *Westminster Theological Journal* 55 (1993), 73–86.

Knight, Janice, *Orthodoxies in Massachusetts: Rereading American Puritanism* (Cambridge: Harvard University Press, 1994).

Lee, Sang Hyun, 'Jonathan Edwards's Theory of the Imagination', *The Michigan Academician.* 23 (1972), 233–41.

—*The Philosophical Theology of Jonathan Edwards* (Princeton: Princeton University Press, 1988).

—'Edwards on God and Nature', in *Edwards in Our Time: Jonathan Edwards and the Shaping of American Religion* (ed. Sang Hyun Lee and Allen C. Guelzo; Grand Rapids: Eerdmans, 1999), 15–44.

—*The Philosophical Theology of Jonathan Edwards* (Princeton: Princeton University Press, 2000).

—'Grace and Justification by Faith Alone', in *The Princeton Companion to Jonathan Edwards* (ed. Sang Hyun Lee; Princeton: Princeton University Press, 2005).

—'God's Relation to the World', in *The Princeton Companion to Jonathan Edwards* (ed. Sang Hyun Lee; Princeton: Princeton University Press, 2005), 59–71.

Locke, John, *An Essay Concerning Human Understanding* (Great Books in Philosophy; Amherst: Prometheus, 1995).

Marsden, George, 'Challenging the Presumptions of the Age', in *The Legacy of Jonathan Edwards: American Religion and the Evangelical Tradition* (ed. D. G. Hart, Sean Michael Lucas and Stephen J. Nichols; Grand Rapids: Baker Academic, 2003), 99–113.

Mastricht, Peter van, *A Treatise on Regeneration* (Morgan: Soli Deo Gloria Publications, 2002).

Mather, Cotton, *Blessed Unions* (Boston: B. Green and J. Allen, 1692).

McClenahan, Michael, 'Jonathan Edwards's Doctrine of Justification in the Period up to the First Great Awakening' (unpublished doctoral dissertation, University of Oxford, 2006).

McClymond, Michael J., *Encounters with God: An Approach to the Theology of Jonathan Edwards* (Oxford: Oxford University Press, 1998).

—'Hearing the Symphony: A Critique of Some Critics of Sang Lee's and Amy Pauw's Accounts of Jonathan Edwards' View of God', in Schweitzer (ed.), *Jonathan Edwards as Contemporary*, 68–92.

—and Gerald R. McDermott, *The Theology of Jonathan Edwards* (Oxford: Oxford University Press, 2012).

McCormack, Bruce L. (ed.), *Engaging the Doctrine of God: Contemporary Protestant Perspectives* (Grand Rapids: Baker Academic, 2008).

McDermott, Gerald R. *One Holy and Happy Society: The Public Theology of Jonathan Edwards* (University Park: Pennsylvania State University Press, 1992).

—*Jonathan Edwards Confronts the Gods: Christian Theology, Enlightenment Religion, and Non-Christian Faiths* (Oxford: Oxford University Press, 2000).

—'Jonathan Edwards on Justification by Faith – More Protestant or Catholic', *Pro Ecclesia: A Journal of Catholic and Evangelical Theology* 27, no. 1 (2008), 92–111.

McDonald, Suzanne, 'Beholding the Glory of God in the Face of Jesus Christ: John Owen and the "Reforming" of the Beatific Vision' (paper delivered at the John Owen Today Conference, Westminster College, Cambridge, 2008).

Merriell, D. Juvenal, 'Trinitarian Anthropology', in *The Theology of Thomas Aquinas* (ed. Rik Van Nieuwenhove and Joseph Peter Wawrykow; Notre Dame: University of Notre Dame Press, 2005), 77–98.

Miller, Perry, *Jonathan Edwards* (Amherst: University of Massachusetts Press, 1981).

Morimoto, Anri, *Jonathan Edwards and the Catholic Vision of Salvation* (University Park: Pennsylvania State University Press, 1995).

Morris, William S., 'The Genius of Jonathan Edwards', in *Reinterpretation in American Church History* (ed. Jerald C. Brauer; Chicago: University of Chicago Press, 1968), 29–65.

Muller, Richard A., *Dictionary of Latin and Greek Theological Terms: Drawn Principally from Protestant Scholastic Theology* (Grand Rapids: Baker, 1985).

—'Scholasticism Protestant and Catholic: Francis Turretin on the Object and Principles of Theology', *Church History* 55, no. 2 (1986), 193–206.

—*The Divine Essence and Attributes* (Post-Reformation Reformed Dogmatics, vol. 3; Grand Rapids: Baker Academic, 2nd edn, 2003).

—*Prolegomena to Theology* (Post-Reformation Reformed Dogmatics, vol. 1; Grand Rapids: Baker Academic, 2nd edn, 2003).

—*The Triunity of God* (Post-Reformation Reformed Dogmatics, vol. 4; Grand Rapids: Baker Academic, 2nd edn, 2003).

Owen, John, *The Glory of Christ* (trans. William H. Goold; The Works of John Owen, vol. 1; London: Banner of Truth Trust, 1965).

—*The Gospel Defended* (trans. William H. Goold; The Works of John Owen, vol. 12; London: Banner of Truth Trust, 1966).

—*The Holy Spirit* (trans. William H. Goold; The Works of John Owen, vol. 3; London: Banner of Truth Trust, 1966).

—*Biblical Theology, or, the Nature, Origin, Development, and Study of Theological Truth, in Six Books: In Which Are Examined the Origins and Progress of Both True and False Religious Worship, and the Most Notable Declensions and Revivals of the Church, from the Very Beginning of the World* (Morgan: Soli Deo Gloria Publications, 1994).

Pauw, Amy Plantinga, *The Supreme Harmony of All: The Trinitarian Theology of Jonathan Edwards* (Grand Rapids: Eerdmans, 2002).

—'"One Alone Cannot Be Excellent": Edwards on Divine Simplicity', in *Jonathan Edwards: Philosophical Theologian* (ed. Oliver Crisp and Paul Helm; Aldershot: Ashgate, 2003), 115–26.

—'A Response from Amy Plantinga Pauw', *Scottish Journal of Theology* 57, no. 4 (2004), 468–89.

Pfizenmaier, Thomas C., *The Trinitarian Theology of Dr. Samuel Clarke (1675–1729): Context, Sources, and Controversy* (New York: Brill, 1997).

Phillips, Timothy Ross, 'Francis Turretin's Idea of Theology' (unpublished doctoral dissertation, Vanderbilt University, 1986).

Rehnman, Sebastian, *Divine Discourse: The Theological Methodology of John Owen* (Texts and Studies in Reformation and Post-Reformation Thought; Grand Rapids: Baker Academic, 2002).

Sanders, Fred, *The Image of the Immanent Trinity: Rahner's Rule and the Theological Interpretation of Scripture* (Issues in Systematic Theology; New York: Peter Lang, 2005).

Schafer, Thomas A., 'Jonathan Edwards and Justification by Faith', *Church History* 20, no. 4 (1951), 55–67.

Schweitzer, Don, 'Jonathan Edwards' Understanding of Divine Infinity', in Schweitzer (ed.), *Jonathan Edwards as Contemporary*, 49–65.

Schweitzer, Don (ed.), *Jonathan Edwards as Contemporary: Essays in Honor of Sang Hyun Lee* (Festschrift Sang Hyun Lee; New York: Peter Lang, 2010).

Schweitzer, William M., *God is a Communicative Being: Divine Communicativeness and Harmony in the Theology of Jonathan Edwards* (T&T Clark Studies in Systematic Theology; London: T&T Clark, 2012).

—'Interpreting the Harmony of Reality: Jonathan Edwards' Theology of Revelation' (unpublished doctoral dissertation; University of Edinburgh, 2008).

Sibbes, Richard, *The Works of Richard Sibbes* (vol. 2; Edinburgh: James Nichol, 1863).

—*The Works of Richard Sibbes* (vol. 4; Edinburgh: James Nichol, 1863).

—*The Works of Richard Sibbes* (vol. 5; Edinburgh: James Nichol, 1863).

—*The Works of Richard Sibbes* (vol. 6; Edinburgh: James Nichol, 1863).

Smith, John E., *Jonathan Edwards: Puritan, Preacher, Philosopher* (Outstanding Christian Thinkers; Notre Dame: University of Notre Dame Press, 1992).

Stout, Harry, 'Jonathan Edwards's Tri-World Vision', in *The Legacy of Jonathan Edwards: American Religion and the Evangelical Tradition* (ed. D. G. Hart, Sean Michael Lucas and Stephen J. Nichols; Grand Rapids: Baker Academic, 2003), 27–46.

Strobel, Kyle, 'By Word and Spirit: Jonathan Edwards on Redemption, Justification, and Regeneration', in *Jonathan Edwards and Justification* (ed. Josh Moody; Wheaton: Crossway: 2012), 45–69.

—'Jonathan Edwards's Polemics of *Theosis*', Harvard Theological Review, 105:3 (July 2012): 259–79.

—'Jonathan Edwards's Reformed Doctrine of the Beatific Vision', in *Jonathan Edwards and Scotland* (ed. Ken Minkema, Adriaan Neale and Kelly van Andel; Edinburgh: Dunedin Academic Press, 2011), 171–88.

—'Review of *Jonathan Edwards as Contemporary: Essays in Honor of Sang Hyun Lee*', *Themelios* 36:3 (November 2011).

Studebaker, Steven M., 'Jonathan Edwards's Social Augustinian Trinitarianism: A Criticism of and an Alternative to Recent Interpretations' (unpublished doctoral dissertation, Marquette University, 2003).

—'Jonathan Edwards's Social Augustinian Trinitarianism: An Alternative to a Recent Trend', *Scottish Journal of Theology*, no. 56 (2003), 268–85.

—'Jonathan Edwards's Trinitarian Theology in the Context of the Early-Enlightenment Deist Controversy', in *The Contribution of Jonathan Edwards to American Culture and Society: Essays on America's Spiritual Founding Father* (*The Northampton Tercentenary Celebration, 1703–2003*), (ed. Richard A. S. Hall) (Lewiston: The Edwin Mellen Press, 2008), 281–301.

—'Supreme Harmony or Supreme Disharmony? An Analysis of Amy Plantinga Pauw's "The Supreme Harmony of All": The Trinitarian Theology of Jonathan Edwards', *Scottish Journal of Theology* 4, no. 57 (2004), 479–85.

—*Jonathan Edwards's Social Augustinian Trinitarianism in Historical and Contemporary Perspectives* (Gorgias Studies in Philosophy and Theology; Piscataway: Gorgias Press, 2008).

Tan, Seng-Kong, 'Trinitarian Action in the Incarnation', in Schweitzer (ed.), *Jonathan Edwards as Contemporary*, 127–50.

Trueman, Carl, *Claims of Truth: John Owen's Trinitarian Theology* (Carlisle: Paternoster, 1998).

—*John Owen: Reformed Catholic, Renaissance Man* (Great Theologians Series; Aldershot: Ashgate, 2007).

Turretin, Francis. *Institutes of Elenctic Theology* (ed. James T. Dennison; trans. George Musgrave Giger; vol. 1; Phillipsburg: P&R, 1992).

—*Institutes of Elenctic Theology* (ed. James T. Dennison; trans. George Musgrave Giger; vol. 2; Phillipsburg: P&R, 1992).

—*Institutes of Elenctic Theology*(ed. James T. Dennison; trans. George Musgrave Giger; vol. 3; Phillipsburg: P&R, 1992).

Veto, Miklos, 'Spiritual Knowledge According to Jonathan Edwards', *Calvin Theological Journal* 31 (1996), 161–81.

Vliet, Jan van, 'William Ames: Marrow of the Theology and Piety of the Reformed Tradition' (unpublished doctoral dissertation, Westminster Theological Seminary, 2002).

Waddington, Jeffrey C., 'Jonathan Edwards's "Ambiguous and Somewhat Precarious" Doctrine of Justification', *Westminster Theological Journal* 66 (2004), 357–72.

Walton, Brad, *Jonathan Edwards, Religious Affections, and the Puritan Analysis of True Piety, Spiritual Sensation, and Heart Religion* (Studies in American Religion; Lewiston: The Edwin Mellen Press, 2002).

Wilson-Kastner, Patricia, 'God's Infinity and His Relationship to Creation in the Theologies of Gregory of Nyssa and Jonathan Edwards', *Foundations* 21, no. 4 (1978), 305–21.

Zakai, Avihu, *Jonathan Edwards's Philosophy of History: The Re-Enchantment of the World in the Age of Enlightenment* (Princeton: Princeton University Press, 2003).

Index

actus purus 27n. 9, 31, 39, 40, 45, 55, 59,
    80n. 17, 88–9, 91, 219, 222
affective knowledge *see also* spiritual
    knowledge 5, 11, 16, 57, 71, 82, 104,
    150, 153–5, 157, 159, 166–7, 173,
    178–9, 183, 209–14, 221, 223, 228–9
angels 106, 109–23, 139n. 163
Anthropology *see* personhood
anti-trinitarians 28–9n. 12, 29, 31–4, 39,
    48–9, 51, 58, 63, 65–6, 69
archetypal knowledge 4, 16, 27, 127, 135,
    150, 152–76, 179, 183, 207, 209–10,
    223, 225, 228
Aquinas, Thomas 125–6, 130–1, 190n. 56,
    219n. 37
Asselt, William J. van 156nn. 23–4, 168
Augustine (*or* Augustinian) 65–8, 173n. 87,
    236

Barth, Karl 43n. 60
Bavinck, Herman 102
beatific vision 4–5, 14, 16, 26–7, 30, 37, 57,
    70, 106, 115–46, 150–76, 206, 210,
    223, 228
Beilby, James 80n. 17, 88n. 47, 93n. 67
biblicism 33, 33n. 30, 56
Biehl, Craig 149n. 1
Bombaro, John 18n. 35, 190n. 56, 232n. 80
Brown, Robert 6n. 8, 151n. 3, 166n. 61

Caldwell, Robert 24n. 5, 35n. 38, 65n. 129,
    76n. 3, 109, 112n. 29, 117n. 53, 118n.
    55, 121, 125–6n. 95, 149n. 1, 169,
    192, 203
Calvin, John 62n. 121, 169n. 74, 204

Canlis, Julie 169n. 74
Carse, James 170n. 78
Cherry, Conrad 181n. 15, 191n. 60
Christology 10, 25n. 7, 35n. 38, 97n. 84,
    105–43, 144, 152–4, 162, 166–71,
    173–4, 226
Clarke, Samuel 29n. 12, 29nn. 13, 15, 31,
    31n. 20, 32nn. 23, 28, 33nn. 30–1,
    34nn. 33–6, 36n. 41, 38nn. 45–7,
    40n. 50, 48–9, 49nn. 76–7, 58n. 108,
    60nn. 113–14
communicative, God is 4, 15, 17, 77,
    80n. 17, 81–108, 115, 118n. 55,
    119–20, 123n. 82, 124, 137n. 148,
    143–7, 154, 157, 165, 176, 183n. 26,
    191, 194–7, 200n. 104, 201–4, 209,
    212, 216, 220n. 42, 223–4, 229,
    240n. 28
Crisp, Oliver 18nn. 34–6, 26, 27n. 9,
    39n. 49, 40n. 51, 48n. 73, 52,
    61n. 116, 64n. 127, 80n. 17, 87n. 47,
    88, 234–42
Cross, Richard 240n. 29

Danaher, William 24, 30, 50, 51n. 82, 65,
    66n. 131, 68, 76n. 4, 97n. 83, 100n.
    93, 193n. 69, 222, 236
Daniel, Stephen 151n. 2
dispositions, human or divine 26n. 8, 45–6,
    79, 83, 84–5n. 37, 87–92, 94, 182,
    187, 195n. 82, 205, 224, 229
divine attributes 4, 14, 26, 33–4, 39, 46–7,
    53, 58–62, 64n. 127, 65, 79–81, 85,
    89, 91, 94–5, 115, 136–7, 140, 155,
    161, 182, 226, 234–42

divine essence 14, 26, 33, 39–44, 46–50,
54–7, 59, 62–3, 65, 85, 88–91,
106n. 2, 127–8, 136, 166, 182, 194,
196, 221, 226, 234–42

ectypal knowledge 16, 116–18, 127–9, 144,
152–76, 179, 183, 209–10, 224–5, 227
emanation 4–5, 13, 15–16, 27, 33n. 31,
37, 39, 57, 59n. 109, 70, 73, 75–7,
80n. 18, 82n. 25, 83–9, 91n. 60, 93,
95–7, 100–5, 119, 136, 144, 146,
149–50, 154, 157, 164n. 53, 171,
176, 179, 183, 196, 209, 211, 222–4,
227
Ezekiel 1 (*or* wheels within wheels) 7–10,
15n. 29, 19, 79, 80n. 16, 114, 146,
211, 225

faith 11, 16, 127, 129, 153, 158, 162–3, 173,
176, 186, 212

glory 2, 5–7, 10–11, 13, 15, 15n. 29, 20,
35nn. 36–7, 56n. 100, 70, 73, 77,
82–4, 89n. 52, 94–5, 97, 99–102,
106–8, 112–13, 115, 118, 120–1,
123–4, 127–9, 132, 134, 137–8,
142–3n. 178, 144–6, 154, 182, 206,
210, 212, 217, 221–3, 226
grace 45n. 67, 58n. 106, 108, 111, 124–5,
127n. 100, 140n. 169, 142, 143n. 178,
150, 153, 155, 177, 181–2, 188,
190–207, 214

harmony 2, 12, 30, 217, 228n. 61, 229, 232
heaven 9–11, 81, 105–25, 137, 175–6, 212,
216–19, 221–2, 226, 228
hell 9–12, 108
Helm, Paul 39n. 49, 52, 52n. 84, 53n. 86,
54n. 92, 151n. 3
Holmes, Stephen 18n. 34, 19, 24n. 5, 26,
35, 39n. 49, 60n. 115, 61n. 116,
76nn. 4–5, 77, 78n. 11, 80n. 17,
84n. 33, 87n. 47, 88, 93, 96n. 78,
97n. 83, 100n. 93, 231n. 75, 234–9

immutability 21, 29n. 14, 39, 60–1, 78n. 11,
80n. 17, 81, 84n. 35, 88–9, 91–2, 93n.

63, 97n. 81, 97n. 83, 99, 106–9, 157,
221n. 46, 235–7
infinity 39, 45, 49, 53, 59–60, 63, 79, 81n. 22,
82–3, 86, 91–2, 94–5, 101, 103n. 107,
106–8, 116, 125, 132–3, 137, 142, 155,
157, 161, 170, 219–20

Jenson, Robert 24n. 5, 30, 76n. 4, 149n. 1

Knight, Janice 91n. 60, 120n. 68

Lee, Sang Hyun xi, 18–19, 23–4, 26n. 8, 39n.
49, 40n. 51, 66n. 131, 70n. 140, 76n.
4, 78n. 11, 80n. 17, 87n. 47, 88–91,
94, 97n. 83, 102, 104n. 110, 151n. 2,
190n. 56, 228, 231–2
Locke, John 53n. 86, 54n. 92, 151, 176, 187,
214n. 13

Mastricht, Peter van 6, 37n. 44, 177–8, 179n.
8, 180, 183n. 25, 184nn. 29–30, 192,
204–5, 241n. 34
McClenahan, Michael 17n. 30, 170n. 75,
177, 181n. 15, 190–7, 227
McClymond, Michael xi, 8–9n. 16, 25n. 7,
61n. 116, 76n. 4, 83n. 28, 91n. 60, 151,
152n. 6, 194n. 74, 203n. 121, 228–2
McDermott, Gerald xi, 18n. 34, 190n. 56,
228n. 61, 229n. 62, 229n. 67,
230n. 69
McDonald, Suzanne 125–6, 129–32, 134–5, 142
Miller, Perry 1, 19n. 38, 151
Morimoto, Anri 18n. 34, 190n. 56
Muller, Richard 32n. 27, 33n. 30, 34, 37,
41n. 53, 48, 55n. 99, 58n. 107,
61n. 117, 62, 62nn. 119–20, 62n. 122,
63n. 125, 87n. 45, 89, 137n. 151,
155n. 21, 156, 156n. 27, 203n. 122,
237n. 17, 238n. 24, 241n. 34, 242

nature, divine or human 11, 17, 27, 32, 38,
45n. 67, 55–7, 61nn. 116–17, 62n.
121, 67, 73, 80n. 18, 81n. 22, 83–91,
93, 96n. 79, 98, 100, 104–5, 119, 128,
138, 138n. 160, 140, 143n. 178, 144,
146, 154, 161, 167, 169, 178, 182,
184, 185n. 34, 187–8, 190, 193–205

Owen, John 6–7, 31, 40n. 50, 113, 125–34, 138, 139n. 163, 140–1, 143, 153n. 10, 155, 158n. 29, 162, 176–7, 180, 182n. 19, 183n. 25, 184nn. 29–30, 188–92, 196n. 85, 210, 218n. 29, 227

participation 5, 13, 15, 73, 82–3, 97–101, 104, 126n. 96, 140–1, 143, 145, 152n. 6, 154, 169n. 74, 173, 177, 183n. 26, 190, 196, 198, 201–2, 206, 217–18, 222–3, 226–7, 229–30, 232, 240n. 28
Pauw, Amy Plantinga 24, 30, 38n. 49, 50, 55n. 99, 61n. 116, 65–6, 68–9, 228, 231–2
'personal beatific-delight' 4–5, 13–17, 19–20, 26–30, 35–7, 45, 52, 55–7, 64n. 127, 65, 67n. 135, 70, 75–6, 79, 82n. 26, 84, 100–2, 104–7, 119, 125, 136, 140, 142, 144–6, 150–4, 157, 167, 179, 192, 195, 209, 211, 217, 220–1, 223–8, 232, 238, 242
personhood 4, 14, 26–9, 33–4, 37–44, 46–53, 55, 57, 59–65, 67n. 135, 69–70, 82, 85, 88, 94, 136, 145, 154, 160–1, 166, 182, 184, 194–6, 206, 209, 212–15, 223–4, 226, 232, 234–42
perichoresis 14, 26–9, 39–41, 43–4, 47–8, 50, 52, 61–5, 225, 239–40n. 28
Pfizenmaier, Thomas 29n. 12, 32n. 23, 33n. 29, 34n. 35, 38n. 45, 49n. 75, 240n. 29
pneumatology 44–6, 57, 58nn. 106–7, 63, 66–7, 86, 100n. 94, 105, 126, 132, 142–3, 150, 168–9, 170n. 75, 171, 179, 180–205, 223, 237
property, the personal attribute of 39, 62, 65, 83, 88–91, 240
psychological analogy 14, 26, 51, 55, 57, 60, 62, 65–6, 67n. 135, 68–9, 89, 189, 242

Ramsey, Paul 97n. 83, 118n. 55, 125, 158n. 30, 170n. 75.
redemption 4–6, 9, 12, 14–15, 17, 19, 23, 58, 70, 77, 82, 96–7, 101–4, 110–17, 120, 125, 135, 146, 149n. 1, 157, 179–80, 183–4, 194–6, 205–6, 210–11, 217, 223, 227

reformed theology 2, 19, 33n. 30, 34, 37, 77, 88–9, 91, 132, 146, 151n. 3, 152, 155–6, 158–9, 180, 204–5, 210, 225–6, 230–2, 237n. 17
regeneration 16, 58, 75, 104, 149–50, 153–4, 177–207, 222, 227
Rehnman, Sebastian 156n. 24, 176
religious affection 16–17, 70, 75, 149–50, 178, 206, 209–24, 227
remanation 5, 13, 15–16, 73, 75–7, 103–5, 119, 144, 146–7, 149–50, 154, 157, 164n. 53, 176, 179, 196–7, 209, 211, 217–18, 222–4, 227
revelation 2, 5–7, 110, 112, 218, 222–3

Schweitzer, William 108n. 12, 126n. 95, 137–8n. 153, 229n. 62
sense of the heart 16, 153, 159, 172–3, 175, 178, 183, 186, 189, 214, 217–18, 220, 223
Sibbes, Richard 87n. 45, 89n. 52, 100n. 91, 158n. 29, 178n. 4, 210
simplicity 31, 39, 39n. 49, 53, 59, 63, 80n. 17, 88–9
spiritual knowledge 4, 16, 75, 115–25, 134–44, 149–76, 179, 188, 207, 209, 212–14, 224, 227
Strobel, Kyle 83n. 28, 125n. 94, 180n. 13, 194n. 74, 202n. 117, 207n. 133, 230nn. 67, 70, 232n. 79
Studebaker, Stephen 24n. 5, 28n. 10, 31n. 21, 34n. 33, 39n. 49, 41n. 52, 50, 65–8, 80n. 17, 210n. 2, 218n. 31, 231n. 75, 231–2n. 77

Tan, Seng-Kong 149n.1, 233n. 81
theological project 5–12, 23, 145
theosis 83n. 28, 98n. 86, 99, 194, 196, 232
trinitarian theology 4, 12–17, 19, 23–5, 28–9, 32n. 27, 50, 58, 100, 119, 145–6, 159, 176, 189–91, 196, 221, 223, 225, 229
Trueman, Carl 7, 31, 162
Turretin, Francis 55, 55n. 99, 57, 125, 130–4, 139n. 163, 156, 177, 180, 181n. 15, 182, 184n. 30, 205, 237, 240, 241n. 31

Veto, Miklos 151, 152n. 6

Walton, Brad 178n. 7, 187nn. 41–2, 206, 209–10, 212, 213–14, 218

Wilson-Kastner, Patricia 76n. 4, 88n. 47, 93n. 66, 97n. 83, 103n. 107

CPSIA information can be obtained
at www.ICGtesting.com
Printed in the USA
LVOW10s0747030317

526053LV00011B/348/P